# From Extractivism to Sustainability

This book investigates how extractive capitalism has developed over the past three decades, what dynamics of resistance have been deployed to combat it, and whether extractivism can ever be transformed into being a part of a progressive development path.

It was not until the 20th century that the extraction of natural resources and raw materials took on a decidedly capitalist form, with the global north extracting primary commodities from the global south as a means of capital accumulation. This book investigates whether extractivism, despite its well-documented negative and destructive socioenvironmental impacts and the powerful forces of resistance that it has generated, could ever be transformed into a sustainable post-development strategy. Drawing on diverse sectoral forms of extractivism (mining, fossil fuels, agriculture), this book analyses the dynamics of both the forces of resistance generated by the advance of extractive capital and alternate scenarios for a more sustainable and liveable future. The book draws particularly on the Latin American experience, where both the propensity of capitalism towards crisis and the development of resistance dynamics to 'extractive' capital have had their greatest impact in the neoliberal era.

This book will be of interest to researchers and students across development studies, economics, political economy, environmental studies, Indigenous studies, and Latin American affairs.

**Henry Veltmeyer** is Senior Research Professor at the Universidad Autónoma de Zacatecas, Mexico, and Professor Emeritus of International Development Studies (IDS) at Saint Mary's University, Canada, with a specialized interest in Latin American development.

**Arturo Ezquerro-Cañete** is Research Fellow at the Center for Advanced Latin American Studies in the Humanities and Social Sciences (CALAS) at the University of Guadalajara, Mexico.

## Routledge Critical Development Studies

*Series Editors*

**Henry Veltmeyer** *is co-chair of the Critical Development Studies (CDS) network; Senior Research Professor at the Universidad Autónoma de Zacatecas, Mexico; and Professor Emeritus of International Development Studies (IDS) at Saint Mary's University, Canada*

**Paul Bowles** *is Professor of Economics and International Studies at UNBC, Canada*

**Elisa van Wayenberge** *is Lecturer in Economics at SOAS University of London, UK*

The global crisis, coming at the end of three decades of uneven capitalist development and neoliberal globalization that have devastated the economies and societies of people across the world, especially in the developing societies of the global south, cries out for a more critical, proactive approach to the study of international development. The challenge of creating and disseminating such an approach, to provide the study of international development with a critical edge, is the project of a global network of activist development scholars concerned and engaged in using their research and writings to help effect transformative social change that might lead to a better world.

This series will provide a forum and outlet for the publication of books in the broad interdisciplinary field of critical development studies—to generate new knowledge that can be used to promote transformative change and alternative development.

The editors of the series welcome the submission of original manuscripts that focus on issues of concern to the growing worldwide community of activist scholars in this field.

To submit proposals, please contact the Development Studies Editor, Helena Hurd (Helena.Hurd@tandf.co.uk).

11 **Agrarian Extractivism in Latin America**
*Edited by Ben M. McKay, Alberto Alonso-Fradejas and Arturo Ezquerro-Cañete*

12 **The Essential Guide to Critical Development Studies (2nd Ed)**
*Edited by Henry Veltmeyer and Paul Bowles*

13 **From Extractivism to Sustainability**
Scenarios and Lessons from Latin America
*Edited by Henry Veltmeyer and Arturo Ezquerro-Cañete*

For more information about this series, please visit: www.routledge.com/Routledge-Critical-Development-Studies/book-series/RCDS

# From Extractivism to Sustainability

## Scenarios and Lessons from Latin America

**Edited by**
**Henry Veltmeyer and**
**Arturo Ezquerro-Cañete**

Routledge
Taylor & Francis Group
LONDON AND NEW YORK

First published 2023
by Routledge
4 Park Square, Milton Park, Abingdon, Oxon OX14 4RN

and by Routledge
605 Third Avenue, New York, NY 10158

*Routledge is an imprint of the Taylor & Francis Group, an informa business*



*British Library Cataloguing-in-Publication Data*
A catalogue record for this book is available from the British Library

ISBN: 978-1-032-29521-3 (hbk)
ISBN: 978-1-032-29522-0 (pbk)
ISBN: 978-1-003-30198-1 (ebk)

DOI: 10.4324/9781003301981

Typeset in Bembo
by codeMantra

# Contents

# Figures

# Tables

# Contributors

**Alberto Alonso-Fradejas** is Postdoctoral Researcher at the Human Geography and Planning Department, Faculty of Geosciences, Utrecht University. Alberto is an Associate Researcher at the Transnational Institute (TNI) in Amsterdam, a Fellow of the Guatemalan Institute of Agrarian and Rural Studies (IDEAR), and Reviews Section Co-Editor for the *Journal of Peasant Studies* (JPS).

**Dario Azzellini** is Professor and Researcher in the Doctoral Program in Development Studies at the Autonomous University of Zacatecas, Mexico, and visiting scholar at the ILR School at Cornell University. His primary research interests are labour studies, local and workers' self-management, and social movements and protest. He has conducted research into social transformation processes for more than 25 years with a specialised focus on Latin America and Europe. He has authored and edited more than 20 books and written more than 100 essays, including book chapters and refereed articles, and 11 documentaries. Recent books include *An Alternative Labour History: Worker Control and Workplace Democracy* (2015); *Vom Protest zum sozialen Prozess: Betriebsbesetzungen und Arbeiten in Selbstverwaltung* (2018); *Communes and Workers' Control in Venezuela: Building 21st Century Socialism from Below* (2017); and *If Not Us, Who? Workers against Authoritarianism, Fascism and Dictatorship* (2021). Together with Oliver Ressler he produced *Occupy, Resist, Produce*, a series of documentaries on recovered factories under workers control in Europe. More information is available on his personal website at: www.azzellini.net.

**David Barkin** is Distinguished Professor at the Universidad Autónoma Metropolitana (UAM), Xochimilco Campus, Mexico City, and was a founding member of the Ecodevelopment Centre, created by the Mexican Science and Technology Council as an independent research organization. He was a recipient of the National Prize in Political Economy in 1979 for his analysis of inflation in Mexico. He was elected to the Mexican Academy of Sciences in 1992 and is Emeritus Researcher at the National Research Council. He collaborates with groups of communities in many parts of Mexico in their efforts to consolidate postcapitalist societies. He was visiting professor at Humboldt University in Berlin as a Georg Forster Fellow during the 2015–2017 period. He is author of more than 200 peer-reviewed articles and 20 books; the latest titles are: *De la Protesta a la Propuesta: 50 años imaginando y construyendo el futuro* (Mexico: Siglo XXI, 2018) and *La Tragedia Ambiental de América Latina y el Caribe* (Santiago de Chile: CEPAL, 2020, with 20 co-authors).

**León Felipe Cubillos** is Professor of Environmental Sciences at the Universidad Tecnológica de Pereira, Colombia. He has a PhD in the Sociology of Development from the Freie Universität Berlín (2006). He is the Director of research related to sociocultural studies and the environmental problematic (www.iespautp.tk). He has also served as Head of the Department of Interdisciplinary Studies and the doctoral program in Environmental Sciences (2010–2013) with the Universidad del Valle, the Universidad del Cauca, and the Universidad Tecnológica de Pereira. His publications include *La interdisciplinariedad en ciencias ambientales: la problemática ambiental del territorio como categoría de investigación para estudios ambientales* (Red Colombiana de Formación Ambiental, 2020). He is currently part of a team of experts working with the Solidarity Council of the Ríos Vivos de Colombia movement (www.riosvivoscolombia.org) heading the resistance against the construction of the mega-dam Hidroituango.

**Raúl Delgado Wise** is Professor and former director of the Doctoral Program in Development Studies at the Autonomous University of Zacatecas, Mexico, general coordinator of the UNESCO Chair on Migration, Development and Human Rights, and member of the advisory board of the UNESCO-Management of Social Transformations (MOST) committee in Mexico. He is also President and Founder of the International Network on Migration and Development and co-Director of the Critical Development Studies Network. He has authored and edited 30 books and written more than 200 essays, including book chapters and refereed articles. Recent books include *Mexico's Economic Dilemma: The Developmental Failure of Neoliberalism* (2011); *Critical Development Studies. An Introduction* (2018); and *Migration, Civil Society and Global Governance* (2019).

**Arturo Ezquerro-Cañete** is Research Fellow at the Center for Advanced Latin American Studies in the Humanities and Social Sciences (CALAS) at the University of Guadalajara. He holds a double PhD in International Development Studies from Saint Mary's University and the Autonomous University of Zacatecas. His research focuses on the dynamics of agrarian transformations and new peasant movements in Paraguay. He is the co-editor of *Agrarian Extractivism in Latin America* (Routledge, 2021).

**Gabriela Gallardo** is a candidate for the Doctoral degree in Development Studies at the Universidad Autónoma de Zacatecas in Mexico.

**Stefanie Garry** is Economic Affairs Officer at the United Nations Conference on Trade and Development (UNCTAD) in Geneva, Switzerland.

She works in the Office of the Director, Division for Africa, Least Developed Countries and Special Programmes. She has also served the Economic Commission for Latin America and the Caribbean (ECLAC) in Mexico City and the International Labour Organization (ILO)—with specialized interests in economics and development, planning, value chains, employment, and labour market statistics.

**Eduardo Gudynas** is Director and Senior Researcher at the Latin American Centre for Social Ecology (CLAES). His expertise is in social ecology and political ecology of the interactions between environment and development. He works closely with social movements in Latin America and has been research associate at the Department of Anthropology, University of California, Davis; was Arne Naess chair on environmental and global justice at the University of Oslow; fellow at the Center for the Advanced Studies at LMU Munich University, and member of the Club of Rome's high commission for the transformation of economies. Ha has been listed among the 74 key thinkers in environment and development and is one of the 50 most influential intellectuals in Latin America. His most recent books are on extractivisms (English edition by Fernwood), alternatives on development and nature's rights, published in eighth Latin American countries.

**Carolina Arias Hurtado** is Professor and Researcher on sociocultural studies and the environmental at the Universidad Tecnológica de Pereira—UTP (Colombia). She has an MSc in Heritage and Territorial Development at the Universidad Mayor de San Simón (UMSS) in Bolivia and a PhD in Development Studies from the Universidad Autónoma de Zacatecas (UAZ) in Mexico. Her recent publications include 'Extractivismo del siglo XXI en los Potosís mexicano y colombiano' (2021), 'Análisis comparativo de los procesos interculturales de construcción territorial agrícola y minera en Quinchía (Colombia)' (2020), 'Entre la renta y la vida: defensa del Bosque de Álamos en Pereira, Colombia' (2020), 'Análisis de la jurisprudencia de la Corte Ambiental en la protección de los derechos constitucionales en Marmato frente a la gran minería' (2018), and 'Neo-extractivismo en América Latina y Colombia: una reflexión desde la ecología política' (2017).

**Fernando Leiva** is Professor of Latin American Studies at the University of California, Santa Cruz, and specialist in development economics, globalization, labour and social movements, and the political economy of Latin American development. He coordinates the Research Cluster on Critical Cultural Political Economy of Extractivism. Recent publications include *Latin American Neostructuralism: The Contradictions of Post-Neoliberal Development* (University of Minnesota Press) and *The Left Hand of Capital: Neoliberalism and the Left in Chile* (SUNY Press).

**Pabel Camilo López Flores** is Bolivian-Italian social researcher, with a PhD in Sociology from Scuola Normale Superiore/University of Milan

'Bicocca' (Italy, Associate Researcher in Postgraduate in Development Sciences, Universidad Mayor de San Andrés CIDES-UMSA (Bolivia), and postdoctoral researcher fellow at the Institute of Latin American and Caribbean Studies of the University of Buenos Aires, IEALC-UBA (Argentina). Member of the Working Group: 'Territorialities in dispute and re-existence' at the Latin American Council of Social Sciences (CLACSO). His current research activities are situated in the fields of political sociology, the sociology of social movements and the sociology of territorial development from a trans-disciplinary perspective. E-mail: velpalopezflo@gmail.com.

**Ben M. McKay** is Associate Professor of Development and Sustainability in the Department of Anthropology and Archaeology at the University of Calgary in Canada. His research focuses on the political economy and ecology of agrarian change in Latin America, agrarian extractivism, and food sovereignty alternatives. He is the author of *The Political Economy of Agrarian Extractivism: Lessons from Bolivia* (Fernwood, 2020) and co-editor of *The Elgar Handbook of Critical Agrarian Studies* (Edward Elgar, 2021) and *Agrarian Extractivism in Latin America* (Routledge, 2021).

**J.C. Moreno-Brid** is Professor of Economic Development and Economic History at the National Autonomous University of Mexico (UNAM). From 2000 to 2015, he served as Deputy Director and Research Coordinator of the Mexico Headquarters of the Economic Commission for Latin America and the Caribbean (ECLAC—UN), after five years as Research Associate at the David Rockefeller Center for Latin American Studies at Harvard University. He has published multiple chapters and articles in international journals. His recent books include Structural Change and Growth in Central America and the Dominican Republic (ECLAC, 2014) and *Development and Growth in the Mexican* Economy: A Historical Perspective (Fondo de Cultura Económica, 2014; Oxford University Press, 2009).

**Isabel Rodríguez Peña** is Research Professor in the Department of Economics and Business at the Universidad Anáhuac México, Campus Norte and Lead Researcher on a collaborative interinstitutional research project on the integration of Mexico into the new international energy situation. Recent publications include/La seguridad energética en Estados Unidos, una discusión entre disponibilidad energía y sostenibilidad Ambiental/ (energy security in the USA, a discussion between energy supply and environmental sustainability), *The Anáhuac Journal: Business and Economics*, Vol. 20, núm. 1, 2020; and 'Re-primarización con financiarización, un análisis desde el mercado petrolero en América Latina' (Reprimarization with Financialisation…), pp. 239–73 in *Financiarización y Crisis en las Estructuras Productivas en Economías en Desarrollo*. Financiarización y crisis de las estructuras productivas en países en desarrollo (Ed.) Levy Noemi. Mexico City: UNAM.

**Anna Preiser** is Assistant Professor (Pre-Doc) at the Institute of Political Science, University of Vienna, Austria. Her PhD thesis, written from a political economy and political ecology perspective, focuses on socio-ecological/eco-territorial conflicts in relation to mining and environmental policy in Peru.

**Alicia Puyana Mutis** is Research Professor with FLACSO-Mexico and a founding member of the International Development Economics IDEAS, of the Mexican Academy of Sciences. She is the author and editor of a number of books on economic growth and unequal world development, and the insertion of Latin America in the global economy, as well as articles on topics such as horizontal inequality, structural discrimination against Indigenous peoples, and oil and energy security. Recent publications include *Elements of Structural Discrimination and Labour Inequality Gaps* (2019), and *Buen Vivir: Economic Theory in Context* (Renewal and Innovation Debate Series of the Social Sciences, 2020).

**Jewellord Nem Singh** is Senior Lecturer/Assistant Professor of International Development at the International Institute of Social Studies, part of the Erasmus University Rotterdam, the Netherlands. He is Principal Investigator of *Green Industrial Policy in the Age of Rare Metals: A Trans-regional Comparison of Growth Strategies in Rare Earth Mining (GRIP-ARM).* This project has received funding from the European Research Council (ERC) under the European Union Horizon 2020 Research and Innovation Programme under Grant Agreement No. 950056. Nem Singh is co-editor of two special issues, *Developmental States beyond East Asia* (Third World Quarterly, 2018) and *Resource Governance and Norm Domestication in the Developing World* (Environmental Policy and Governance, 2020), as well as author of several chapters and journal articles on political economy of development in Latin America and East Asia. He is also the author of *Business of the State: Why State Ownership Matters in Resource Governance* (forthcoming, 2022).

**Darcy Tetreault** is Professor and Researcher in the Department of Development Studies (Unidad Académica en Estudios del Desarrollo) at the Autonomous University of Zacatecas. He has a PhD in Social Science from the University of Guadalajara, Mexico, and a Master of Arts degree in International Development Studies from Saint Mary's University in Halifax, Canada. His research interests include extractivism, environmental conflicts, agrarian transformation, and peasant and Indigenous movements. Recent journal publications include (2021) 'Distilling agro-extractivism: Agave and tequila production in Mexico' (with Cindy McCulligh and Carlos Lucio), *Journal of Agrarian Change* 21 (2); and (2020) 'The new extractivism in Mexico: Rent redistribution and resistance to mining and petroleum activities', *World Development* 126. https://orcid.org/0000-0002-1157-7839.

**Henry Veltmeyer** is Senior Research Professor at the Universidad Autónoma de Zacatecas, Mexico, and Professor Emeritus of International Development Studies (IDS) at Saint Mary's University, Canada, with a specialized interest in Latin American development. In 2020, he was awarded the distinction Emeritus National Researcher by Conacyt, Mexico's National Research Council. In addition to holding a Senior Research Fellowship in advanced Latin American Studies at the University of Guadalajara, he is co-Chair of the Critical Development Studies (CDS) network and co-editor of Routledge's Critical Development Studies book series. He has authored and edited over 50 books on Latin America and the political economy of international development, including *Poverty and Development in Latin America: Public Policies and Development Pathways* (2013), *New Extractivism in Latin America* (2015), *The Politics of Agrarian Reform in Brazil: The Landless Rural Workers Movement* (2015), and *Development in an Era of Neoliberal Globalization* (2016). Recent publications include *Latin America in the Vortex of Social Change* (2018) and *Critical Development Studies: An Introduction* (2018).

# Acknowledgements

The editors acknowledge with gratitude the critical organizational support of CALAS (The Maria Sibylla Merian Center for Advanced Latin American Studies – Guadalajara) in hosting a webinar on the theme of the book and making available the use of both their facilities at the Universidad de Guadalajara and the invaluable services provided by the director Jochen Kenner. The program of this webinar brought together most of the contributors to the book, allowing for a fruitful debate and feedback on the working papers prepared in anticipation of this publication.

The editors also acknowledge with appreciation the occasional conference grant provided for the research and publication project by the Social Sciences and Humanities Research Council of Canada (SSHRC). This grant provided direct research support to some of the contributing authors and facilitated the participation of the contributing authors in the CALAS webinar. The grant provided by SSHRC also supported the publication of this book, including the translation into English of some of the chapters and construction of the index.

In particular, the editors acknowledge with appreciation of his professional skills the invaluable services of Mark Rushton in regard to the logistics of organizing the CALAS webinar, his expert translation of book chapters that were written in Spanish, and copyediting the entire manuscript in preparing it for publication.

Finally, the editors acknowledge the expertise and professionalism of the people at Routledge who were responsible for managing the contributions of more than 20 authors and shepherding with meticulous care such a complex project to completion. Thanks in particular to Helena Hurd, Rosie Anderson, and Matt Shobbrook.

# Introduction

*Arturo Ezquerro-Cañete*

Extractivism, or foreign investment in the extraction of natural resources to the purpose of their exportation in primary commodity form, constitutes a major model of economic development and has done so since the beginning of the era of European colonialism and imperialism in the early 1500s. For the first three centuries, the dynamics of development and resistance associated with this model took form within the centre-periphery structure of what would evolve into the world capitalist system (Wallerstein, 1974). Although capitalism as such, i.e., as a system of commodity production based on the capital-labour relation, did not materialize until well into the 19th century, its origins can be traced to the dispossession of the aboriginal population or Indigenous communities, the super-exploitation of their labour power, and the accumulation of merchant capital in a process based on the transfer of natural and human resources from the periphery of the system to its metropolitan centre. Given that the logic or aim of the system engaged by this transfer of resources from the periphery to the centre was not to accumulate capital, but rather to enrich the ruling classes of Western European societies, and to finance the oligarchic state (monarchism), extractivism in this historic colonial context can best be understood not as capitalism but as imperialism (Girvan, 2014). It was not until the turn into the 20th century that extractivism as we understand it today assumed a decidedly capitalist form—that is, as a modality of capital accumulation and a particular form of capitalist development based on natural resource extraction, and the exchange of raw materials and commodities in primary form from the Southern periphery of the world system to its metropolitan centre in what we might describe as the 'Global North.' Another dimension of this unequal exchange was a reliance of peripheral economies on low- or no-valued added labour, allowing economies at the centre of the system, with access to capital- and technology-intensive lines of industrial production to not only capture surplus value, but also both ground and technology rents (Delgado Wise, 2020). It was not until the 1980s, with the installation of a new world order based on the neoliberal doctrine of free market capitalism, that we can conceive of extractive capitalism as such, a system based on the advance of extractive capital in the development process within the centre–periphery structure of international

DOI: 10.4324/9781003301981-1

trade. This book is an exploration of the complex development and resistance dynamics of this process in Latin America over the past three decades.

The central question addressed in the book is whether extractivism, notwithstanding its well-documented negative and destructive socioenvironmental impacts and the powerful forces of resistance that it has generated, can form a part of a sustainable post-development[1] strategy that reaches beyond capitalism as well as neoliberalism. There are essentially three answers to this question.

One is provided by the economists and policymakers at or associated with the World Bank and the governments and other intergovernmental organizations in the mainstream of economic development thought and practice. The argument advanced here is that the endowment of natural resources available to so many developing countries on the periphery of the world system provides an economic opportunity of which these countries should avail themselves by means of a strategy of sustainable resource development and inclusive growth. A review of the literature points towards two variations in this approach. One is embodied in the notion of 'inclusive economic growth' based on the agency of the 'private sector' (in the form of multinational corporations) and driven by the operations of these corporations in the extractive sector (see Canada, House of Commons, 2012). From this perspective, an extractivist strategy of inclusive economic growth and sustainable resource development is predicated on an institutional and policy framework and system of global governance (neoliberal globalization) that allows for corporate self-regulation within a regime of corporate social responsibility (Gonzalez-Perez and Leonard, 2013; Sagebien and Whellams, 2010). An important variation of this approach is associated with an institutional and policy framework constructed by economists at United Nations Economic Commission for Latin America and the Caribbean (ECLAC), known as neostructuralism (see Leiva, 2008). Within this framework, it is assumed that the agency of the private sector is a critical factor in the process of sustainable development and inclusive growth, but that their operations in the extractive sector need to be regulated, providing here an important role for the state. The belief shared by these neoliberal theorists and proponents of economic globalization (integration into the system of global governance) is that capitalism provides fundamental system requirements for a process of sustainable and inclusive development, but that the operations of the companies in the sector need to be regulated to ensure the mitigation of any destructive outcomes and negative socioeconomic impacts and to ensure that the impacted communities on the extractive frontier are properly consulted with respect to any extractive project and their rights respected (Gonzalez-Perez and Leonard, 2013).

A second school of thought on extractivism as a development model has been articulated by the social movements formed by the Indigenous and peasant communities on the extractive frontier with the support of civil society environmental activists. The basic position of these groups and organizations is that mega-mining and other extractive projects and operations are destructive of nature and the ecological foundations of their way of life and rural livelihoods. The argument advanced in support of this position is that capitalism in its different forms (financial, monopoly, industrial, extractive) cannot overcome or get away from its fundamental built-in contradictions—the fundamental drive to accumulate and its associated dynamics of incessant economic growth dynamics.

Both the first and second schools of thought on extractivism are supported by an extensive body of research and argumentation. The arguments advanced in this context are clear enough. Extractivism is seen as either viable and an essential component of a sustainable development strategy, or on the contrary, extractivism is viewed as unsustainable and destructive of nature, the environment, and rural livelihoods—that there is no room for extractivism in an imagined alternative post-development future or a sustainable development path. Less clear is whether there is any room for a possible or solid alternative argument within these two polarized standpoints—that extractivism can be transformed into or be a vital part of a progressive development path.

## This is the central question addressed by this book

Some theorists in the areas of extractivism and development, including Álvaro García Linera, a renowned sociologist but also the former vice-president of Bolivia in the policy regime headed by Evo Morales (2006–2019), the first Indigenous politician in contemporary history to have achieved state power, prefer to treat 'development' (viz. construction of a new industrial policy for countries on the periphery of the world system) and extractivism as compatible and symbiotic. The empirical evidence for this, however, is rather thin. In Latin America, the best cases would be Mexico and Brazil, but many analysts regarding the political economy of capitalist development in both these countries would cast serious doubts on this proposition or the extent of their success. Hence, perhaps we need to place this conundrum at the heart of the extractive development model: is it possible to promote manufacturing-based industrial policy alongside extractivism or can the extractive sector generate spill-over effects to overcome the problems of resource specialization? Conversely, does this tension not explain why the rest of the region appears to have failed to pursue industrialization in the 20th century?

Of course, another explanation advanced in the literature has to do with the fundamental contradiction of centre-periphery relations within the world capitalist system, with reference here to what has been described as the 'new dependency' brought about by and associated with the associated with extractivism and neoliberal globalization. The proponents of this theory argue that this latest advance of global extractive capital has created a neocolonial system of global production in which Latin American countries are forced into a new relation of dependency in the exchange of resource-based commodities for industrial products and financial services (Borón, 2008; Vidal and Guillén, 2007).[2]

## *Part I*

Part I of the book is designed as an introduction to the complex dynamics associated with the advance of resource-seeking 'extractive' capital in the development process. The aim here is to provide a theoretical framework for the subsequent analysis and for the chapters that follow.

**Raúl Delgado Wise**, in Chapter 1, places the advance of extractive capital in the development process in a broader context of a system in crisis defined by the interaction of diverse forms of capitalism in what he understands as the neoliberal era of 'generalized monopolies.' Following Marx as well as David Harvey, this argument is advanced with reference to a theoretical framework focused on the fundamental propensity of the system towards crisis, a problem resulting from the workings and interaction of three fundamental contradictions endemic to the capitalist system. The first and arguably key contradiction relates to the capital–labour relation, a contradiction manifest in the dynamics of a class struggle for wages and land—and in the current context, for access to potable water and the global commons. A second contradiction relates to the structure of international trade—the centre-periphery relation, as theorized and analysed by proponents of a Latin American theory of dependency (see the discussion above). In addition to these two contradictions, the dynamics of which were analysed predominantly in the context of the advance of industrial capital in the development process, the advance and operations of extractive capital have exposed a third contradiction based on the metabolic relation between nature and society, manifest in the emergence of an environmental crisis of global proportions and the dynamics of a socioenvironmental movement on the frontier of extractivism. Thus, as Delgado Wise sees it, contemporary capitalism is characterized by the emergence of new modalities of unequal economic and ecological exchange and a trend towards a new predatory form of extractive capital that has accentuated the three principal contradictions of the system and a propensity towards crisis, a multidimensional crisis of global proportions. The operation of the General Law of Capital Accumulation on a world scale, a central proposition of Marx's theory of Capital, is at the core of this trend. In the context of the current epochal crisis that embraces all aspects of the system and its interactions with the natural environment, the relationship between industrialization and development has experienced a meaningful shift. The current mode of industrialization in the periphery, based on assembly plants, cannot be conceived of as a pathway for counteracting unequal exchange relations across the North-South or centre-periphery divide. On the contrary, it implies a new form of 'robbery' that expands beyond natural resources, giving rise to the configuration of new types of enclave economies.

In Chapter 2, **Henry Veltmeyer** provides a theoretical framework for understanding these new geoeconomics of capital in the context of Latin America, where both the propensity of capitalism towards crisis and the development and resistance dynamics associated with the advance of resource-seeking 'extractive' capital in the neoliberal era have had their greatest impact and resonance. Latin America has also been the locus of diverse experiments with alternative models and post-development pathways that reach beyond the capitalist system towards what has been described as the 'socialism of the 21st century.' According to the author the activism of the peasant movement, with its social base in Indigenous communities and in the semi-proletariat of landless rural workers, created the conditions for a 'progressive cycle' of policy regimes oriented towards neodevelopmentalism and neoextractivism, consisting of the use of foreign investments destined to the extraction of resources to finance a new policy of inclusive development and poverty reduction. With reference to this 'development,' the chapter raises a series of critical issues for debate, which are addressed by other authors in this volume. They include reference to (i) the contradictions of capitalism and neoextractivism as a model of accumulation, as well as the emergence of socioecological conflicts in a post-extractivist horizon; (ii) mining as a classical form of extractivism (see Chapter 3); (iii) the dynamics of agro-extractivism (see Chapter 4); and (iv) social movements on the extractive frontier associated with the resistance of communities on the extractive frontier (see Chapters 9–11). The chapter elucidates critical dimensions of this process that have to do with the development and resistance dynamics resulting from the forces of change released in the development process within the institutional and policy framework of the new world order.

## *Part II*

Part II delves into the dynamics of extractivism in three key extractive sectors of the economy—mining, agriculture, and water.

In Chapter 3, **Darcy Tetreault** critically examines Mexico's extractive policies during the first three years of the administration of the current president Andrés Manuel López Obrador (AMLO). To evaluate the extent to which AMLO's petroleum and mining policies constitute steps towards progressive neoextractivism, the author employs an analytical framework focused on three main areas of policy orientation: ownership of subsoil resources and extractive enterprises, mechanisms to capture and redistribute resource rents, and environmental policy, including state mediation of social environmental conflicts around extractive activities. With many nuances and some countertendencies, Tetreault's findings show that despite projecting a discourse of neoextractivism, López Obrador's government has so far given continuity to the overarching institutional framework that was put in place during the neoliberal era to provide private and foreign capital access to the country's natural resources and to (under)regulate extractive activity. Evidently, policies aimed at increasing the rates of extracting hydrocarbons, metals and minerals fly in the face of the climate crisis and relegate to a second level of importance the environmental and social impacts of petroleum and mining activities on the local level. All of this is likely to lead to further environmental damage and social conflict in rural Mexico, with unpredictable outcomes that hinge on the struggles that are unfolding in and over specific territories.

In Chapter 4, **Arturo Ezquerro-Cañete, Alberto Alonso-Fradejas, and Ben McKay** elaborate on the relatively new notion of agro-extractivism which is characterized by corporate control over the value chain, a dependence on externally produced inputs, and large-scale plantation monocultures (see McKay et al., 2021). They explore the political dynamics that justify, legitimize, and ultimately allow for heightened biomass extractivism in current transitions to sustainability within the agricultural sector in Bolivia, Guatemala, and Paraguay. In Bolivia, Evo Morales suffered a crisis of legitimacy that was years in the making. His authoritarian tendencies, alliances with classes of capital, and reliance on the extractive economy ultimately led to his downfall as he lost support from his social bases and was unwilling to give up state power. An analysis of the politics behind the rise of the flex sugarcane and oil palm complexes in Guatemala since the mid-2000s shows that an authoritarian corporate populist agenda is on the rise. This involves political concessions to the underprivileged through public grants and multistakeholder governance. But additionally, and distinctively, authoritarian corporate populism involves concessions to working people and the environment in the sphere of private relations of production. Violence, however, remains foundational to this political agenda, even if it is now cloaked in the rule of law. In Paraguay, the fierce rejection of Fernando Lugo's tepid attempts to regulate the agribusiness sector culminated in a 'parliamentary coup,' orchestrated by the landlord class, and preceded by spectacular acts of violence against campesinos. In its aftermath, we have witnessed the continuing expansion of an agro-extractive export model characterized by the adoption of new genetically modified soy varieties, recurring state violence, and increasing campesino and Indigenous dispossession and marginalization. Despite the 'green' discourse of dominant models of 'sustainable agriculture,' the authors argue that strategic alliances among political and capitalist elites are paving the way for enhanced resource extractivism in mainstream sustainability transitions today.

In Chapter 5, **Carolina Arias Hurtado and Léon Felipe Cubillos Quintero** analyse the development and resistance dynamics of extractivism around water, land, and gold in Colombia. This analysis is framed by the theoretical perspective of sociocultural studies and the geoeconomics of extractive capital. With an analytical focus on the environmental situation brought about by the development dynamics of extractivism the authors focus on three expressions of the extractivist model: hydroelectric projects, agro-industry, and mega-mining, which, prior to the crisis brought on by the COVID-19 pandemic, was widely viewed as the motor of the development process, and the primary source of financing the peace and economic reactivation process. The central focus of the authors in this context is on the discursive disputes and development practice concerning the agency of the private sector, the role of the State, and the activism of social movements. The chapter here provides a case study of the municipality of Quinchía located in the Coffee Cultural Landscape of Colombia, one of the areas most affected by the armed conflict, where hydroelectric projects, the Hass avocado agribusiness, forest plantations, and mining megaprojects are advancing vertiginously. This case allows the authors to illustrate how this new environmental situation exacerbates old problems and conflicts in the territory. The main argument advanced is that extractivism in the current context is environmentally, culturally, and socially unsustainable and a major obstacle in the search for, and construction of, peace in Colombia on the heels of a long class war.

### *Part III*

Part III examines the prospects for a new industrial policy in the region that retains and combines both industrialization and extractivism as essential parts of a progressive development model as part of a wider transition towards clean energy.

In Chapter 6, **Juan Carlos Moreno-Brid, Stephanie Garry, and Alicia Puyana** address the challenge of transforming extractivism into a progressive development path. The question is whether the greening of extractivism is possible. The authors preface their analysis of the challenges posed by the incorporation of extractivism into a new industrial policy for Latin America, with a discussion of the negative consequences that both industrialism and extractivism have had on the environment. As they see it, at issue in these negative consequences is not only the sustainability of extractivism as a model of development but also three brutal contradictions that put pressure on the growth rate of the economy, contradictions that are inherent to capitalism and thus difficult, if not impossible, to escape even with the strenuous efforts of governments and policymakers to construct a sustainable development policy regime. The problem, they argue, is that in the Latin American context (with reference to the gaps and problems such as poverty and inequality, and slow growth, created by these contradictions), the proposal of a 'no growth' development path advanced in some forums is simply not an option. The ideal for Latin American governments in their macroeconomic policies would be to move away from extractivism and towards inter-industrial chains of added value and employment. However, the region's peripheral status within the world capitalist system creates conditions that reproduce and reinforce the structure of dependency and economic underdevelopment and that severely constrain the governments' options and ability to respond to the fundamental challenges that they face in the current context. All that they can realistically do at the level of macro- and micro-policy in the current context of capitalist development (a wealth of natural resources, the lack of capital and limited fiscal resources) and crisis (deepening social inequalities, environmental degradation, spread of the coronavirus) is to invite global companies in the extractive sector to invest in the exploitation of their country's natural resource wealth.

In Chapter 7, **Alicia Puyana and Isabel Rodriguez Peña** address the question of transforming extractivism into a sustainable development model. The analysis provided by the authors is focused on the paths pursued by Canada, Mexico, and the US in regard energy security and energy transition policies. Each of these paths, traced out over the period 1980–2016, point to the little progress made by green energies across North America, as revealed by the continuing importance of oil across the energy matrix and difficulties of moving towards less $CO_2$-emitting productive structures supported by a secure affordable clean energy supply—what could be described as the greening of extractivism. Puyana and Rodriguez Peña argue that substituting energy from fossil fuels (coal, oil and gas) for renewables sources (wind, solar, hydroelectric, nuclear), will actually amplify and perpetuate extractivism through the privatization of public goods, including the sun, wind, water and land, to transform them into electricity or fuel and reap rents from their sale on domestic and foreign markets. Additionally, low-emission technologies will increase the production and consumption of strategic metals and minerals. Thus, the greening of extractivism—an approach that stimulates industrialization, generates more and better-paying jobs, reduces inequality and poverty, and reverts environmental damage—regardless of its vital urgency, seems to be an impossibly difficult task.

**Jewellord Nem Singh**, in Chapter 8, turns his attention to the environmental dimension of the global crisis. In the current global and regional context of capitalist development, the transition to clean technologies has emerged as the overarching solution to the crisis. This, in turn, entails a worldwide shift from fossil fuel dependence towards a diversified energy source. Through the Paris Agreement, the industrialized world—including China—has committed to progressively reduce their carbon emissions. However, recent studies by international organizations have made clear that an exponential increase in wind power, solar energy, and other renewables will require the extensive and intensive exploitation of 'critical raw materials' (CRMs) that are widely used across a range of intermediate and final output manufacturing sectors. Latin America—and Africa—are expected to fuel the extraction of these minerals to support the global transition to clean energy. In this context, the chapter seeks to examine the place of Latin America in this emerging global value chain, and the extent to which a renewed industrial strategy can be crafted to enable regional governments to take advantage of this new boom in resource production. Nem Singh argues that in the current situation only a few countries have been prepared to exercise strategic control for these minerals. He proceeds to document how existing mining policies are insufficient to enable Latin America states from taking advantage of this new opportunity in two ways: (i) existing mining policies are still unable to establish sectoral linkages to enable greater control over the supply chain and (ii) there is very little political discussion linking industrial policy, clean energy transition, and climate change solutions. The chapter argues that a new industrial strategy is vital in pushing Latin American governments to maximize the potential benefits and to commit towards greener forms of industrial policy. The chapter moves the debate regarding mining governance and industrial policy forward by stressing the need to explore new research inquiries in the context of green transition that have thus far been neglected by Latin American political economy scholarship.

### *Part IV*

Part IV focuses on the dynamics of resistance to the advance of extractive capital(ism) mounted by the Indigenous and peasant communities on the extractive frontier.

In Chapter 9, **Pabel Camilo López Flores and Anna Preiser** expand on the socioecological crisis and conflicts that neoextractivism generates between the companies in the extractive sector, the states that support their extractive ventures, and the active resistance of the communities on the extractive frontier. Resistance in this context takes is shaped by the destructive impacts of mining and other extractive projects, as well as the struggle of these communities to reclaim their territorial rights and demands to protect their ways of living and their livelihoods. The authors dissect the dynamics of these conflicts and disputed territorialities as they relate to and play out in the context of local community-based development. They argue that neoextractivism can be conceptualized as an inherent part of global capitalist accumulation and as such a 'glocal' phenomenon—conditioned by globalization but anchored locally, a phenomenon that has led to an increasing number of conflicts and increased violence against movements resisting extractivism and its destructive socioenvironmental impact on the communities. One of the conclusions reached by López Flores and Preiser in their analysis of several local cases of extractivism is that the advance of extractive capital and the expansion of extractive frontier is promoted by both neoliberal and 'progressive' regimes. The authors also bring into analytical focus the dynamic of various imagined futures and post-extractivist transition scenarios presented by diverse agencies and forces of resistance. These proposals include ideas associated with the Indigenous cosmovision of '*buen vivir*' and the notion of 'the commons' as a public good, as well as ideas associated with 'eco-feminism' and 'the indigenous perspective.'

The central focus of Chapter 10 by **Fernando Leiva** is on the new territorial management strategies used by the mining companies to defeat community-based resistance. Chile is what can be regarded as a classic case of a country heavily dependent on mining for its development, being one of the largest producers of strategic minerals and industrial metals (copper) in the world. It is also the site of some of the most virulent forces of community-based resistance, which has resulted in a relation of conflict between the companies in the mining sector and the Indigenous communities contiguous to the sites of extraction. Many mining companies in the country over the past two decades have confronted this resistance by pursuing a strategy concerted with several imperial nation states that have promoted the extractive industries as an opportunity for their economic development. The dominant strategy has taken the form of corporate self-regulation in the form of corporate social responsibility (CSR), a strategy premised on the ability of the mining companies to obtain a 'social license'—the support and approval of the communities on the extractive frontier, and their 'informed consent.' However, Leiva traces out the evolution of ideas and diverse strategies for territorial embedding pursued by the mining companies designed to overcome and defeat community resistance. As Leiva sees it, Chile represents the vanguard of the most advanced response and counter-strategy of the mining companies to community resistance in the world. His analysis has enormous significance for the worldwide resistance to the advance of extractive capital in the development process, posing new challenges for activists, communities, and scholars as they further narrow possibilities for building genuinely democratic societies.

**David Barkin**, in Chapter 11, moves beyond the issue of extractivist conflict and resistance on the extractive frontier to the broader question that has bedevilled the critics and opponents of capitalism throughout the 20th century: the search for an agency of revolutionary change and social transformation. Marxists throughout the 20th century had identified the working class or proletariat, as the most likely candidate to constitute an effective agency of revolutionary change, an actor conscious of its mission to help bring about the end of capitalism. Barkin advances the argument that the communities on the extractive frontier could very well serve as an agent of transformative change, reviving the search for and dwindling hopes on the political left for a social force with the capacity to instigate if not lead a process of revolutionary change. In this context, the resistance has taken and is taking, the form of self-conscious proposals to build new plural societies on the margins of the world capitalist system. Some observers and analysts in diverse regional contexts have argued that many Indigenous communities across the world are disempowered and lack the resources to develop alternatives. However, the current effervescence of rural and Indigenous communities in Latin America belies this. Indeed, it might be just as Latin America is on the frontlines of the global resistance against the neoliberal policy agenda and extractive capitalism so does the activism of Indigenous communities in Latin America in constructing alternative futures provide important lessons for activists and communities elsewhere.

### *Part V*

With Part V the book shifts from a concern with the dynamics of popular resistance to the question of post-extractivist transitions and alternative proposals for social transformation in conditions of a multidimensional crisis. The concern in these chapters is to draw out the lessons from an analysis of idea- and experiment-related alternative pathways beyond both neoliberalism and capitalism: a sustainable form of inclusive resource development based on social solidarity, social and environmental justice, and harmony with nature—*Pachamama* (mother earth), as described in Inca mythology.

In Chapter 12, **Eduardo Gudynas**, senior researcher at the Latin American Centre for Social Ecology (CLAES), provides his post-development perspective on the dynamic forces of social transformation that are at work in Latin America and the alternative futures that they envision. The chapter summarizes the diverse proposals associated with the notion of 'post-extractivist transitions' as it has been constructed in Latin America over the last 15 years of active resistance to the advance of extractive capital and the neoliberal policy agenda in the development process. Extractivisms in this context are briefly defined to distinguish them from other types of appropriation of natural resources, and the concept of 'post-extractivist transitions' is discussed. Some key contributions to the debate about the alternative development pathways in this transition are reviewed, including the transition to the socialism of the 21st century and transitions based on the agency of grassroots organizations and civil society. The chapter includes a discussion of the concept of post-extractivist transitions in terms of its contents, sequences, actions and associated public policies. These transitions are divided into a phase of emergency and urgency measures and a phase of transformative structural change. In this context, the policy options associated with the reduction versus the continued exportation of the country's wealth of natural resources in primary commodity form are discussed. This discussion includes consideration of the (economic) benefits and (socioenvironmental) costs associated with an industrial policy—to process and industrialize the country's wealth of natural resources before exporting them—versus the benefits and costs of reducing the exportation of these resources to capitalist markets, including weighing the impact of this reduction on fiscal revenues derived from commodity exports against the benefits of preserving both the country's natural heritage and protecting rural livelihoods as well as the way of life associated with Indigenous communities. At issue in this discussion of post-extractivist transitions is the possibility of 'greening' extractivism and reversing the spillover effects of extractivist projects on politics, and especially on democracy and the rights of both people and Nature.

In Chapter 13, **Gabriella Gallardo** picks up on the 'post-development' debate that has taken place in recent years around the Indigenous cosmological conception of *Buen Vivir* or *Vivir Bien* (*Sumak Kawsay*, in Quechua), as a new way of thinking about 'development,' which has been incorporated into the constitution promulgated by the governments of Ecuador and Bolivia. Drawing on a discourse analysis of a series of interviews with Indigenous and peasant women leaders, Gallardo provides a decolonial feminist critique of *Sumak Kawsay*, highlighting how its conceptualization has been constructed without a serious questioning or deep understanding of the lives of subaltern women—a matter of both class and gender-based inequalities and oppression. Given the relatively few encounters between the feminist and Indigenous movements and *Sumak Kawsay*, there is a clear need to democratically reconstruct the concept from an intersectional perspective that takes into account the voices of subaltern women and challenges the power matrix of male domination. Against this backdrop, Gallardo contributes to a collective reconstruction of the concept of *Sumak Kawsay*, both in terms of debates surrounding extractivism and the struggle of women to escape and improve their social condition. As she maintains, *Buen Vivir* is not possible without gender equality.

In Chapter 14, **Dario Azzellini** analyses the dynamics of a broad movement to construct an alternative 'social and solidarity' form of society based on cooperativism, autonomism and worker self-management, and local community-based development within the context of popular power (*poder popular*), revolutionary democracy and the 'socialism of the twenty-first century.' Azzellini notes that while the institution of communal councils emerged from the grassroots within civil society, their leading role and revolutionary form, as well as their exponential growth in recent decades, owes much to state support, particularly in the case of Venezuela. For example, he notes Chávez presented them publicly at various times before promulgating the Law of Communal Councils in 2006, explaining how they were made up and how they functioned. The law specified that the councils were to be autonomous bodies of popular power that assured or allowed for public policies to 'respond to the necessities and aspirations of the communities in the building of a society of equality and social justice.' At the same time the state has also an inherent tendency to inhibit the development of autonomous structures and tends to control and subordinate social processes. This contradiction became increasingly accentuated the more communities developed the structures of self-government.

The concluding Chapter 15 provides an assessment of the alternative proposals for transformative change and post-extractivist transition associated with the 'progressive cycle' in Latin American politics—the 'pink tide' of post-neoliberal policy regimes that emerged in South America in conditions of a global crisis and disenchantment with and rejection of neoliberalism—as well as the diverse forces of social change and resistance that civil society organizations formed on the extractive frontier. The aim is to draw out the lessons provided by these diverse experiments throughout the region in terms of the possibility and the conditions under which these forces and alternative models can help bring about a process of social transformation in the direction of another world of more inclusive and sustainable post-capitalist development.

## Notes

1 The concept of post-development originated in the 1980s in a debate advanced with reference to a 'theoretical impasse' rooted in the rejection of social science, i.e., 'structuralism' and materialism, as a way of thinking about development, and

a focus on the cultural dimension of the development process. For this theoretical impasse and a proposed (post-structuralist) conception of post-development, see Gudynas (2021).

2 For the original variations in this Latin American theory of 'dependency' and its contributions to development theory, see, inter alia, Kay (1989).

## References


Borón, A. (2008). "Teoria(s) de la Dependencia." *Realidad Economíca*, 238: 20–43.

Canada, House of Commons. (2012). *Driving Inclusive Economic Growth: The Role of the Private Sector in International Development.* Report of the Standing Committee on Foreign Affairs and International Development, House of Commons. Ottawa: Public Works and Government Services Canada.

Delgado Wise, R. (2020). "Unravelling Monopoly Capital in the 21st Century and the Role of the Imperial Innovation System. Silicon Valley and Counter-Hegemonies," in Hosseini, H., Goodman, J., Motta, S.C., and Barry, K. Gills (eds.), *The Routledge Handbook of Transformative Global Studies*, pp. 331–342. Abingdon: Routledge.

Girvan, N. (2014). "Extractive Imperialism in Historical Perspective," in Petras, J., and Veltmeyer, H. (eds.), *Extractive Imperialism in the Americas*, pp. 49–61. Leiden: Brill Books.

Gonzalez-Perez, M., and Leonard, L. (2013). *International Business, Sustainability and Corporate Social Responsibility.* Bingley: Emerald Group Publishing.

Gudynas, E. (2021). "Post-Development and Other Critiques of Development," in Veltmeyer, H., and Bowles, P. (eds.), *The Essential Guide to Critical Development Studies*, pp. 49–56. London: Routledge.

Kay, C. (1989). *Latin American Theories of Development and Underdevelopment.* London: Routledge.

Leiva, F.I. (2008). *Latin American Neostructuralism: The Contradictions of Post-Neoliberal Development.* Minneapolis: University of Minnesota Press.

McKay, B.M., Alonso-Fradejas, A., and Ezquerro-Cañete, A. (eds.). (2021). *Agrarian Extractivism in Latin America.* London: Routledge.

Sagebien, J., and Whellams, M. (2010). "CSR and Development: Seeing the Forest for the Trees." *Canadian Journal of Development Studies*, 31 (3–4): 483–510.

Vidal, G., and Guillén, A. (eds.) (2007). *Repensar la Teoría del Desarrollo en un Contexto de Globalización: Homenaje a Celso Furtado.* Buenos Aires: CLACSO.

Wallerstein, I. (1974). *The Modern World-System: Capitalist Agriculture and the Origins of the European World-Economy in the Sixteenth Century.* New York: Academic Press.

# Part I

# The Contemporary Dynamics of Global Capitalism

# 1 The contradictions and verities of capitalism

*Raúl Delgado Wise*

Research into the historical and regional dynamics of capitalist development—i.e., the development of the forces of production within the institutional framework of what has evolved as the world capitalist system—has yielded awareness of some truisms regarding capitalism, what we might term the verities of capitalist development.

One is that the development of the forces of production is predicated on and requires the accumulation of capital in diverse forms—including *industrial* (investment in labour, raw materials, production and technology), *financial* (investment in financial instruments) and *extractive* (investment in the extraction of natural resources for exportation in primary commodity form).

A second truism is that these diverse forms of capital do not exist in isolation but are always found in some combination, as is manifest in the current phase of capitalist development that features the advance of both monopoly capital and resource-seeking 'extractive' capital. In the current context, the development process in Latin America and its dynamics can best be understood in terms of the interaction between corporate monopoly capital and resource-seeking 'extractive' capital, with the domination of the latter in the southern hemisphere. This truism is exemplified by the development dynamics of agro-extractivism as discussed in Chapter 4 and the dynamics of rare earth extraction discussed in Chapter 8.

A third truism is that the accumulation of capital and the process of capitalist development is based on the capital-labour relation, i.e., the exploitation and commodification of labour, a social relation of capitalist production that is manifest in the dynamics of a class struggle.

Another truism, which features in Marx's theory of Capital as the General Law of Capital Accumulation, is manifest as a twofold tendency towards, on the one hand, the concentration and centralisation of capital in monopoly form, and on the other hand, the formation of a reserve army of surplus labour and industrial proletariat based on the conversion of peasant farmers and small-scale producers into an industrial proletariat, a wage-labouring working class. Both trends (economic concentration and the development of monopoly capital, the proletarianisation of the peasantry) can be traced out in diverse regional contexts throughout the 20th century, but they were seen

DOI: 10.4324/9781003301981-3

to greatly accelerate within the institutional and policy framework of the new world order of neoliberal globalisation established in the 1980s. The dynamics associated with the concentration and centralisation of capital, including the formation of an industrial reserve army and the production of a global labourforce, are briefly discussed below.

A fifth truism is that each advance of capital in the development process generates commensurate forces of resistance, a dynamic tendency that is manifest in the development process that has unfolded over the past seven decades—a period that featured three decades of state-led development (developmentalism) and four decades of neoliberal globalisation and neodevelopmentalism. These dynamics of capitalist development can be traced out in the form of three cycles: first, a cycle in the 1950s–1970s that saw the resistance in the form of a class struggle for higher wages and a rural land struggle. In the 1980s and 1990s, the resistance, led by the rural landless workers generated by decades of capitalist development in the agricultural sector, took the form of opposition to the neoliberal policy agenda of governments in the region. And then, in the opening decades of the new millennium, the resistance at the level of national politics took the form of a cycle of 'progressive' (post-neoliberal) policies, whereas at the level of civil society the communities on the extractive frontier mobilised the forces of resistance against the destructive operations of extractive capital in a struggle to reclaim their communal territorial rights and the rights of nature that were violated by the destructive operations of the capitalist enterprises in the extractive sector. On these resistance dynamics, see Chapters 9–11 in this volume.

A sixth truism, advanced in Latin America as a theory of dependent capitalist development ('dependency'), is that the international division of labour formed by nations at the centre of the world system with those on the periphery functioned as a system of unequal exchange—the exportation of raw materials and primary commodities in exchange for manufactured goods. This relation of unequal exchange in turn served as a mechanism of exploitation—appropriation of the surplus value produced by the working class and the direct producers on the periphery of the system. This relation of dependency and exploitation among nations formed along a North-South axis which can be traced back to an international division of labour formed at the turn into the 20th century at an advanced stage of capitalist development conceptualised by Lenin as 'imperialism' (Petras and Veltmeyer, 2014). This system of unequal economic exchange (raw materials and natural resources in exchange for manufactured and industrialised goods), a feature of both extractive imperialism and extractive capitalism, was reinforced by the response of Latin American governments to both the influx of resource-seeking capital in the 1990s and the 2000s and the demand for natural resources in capitalist markets. For a discussion of these dynamics, see Chapter 2 in this volume.

A seventh truism, an all-too-evident fundamental feature of capitalism, is that development in this systemic form is driven by built-in contradictions and forces that lead to both the system dynamics of a class struggle and relations of political conflict, as well as a propensity towards crisis, a feature which in the current context is manifest in the unfolding of a multidimensional systemic crisis of global proportions. Although we do not have space in this chapter to elaborate on the contradictions inherent to capitalist systems—David Harvey (2014) has identified 17 of them—they include a relation of conflict between the forces and the social relations of production, which implicate both the capital-labour relation and the centre-periphery structure of international relations, as well as a propensity towards overproduction, which Marx theorised in terms of a systemic tendency towards a falling rate of profit.

Another fundamental system-defining contradiction, which Marx did not fully theorise but that is particularly relevant to the current debate on extractivism, has to do with the society-nature relation—a contradiction that has been exposed by the destructive operations of extractive capital and the resulting global ecological crisis. Foster (2002) elaborates on the fundamental contradiction between society and nature under capitalist relations of production with reference to Marx's metabolic rift theory, which posits that the growth of industry and large-scale agriculture under capitalism has created an 'irreparable rift' in the 'metabolic interaction' between human beings and the natural environment. For a discussion of this contradiction and its dynamics, and the unresolved question as to whether the capitalist system is sufficiently resilient to enable it to transcend the metabolic rift between humans and nature and elude or recover from the ecological crisis caused by this rift, see Foster, Clark and York (2010) and Foster and Clark (2020).

A contradiction, which cannot be understood in systemic terms as a verity of capitalism, but rather as a conjunctural matter that relates to the new geopolitics of capital in the region, is manifest in the policy regime established by both Evo Morales in Bolivia during his presidency (2006–2019) and Rafael Correa during his in Ecuador (2007–2017). Both regimes have been widely regarded as the most progressive regimes on the continent in terms of both inclusive development and protection of the rights of nature, which are enshrined in the constitutions of the plurinational and multi-ethnic states. There is no space in this chapter to discuss the contradiction between the stated goal of creating a new society based on the principles of *Buen Vivir*, how to live well in social solidarity and harmony with nature, and the actual policies implemented within the framework of modernist developmentalism. But see, inter alia, Acosta, Cajas-Guijarro, Hurtado-Caicedo and Sacher (2020) and Farah and Vasapollo (2011).

The purpose of this chapter is twofold. One is to provide elements of a theoretical framework for the analysis provided by the contributing authors. The second is to analyse the form taken by these system dynamics of capitalist development in the Latin American context, with particular emphasis on the emergence of a new international division of labour associated with the exportation of the large reserves of labour power, a fundamental legacy of capitalist development in the agricultural sector, and also the notable advance of resource-seeking 'extractive' capital (neoextractivism) in the development process (Veltmeyer and Petras, 2014).

In the first stage, this process involves the separation of the direct producers and peasant farmers in the agricultural sector from their means of production and their expulsion, so producing a reserve of low-skilled labour, adding to this reserve army of surplus labour generated by the dismantling of the production apparatus in both agriculture and industry and the destruction of built-up forces of production on the periphery of the system. On this phenomenon, and its rearticulation with the major imperialist powers through the mechanism of a global value chain in capitalist markets, see Delgado Wise (2021).

In the second stage, the process comprises the exportation of highly skilled labour (via the mechanism of international migration) to service the production and labour requirements associated with the concentration and centralisation of human capital in the form of scientific knowledge and technological innovation tied to a restructured global production apparatus in a process of research and development (R&D) and carried out in centres of technological research and innovation such as Silicon Valley, which are at the forefront of a global restructuring process associated with the production of technological innovation systems.

This new international division of labour, encompassing the direct and disembodied exportation (or the extraction and subsequent exploitation of labour) of both low- and highly skilled labour, together with the extraction of natural resource wealth in the form of industrial minerals and metals, fossil fuels and agro-food products, has reconfigured or restructured the relation of dependence and exploitation among nations on a North-South or core-periphery axis, giving rise to new modalities of unequal economic and ecological exchange. We expand on this point below.

## Theoretical considerations

Unequal economic exchange and development is a key issue for understanding contemporary capitalism and imperialism, and it has sparked multiple debates regarding the nature of North-South or core-periphery relations. Without going into much detail, the first thing that should be noted is that at the most general level of abstraction the primary source of unequal development is the relationship between capital and labour based on the exchange of two commodities: money and labour power. But in the current context of capitalist development, another element has been added to the development matrix and needs to be factored into an analysis of its dynamics, namely unequal *ecological* exchange based on the extraction of natural resources and their exportation in primary commodity form. A dominant feature of unequal ecological exchange is that the benefits accrue predominantly to the North in the form of both access to raw materials for industrial development and super profits, which ignited and fuels the capital accumulation and production process; meanwhile, the social and environmental costs of this development in terms of lost livelihoods, an assault on territorial rights and the rights of nature, as well as ecological damage that reaches to the foundation of the production process and life itself, are borne disproportionately by the rural poor and the communities that inhabit and are seeking to eke out a living on the extractive frontier.

For the most part, the debate on unequal exchange, particularly that which arose around the question of development (within the framework of the Marxist dependency school of thought), departs from the formation of the prices of production. In this regard, through the configuration of the average rate of profit and the social distribution of surplus value between capitals and branches of production/commerce, it is possible to understand unequal exchange relations between primary goods and industrialised goods in line not only with the economic structure of extractive capitalism and the theory of dependency but also with Marx's theory of value. At the level of abstraction of Volume iii of Capital, all exchange—as Andrea Ricci (2019) appropriately points out—is unequal. However, when analysing international trade several critical issues such as wage differentials (Emmanuel, 1972) and structural differences in the organic composition of capital across the North-South divide (Amin, 1974) come into play.

Beyond these and other issues such as the potentiation of labour, global labour arbitrage and the problem of transformation in an international context (Astarita, 2006; Finger, 2020; Garay, 1980; Katz, 2018) currently debated, it is important to recognise that:

1. Unequal exchange involves both wage differentials and uneven development of the forces of production in the centre and the periphery of the capitalist world system (Dussel, 2019; Marini, 1974). In this system, the development of the forces of production at the centre is predicated on the underdevelopment of these forces on the periphery, hence the notion 'the development of underdevelopment' popularised by André Gunder Frank (1970) or the more theoretically precise concept of 'uneven capitalist development'.
2. The debates on unequal exchange have underestimated the importance of the General Law of Capital Accumulation postulated by Marx for understanding the dynamics of uneven development and unequal exchange. This law, which synthesises two fundamental contradictions of capitalist development—the capital-labour relation and the centre-periphery structure of international relations—is related to the advance and growing importance acquired, on the one hand, by monopoly capital, and on the other hand, by the proletarianisation of the peasantry with the resulting formation of an 'industrial reserve army of labour'. The uneven distribution of both developments along the core-periphery axis of the world system—i.e., the concentration of capital in the metropolitan centre of the system and the formation of a mobile labourforce—is

crucial for understanding the dynamics of unequal exchange in relation to the global capital accumulation process.

3 The international division of labour has been, and continues to be, a focal point in the analysis of unequal economic exchange. However, contrary to what many analysts of unequal exchange postulate, this division is neither static nor unidimensional. We posit that the turn from the 20th century into the first two decades of the new millennium has engendered a new double dynamic of peripheral capitalist development: (a) the exportation of natural resources needed for industrial development at the centre of the world system and expropriated in large part from the ancestral lands and territory of the Indigenous population and (b) the exportation of labour power, an essential commodity produced under similar conditions of 'accumulation by dispossession', namely, the displacement and impoverishment of the rural population.

4 The precondition of this dynamic is provided by the advance of industrial capital in dispossessing the direct producers and peasant farmers from the land and thus their means of production, and the advance of extractive capital in dispossessing the Indigenous communities by means of pollution and environmental degradation. The end result of this double dynamic—accumulation by dispossession—is variegated but it basically means that the dispossessed population, which is moreover often denied access to the commons, (i) is either displaced and impoverished, (ii) is forced to take the road out of rural poverty offered by the agencies of international cooperation (namely, migration and labour), (iii) pursues community-based development in the form of a social and solidarity economy or (iv) mobilises the forces of resistance in the form of a social movement, forming alliances across localised struggles (on this resistance dynamic see Barkin, Chapter 11 in this volume).

5 Equally important in regard to the problematic of uneven development, and central to our understanding of the development and resistance dynamics of extractive capital, is the phenomenon of *unequal ecological exchange*, which Foster and Clark (2020), following Marx, trace back to a biological rift, a fundamental contradiction between exchange and use value, which in some contexts leads to the destruction of the fundamental metabolism between human beings and nature. We elaborate on this point below.

## Dynamics of unequal economic exchange and uneven development

As of the end of the 1970s, large multinational corporations initiated a deep restructuring process, transferring part of their production processes to peripheral regions in the search for cheap and flexible labour as well as natural resources. This strategic shift entailed what has been described as the 'new nomadism' in the global production system, including commercial and services endeavours, that are supported by the enormous wage differentials that exist and are reproduced along the North-South divide—the so-called global labour arbitrage (Foster, McChesney and Jonna, 2011a: 18). This, in turn, led to a reconfiguration of global value chains, or more precisely, global networks of monopoly capital, through the establishment of export platforms that operate as enclave economies in peripheral countries (Delgado Wise and Martin, 2015). The resulting strategic shift in the organisation of industrial production has been spectacular:

> The top one-hundred global corporations had shifted their production more decisively to their foreign affiliates [mainly in the South], which now account for close to 60 per cent of their total assets and employment and more than 60 per cent of their global sales.
>
> (UNCTAD, 2010)

In a similar vein, it is estimated that in the periphery around 100 million workers are directly employed in assembly plants established in more than 5,400 processing zones that operate in at least 147 countries (UNCTAD, 2020). This significantly transformed the global geography of production to such an extent that most of the world's industrial employment (more than 70 per cent) is now located in countries on the periphery (Foster, McChesney and Jonna, 2011b).

It is important to highlight that this phenomenon does not imply an industrialisation of the periphery, but rather a doubly regressive process that we have conceptualised as economic sub-primarisation (Cypher and Delgado Wise, 2008). This means that, far from moving towards a manufacturing export-led model, what is actually being exported under the guise of manufactured exported goods and without leaving the country is not surplus value but the labourforce itself. It should not be forgotten that the assembly plants installed in peripheral countries operate with imported inputs and tax exemption regimes, meaning that the substance of the manufacturing goods exported by them is the labour power incorporated into the productive process. Hence, it entails an indirect or disembodied export or extraction of labour power in the guise of exporting manufactured products (Cypher and Delgado Wise, 2012).

Three considerations in relation to the genesis and implications of this peculiar export or extraction modality are relevant here. The first refers to the implementation of 'structural reforms' in macroeconomic policy mandated under the Washington Consensus—a commercial opening of the economy to capitalist markets freed from regulatory constraint of the development state (*globalisation*, in development discourse), *privatisation* (of the means of production and state enterprises), *liberalisation* (of the flow of capital and commerce) and *deregulation* (of the market). The aim and underlying objective of these 'structural reforms' and the associated vaunted Structural Adjustment Programs (SAPs), imposed by the World Bank and the International Monetary

Fund as pillars of the neoliberal restructuring process, was and continues to be the dismantling and disarticulation of the productive apparatus of these economies for the purpose of rearticulating diverse production processes in an asymmetric and subordinate relation to the dynamics of accumulation in the major imperialist powers under the command of monopoly capital. On the dynamics of this neoliberal restructuring process, see, inter alia, Harvey (2003) and Petras and Veltmeyer (2001) and also Chapter 2 in this volume.

The second consideration, as a corollary or consequence of this momentous shift, is a destruction of the labour markets in the formal economy of nations on the periphery of the world system, which have created what analysts (Sotelo Valencia, 2015; Standing, 2011) have described as a peri-urban semi-proletariat or 'precariat', generating in the process a surplus population thrown into the ranks of informality or forced to emigrate in a South-North direction. The direct and indirect exportation of labour power through international labour migration is subjected to high vulnerability and severe restrictions regarding the labour and human rights of migrant workers. This immigrant labourforce, often categorised and treated as 'illegal' regardless of the labour market demand, is generally subjected to conditions of super-exploitation, discrimination and xenophobia, a situation that not only obscures the significant contributions that migrants make to destination economies and societies but also contributes to criminalising them and turning them into 'public enemies' with important political dividends for the neoliberal far right.

We must also bear in mind that these repositories of surplus migrant labour did not appear in a spontaneous manner. Nor were the migrants educated for free regardless of the labour time expended on the social reproduction of the labourforce. The costs of social reproduction, education and training, etc. are either assumed by the State in their countries of origin on the periphery of the world system or are assumed by the families of the migrants. These costs, when weighed against the remittances that are returned to their countries of origin, tend to be onerous. This implies that contrary to what is proclaimed by the World Bank and other institutions at the service of the interests of the US and other imperialist powers, remittances—and therefore labour migration—do not represent a North-South subsidy, but precisely the opposite: a South-North subsidy (Delgado Wise and Gaspar, 2018), which is to say, a disguised modality of unequal exchange.

The third consideration is that in addition to the direct exportation of labour power, its indirect or disembodied form of exportation deepens the relation of unequal exchange between peripheral countries and those located in the core, given the fact that through the assembly plants—most of them involving intra-firm trade—what is actually being transferred abroad are total profits, i.e., the entire stock of surplus value incorporated into the exported goods, as well as a supplementary labourforce for the accumulation of industrial capital in the centre of the system. It represents a modality of unequal exchange that on an international scale resembles the exchange that occurs between labour and capital at the heart of the production process. It is difficult to imagine a more exacting modality of unequal exchange between countries, with the added aggravation that what remains in the country of origin are wages and benefits that are much lower than those that would be granted in the country of destination.

Thus, we have the foundation of a new international division of labour based on the direct and indirect or disembodied exportation and extraction—and the subsequent exploitation—of labour power, although at this initial stage it is nourished by an unlimited supply of low or relatively low-skilled labour.

The exportation of labour power acquires its broader meaning by incorporating a repository of highly qualified labour in the workforce. This development is a relatively recent phenomenon associated with the profound restructuring process undergone by the most advanced innovation systems worldwide. The most salient features of this restructuring process, taking as a reference what we conceive of as Silicon Valley's Imperial Innovation System (Delgado Wise, Chávez and Gaspar, 2021), are: (i) the internationalisation of research and development (R&D) activities; (ii) the creation of scientific cities where collective synergies are engendered to accelerate innovation processes; (iii) the implementation of new forms of control and appropriation of the products of scientific-technological labour by the large multinational corporations; (iv) expansion along the North-South horizon of the labourforce in the areas of science, technology, engineering and mathematics (STEM areas); (v) monopoly control over agribusiness and the commodification and exportation of staple agricultural products; and (vi) the creation of an ad hoc institutional framework aimed at the concentration and appropriation of the products of the scientific-technological knowledge, or human capital, through a process of patenting, under the tutelage of the World Intellectual Property Organization (WIPO) in agreement with the World Trade Organization (WTO).

## The extractivist dynamics of unequal ecological exchange

In Indigenous cosmology, humanity is viewed as an integral part of nature, existing in harmony with it rather than in an antagonistic relation of domination and exploitation. The Indigenous population, which over five centuries of development have served as a repository of resources and wealth for the capitalist system, a mechanism or lever of capital accumulation, in this context is and has always tended to be highly respectful of 'mother earth' and its bounty, viewing itself as custodians of its integrity. However, with the beginnings of the modern era a rather different and contradictory view of nature, as a repository of wealth to be exploited and appropriated at will and subject to human domination, emerged. And with the advent of capitalism, we have the additional notion that nature is constituted by resources that are entirely at the disposal of capital to exploit and commodify for the purpose of both capital accumulation and economic development. The earth in this context was essentially viewed in terms of the idea that it was a 'gift' of Nature available for exploitation by Capital, an argument that, as Foster and Clark (2020) point out, was propounded by Malthus long before Marx. As for Marx, they note (p. 167) that while he accepted this as a reality of capitalist production, he 'nonetheless was aware of the social an ecological contradiction embedded in such a view'.

To briefly expand on this point, the wealth embodied in nature's bounty is a matter primarily not of exchange value or commodification but of use value—the uses that can be made of it. But as to the value of natural resources as commodities, i.e., when produced for sale on the market, it is an entirely different matter. 'To be sure', Foster (2000) notes, Marx agreed with classical liberal political economy that under the law of value 'nature' was accorded no value in itself. 'The earth', he wrote (as quoted by Foster), 'is active as an agent of production in the production of a use-value, a material product, say wheat'. But, Marx continues, it has nothing to do with producing the value of the wheat. The value of the wheat, as with any commodity under capitalism, including labour power, can be determined by measuring the hours of labour—labour power—consumed and used up in its production.

For Marx, however, this merely pointed to the very narrow, limited conception of wealth associated with capitalist commodity relations and a system built around exchange value. Genuine wealth, he argued, consists of use values—the characteristic of production in general, transcending its specifically capitalist form. Indeed, it is the contradiction between use value and exchange value engendered by capitalism that Marx considered to be one of the foremost contradictions of the entire dialectic of capital (Foster and Clark, 2020). Another contradiction, viewed from an Indigenous cosmological as opposed to a Marxist perspective, is that between nature and society. The contradiction consists in the fact that an unhindered exploitation of nature's bounty inevitably leads to environmental degradation or ecological destruction, which then threatens to undermine the ecological foundation not only of production but of life itself. The literature on this fundamental contradiction in the context of several decades of rapacious development on the extractive frontier in Latin America (and elsewhere, of course) is voluminous—and an indictment of the environmental destruction and devastation associated with the advance of extractive capital in the development process.

Nature, which contributes to the production of use values, arguably is just as much a source of wealth as labour—even though its contribution is not normally taken into account or measured in an accounting of the costs and benefits of 'development' (of the forces of production), or in a calculation as to what percentage of the total value of the product on capitalist markets is exported, that is appropriated by Capital.

To expand on this point, the value of the natural resources that are extracted from the earth, as measured by or reflected in its final sale price, clearly reflects not only the value added to the product by labour, i.e., the value of labour power, but also the contribution of Nature, which is appropriated not as surplus value but as resource rent and ground rent, which is normally shared by Capital (as a source of super profits) and the State (in the form of royalties and taxation). However, as noted, the contribution of nature to the total value of primary commodities on capitalist markets is usually not taken into account, adding to the failure of many analysts to appreciate the magnitude of capitalist and imperialist exploitation in the current context of extractive capitalism. For example, it has been estimated that up to 80 per cent of the total value of the minerals and metals exported from Bolivia to capitalist markets over the past decade was appropriated by Capital via the mechanism of commodity trade. Meanwhile, the State was able to appropriate an estimated maximum of 10 per cent of this value in the form of rent (concession fees, royalties, export duties and taxation of sales), around the same share received by workers in the form of wages.

This scenario, and the depth of imperialist exploitation (the appropriation of wealth generated by labour), is even more extreme in the case of Mexico, where the Auditor-General estimated that in the period 2005–2010 the government received barely 1.2 per cent of the total value of exported minerals and metals while the lion's share was appropriated by Capital and exported (Bárcenas, 2012). In the case of Colombia, the distribution of the wealth generated by the export sale of minerals on capitalist markets is even more uneven—less than one per cent of the mineral wealth generated was retained by the country (Colombia, Portal de Información Minera. http://www.imcportal.com).

The exploitation of the wealth created by labour and the pillage of the bounty of nature are reciprocal and equally important conditions of unequal economic exchange and uneven economic development. However, as Marx observed, there is an additional dynamic that needs to be taken into account. As he puts it, '[t]o a large extent the current wealth of the rich countries has been based on a historical system of ecological robbery', which, Foster and Clark (2020: 259) argue, has led to a process of unequal ecological exchange. As they see it, '[t]he only just and sustainable solution is one of contraction and convergence, whereby global per capita carbon emissions and ecological footprints are equalised, along with the elimination of imperialist rent (including both economic and ecological unequal exchange)'.

Foster and Clark argue this point as follows: 'The ecological problem under capitalism is a complex one. An analysis at the level of the entire globe is required'. In effect,

> ecological degradation at this universal level is related to the divisions within the world capitalist system, arising from the fact that a single world economy is nonetheless divided into numerous nation-states, competing with each other both directly and via their corporations. It is also divided hierarchically into centre and periphery, with nations occupying

> fundamentally different positions in the international division of labour, and in a world-system of dominance and dependency.

All of this, Foster and Clark add, makes the analysis of extractive imperialism complicated enough, but understanding has also been impeded by the under-development of an ecological materialist analysis of capitalism within Marxist theory as a whole. Nevertheless, it has long been apparent—and was stipulated in Marx's own work—that transfers of economic values and the extraction of surplus value or labour power are accompanied by real 'material-ecological' flows that transform relations between city and country, and between global metropolis and periphery. Control of such flows is a vital part of competition between rival industrial and financial centres.

Extractive or ecological imperialism, as Foster and Clark see it, presents itself most obviously in the following ways:

1 pillage of the resources of some countries by others and the transformation of whole ecosystems upon which states and nations depend;
2 massive movements of population and labour that are interconnected with the extraction and transfer of resources;
3 the exploitation of ecological vulnerabilities of societies to promote imperialist control;
4 the dumping of ecological wastes in ways that widen the chasm between centre and periphery; and overall
5 the creation of a global 'metabolic rift' that characterises the relation of capitalism to the environment, and at the same time limits capitalist development (p. 187).

Foster and Clark (2020), both political economists and ecologists who have provided the most relevant theoretically informed and profound analysis of the ecological contradiction of capitalist development, have themselves drawn the following conclusions from their investigations into the dynamics associated with this development:

1 'The growing race for resources behind the current geopolitical struggle is feeding a new extractivism, extending to every corner of the earth, and increasingly to the Arctic—where melting sea ice from climate change is opening up new realms for oil exploration'.
2 'Economically, the outward movement of generalised-monopoly capitalism is propelled primarily by the competitive struggle for low-cost position via global sourcing of labour and increasingly scarce raw materials, and the monopoly rents that all of this generates'.
3 The result…is enormous cost savings in production for individual monopolistic enterprises, generating widening profit margins, which, coupled with more traditional forms of tribute, leads to a continual inflow of imperial rent to the centre of the system.

4 The full extent of extracted surplus is disguised by the enormous complexity of global value chains, exchange ratios, hidden accounts, and above all by the nature of capitalist GDP accounting (in which the contributions of both labour and nature are underestimated or hidden, and ecological costs are externalised).

## Conclusion

Latin America in the current context of capitalist development is embroiled in the vortex and maelstrom of contradictory forces of social change generated by the recent advances of both monopoly capital and resource-seeking 'extractive' capital. Extractive capitalism in particular, in regard to both the exportation of raw materials and labour, poses a serious challenge because it has unleashed forces that not only threaten the livelihoods and lives of countless individuals and communities on the extractive frontier but also have led to a multidimensional crisis of global proportions. At issue in the debates that have surrounded these developments are a number of questions addressed in this volume, in particular the question as to the nature and power of the forces of resistance generated in this context, questions about the design of alternative models and possible pathway towards a post-extractivist transition, and in particular the role of extractivism as a vital part of a strategy of sustainable and inclusive development going forward along this path.

The authors who have collaborated to contribute a chapter to this volume are by no means of one mind regarding these issues. While none espouse the position taken by the guardians of the capitalist system and agencies of international cooperation such as the World Bank—that an extractivist model and policies provide economic opportunities for inclusive growth and development of which developing countries should avail themselves—they are divided as to the best way forward in a complex situation. Some of the contributors to this volume are of the view that there is no role for an extractivist approach towards development in the transition towards a more sustainable alternative to neoliberalism and capitalism. Animated by a vision of an alternative system that is sustainable in terms of both livelihoods and the environment, as well as social inclusion and environmental justice, and concerned for both territorial rights and the rights of nature, they argue that the only way forward is a world without extractivism, i.e., without resource extraction as a modality of capital accumulation. On the other hand, several contributors and some analysts (such as García Linera, the former vice-president of Bolivia) see and have conceptualised a third way, an alternative to embracing extractivist capitalism or rejecting it entirely (Bebbington, 2009). This 'third way' or intermediate position on the question of extractivism—the 'new extraction'—is predicated on 'resource nationalism' (taking ownership and control of the country's wealth of natural resources, reducing dependence on foreign investment) and includes both state control of vital industries and the industrialisation and commercialisation of the country's natural resources, as well as what might be conceived of as communal socialism, or community-based resource management—not merely incorporating the Indigenous groups and communities in the development process, or offering them a share in the proceeds and the bounty of nature, but recognising and fully respecting their autonomy (resource sovereignty) and territorial rights, and empowering them as custodians of mother earth.

## References

Acosta, A., J. Cajas-Guijarro, F. Hurtado-Caicedo and W. Sacher. (2020). *El festín minero del siglo XXI ¿Del ocaso petrolero a una pandemia megaminera?* Quito: Abya-Yala. https://bit.ly/2OLGWcc.

Amin, S. (1974). *Accumulation on a World Scale. A Critique of the Theory of Underdevelopment.* New York: Monthly Review Press.

Astarita, R. (2006). *Valor, mercado mundial y globalización.* Buenos Aires: Kaicron.

Bárcenas, F. (2012). "Detener el saqueo minero en México," *La Jornada*, sfebrero 28. http://www.jornada.unam.mx/2012/02/28/opinion/023alpol.

Bebbington, A. (2009), "The New Extraction: Rewriting the Political Ecology of the Andes?," *NACLA Report on the Americas*, 42(5): 12–21.

Cypher, J. and R. Delgado Wise (2008). "Mexico and the North American Free Trade Agreement: Re-Peripheralisation under the Labour Export-LED Model," in P. Bowles, T. Broomhill, T. Gutiérrez-Haces and S. McBride (eds.), *International Trade and Neoliberal Globalism. Towards re-peripheralization in Australia, Canada and Mexico?* Abingdon: Routledge.

Cypher, J. and R. Delgado Wise (2012). *México a la deriva. Génesis, desempeño y crisis del Modelo Exportador de Fuerza de Trabajo.* Mexico: Miguel Ángel Porrúa.

Delgado Wise, R. (2021). "21st Century Imperialism and the Export of Labour Power," *Forum Wissenschaft*, 36(3): 18–22.

Delgado Wise, R., M. Chávez and S. Gaspar. (2021). *La Migración Mexicana Altamente Calificada de Cara al Siglo XXI. Problemática y Desafíos.* Mexico: CONACYT.

Delgado Wise, R. and S. Gaspar. (2018). "Claves para descifrar la arquitectura de la globalización neoliberal: exportación de fuerza trabajo e intercambio Desigual," in J.L. Calva (ed.), *La Globalización Neoliberal en Crisis.* Mexico: Juan Pablos: 159–186.

Delgado Wise, R. and D. Martin. (2015). "The Political Economy of Global Labour Arbitrage," in K. van der Pijl (ed.), *Handbook of the International Political Economy of Production.* UK: Edward Elgar Publishing: 59–75.

Dussel, E. (2019). *La producción teórica de Marx. Un comentario a los Grundrisse.* México: Siglo XXI.

Emmanuel, A. (1972). *Unequal Exchange: A Study of the Imperialism of Trade.* New York & London: Monthly Review Press.

Farah, I. and L. Vasapollo, (eds.) (2011). *Vivir bien. ¿Paradigma no-capitalista*? La Paz: CIDES-UMSA.

Finger, B. (2020). "Unequal Exchange: Key Issues for the Labor Theory of Value," *Journal of Socialist Theory*, 48(2–3): 169–187.

Foster, J.B. (2000). *Marx's Ecology: Materialism and Nature.* New York: Monthly Review Press.

Foster, J.B. (2002), "Capitalism and Ecology: The Nature of the Contradiction," *Monthly Review*, 54(4): 6–16.

Foster, J.B. and B. Clark. (2020). *The Robbery of Nature: Capitalism and the Ecological Rift*. New York: Monthly Review Press.

Foster, J.B., B. Clark and R. York. (2010). *The Ecological Rift. Capitalism's War on the Earth*. New York: Monthly Review Press.

Foster, J. B., R. W. McChesney and J. Jonna. (2011a), "The Internationalization of Monopoly Capital," *Monthly Review*, 63(2): 3–18.

Foster, J.B., R.W. McChesney and J. Jonna. (2011b). "The Global Reserve Army of Labour and the New Imperialism," *Monthly Review*, 63(6): 1–15.

Frank, A. G. (1970) *Latin America: Underdevelopment or Revolution: Essays on the Development of Underdevelopment and the Immediate Enemy*. New York: Monthly Review Press.

Garay, L.G. (1980). "Hacia una crítica interna de la teoría del intercambio desigual de Emmanuel," *Cuadernos de Economía*, 1(2): 53–114.

Harvey, D. (2003). *The New Imperialism*. Oxford: Oxford University Press.

Harvey, D. (2014). *Seventeen Contradictions and the End of Capitalism*. London: Profile Books.

Katz, C. (2018). *La Teoría de la Dependencia, cincuenta años después*. Buenos Aires: Batalla de Ideas.

Marini, R.M. (1974). *Dialéctica de la Dependencia*. México: Era.

Petras, J. and H. Veltmeyer (2001). *Globalization Unmasked: Imperialism in the 21st Century*. London: ZED Press.

Petras, J. and H. Veltmeyer (2014). *Extractivist Imperialism in the Americas*. Leiden: Brill Books.

Ricci, A. (2019). "Unequal Exchange in the Age of Globalization," *Review of Radical Political Economics*, 51(2): 225–245.

Sotelo Valencia, A. (2015). *The Future of Work: Super-Exploitation and Social Precariousness in the 21st Century*. Boston: Brill.

Standing, G. (2011). *The Precariat: The New Dangerous Class*. London: Bloomsbury.

UNCTAD (2010). *World Investment Report 2010*. Nueva York: United Nations.

UNCTAD (2020). "Special Economic Zones and Urbanization." https://unhabitat.org/special-economic-zones-sezs-and-urbanization.

Veltmeyer, H. and J. Petras (2014). *The New Extractivism*. London: Zed Books.

# 2 The geoeconomics and geopolitics of extractive capital in Latin America

*Henry Veltmeyer*

Capitalism as a system of commodity production is commonly viewed as both a powerful engine of economic growth and a monster that wreaks havoc on society and nature, not out of malice or because of the self-seeking behaviour and greed that it engenders, but simply by virtue of its nature as a system. Nothing has propelled this view of capitalism as much as the aftermath and outcomes of forces set in motion in the 1980s with the installation of what was then a 'new world order'. This new world order, dubbed by many as 'neoliberal globalisation', not only set new rules for international trade and the free flow of investment capital but also required prospective entrants—governments seeking to integrate their economies into the global economy—an adjustment of their macroeconomic policies in the direction of globalisation, privatisation, deregulation and liberalisation (Petras and Veltmeyer, 2001). Nowhere was this 'structural adjustment program' and the associated 'structural reform' agenda implemented as fully as it was in Latin America, where—under conditions of a 'third world' debt crisis—the implementing agencies of this program (the World Bank, the IMF) had acquired the requisite leverage to impose it. The outcome of this Latin American turn towards free market capitalism based on the ideas of the Mont Pelerin Society includes a neoconservative counterrevolution in development thought and practice, the financialisation of production and an associated propensity towards crisis and the emergence of powerful forces of popular resistance against the neoliberal policy agenda. Together, these changes constituted an epoch-defining shift in the form taken by capitalism in Latin America, namely, 'inclusionary state activism'—neodevelopmentalism combined with the extraction of natural resources and the (re)primarisation of exports.

This chapter elucidates some critical dimensions of this process relevant to the development and resistance dynamics resulting from the forces of change released in the development process within the institutional and policy framework of the new world order. Our aim in advancing this argument is twofold. The first is to provide a context for the diverse analytical probes into the development process unfolding in the region provided by the collaborating authors in this book. Secondly, the aim is to bring into focus the powerful forces of change generated by three fundamental contradictions inherent to

DOI: 10.4324/9781003301981-4

capitalism (on these contradictions and their dynamics see Chapter 1). A third ancillary aim is to establish the difference between two major forms of capital (and capitalism), one based on the capital-labour relation (the exploitation of labour power) and the other based on the extraction or pillage of the natural resource wealth (i.e. natural capital) provided by the bounty of nature rather than the exploitation of labour. These two forms of capital, as well as others (financial, industrial, human), do not exist in isolation but in every conjuncture of the development process are always found to interact in some combination. Another aim of the chapter is to establish the economic and political dynamics resulting from and associated with the advance of resource-seeking 'extractive' capital in the development process—dynamics that are elucidated in the other chapters of the book.

Our focus regarding the political dynamics of capitalist development in the region is on the response of the post-neoliberal policy regimes formed in the wake of what has been widely interpreted as a progressive cycle of Latin American politics—a cycle that appears to have come to an end with the downward turn in the primary commodities boom and another pendulum swing of regime change from the progressive left back to the reactionary right.

The chapter briefly outlines the responses made to the forces of social change and capitalist development by the mass of semi-proletarianised and impoverished 'peasant' farmers (the 'rural poor', in the development discourse of economists at the World Bank) dispossessed from their means of production in the capitalist development process in the agricultural sector (for the development dynamics in this sector, see Chapter 4). This semi-proletariat of rural landless workers, self-identified as peasants, has made two strategic and political responses to the advance of capital in the agricultural sector. One was to take the pathway out of rural poverty staked out and advocated by the World Bank and the other agencies of International Cooperation, namely migration and labour (on this see Delgado Wise and Veltmeyer, 2016). The other response (see Part IV—Chapters 9–11) was in the form of collective action—for the communities on the extractive frontier negatively impacted by the destructive operations of extractive capital to mobilise the forces of resistance against the advance of capital and extractivism and to reclaim their ethnic and communal territorial rights as well as their access to the commons.

This argument is constructed as follows. First, we describe the dynamic pattern in the inflows of capital (foreign direct investments—FDI) unleashed by the neoliberal policy agenda. This form of capital, in the first instance, was to a significant extent directed towards the purchase of the assets of the state enterprises put up for sale by the neoliberal regimes that came to power in the 1990s. But in response to changing conditions in the world market that included a demand for primary commodities, an increasing proportion of these capital flows were 'resource-seeking', driven by the search for the commodities that would supply this demand.

The second part of the chapter outlines the changing role of the state in this process, with particular reference to the left-leaning or 'progressive' post-neoliberal governments that were formed in South America in a tidal wave of regime change. These regimes were the primary recipients of the rapidly expanding wave of resource-seeking foreign investments, which we term 'extractive capital'. By the same token, these regimes were eager to take advantage of the growing demand for natural resources or commodities and to strike a deal with the agents of extractive capital and the multinational corporations in the extractive sector.

In Part III, we briefly discuss the policy dynamics of the post-neoliberal regimes formed in the first decade of the new millennium, and also the search for a new economic model based on two pillars—'inclusionary state activism' or the 'new developmentalism', a policy regime proposed by economists at CEPAL (Bresser-Pereira, 2007), and what has been described as the 'new extractivism' (the allocation of the resource rents collected in the process of 'natural resource development') in the direction of social programs oriented towards inclusive development, i.e. poverty reduction (Infante and Sunkel, 2009). Various dimensions of this neoextractivism are discussed before we bring into focus the forces of popular resistance engendered by the operations of extractive capital.

## The new geoeconomics of capital

The neoliberal reforms implemented as the price of admission into the new world order not only released the 'forces of economic freedom' from the regulatory constraints of the developmental state but also generated a massive inflow of capital in search of profit-making opportunities related to assets, resources and markets. This was in the 1990s, which saw a sixfold increase in the inflows of capital in the form of FDI in the first four years of the decade and then another sharp increase from 1996 to 2001, which tripled, in fewer than ten years, the foreign capital accumulated in the region in the form of foreign-company subsidiaries (ECLAC, 2012: 71).

Another major inflow occurred in the first decade of the new millennium, in conditions of a primary commodities boom that worldwide affected primarily South America. In 2009, Latin America received 26 per cent of the capital invested globally in mineral exploration and extraction (Sena-Fobomade, 2011). According to the Metals Economics Group, a 2010 bonanza in world market prices led to another increase of 40 per cent in investments related to mineral exploration, with governments in the region, both neoliberal and post-neoliberal, competing fiercely for this capital. In 2011, South America attracted 25 per cent of global expenditures related to mining exploration (Kotze, 2012).

The growth of FDI flows to Latin America over the past two decades have been in the direction of services (particularly banking and finance) and the natural resources sector—the exploration, extraction and exploitation of fossil and biofuel sources of energy, precious metals and industrial minerals and agrofood products. In the earlier era of state-led development, FDI had predominantly served as a means of financing the capitalist development of industry and a process of 'productive transformation' (technological conversion and modernisation), reflected in the geoeconomics of global capital and the dynamics of FDI flows at the time. However, the new world order and two generations of neoliberal reforms changed and dramatically improved conditions for capital. For one thing, it opened up in Latin America a market for US technology and investment, and goods manufactured at the centre of the system. It also provided greater opportunities for resource-seeking capital—consolidating the role of Latin America as a source and supplier of natural resources and exporter of primary commodities—a role reflected in the flows of productive investment away from manufacturing and services towards the extractive sector, a trend that unfolded over the years of the primary commodities boom (see Table 2.1).

The year 2008 saw the beginnings of a downward trend in resource-seeking investments, which corresponded closely to a decline in the price of many commodities on the world market. In some economies, such as Colombia, Ecuador and the Plurinational State of Bolivia, the natural resources sector continued to receive a large share of FDI inflows, but even in these economies, that share is waning. The reason for this is a general decline in the prices of minerals and a sharp fall in the price of oil, a trend that can be traced out as of 2012 but is only now (in mid-2021 when prices began to rebound) starting to affect FDI inflows. However, the end of the boom has led to a significant change in the sectoral distribution of FDI (see Table 2.1) as well as a slowdown in the rate of GDP growth for many countries, especially those like Venezuela that are heavily resource export dependent.

The sectoral shift in the distribution of FDI was particularly evident in the wake of what has been described as a 'global financial crisis'—a phenomenon that had such minimal repercussions in Latin America that some analysts (e.g. Porzecanski, 2009) would ask, 'What crisis?' In the midst of this supposed crisis, the inflow of resource-seeking investments in 2008 reached unprecedented levels, accentuating the trend towards primarisation—or, more precisely, reprimarisation—that can be traced back to the new millennium in the context of the growing demand for energy and minerals, and foodstuffs for the expanding middle class in the emerging markets of China and the other BRIC countries.

*Table 2.1* Percentage distribution of FDI by sector in a commodities boom

| | *'00* | *'01* | *'02* | *'03* | *'04* | *'05* | *'06* | *'07* | *'08* | *'09–13* | *'14* |
|---|---|---|---|---|---|---|---|---|---|---|---|
| Resources | 10 | 12 | 12 | 11 | 12 | 13 | 12 | 15 | 30 | 24 | 17 |
| Manufacturing | 25 | 26 | 38 | 35 | 38 | 37 | 36 | 35 | 22 | 38 | 35 |
| Services | 60 | 61 | 51 | 48 | 46 | 48 | 51 | 49 | 47 | 38 | 48 |

*Source:* Arellano (2010); ECLAC (2014: 23).

*Table 2.2* Trendlines of commodity exports, per cent of total exports

| | *1990* | *2000* | *2004* | *2006* | *2008* | *2011* | *2013* |
|---|---|---|---|---|---|---|---|
| Argentina | 70.9 | 67.6 | 71.2 | 68.2 | 69.1 | 68.0 | 66.9 |
| Bolivia | 95.3 | 72.3 | 86.7 | 89.8 | 92.8 | 95.5 | 96.0 |
| Brazil | 48.1 | 42.0 | 47.0 | 49.5 | 55.4 | 66.2 | 63.6 |
| Chile | 89.1 | 84.0 | 86.8 | 89.0 | 88.9 | 89.2 | 86.1 |
| Colombia | 74.9 | 65.9 | 62.9 | 64.4 | 68.5 | 82.5 | 82.4 |
| Ecuador | 97.7 | 89.9 | 90.7 | 90.4 | 91.3 | 92.0 | 93.3 |
| Mexico | 56.7 | 16.5 | 20.2 | 24.3 | 27.1 | 29.3 | 23.8 |
| Peru | 81.6 | 83.1 | 83.1 | 88.0 | 86.6 | 89.3 | 85.4 |
| Venezuela | 89.1 | 90.9 | 86.9 | 89.6 | 92.3 | 95.5 | ... |
| LA | 66.9 | 40.9 | 46.2 | 51.3 | 56.7 | 59.8 | 53.0 |

*Source:* ECLAC (2004, 2012, 2014: 102).

The scope of this reprimarisation process, and the increasing reliance of neoliberal and post-neoliberal regimes in South America on the export of primary commodities for foreign exchange and fiscal revenues, is evident in the data presented in Table 2.2.

At the turn into the new millennium the service sector still accounted for almost half of FDI inflows, but Table 2.3 points towards a steady and increasing flow of capital towards the natural resources sector, at least in South America and especially as regards mining, over the past decade. In 2006, it grew by 49 per cent to reach US$59 billion, exceeding the total FDI inflows of any year since economic liberalisation began in the 1990s (UNCTAD, 2011: Figure II.18). Income on FDI (i.e. profits on capital invested in the resource sector) was particularly high in Brazil and Chile, US$14 billion and US$20 billion, respectively, leading to a surge in the share of retained earnings in total FDI inflows. In the South American countries for which data are available, income on FDI soared from an average of 10 per cent in 2000–2003 to 61 per cent in 2006 (ECLAC, 2012). Despite the global financial and economic crisis at the time, FDI flows towards Latin America and the Caribbean reached a record high in 2008 (US$128.3 billion), an extraordinary development considering that FDI flows worldwide at the time had shrunk by at least 15 per cent (ECLAC, 2012). This counter-cyclical trend signalled the continuation of the primary commodities boom and the steady expansion of resource-seeking capital in the region.

The rapid expansion in the flow of FDI towards Latin America in the 1990s reflected the increased opportunities for capital accumulation provided by the neoliberal policy regimes in the region. In the new millennium, however, conditions of capital accumulation and the context for capitalist development had radically changed. In this context, which included a major realignment of economic power and relations of trade in the world market (especially the emergence of the BRICS) and the growth in both the demand for and the prices of primary commodities, the shift of FDI towards Latin

*Table 2.3* Net inflows of FDI, by leading countries (US$ billions)

| | *2000* | *2002* | *2004* | *2006* | *2008* | *2010* | *2012* | *2014* |
|---|---|---|---|---|---|---|---|---|
| Argentina | 10.4 | 2.2 | 4.1 | 5.5 | 9.7 | 7.9 | 12.6 | 6.6 |
| Bolivia | 0.7 | 0.7 | 0.1 | 0.3 | 0.5 | 0.6 | 1.1 | 0.7 |
| Brazil | 32.8 | 16.6 | 18.2 | 18.8 | 45.1 | 48.5 | 65.3 | 62.5 |
| Chile | 4.9 | 2.6 | 7.2 | 7.4 | 16.8 | 15.4 | 30.3 | 22.9 |
| Colombia | 2.4 | 2.1 | 3.0 | 6.7 | 10.6 | 6.8 | 15.8 | 16.1 |
| Mexico | 18.0 | 23.7 | 23.7 | 19.3 | 22.0 | 21.4 | 13.4 | 22.8 |
| Peru | 0.8 | 2.2 | 1.6 | 3.5 | 4.1 | 8.5 | 12.2 | 7.6 |
| Venezuela | 4.7 | 0.8 | 1.5 | 0.6 | 1.7 | 1.9 | 3.2 | 0.3 |

*Source:* ECLAC (2012: 50, 2015: Table 1.6).

America signified a major change in the geoeconomics and geopolitics of global capital. For the first time, flows of FDI into Latin America from 2000 to 2007 exceeded that into the United States, surpassed only by flows into Europe and Asia.

The global financial crisis brought about an even more radical change in the geoeconomics of global capital, both in regard to its regional distribution (increased flows to Latin America) and sectoral distribution (concentration in the extractive sector). In 2010, in the throes of a financial and production crisis, the advanced capitalist economies at the centre of the system and the epicentre of the crisis (the US and the EC) received less than 97 per cent of global investment capital—for the first time since UNCTAD has tracked and kept records of these flows, i.e. since 1970 (Zibechi, 2012). In 2005, the 'developing' and 'emerging' economies attracted only 12 per cent of global flows of productive capital. But in 2010 FDI flows into Latin America increased by 34.6 per cent, well above the growth rate in Asia, which was only 6.7 per cent (UNCTAD, 2012).

The flow of productive capital into Latin America over the past decade has been fuelled by two factors: commodity prices, which remained high through most of this period, attracting 'natural resource-seeking investment', and the solid economic growth of the South American sub-region, which encouraged market-seeking investment. This flow of FDI was concentrated in four South American countries—Argentina, Brazil, Chile and Colombia—which accounted for 89 per cent of the sub-region's total inflows. The extractive industry in these countries, particularly mining, absorbed the greatest share of these inflows. For example, in 2009, Latin America received 26 per cent of global investments in mineral exploration (Sena-Fobomade, 2011). And together with the expansion of oil and gas projects, mineral extraction constitutes the single most important source of export revenues for a majority of countries in the region.

> Although the flow of resource-seeking capital is concentrated in four South American countries, Brazil accounted for the bulk of FDI flows.

> FDI flows to it reached a new high in 2008 of US$45 billion, 30 per cent above the record level posted the year before (ECLAC, 2012). Mexico, the second largest recipient of FDI in the region, was hit hard by the financial crisis and consequently saw FDI inflows fall 20 per cent over the same year. Much of this fall can be attributed to the decline of FDI in the services and manufacturing sectors, and reduced US imports. In contrast, natural resource seeking FDI drove an expansion of capital flows into Argentina, Chile and Colombia, especially in the mining sector. Thus, while efficiency- and market-seeking FDI have more weight in private capital flows into Mexico and the Caribbean, resource-seeking FDI accounts for the bulk and weight of FDI in the region.
>
> (UNCTAD, 2007: 122–123)

Thus, South America today is the centre of gravity for the new geoeconomics and geopolitics of global capital—the new extractivism and the post-neoliberal state.

## Progressive extractivism: a new model for Latin America?

The new millennium opened with a boom—a primary commodities boom. This was stimulated by changes in the global economy, specifically, the ascent of China as an economic power and the associated demand by industry and the middle class for raw materials (minerals, fuel and food). The demand for these commodities was stimulated by security needs of some governments related to energy and food as well as the 'economic opportunities' perceived by the multinational corporations in the extractive sector. This demand led to the growth of what the Food and Agriculture Association of the United Nations (FAO, 2011) and the World Bank (2010) describe as 'large-scale foreign investment in the acquisition of land'—'landgrabbing', in the parlance of critical agrarian studies (Borras, Franco, Gomez, Kay and Spoor, 2012). On the global dynamics of landgrabbing, see Kaag and Zoomers (2014).

The volume of the capital deployed to this end (the extraction of non-renewable natural resources) and the profits made in the process are staggering. Higginbottom (2013: 193) estimates that from 1997 to 2010 the multinationals that dominate the world economy extracted a total of US$477.6 billion in profit and direct investment income from Latin America, most of it derived from primary commodity exports. As for the financial returns to other foreign investors, the *Financial Times* reported that trades in commodities, in the context of the primary commodities boom and the financialisation of capitalist production, led to the accumulation of large reserves of capital and huge fortunes (Blas, 2013). As Blas observed: 'The world's top commodities traders have pocketed nearly $US250 billion over the last decade, making the individuals and families that control the largely privately-owned sector big beneficiaries of the rise of China and other emerging countries'—and, one might add, beneficiaries of the turn towards extractivism and export primarisation.

A wave of resource-seeking FDI was a major feature of the political economy of global capitalist development at the turn into the first decade of the new millennium. Another was neoliberalism's fall from favour as an economic doctrine and model in several countries in Latin America, where powerful social movements successfully challenged this model. Over the past decade, as a result of social movement activism, a number of countries in South America underwent a process of regime change—a tilt towards the left in what has been described as 'progressive extractivism'. The political victories of these democratically elected 'progressive' regimes opened a new chapter in Latin American history. At the same time, the wide embrace of resource-seeking FDI has generated deep paradoxes for these progressive regimes committed to addressing what UNDESA (2005) has described as Latin America's 'inequality predicament' (the most unequal distribution of wealth and income in the world) and what diverse organisations representing the Indigenous movement have described as 'the crisis of nature'.

Some leaders and social movements in this context speak of revolution—Venezuela's 'Bolivarian' revolution, Bolivia's 'democratic and cultural revolution' and Ecuador's 'citizens' revolution'—and, together with several governments that have embraced the new developmentalism (the search for a more inclusive form of development), these regimes have indeed taken some steps in the direction of poverty reduction and social inclusion, using the additional fiscal revenues derived from resource rents to this purpose. Yet, like their more conservative neighbours—regimes such as Mexico's and Colombia's, committed to both neoliberalism and an alliance with 'imperialism'—the left-leaning progressive regimes in the region find themselves entangled in a maze of renewed dependence on natural resource extraction (the 'new extractivism') and primary commodity exports ('reprimarisation'). Further, as argued by Gudynas (2009), this new 'progressive' extractivism is much like the old 'classical' extractivism in its destruction of both the environment and livelihoods and its erosion of communal territorial rights and the autonomy of Indigenous communities most directly affected by extractive development, which continues to generate relations of intense social conflict.

Despite the use by the 'progressive' centre-left governments of resource rents as a mechanism of social inclusion and direct cash transfers to the poor, it is not at all clear whether these governments are able or disposed to pursue revolutionary measures in their efforts to bring about more inclusive and sustainable forms of democratic development while continuing to toe the line of extractive capital and its global assault on nature and livelihoods. The problem here is twofold. One is a continuing reliance of these left-leaning post-neoliberal regimes (indeed, all but Venezuela) on neoliberalism ('structural reforms') at the level of macroeconomic public policy. The other relates to the so-called 'new extractivism' based on 'inclusionary state activism' and continued reliance on FDI—on striking a deal with global capital in regard to sharing the resource rents derived from the extraction process.

The problem here relates to several contradictions intrinsic to extractive capitalism and the machinations of the imperial state in support of extractive capital. These contradictions are reflected in a process of uneven economic and social development—economic concentration tending towards the extremes of wealth at the centre of what has morphed into a world system and poverty on the periphery—in addition to what some economists call 'the resource curse' (the fact that so many resource-rich countries are developmentally poor, while many resource-poor countries have achieved a high level of economic and social development).

One expression of this resource curse is what economists term the 'Dutch disease', reflected in the slowdown currently experienced by Brazil in its engine of economic growth—down from an average of over six per cent a year from 2003 to 2010 to only 0.9 per cent in 2012 (BBC News, 2013). Another is the boom-bust cycle characteristic of extractivism and natural resource development. The slowdown of the commodity super-cycle in the same year (Konold, 2013) suggests that extractive capitalism has not yet outgrown this propensity. A third manifestation of the resource curse is that sites of natural resource extraction cannot be established by design so as to take locational advantage of existing infrastructure, markets and labour supply. Development projects based on natural resource extraction are necessarily localised in enclaves with linkages to the global market but with very few to other sectors of the local and national economy, with the inevitable result of relatively few multiplier effects regarding a broader development process.

The 'resource curse' can also be understood and explained in terms of a series of fundamental contradictions but that assume more extreme proportions under conditions of extractive capitalism, which is based on the exploitation of natural resource wealth, rather than the classic form of capitalism, which is based on the exploitation of labour. This relates to what the French economist Piketty (2014) describes as the 'central contradiction' of capitalism, that is, its tendency to produce ever-greater levels of inequality.

Whether, as argued by Piketty, uneven development and expanding social inequalities are the central contradictions of capitalism, there is no question that extractive capitalism is more inequality-generating than the capitalism of the post-Second World War years. The latter was based on the exploitation of the 'unlimited supplies of surplus labour' released in the process of capitalist development of agriculture while the former is technology-intensive and uses relatively little labour in the production process. As a result, labour receives a reduced and disproportionately small share of the social product, particularly in the mining sector.

Even in Bolivia, where the government 'nationalised' the country's reserves of non-renewable fossil fuels and sub-soil mineral resources, it is estimated that labour receives less than 10 per cent of the world market value of exported minerals—six per cent in the case of Argentina and Chile

(Solanas, 2007: 2)—and as little as 1.2 per cent in the case of Mexico. Evidently, workers in the sector have not benefitted from the extraction of minerals and primary commodity exports. James Cypher (2012) reports that after four years of booming exports (from 2002 to 2006) the index of the value of real wages in the extractive sector had grown by less than 0.5 per cent. This is in contrast with the well-established pattern of cumulative wage increases in the era of post-war state-led development based on 'labour-seeking' FDI, human resource development and industrialisation. In this context, the share of labour (wages and salaries) in the social product (i.e. in the income derived from the production process) settled at a much higher rate—as much as 60 per cent—with undeniably positive (although contradictory) development outcomes and implications.

Another contradiction of capitalist development relates to the historical process of transforming traditional forms of agrarian society based on diverse precapitalist relations of production into a modern industrial capitalist system. As some Marxists in the political ecology tradition (e.g. Foster, 2000) understand it, the contradiction—between nature and society, or between the logic of capital accumulation and the ecological foundations of society and the economy—is manifest in the ecological unsustainability of industrial capitalism. However, the destructive operations of extractive capital in the new millennium, and the emergence of an evidently new phase in the development process (extractive capitalism), have brought into sharp relief the contours and dynamics of this fundamental contradiction. It could even be argued that in the contemporary context this contradiction between economic development and the biophysical world trumps both the so-called first contradiction (and relation of conflict), that between labour and capital, and the secondary 'north-south' contradiction (Farah and Vasapollo, 2011).

Perhaps the most serious 'contradiction' of natural resource development is that a large part of the benefits of economic activity is externalised, i.e. appropriated by groups outside the country and region, while virtually all of the costs—economic, social and environmental—are internalised and disproportionately borne by the Indigenous and farming communities contiguous to the open pit mines and other sites of extraction. These costs have given rise to powerful forces of resistance—socioenvironmental movements concerned with preventing further enclosures of the global commons (land, labour, natural resources) and with the negative impacts of extractivism on their livelihoods.

## The resistance and class struggle on the frontier of extractive capital

Socioenvironmental conflicts have been part of South America for a long time. They generally involve communities struggling against the unequal distribution of costs and benefits of natural resource extraction and the negative impact this extraction has on their livelihoods.

There is a burgeoning literature that analyses the emergence of socioenvironmental conflicts related to the extractive sector. This literature can be placed into four categories. First, there are those studies that explore the sociopolitical and cultural implications of such conflicts for development policies and processes (Chaparro, 2006; CIDSE/ALAI, 2009; Escobar, 2010; Svampa and Antonelli, 2009).

A second set of studies stress the implications of these conflicts on state-building processes as part of shifting interrelations between social movements, corporations and states (Bebbington, 2009).

A third set of studies explores the negative socioenvironmental impacts of extractivism and the political responses of local communities directly affected by them, which is to demand respect for their territorial and human rights and the accountability of powerful state and corporate interests for undermining their sources of livelihood (Martinez-Alier, 2003; Rodriguez and Carruthers, 2008; Tetreault, 2014). As Martinez-Alier sees it, conflicts emerge when there are asymmetric expectations and understandings concerning the economic, ecological, social and cultural values of different resource-sensitive projects.

A fourth small group of studies have begun to explore the regional and international dimensions of extractivism and related socioenvironmental conflicts (Ceceña et al., 2007; Saguier, 2014).

A fifth approach focuses on how these conflicts can be managed (Collier and Venables, 2011). From this conflict resolution perspective, the problems associated with the political economy of natural resource extraction are not systemic or endemic but can be 'managed', and the negative impacts or social and environmental costs mitigated. Resource conflict management, it is argued, is a matter of 'corporate social responsibility' and 'good governance', which includes engagement of the communities, even 'civil society', in the process of securing a 'social licence' to operate (explore and extract) in addition to a government-issued concession to explore for resources and a licence to operate.

In addition and in contrast to these studies, a number of scholars have begun to explore the social class dynamics of these socioenvironmental movements that have sprung up on the latest frontier of capitalist development (e.g. Veltmeyer and Petras, 2014). From this class analysis perspective, extractivism represents the emergence of a new form of rentier capitalism based on the pillage of natural resources rather than the more customary exploitation of labour. It can also be seen as a new form of imperialism, which, according to Girvan (2014), in the historical context of the Americas has always involved pillage.

From this perspective, the socioenvironmental conflicts and resource wars that have surrounded the contemporary operations of extractive capital are viewed as a new form of 'primitive accumulation' as Marx had it (to separate the direct producers from their means of production, forcing their expulsion from the land and leading to their proletarianisation). Essentially, it is argued that the operations of extractive capital represent a new form of enclosing the commons—denying the Indigenous and farming communities close to the mines and extractive operations of capital access to the global commons of land, water and resources, and denying any respect for the rights claimed by the Indigenous communities.

The mechanism of 'enclosure' in this analysis is the concession granted by the state to the corporations to explore and extract the sub-soil resources (oil and gas, minerals and metals) from land occupied or owned by these communities or their members. Therefore, the form taken by the resistance on the new frontier of extractive capital includes rejection of the economic model used by the governments to make public policy in the area of economic development and the demand that their territorial and human rights be respected and, above all, protests against the negative impact of extractivism on both their livelihoods and the environment on which they depend (see Gustafson, this volume).

The destruction of the livelihoods of the communities contiguous to and most directly affected by the operations of extractive capital stems not only from their negative socioenvironmental impacts but also from the contradictory practices and policies associated with resource-driven 'economic development' discussed above. These practices reflect what has been defined as the logic of 'accumulation by dispossession' (Harvey, 2003). This refers to a mode of generating material wealth that comes at the expense of depriving people of their rights and causing ecological destruction. Accumulation by dispossession has been characteristic of diverse and prevailing forms of capitalism where accumulation depends on expanding the boundaries of a global market via the privatisation and commodification of nature, i.e. land, water and natural resources such as sub-soil minerals, fauna and the forest. Some suggest that Indigenous peoples are particularly vulnerable in this regard since they are directly dependent on nature, the rich biodiversity of rain forests, rivers and land, not only for their livelihood and material subsistence but also for their social and cultural reproduction, which is to say, their very existence.

Large-scale mining, particularly in the form of open pit mining, with the use of cyanide and mercury in the mineral extraction process, is responsible for the pollution of the region's precious water reserves. This could potentially lead to the decimation of fish in rivers, health problems for people exposed to contaminated water, loss of fertile land and shortages of clean water for human and animal consumption. Needless to say, fishing and the husbandry activities of communities located near mining sites are put at risk or are compromised.

As already mentioned, the communities of peasant farmers and Indigenous peoples are particularly vulnerable (CIDSE/ALAI, 2009). In the region of the Southern Andes—and the border between Chile and Argentina—large-scale mining activities have been responsible for the pollution of mountain glaciers and downstream water, such as in the case of Barrick Gold's Pascua Lama project. Mining is a particularly environment-sensitive industry that

*Table 2.4* Socioenvironmental conflicts related to mining in Latin America, 2006–2010

| *Countries (selected)* | *Conflicts* | *Projects* | *Companies* | *Communities* |
|---|---|---|---|---|
| Argentina | 24 | 30 | 43 | 37 |
| Bolivia | 5 | 6 | 7 | 21 |
| Brazil | 21 | 21 | 37 | 34 |
| Chile | 25 | 28 | 42 | 34 |
| Colombia | 16 | 32 | 21 | 20 |
| Ecuador | 4 | 5 | 4 | 5 |
| Guatemala | 4 | 4 | 7 | 4 |
| Mexico | 13 | 13 | 17 | 15 |
| Peru | 26 | 26 | 42 | 28 |

*Source*: OCMAL. http://www.olca.cl (retrieved January 28, 2011).

has led to conflict in connection to its negative social and ecological consequences. Throughout Latin America, out of a total of 184 ongoing resource conflicts, 154 are mining related (Table 2.4). These conflicts have affected 222 communities (179 of them in South America) and involve 247 companies (Saguier, 2014: Table 7.1. N.6).

## Social movement resistance dynamics

A class analysis of these socioenvironmental conflicts and associated struggles and social movements is concerned with three sets of issues, each a matter of debate. The first has to do with the social base of these social movements, establishing the social relation of community members to the system of economic production. The second concerns the matter of understanding the relationship of the communities affected by the operations of extractive capital with both the state and the companies involved, as well as the relationship of capital to the state. A third issue, which is not explored here, concerns the political dynamics of the associated class struggle.

On the first issue, the prevailing view is to see community members as a proletariat, the latest victims of the capitalist development process in which the direct producers are separated from their means of production as a mechanism of capital accumulation—'accumulation by dispossession', as Harvey has it. In the classical context analysed by Marx the mechanism of accumulation—the generation of a proletariat, or a class for hire, and with it a reserve army of surplus labour—involved the enclosure of the commons needed by the communities of small-scale direct producers, or peasant farmers, to subsist. In the contemporary context analysts have established two mechanisms of dispossession: one is large-scale foreign investment in the acquisition of land, or 'landgrabbing'; the other is enclosure of the commons by means of a public policy of privatisation and commodification, converting natural resources into means of production and productive resources or assets.

Extractivism in the current context is taking diverse forms, including 'landgrabbing' and enclosures of the commons: large-scale foreign investments in the acquisition of land with the aim of securing access to natural resources for extraction and sale on the world market. Although it has not generated significant forces of resistance or any social movements, it has resulted in a relation and condition of conflict with the local communities who are pressured to abandon the land either by the local agents of the foreign or local investors, or by legislative or administrative fiat.

A second dimension of the class struggle on the expanding frontier of capitalism is the relationship of the communities that are negatively impacted by the mining of minerals and metals and by the commodification and extraction of water and other resources, to the companies in the extractive industry and the state. The relation of these communities to the companies is one of economic exploitation and political conflict. However, the role of the state in this struggle is very much at issue. By a number of accounts (see, for example, the case studies in Veltmeyer and Petras, 2014), because of a coincidence of economic interest (resource rents and additional fiscal resources for the government, super-profit for the companies) the state tends to side with the companies in their relation of conflict with the communities negatively affected by the operations of extractive capital.

A good example of this is Peru under President Humala who came to power in June 2011 with a promise to support local communities against the mining companies (on a platform of 'water before gold'). However, when open and violent protests erupted during his term between the Canadian mining company Minera Afrodita and the Awajun Indigenous communities in the town of Bagua, the Armed Forces turned against the protesters, resulting in 33 deaths, 200 wounded and 83 detentions. This event, on June 29, 2013, was the last episode of a long process of protests led by the Awajun to oppose the concessions of exploration and exploitation rights to Afrodita in an area located in the Cordillera del Condor region where there has been a long-standing relation of confrontation and conflict between the government, Indigenous communities and the companies in the extractive sector.

Prior to the decade of the 1990s, the resistance and the popular movements in Latin America were primarily concerned with issues of social class relating to the struggle over land in the countryside and wages and working conditions in the urban centres. In the 1990s, however, the popular movements, with the agency of class-based and community-based social movements, mobilised against the policies of the neoliberal state (and the governing regimes). By the end of the decade, a number of these movements, led by proletarianised peasant farmers, rural landless workers and Indigenous communities (for example in Chiapas, Brazil, Ecuador and Bolivia) achieved major gains in their struggle, placing the existing neoliberal regimes on the defensive and provoking a legitimation crisis for the neoliberal state. At the turn of the 21st century, for all intents and purposes, neoliberalism was in decline if not dead, no longer able to serve its legitimating function in regard to the idea of globalisation and the new world order.

The key agents involved in this 'politics of resistance' against the imperial incursions of capital in the exploitation of natural resources—at least in the Latin American context—were and remain the predominantly Indigenous communities that populate the areas ceded by the different governments (be they neoliberal or post-neoliberal in form) to the foreign mining companies for the exploration and exploitation of natural resources in their territorial lands. However, they also include a variety of civil society groups and NGOs that have been drawn into the conflict between global capital and local communities. And the forces of resistance to resource imperialism include new social movements formed to protest against the damage caused by resource extraction to the environment, as well as against its effects on the health and livelihoods of the local population and the miners themselves, who face life-threatening working conditions and health concerns. In other words, many of these movements are rooted in those negatively affected by the impacts of resource extraction and mining operations (for example, *Red Mexicana de Afectados por la Minería* and the *Confederación Nacional de Comunidades del Perú Afectadas por la Minería* or CONACAMI).

The social actors who engage these forces of resistance use tactics such as marches and demonstrations, road and access blockades and other forms of direct collective action to impede mining operations. According to a forum of people, communities and groups affected by the operations of mining capital, the exploitation of the region's mineral resources in 2009 had reached levels never before experienced (*Foro de los Pueblos Indígenas Minería, Cambio Climático* y *Buen Vivir* 2010). Of particular concern was the Amazon region, where abundant deposits of gold, bauxite, precious stones, manganese, uranium and other materials are coveted by the companies operating in the mining sector.

Another concern was the perceived connection between the multinational corporations in the sector and a host of foundations and NGOs with an alleged humanitarian or religious concern for the environment and the livelihoods of Indigenous peoples and communities. In this connection, Eddy Gómez Abreu, president of the *Parlamento Amazónico Internacional*, declared that they had 'incontrovertible evidence of these transnationals and foundations, under the cover of supposed ecological, religious or humanitarian concerns, collaborat[ing] in the effort to extract… strategic minerals', as well as espionage and illegal medical experiments on the Indigenous population (Sena-Fobomade, 2011). In effect, he alleged that the mining companies regularly used foundations and other NGOs as one of their tactics to secure the consent of the local population to their projects and operations and to manipulate them. If this be the case, these NGOs are engaged to continue the long, sordid history of colonial rule, dispossession, expropriation and exploitation.

## Conclusion

The growing protest movement against mining capital and extractivism in the region has engaged the forces of resistance not just against neoliberalism and globalisation, but against the underlying operative capitalist system. Thus, the so-called politics of natural resource extraction is not merely a matter of better resource management, a post-neoliberal regulatory regime, a more socially inclusive development strategy or a new form of governance—securing the participation of local communities and stakeholders in decisions and policies in which they have a vital interest. Given the interests that the state represents and the coincidence of these interests with those of the 'transnational capitalist class' (to use the phrase of some globalisation sociologists), the officials and managers of the post-neoliberal state generally side with capital against labour and have not reacted well to the civil society organisations that criticise or resist their mineral policies or extractive projects. The anti-extractivist protests in the region have received international activist (and academic) recognition as part of a global environmental justice movement, but the agents and progressive officials of the post-neoliberal states simply ignore them—and proceed with their geopolitical project: to advance the exploitation of the country's natural resources by global capital in the public interest. Thus, the politics of natural resource extraction resolves into a matter of class struggle—of combatting the workings of capitalism and imperialism in the economic interests of the dominant class and mobilising the forces of resistance, found in the Indigenous communities of semi-proletarianised peasant farmers, against these interests.

## References

Arellano, M. (2010). "Canadian Foreign Direct Investment in Latin America," *Background Paper*, North–South Institute, Ottawa, May.

BBC News. (2013). "Brazil Economy Grew 0.9% in 2012," March 1. www.bbc.co.uk/news/business-21630930.

Bebbington, A. (2009). "The New Extraction: Rewriting the Political Ecology of the Andes?," *NACLA Report on the Americas*, 42(5): 12–21.

Blas, J. (2013). "Commodity Traders Reap $250bn Harvest," *Financial Times*, April, 14.

Borras, S. Jr., J. Franco, S. Gomez, C. Kay and M. Spoor (2012). "Land Grabbing in Latin America and the Caribbean," *Journal of Peasant Studies*, 39(3–4): 845–872.

Bresser-Pereira, L.C. (2007). "Estado y mercado en el nuevo desarrollismo," *Nueva Sociedad*, 210, July–August: 110–125.

Ceceña, A., P. Aguilar and C. Motto. (2007). *Territorialidad de la dominación. Integración de la Infraestructura Regional Sudamericana (IIRSA)*. Buenos Aires: Observatorio Latinoamericano de Geopolítica.

Chaparro, E. (2006). *Industrias extractivas y desarrollo sostenible en América Latina*. Santiago: CEPAL.

CIDSE/ALAI. (2009). *América Latina: Riqueza privada, pobreza pública*. Quito: CIDSE/Alianza de organizaciones católicas para el desarrollo & ALAI/Agencia Latinoamericana de Información.
Collier, P. and A. J. Venables. (2011). *Plundered Nations? Successes and Failures in Natural Resource Extraction*. London: Palgrave Macmillan.
Cypher, J. (2012). "Neoextracciónismo y Primarización: ¿la subida y decadencia de los términos del intercambio en América del Sur?," *Presented at the International Seminar 'Como Sembrar el Desarrollo en América Latina'*, UNAM, Instituto de Investigaciones Económicas, México, DF, October 29–31.
Delgado Wise, R. and H. Veltmeyer. (2016). *Agrarian Change, Migration and Development*. Halifax: Fernwood Publications.
ECLAC – Economic Commission for Latin America and the Caribbean. (2004, 2012, 2014). *Statistical Yearbook for Latin America and the Caribbean*. Santiago: United Nations.
ECLAC – Economic Commission for Latin America and the Caribbean. (2015). *Foreign Direct Investment in Latin America and the Caribbean*. Santiago: United Nations.
Escobar, A. (2010). "Latin America at the crossroads," *Cultural Studies*, 24(1): 1–65.
FAO – Food and Agricultural Organization of the United Nations. (2011). *Land Tenure and International Investments in Agriculture*. Rome: FAO.
Farah, I. and L. Vasapollo (eds.). (2011). *Vivir bien. ¿Paradigma no-capitalista*? La Paz: CIDES-UMSA.
*Foro de los Pueblos indígenas, minería, cambio climático y buen vivir*. (2010). *Suscribe Declaración*. Lima: Servicios en Comunicación Intercultural Servindi, 23 November.
Foster, J. B. (2000). *Marx's Ecology: Materialism and Nature*. New York: Monthly Review.
Girvan, N. (2014). "Extractive Imperialism in Historical Perspective," in J. Petras and H. Veltmeyer, *Extractive Imperialism in the Americas*. Leiden: Brill Books.
Gudynas, E. (2009). "Diez tesis urgentes sobre el nuevo extractivismo. Contextos y demandas bajo el progresismo sudamericano actual," pp. 187–225 in *Extractivismo, Política y Sociedad*. Quito: CLAES/CAAP.
Harvey, D. (2003). *The New Imperialism*. Oxford: Oxford University Press.
Higginbottom, A. (2013). "The Political Economy of Foreign Investment in Latin America Dependency Revisited," *Latin American Perspectives*, 40(3): 184–206.
Infante, R. and O. Sunkel. (2009). "Chile: Towards Inclusive Development," *CEPAL Review*, 97, April: 133–152.
Kaag, M. and A. Zoomers. (2014). *The Global land Grab: Beyond the Hype*. London: Zed Books.
Konold, M. (2013). "Commodity Supercycle Slows Down in 2012," *Worldwatch Institute*, October 10.
Kotze, C. (2012). "South American Mining Sector to Continue as Resource-Based Economy," *Mining Weekly*, June 15. http://www.miningweekly.com/article/south-american-mining-sector-to-continue-as-resource-based-economy-2012-06-15.
Martinez-Alier, J. (2003). *The Environmentalism of the Poor: A study of Ecological Conflicts and Valuation*. London: Edward Elgar Publishing.
Petras, J. and H. Veltmeyer. (2001). *Unmasking Globalization: The New Face of Imperialism*. Halifax: Fernwood Books.
Piketty, T. (2014). *Capital in the Twenty-First Century*. Cambridge: Belknap Press of Harvard University Press.

Porzecanski, A. (2009). "Latin America: The Missing Financial Crisis," pp. 1–37 in *ECLAC Studies and Perspectives, No. 6*. Washington, DC: ECLAC.

Rodriguez, P. and D. Carruthers. (2008). "Testing Democracy's Promise: Indigenous Mobilization and the Chilean State," *European Review of Latin American and Caribbean Studies*, 85, October: 3–21.

Saguier, M. (2014). "Minería para el desarrollo integral en la estrategia de UASUR," *Conference ISA/FLACSO*, Buenos Aires, July 23–25.

SENA-Fobomade. (2011). *Se intensifica el extractivismo minero en América Latina. Foro Boliviano sobre Medio Ambiente y Desarrollo, 03–02, 2005*. http://fobomade.org.bo/art-1109.

Solanas, F. (2007). "El despojo de los metales argentinos (Parte IV)," *Rebelión*, July 31: 1–9. http://www.rebelion.org/seccion.php?id=9.

Svampa, M. and M. Antonelli. (2009). *Minería Transnacional, Narrativas del Desarrollo y Resistencias Sociales*. Buenos Aires: Editorial Biblos.

Tetreault, D. (2014). "Mexico: The Political Ecology of Mining," pp.172ff. in H. Veltmeyer and J. Petras, *The New Extractivism*. London: Zed Books.

UNCTAD – United Nations Conference on Trade and Development. (2007). *World Investment Report 2007: Transnational Corporations, Extractive Industries and Development*. Geneva: United Nations.

UNCTAD – United Nations Conference on Trade and Development. (2011). *World Investment Report. Non-Equity Modes of International Production and Development*. Geneva: United Nations.

UNCTAD – United Nations Conference on Trade and Development. (2012). *"Investment Trend Monitor," No. 8*. New York: United Nations, January 24.

UNDESA – United Nations Department of Economic and Social Affairs. (2005). *The Inequality Predicament: Report on the World Social Situation*. New York: United Nations.

Veltmeyer, H. and J. Petras. (2014). *The New Extractivism*. London: Zed Books.

Zibechi, R. (2012). La nueva geopolítica del capital," *La Linea de Fuego*, April 27. https://lalineadefuego.info/la-nueva-geopolitica-del-capital-por-raul-zibechi/.

# Part II

# Extractivism in the Mines and the Countryside

# 3 Mexico's mining and petroleum policies under AMLO

## A turn to neoextractivism?

*Darcy Tetreault*

Until recently, Mexico's extractive policies were considered to be representative of 'classical extractivism' (Veltmeyer and Petras, 2014), especially because of the favourable conditions afforded to foreign mining capital, including low effective taxation, no royalties, lax enforcement of environmental laws and cheap and flexible labour. Moreover, since the 1990s, successive federal governments in Mexico have taken steps to allow and encourage private investment in petroleum and electricity, culminating in the energy reform that was carried out in 2013 and 2014. In these ways and others, since the 1980s Mexico's extractive policies have been increasingly aligned with the neoliberal principles of privatisation, free trade, labour flexibility and market-led development.

Andrés Manuel López Obrador (AMLO) promised to put an end to neoliberalism. The former mayor of Mexico City (from 2000 to 2005) was a presidential candidate in 2006 and 2012, before finally winning the presidential election of 2018 by a landslide. In the years leading up to his electoral victory, AMLO toured the country declaring solidarity with diverse resistance movements to extractive projects and denouncing corruption, neoliberalism and the energy reform in particular. He quit the left-of-centre Democratic Revolution Party (PRD in its Spanish acronym) in early 2013, when its leaders agreed to go along with the energy reform by signing the *Pact for Mexico*, and he went on to form a new political party, the National Regeneration Movement (MORENA), which gained control of both the Senate and the Chamber of Deputies in 2018, thereby providing AMLO with unhampered parliamentary support for his political agenda during the first three years of his administration.

What policy changes has AMLO's government introduced to the mining and petroleum sectors during this three-year period? In what ways can these be considered steps towards progressive neoextractivism? And what has remained the same? These are the main questions that this investigation seeks to address. The analysis proceeds as follows: First, some key points of reference in the emerging literature dealing with extractivism in Latin America are reviewed in order to identify the core policy orientations associated with neoextractivism. The following three sections investigate manifestations of

DOI: 10.4324/9781003301981-6

neoextractivism in Mexico's extractive policies along lines of continuity and change. Section 2 deals with the ownership of subterranean resources and the legal conditions for private-sector participation in mining and petroleum activities. Section 3 analyses the mechanisms in place for capturing and distributing resources rents; and Section 4 examines environmental policy and state mediation of conflicts around extractive activities. While recognising that forms of extractivism exist beyond the exploitation of subterranean resources—for example, in agriculture, forestry, dam building and wind farms—because of space limitations, this chapter focuses on the mining and petroleum sectors.

The findings of this analysis point to manifestations of neoextractivism in the current government's actions to strengthen the parastatal company *Petróleos Mexicanos* (Pemex), to increase refining capacity to reach higher levels of self-sufficiency in gasoline and diesel production and to try to nationalise lithium reserves that have not already been granted to private companies through concessions. Notwithstanding these initiatives, the main finding to emerge from this analysis is that AMLO's government has so far given continuity to the overarching institutional framework that was put in place during the neoliberal era to exploit subterranean resources, regulate extractive activity and capture and redistribute rent. In this context, community-based groups and solidarity organisations struggling to defend territories from the imposition of large-scale extractive projects have found themselves at loggerheads with the current government's agenda to expand mining and petroleum activities. The last section of this chapter seeks to nuance these findings by summing up the main lines of continuity and the most important changes brought by AMLO's government to extractive policies during the first half of his six-year mandate.

## Classical extractivism versus neoextractivism

Neoextractivism (also called 'new extractivism') has been described as a policy-orientation trend among progressive governments in Latin America that emerged during the first decade of the 21st century, oriented towards increasing the rate of extracting natural resources, while also increasing the state's share of resource rents in order to finance progressive social policies (Gudynas, 2010; Veltmeyer and Petras, 2014; Burchardt and Dietz, 2014). At its conception, a 'pink tide' in electoral politics coincided with a primary commodities boom, largely driven by rapid economic growth in China (Cypher, 2010). The first wave of this tide included the governments formed under Hugo Chávez in Venezuela, 'Lula' in Brazil, Nestor Kirchner in Argentina, Evo Morales in Bolivia, Tabaré Vázquez in Uruguay and Rafael Correa in Ecuador. In the context of high international prices for primary commodities, these governments were able to assert greater economic and political control over the exploitation of natural resources in order to garner for the state a greater share of the rents derived from their extraction and exportation.

Moreover, these resource rents 'have been invested in ambitious social policies and infrastructure for economic development assuring the legitimacy of the incipient post-neoliberal state and ensuring continuing popular support of the extractivist drive especially among the urban and peri-urban working classes' (Arsel et al., 2016: 881).

In some of the literature dealing with neoextractivism, this progressive policy orientation is contrasted with classical extractivism (alternatively called 'conventional' or 'traditional' extractivism), thereby setting up a dichotomy of prototypes. Gudynas (2010: 26), for example, relates classical extractivism to the policy trends that held sway during the neoliberal era, when 'the imposition of taxes, tariffs, and licenses was reduced, and thus the collection of surpluses by the state was limited and depended on the trickle-down effect'. This is juxtaposed with neoextractivism, where 'the state is much more active in capturing surpluses', either indirectly through the imposition of higher taxes and royalties, or directly by strengthening state-run extractive enterprises.

Adopting the same dichotomy, Veltmeyer and Petras (2014: 225) distinguish between classical extractivism exemplified by Colombia and Mexico, 'where the governing regime continues to follow a neoliberal path towards national development within the orbit of the Washington Consensus and US imperialism' and what has been described as 'progressive extractivism' and 'post-neoliberal developmentalism', associated with the extractive and social policies of the countries mentioned above. With regard to Mexico, the same binary lenses have been employed to argue that the country's extractive policies moved in some ways towards the model of new extractivism in 2014, when new mechanisms were introduced to capture resource rents and to use them to finance social development programs in extractive regions (Tetreault, 2020).

The common denominator between classical and neoextractivism is an export-oriented capitalist development strategy geared towards achieving high rates of economic growth. This implies using the state apparatus to promote increasing the rate of extracting subsoil resources, with private-sector participation. This is what Svampa (2018) refers to as the commodity consensus. Along these lines, Latin American governments from across the political spectrum responded to the primary commodities boom by taking measures to expand the extractive frontier, in order to increase the exportation of raw materials, resulting in the primarisation of their economies (Cypher, 2010). Moreover, this drive to accelerate natural resource exploitation continued after 2012, when primary commodity prices fell, in an effort to make up for lost revenue (Svampa, 2018); and it has received renewed impetus from rising prices for primary commodities in the context of the COVID-19 pandemic.

Having established this common denominator, it is important not to lose sight of the differences between the policies implemented by progressive governments and those employed by 'neoliberal' or 'conservative' ones. As Ellner (2021: 6) suggests: 'Important policies related to extractivism differentiate not only Pink Tide governments from conservative ones but also governments within both categories'. What is more, extractive policies within a given country can vary from one sector to another; for example, in Bolivia, where state interventions and policies for mining and petroleum exploitation are representative of the new extractivism, while 'a somewhat laissez-faire strategy in the agricultural sector' (McKay, 2017: 203) has given rise to a form of extractivism in soybean production that can be said to be representative of the classical model. As analysed below, similar incongruities exist between the mining and petroleum sectors in Mexico.

## Ownership and private-sector participation in extractive activities

Article 27 of the Mexican Constitution, established in 1917 after seven years of revolutionary war, states that mineral and hydrocarbon resources are the property of the nation. Nonetheless, private and foreign firms continued to have access to the country's subsoil resources after the Mexican Revolution, through concessions granted by the federal government. This situation came to an end in the petroleum sector when it was nationalised in 1938. It has continued to this day in the mining sector, with modifications in ownership patterns over time.

Mexico's petroleum sector was opened completely to private and foreign investment by Enrique Peña Nieto's government in December 2013, when changes were made to Article 27 of the Constitution to allow private enterprises to invest in all phases of hydrocarbon exploitation. While petroleum resources technically remain the property of the state, private firms have since been allowed to book proven reserves and take ownership of oil and gas at the wellhead. The tendering process for awarding upstream contracts to private companies began in 2014 with 'round zero' to set aside reserves for Pemex, where it had the capacity to exploit them. The following three rounds resulted in the Mexican government awarding 111 contracts to private firms, of which 76 are licence contracts and the rest either profit- or product-sharing agreements.

AMLO has put an end to these bidding rounds. At the same time, he has promised to respect the contracts signed between 2014 and 2018. In public discourse, he frequently admonishes the private firms that hold exploration and production contracts for not investing nor producing enough. This is indicative of his main focus, which is to increase the rate of extracting hydrocarbons in order to generate public revenue to finance his administration's social policies and development initiatives. Accordingly, he has opened new avenues for private-sector participation in the petroleum sector via Integral Contracts for Exploration and Extractive Services. These contracts have a duration of between 15 and 25 years; Pemex maintains ownership of entitlements and continues as an operator, and private firms are remunerated through a fee in dollars per unit of hydrocarbon produced. According to

Pemex's Business Plan 2019–2023, the government expects to attract 108 billion pesos of private investment through these contracts between 2020 and 2023 (equal to about US$5 billion) (Pemex, 2019: 192).

Another important opportunity for private-sector participation in Mexico's petroleum sector is in the refinery that is being built at the Dos Bocas port in the state of Tabasco. This is one of AMLO's flagship megaprojects. It is meant to reduce the dependence that Mexico has on importing refined hydrocarbons from the United States, which in 2018 supplied more than three quarters of the gasoline consumed in the country. It is a controversial project, among other reasons because of the large amounts of carbon dioxide the refinery is expected to emit and because it is being built in a coastal zone that is prone to flooding. Initially, AMLO tried to auction off the project in its entirety to a limited number of foreign companies who were invited to participate. However, in May 2019, he announced that none had submitted a proposal that fits within the project's budget (US$8 billion) and timeframe (to be completed by the end of 2022); and that his government was planning to go ahead with the project under the supervision of the Ministry of Energy and Pemex, with private sector participation. For this purpose, a bidding process was organised around five 'packages' of the refinery's infrastructural components and a select group of companies were invited to participate. In July 2019, it was announced that six firms had submitted successful bids and soon thereafter they were contracted to initiate the refinery's construction: Fluor Enterprises, ICA Fluor, Samsung Engineering, Asociados Constructores DBNR, Kellogg Brown and Root and Constructora Hostotipaquillo.

Besides the new refinery, AMLO's government has Pemex revamping the country's six existing refineries, which in 2019 were operating at under 40 per cent of their combined total capacity. Originally, the plan was to increase Pemex's refining capacity from 612 thousand barrels per day (TBPD) in 2019 to 1,470 TBPD by 2023—when the refinery at Dos Bocas was expected to be operating at its full capacity (340 TBPD), in order to meet 70 per cent of the country's projected demand for gasoline and 93 per cent of the demand for diesel (Pemex, 2019: 188–189). However, on 24 May 2021, AMLO announced the closing of a deal to have Pemex buy Shell's 50 per cent share of the Deer Park refinery in Texas to become the sole owner, at a cost of US$596 million. In this way, according to the president's discourse, the country is now poised to become completely self-sufficient in gasoline and diesel production by 2023.

In May 2021, AMLO's government made changes to the Hydrocarbons Law in an effort to strengthen the state's capacity to revoke permissions from private companies that transport, store and/or distribute hydrocarbons, because of non-compliance with administrative requirements or for infringing the law. Other changes sought to eliminate the asymmetrical regulation imposed on Pemex by the 2013–2014 energy reform. However, these changes were immediately challenged by affected private companies and business groups, whose lawyers flooded the courts with *amparos* (a legal recourse to contest grievances that allegedly violate the Constitution), resulting in the suspension of the reform in accordance with the rulings of judges siding with private-sector interests. Faced with these obstacles, AMLO announced his intention to seek constitutional reform, not only to make changes to the Hydrocarbons Law but also to strengthen the state's role in electricity production and distribution.

As for the mining sector, since parastatal companies were privatised in the late 1980s and early 1990s, large mining projects in Mexico have been carried out exclusively by private capital, both domestic and foreign. Mexican firms own the majority of mines in the phase of operation. They have invested about twice as much capital as foreign mining firms since the early 1990s (Azamar Alonso, 2017: 153). At the same time, foreign capital (especially Canadian) has taken the lead in exploration, with a focus on gold and silver. Today, the largest gold and silver mines in the country are owned and operated by Canadian mining companies.

The federal government delivered over 45 thousand mining concessions to the private sector between 1994 and 2018, covering an area of approximately 105 thousand hectares, equivalent to over half of the country's territory.[1] Since AMLO became president, no additional mining concessions have been granted, because, in his own words, the previous ones 'were obtained not to produce, not to extract minerals, but to speculate financially'. At the same time, there has been no initiative to rescind the mining concessions granted by past governments, nor of changing their terms.

On 1 October 2021, AMLO announced a proposal for constitutional change to nationalise lithium reserves, coupled with his proposal for changes in the energy sector. At the same time, AMLO has promised to respect the conditions of the eight existing concessions granted to foreign companies to extract lithium from Mexico. When this was announced, the only project in the country to be in the stage of construction was the Sonora Lithium Project, owned in equal shares by the English company Bancora and the Chinese company Gangfeng, with the latter in the process of acquiring 100 per cent ownership. With 1.67 million tons of proven reserves and almost twice that of probable reserves, the lithium reserves for this project are considered to be among the largest in the world.

Importantly, no changes were made to Mexico's mining law during the first three years of AMLO's government. Also, his government has given the green light to a number of new toxic mega-mining projects that promise to bring billions of dollars of private investment to Mexico between 2021 and 2024. These include the following open-pit gold and silver mines: *Metates*, in the state of Durango, where Canadian company Chesapeake Gold plans to invest US$3.46 billion; *Media Luna*, in Guerrero, where Canadian company Torex Gold plans to invest US$496 million; *Orisyvo*, in Chihuahua, where Fresnillo PLC (a subsidiary of Industrias Peñoles) has announced that it will invest US$430 million; and *Camino Rojo*, in Zacatecas, where Canadian-based Orla Mining estimates that its initial investment will be US$123 million.

Finally, it is worth noting the priority given to mining and hydrocarbon extraction in the context of the COVID-19 pandemic. When AMLO's government announced on 31 March 2020 the immediate suspension of all non-essential activities in an effort to slow the propagation of the virus, petroleum extraction was exempt and continued uninterrupted, as did the construction of the refinery at *Dos Bocas*. Workers on offshore rigs were particularly vulnerable. By mid-November 2020, 356 Pemex workers had died from COVID-19, by far the highest number of any petroleum company in the world (Stillman, 2020). Mining was initially classified as a non-essential activity, but in the context of soaring prices for gold and other minerals and under intense pressure from business groups, after six weeks AMLO's government reclassified it as essential. In 2020, outbreaks of COVID-19 occurred at several mines in the country, including Equinox Gold's *Los Filos* mine in the state of Guerrero, Newmont and Goldcorp's *Peñasquito* mine in Zacatecas and Great Panther's *Topia* mine in Durango.

## Policies to capture and distribute resource rents

Until 2014, mining companies operating in Mexico did not have to pay royalties, only a token fee for the right to explore and extract minerals: five pesos per hectare during the first two years and increasing to 111 pesos per hectare after ten years. As part of the *Pact for Mexico*, signed on 23 January 2013, Peña Nieto's government promised to introduce royalties to the mining sector. This was brought into law in December of that year by making changes to the Federal Law of Rights to collect royalties equal to 7.5 per cent of the net income declared by mining companies from their operations in Mexico, plus 0.5 per cent on the sale of precious metals. This law went into effect at the beginning of 2014, when prices for minerals and metals were falling.

In effect, the royalties introduced by Peña Nieto's government are similar to the ones that were in place during the late 1970s, when mining companies paid a royalty of seven per cent on the value of their production, nine per cent in the case of gold (Urías, 1980: 956). One important difference, though, is that Peña Nieto's government introduced focusing mechanisms to use mining royalties to finance social development projects in mining regions. For this purpose, the *Fund for the Sustainable Regional Development of Mining States and Municipalities* was created. The changes made in December of 2013 to Article 275 of the Federal Law of Rights stipulate that 77.5 per cent of the royalties collected from mining companies be channelled to this fund, 20 per cent to the Ministry of Finance and Public Credit for infrastructure development and the remaining 2.5 per cent to cover operating expenses. Until modifications to this law were made by AMLO in 2019, 62.5 per cent of the mining fund's resources were channelled to municipalities with mining activities and 37.5 per cent to the corresponding state governments. The types of projects that were supposed to be financed by the mining fund include the remodelling of schools and public spaces, the provision of piped water, sewers, landfill sites, public transport, roads and electricity.

The mining fund received 14.16 billion pesos between 2014 and 2018, equal to approximately US$817 million. A report released in 2016 by Mexico's Chief Audit Office underlined numerous problems, from administrative omissions affecting the collection of royalties, to a severe lack of transparency and accountability in the allocation of resources on all levels. For these reasons, which were frequently reported on by the press, the mining fund gained widespread notoriety by the time AMLO became president. On 12 April 2019, he announced that his government was investigating the embezzlement of the fund's resources and that he was looking for ways to cut out intermediaries, meaning state and municipal governments. Although the investigation has not led to any prosecutions, the executive branch did take measures to change the way in which the fund is managed by centralising its resources in the Ministry of Public Education and by eliminating the mechanisms for concentrating spending in mining regions.

Along these lines, the Federal Law of Rights was modified again on 12 December 2019 to reallocate the mining fund's resources. Now, 85 per cent goes to the Ministry of Public Education and the Ministry of Health, which have been entrusted to carry out the same types of projects as mentioned above; five per cent to the Ministry of Energy 'to carry out actions to strengthen the mining sector' (Article 275); and ten per cent goes to the federal government, to be used for infrastructure development. As observed by Fundar (2019: 2), this reform has 'eliminated the provision that linked the application of the fund to communities and municipalities where there is mining'; what is more, there is no 'transparency or certainty regarding allocation criteria, nor mechanisms to foster participation in the allocation and monitoring of resources'.

Turning now to policies for capturing rent in the petroleum sector, it is worth noting from the start that Pemex has long been the metaphorical goose that lays golden eggs for the federal government. During the post-World War II period, most of Pemex's product was consumed domestically at low cost, literally fuelling the industrialisation process. However, export volumes rose quickly during the 1970s as production came online from the discovery of huge reserves off the coast of Campeche. By the early 1980s, when oil prices were soaring, over half of the country's petroleum was being exported. While in 1973, the taxes levied on Pemex only amounted to 2.2 per cent of the federal government's revenue; by 1982 they represented 44 per cent (Colmenares, 2008: 57). Oil prices crashed thereafter, but the 'petrolisation' of public finances continued.

Between 1994 and 2013, the federal government received over 30 per cent of its income from Pemex, through a complex system of taxes that included nine different types of royalties, the first and most important equal to 71.5 per cent of the value of extracted oil and gas, after permitted deductions. While this allowed successive federal governments to continue with a policy of applying low effective taxes to private enterprises in other sectors of the economy, it left Pemex with a growing debt that by 2012 had reached US$59.6 billion, in spite of high oil prices during the first decade of the new millennium.

The energy reform promised to gradually lower Pemex's debt. The *Hydrocarbon Income Law* that was proclaimed on 11 August 2014, reduced to 65 per cent the amount paid on the value of hydrocarbons extracted after permitted deductions, and it simplified administrative matters by reducing the number of royalties that Pemex must pay to three. Still, with the reform's application coinciding with a fall in oil prices, Pemex's total debt climbed steeply during Peña Nieto's presidential term, reaching US$106.5 billion by the end of it. At the same time, the petroleum sector's contribution to the country's public finances fell to below 20 per cent after 2015. In short, the golden goose was being strangled.

In AMLO's discourse, the petroleum sector is meant to be a 'lever' or 'engine' of development, by providing energy for domestic consumption, job creation and resource rents for the state to expand social policies. Accordingly, he has made 'rescuing Pemex' a central objective. Three main corresponding lines of action have emerged during the first three years of his administration: (1) actions to combat the stealing of hydrocarbons, which according to official reports reduced the volume of stolen petroleum from 20.4 billion barrels in 2018 to 5.1 billion barrels in 2019; (2) increased investment in drilling and infrastructure development, giving priority to accelerating processes of secondary and improved recovery in mature fields and to exploration in adjacent fields (Pemex, 2019: 77); and (3) measures to strengthen Pemex financially. These include the following: (a) reducing the company's most important royalty (called 'shared utility rights') from 65 per cent to 54 per cent of the value of hydrocarbons extracted after permitted deductions; (b) negotiating in May 2019 a debt-restructuring loan for US$8 billion with JP Morgan, HSBC Holdings PLC and the Mizuho Financial Group (which did not by the way prevent Fitch Ratings from downgrading Pemex's debt to junk status the next month); and (c) injecting public resources into Pemex to help the company make its debt payments, starting with US$5 billion in September of 2019.

Before moving on to the next section, it is important to consider the mechanisms that were introduced in 2014 as part of the energy reform to capture and redistribute petroleum rent, as they have remained in place since AMLO took office. Article 2 of the Hydrocarbons Income Law establishes three ways for the state to capture petroleum rent: (i) from Pemex's activities in the areas assigned to it, (ii) from the contracts to come out of the bidding process and (iii) from taxes paid by private oil-and-gas companies and by Pemex. The first is the most important in terms of public revenue. It includes the shared utility rights mentioned above, as well as two fees of lesser importance for exploration and extraction.

As for the second, private firms with contracts to carry out exploration and exploitation activities in Mexico (alone or in association with Pemex) pay the federal government a variety of fees and royalties, whose amount is determined on a case-by-case basis, using parameters that depend on the type of contract and the phase of the field's development. For licence contracts, these include a contract-signing fee, an exploration fee based on surface area and royalties depending on the type and price of hydrocarbons. These last two mechanisms also apply to production and profit-sharing contracts, which in addition stipulate that private firms must pay a percentage of operating profits, depending on the price of hydrocarbons. In all, the fees and royalties collected from contracts involving private oil and gas firms amounted to US$75 million dollars in 2020 (FMPED, 2021: 6).

According to Article 2 of the Hydrocarbons Income Law, these resources are channelled to the Mexican Petroleum Fund for Stabilisation and Development, as are the fees and royalties paid by Pemex in its assigned areas; the latter representing 96 per cent of transfers to the Petroleum Fund in 2020. The Petroleum Fund was created in August of 2014 as a public trust whose purpose is to receive, manage and distribute the income derived from contracts and permits granted to both Pemex and private companies. The Bank of Mexico is its trustee. Article 16 of the Petroleum Fund Law lists the priorities for which the fund's resources are to be used, the first being the *Budget Revenue Stabilisation Fund* to cover shortfalls in financing for the federal government's planned expenditures. The *Petroleum Fund* is designed to channel the equivalent of 4.7 per cent of the country's gross domestic product (GDP) to this sub-fund and four others, and to the Treasury of the Federation, before directing any additional resources to long-term savings. However, largely because of low oil prices since 2014, the Petroleum Fund has not transferred close to this amount in any year since its operations began; the highest level was in 2018, when it transferred the equivalent of 2.4 per cent of GDP.

Finally, Pemex and the private oil-and-gas companies operating in Mexico have to pay two taxes. The first is income tax on earnings obtained from exploration and extraction activities, with a number of deductions allowed, including 100 per cent of investments in exploration and enhanced secondary recovery. Income tax is paid to the federal government's Tax Administration Service. The second is called the *Tax on Hydrocarbon Exploration and Extractive Activities*. It is based on the surface area under contract or assigned to Pemex, and its amount depends on whether the field is in the stage of exploration or extraction.

The latter tax is channelled in its entirety to the *Fund for Hydrocarbon Producing States and Municipalities* (FEFMH). Article 57 of the Hydrocarbon Income Law states that 100 per cent of the FEFMH's resources is to be delivered to the states where oil and gas are extracted and that these states must in turn deliver 20 per cent of the resources they receive to the municipalities where petroleum activity is concentrated. The explicit objective is to compensate these regions for the environmental and social disruption caused by petroleum exploitation, much like how the mining fund worked before AMLO made changes to it. In fact, the types of projects financed by the program are the same as for the mining fund. The main difference is that the FEFMH continues to deliver resources to state and municipal governments and to focus on spending in extractive regions.

## State meditation of conflicts and environmental regulation

As elsewhere in Latin America, in Mexico there has been a growing number of conflicts around extractive projects since the turn of the millennium. These conflicts tend to pit organised groups in affected rural communities and their allies in civil society against governmental agencies and private-sector actors that promote these projects (Tetreault et al., 2018). In an inventory of 560 social–environmental conflicts in Mexico, compiled between 2012 and 2017 by a group of researchers under the direction of Victor Toledo, 173 have to do with mining, 86 with water and 74 with energy projects; these being the three most numerous categories. In another inventory made available online, a team of researchers led by Gisela Zaremberg and Valeria Guarneros Meza systematically reviewed newspaper reports from 2006 to 2020 to detect and digitally map conflicts around the implementation of 336 large-scale extractive projects in Mexico dealing with mining, petroleum extraction, oil and gas pipelines, hydro-electrical dams and wind farms.

To be sure, large-scale projects to extract subterranean resources have met with resistance because they invariably reconfigure local landscapes, infrastructure and ecosystems, causing massive environmental damage and contamination. Affected rural communities struggle to protect, not only healthy living environments and productive assets for small-scale farming but also symbolically significant landscapes and territories for cultural and social reproduction (Tetreault et al., 2018). This is not to say that all conflicts around extractive projects in Mexico involve local groups organised in opposition; in some cases, local groups struggle to negotiate better terms for ceding land and territory, employment opportunities, the fulfilment of unmet promises by extractive firms and/or the mitigation of environmental impacts (Tetreault, 2014). Moreover, many communities are divided by the arrival of extractive projects, leading in some cases to multiple postures and tensions among the affected population (Uribe et al., 2020).

The people involved in collective struggles to defend territories, traditional livelihoods and healthy living environments have suffered various forms of repression from all levels of government. At least 147 people involved in these struggles were murdered in Mexico between 1995 and 2019, including 18 during the first year of AMLO's presidency (Velázquez Hernández, 2020). Another 30 were murdered in 2020, according to Global Witness (2021: 11), whose worldwide reporting indicates that Mexico is second only to Colombia in this grim measure. These numbers indicate that the rate of murdering defenders of land and territory has increased during AMLO's presidency.

While murder is the most extreme form of repression, it is not the only one. The Mexican Centre for Environmental Rights (CEMDA, 2021) registered 566 'attacks' against defenders of land, territory and environment between 2012 and 2020, with 104 occurring in 2019 and 2020, the first two full year of AMLO's presidency, including threats, physical aggressions, criminalisation of protest, intimidation and murders. CEMDA (2020: 27) found that in 2019 the Mexican government—on one level or another (municipal, state or federal)—could be linked to over 40 per cent of these attacks.

As these numbers suggest, while state repression against organised resistance to extractive projects has continued since AMLO became president, some changes have occurred. Significantly, AMLO has promised not to use the federal armed forces to repress peaceful manifestations of protest and demand. One of his oft-repeated mottos is: '*nada por la fuerza, todo por la razón*' (nothing by force, everything by reason). Accordingly, during the first three years of his administration, he did not unleash the federal armed forces to openly commit violent acts of repression comparable to those of previous governments. Nevertheless, AMLO has further militarised zones of mineral extraction and he has resorted to deploying the recently created National Guard to deal with social–environmental conflicts in different parts of the country, including to illegally dislodge peaceful protestors in the state of Morelos, as detailed below. Further, by deriding the people involved in resistance movements to extractive activities and mega-development projects, AMLO has created a hostile environment for them, while impunity reigns for those who murder them.

A case in point is that of organised resistance in the state of Morelos to the construction and now operation of a thermoelectric plant that threatens the water supply of local Indigenous communities and farmers, while posing a danger to human safety among other reasons because of the installation of gas lines to supply the plant in a zone of frequent seismic and volcanic activity. In May 2014, AMLO visited Yecapixtla, one of the towns threatened by the project, to declare solidarity with the resistance movement. On that occasion, he was recorded as saying: 'We don't want that gas pipeline, nor the thermoelectrical plant, and we do not want mines that are going to destroy territory and pollute water'. However, soon after becoming president, his discourse changed to argue that, given that the infrastructure for the thermoelectric plant was almost complete, it would be a waste not to use it.

On 8 February 2019, he announced that the matter would be decided democratically through 'popular consultation', an exercise that he and his supporters had carried out on two previous occasions. It bears mentioning that these consultations have been widely criticised, not only because of their dubious legal basis but also because they dilute the vote of directly affected rural communities by including urban populations that stand to benefit from infrastructure projects, thereby sidestepping the right of communities to free, prior and informed consent.

Two days after this announcement, AMLO labelled those opposed to the thermoelectric plant as 'left-wing radicals, who for me are only conservatives'. Shortly thereafter, on 20 February 2019, just three days ahead of the consultation, Samir Flores—one of the most visible leaders of the Indigenous-based resistance movement—was shot dead outside of his home. AMLO insisted on going ahead with the consultation, in which affected communities refused to participate. The results were, as expected, to go ahead with the project. Legal and direct action by community-based opposition groups continued to prevent the plant's operation until 23 November 2020, when AMLO sent in the National Guard to dislodge opposition groups, in violation of court orders (*amparos*) that were meant to give them legal protection. Meanwhile, no one has been brought to justice for the murder of Samir Flores.

A few days after the popular consultation over the thermoelectric plant in Morelo, AMLO announced the cancellation of another popular consultation which he had planned for the *Cordones* open-pit gold-mining project in the state of Baja California Sur. Organised resistance to this project goes back to Felipe Calderón's presidency (2006–2012), when Canadian mining company Vista Gold presented various proposals under two different names (Paredones Amarillos and Concordia), all of which were rejected by the Ministry of Environment and Natural Resources (SEMARNAT) due to pressure from local organisations and from specialists who underlined the threat the project posed to the sources of water for the cities of Los Cabos and La Paz. The project was taken over by Desarrollos Zapal, a company belonging to Mexican billionaire Ricardo Salinas Pliego (the third richest man in Mexico), and a modified version of its MIA was conditionally accepted by SEMARNAT in June 2014. The resistance movement brought together 37 civil-society organisations and was supported by the heads of local governments.

Beyond political considerations, there are some key differences between these two cases that explain their differential treatment. First, although the thermoelectrical plant in Morelos provided generous contracts for private companies during the construction phase, it is the Federal Electricity Commission's project and one that AMLO considers to be important for increasing the supply of energy to power industrial development in the central region of the country. By contrast, the Cordones project is entirely in the hands of private capital, with fewer benefits for the national economy and more visually dramatic environmental impacts. Also, while the thermoelectrical plant threatens to negatively impact the small-scale farming activities of Indigenous communities, the Cordones mine threatened to impact a lucrative tourist industry in Baja California. These differences speak to AMLO's priorities and focus on achieving economic growth.

In an apparent concession to environmental groups, AMLO has promised not to use hydraulic fracturing or 'fracking' to exploit hydrocarbons. This is a commitment that he made on the campaign trail and one that he has repeated several times since assuming the presidency. However, his government has so far not taken action to translate it into law. In June 2019, reports emerged that the National Hydrocarbons Commission had approved Pemex's plan to use fracking in the exploration of the *Humapa* field located between the states of Veracruz and Puebla. As Hernández Ibarzábal and Bonilla (2020: 4) observe: 'The inconsistencies between the president's commitment to ban fracking, the exploration plans approved by the National Hydrocarbons Commission (CNH), and the USD220 million that will be invested by Pemex in shale oil and gas projects in 2020 indicate that the development of unconventional resources is likely to continue'.

Finally, as regards to environmental policy, it is noteworthy that, during the first three years of AMLO's presidency, no significant changes were made to the environmental laws and institutional framework that were put in place during the neoliberal era to regulate extractives activities. The landmark environmental law that was proclaimed on 28 January 1988, called the *General Law of Ecological Balance and Environmental Protection*, was modified 41 times between 1996 and 2018. AMLO's government has only made minor changes to it, the most significant, on 18 January 2021, to better regulate and control light and noise pollution.

The most important changes made to Mexico's environmental policies during the first three years of AMLO's presidency are the cuts made to SEMARNAT's budget and staff, in the context of a broader initiative towards 'republican austerity'. Although AMLO frequently underlines the importance of the environment in discourse, the resources assigned to SEMARNAT in 2019 were less in nominal terms than any year since 2007 and less than half of the ministry's budget in 2015, when it reached a high of 68 billion pesos (equal to US$4.28 billion in that year). In 2020, SEMARNAT's budget was further reduced by more than a billion pesos to just under 30 billion pesos (equal to US$1.38 billion). In line with these cuts, all of SEMARNAT's state-level delegates and an estimated 30 per cent of the administrative staff on the state level were discharged without replacement (Madrid Ramírez, 2020: 7–8). This, according to Madrid Ramírez (2020: 1), is tantamount to 'the institutional dismantling of the environmental sector'.

## Conclusions

In order to evaluate if and to what extent AMLO's petroleum and mining policies constitute steps towards progressive neoextractivism, the analytical framework employed in this chapter has focused on three main areas of policy orientation: ownership of subsoil resources and extractive enterprises, mechanisms to capture and redistribute resource rents and environmental policy, including state mediation of social–environmental conflicts around extractive activities.

In the realm of ownership, there are some important differences between Mexico's petroleum sector and the mining sector that date back to the nationalisation of the former in 1938. While AMLO's government has not taken measures to change the contracts granted to private companies to carry out hydrocarbon exploration and exploitation, it has put an end to the auctioning of oil and gas fields. Also, his government has taken measures to strengthen Pemex inter alia by injecting it with financial resources and curbing hydrocarbon theft. In addition, the construction of a new refinery and the revamping of existing ones are meant to add value to crude oil, create jobs and attain higher levels of energy self-sufficiency. These actions represent the current government's most important steps towards neoextractivisms as a strategy for achieving development on the national level. In the mining sector, the most significant step in this direction can be found in AMLO's efforts to nationalise lithium reserves that have not already been granted to private companies through concessions. Otherwise, the mining sector continues to be completely dominated by private firms with 50-year-long concessions to exploit them.

AMLO's government has made no significant changes to the institutional framework put in place during the neoliberal era to capture and redistribute resource rents derived from the exploitation of subterranean resources. In the petroleum sector, the most important exception to this continuity can be found in measures to reduce the taxes paid by Pemex, in order to strengthen the state-owned enterprise for the purpose of generating higher resource rents in the longer term. The system of taxes and royalties for private oil and gas companies has remained the same. Likewise, mechanisms to capture rent from private sector firms in the mining sector have remained the same. The most important change in the redistribution of mining rent has been to eliminate the focusing mechanisms that were in place to channel it to the regions where mining activities take place.

As regards to Mexico's environmental policy, the most significant change introduced so far by AMLO's government has been to drastically cut SEMARNAT's budget and administrative staff. While strong environmental policies are not the hallmark of progressive neoextractivism, insofar as these cuts translate into weaker state capacity to regulate extractive activities in Mexico, they represent a step towards deregulation.

Finally, in the mediation of social–environmental conflicts, while AMLO's government has so far avoided engaging in some forms of overt state-sponsored repression that were seen in Mexico during the neoliberal period and before, the president has resorted to deploying the federal government's armed forces to militarise zones of extraction and to dislodging peaceful opposition groups. In addition, his discourse has contributed to creating a hostile environment for the people involved in organised resistance to extractive projects. Since AMLO has become president, there has been an increase in the rate at which defenders of land, water and territory are murdered, while impunity reigns for those who attack and kill them.

In short, in the policy areas examined in this chapter, AMLO has introduced only a few modest steps towards restructuring the country's extractive policies in the direction of progressive neoextractivism, and some contradictory steps in the opposite direction. While his discourse projects themes of neoextractivism, the overall institutional framework for regulating the extraction of non-renewable underground resources in Mexico has retained its general orientation vis-à-vis private-sector participation, international market integration and accelerating rates of extraction. Needless to say, policies aimed at increasing the rates of extracting hydrocarbons, metals and minerals fly in the face of the climate crisis and relegate to a second level of importance the environmental and social impacts of petroleum and mining activities on the local level. All of this is likely to lead to further environmental damage and social conflict in rural Mexico, with unpredictable outcomes that hinge on the struggles that are unfolding in and over specific territories.

## Note

1 https://www.gob.mx/presidencia/prensa/que-sea-un-dia-de-solidaridad-y-fraternidad-con-los-que-sufren-expresa-presidente-en-visperas-de-navidad.

## References

Arsel, M., B. Hogenboom and L. Pellegrinia (2016). "The extractive imperative in Latin America," *The Extractive Industries and Society* 3: 880–887.

Azamar Alonso, A. (2017). *Megaminería en México. Explotación Laboral y Acumulación de Ganancia.* Mexico City: UAM.

Burchardt, H. J. and K. Dietz (2014). "(Neo-)extractivism – a new challenge for development theory from Latin America," *Third World Quarterly* 35(3): 468–486.

CEMDA (Centro Mexicano de Derecho Ambiental) (2020). *Informe sobre la situación de las personas defensoaras de los derechos humanos ambientales.* Mexico City: CEMDA.

CEMDA (Centro Mexicano de Derecho Ambiental) (2021). *Informe sobre la situación en México de los derechos humanos ambientales en el contexto de megaproyectos.* Mexico City: CEMDA.

Colmenares, F. (2008). "Petróleo y crecimiento económico en México 1938–2006," *Economía UNAM* 5(15): 53–65.

Cypher, J. (2010). "South America's commodities boom: developmental opportunity or path dependent reversion?," *Canadian Journal of Development Studies* 30(3–4): 635–662.

Ellner, S. (2021). "Introduction: rethinking Latin American extractivism," pp. 1–28 in S. Ellner (ed.) *Latin American Extractivism. Dependency, Resource Nationalism, and Resistance in Broad Perspective.* London and New York: Rowman & Littlefield.

FMPED (Fondo Mexicano del Petróleo para la Estabilización y el Desarrollo) (2021). *Informe anual 2020.* https://www.fmped.org.mx/transparencia/%7B5E5639DA-A83E-72CC-6F2D-0DF6F2CDD0A7%7D.pdf

Fundar (2019). *Fondo Minero: Preocupaciones y propuestas.* https://fundar.org.mx/wp-content/uploads/2019/11/Fondo-Minero_Posicionamiento_Nov04.pdf

Global Witness (2021). *Last Line of Defense. The Industries Causing the Climate Crisis and Attacks Against Land and Environmental Defenders.* https://www.globalwitness.org/en/campaigns/environmental-activists/last-line-defence/

Gudynas, E. (2010). "El nuevo extractivismo del siglo XXI. Diez tesis sobre el extractivismo bajo el progresismo sudamericano actual," *Revista Memoria* 242/243: 12–17/24–30.

Hernández Ibarzábal, J. A. and D. Bonilla (2020). "Examining Mexico's energy policy under the 4T," *The Extractive Industries and Society* 7(2): 669–675.

Madrid Ramírez, L. (2020). *El desmantelamiento institucional del sector ambiental: un balazo en el pie*. Mexico City: CCMSS.

McKay, B. (2017). "Agrarian Extractivism in Bolivia," *World Development* 97: 199–211.

Pemex (2019). *Plan de negocios de petróleros mexicanos y sus empresas productivas subsidiarias 2019–2023*. Mexico City: Pemex.

Stillman, A. (2020). "How AMLO's Crown Jewel became the world's deadliest Covid Company," *Bloomberg Businessweek*, 10 September. https://www.bloomberg.com/news/features/2020-09-10/oil-producer-pemex-has-the-most-covid-19-deaths-of-any-company-in-the-world

Svampa, M. (2018). *Las fronteras del neoextractivismo en Ámerica Latina. Conflictos socioambientales, giro ecoterritorial y nuevas dependencias*. Guadalajara: Universidad de Guadalajara.

Tetreault, D. (2014). "Resistance and reform in Mexico's mining sector," pp. 194–233 in J. Petras and H. Veltmeyer (eds.), *Extractive Imperialism in the Americas. Capitalism's New Frontier.* Leiden/Boston: Brill.

Tetreault, D. (2020). "The new extractivism in Mexico: Rent redistribution and resistance to mining and petroleum activities," *World Development* 126: 1–10.

Tetreault, D., C. McCulligh and C. Lucio (eds.) (2018). *Social Environmental Conflicts in Mexico. Resistance to Dispossession and Alternatives from Below.* London and New York: Palgrave Macmillan.

Urías, H. (1980). "¿Quién controla la minería mexicana?," *Comercio Exterior* 30(9): 949–965.

Uribe Sierra, S., J. Gómez Alonso and D. Tetreault (2020). "Dos conflictos mineros en Mazapil, Zacatecas: entre la oposición, negociación y la colaboración," *Región y Sociedad* 32: e1373.

Velázquez Hernández, L. (2020). "La defensa del ambiente en México, ¿cuestión de vida o muerte?," *Diálogos Ambientales* 1(1): 41–46.

Veltmeyer, H. and J. Petras (eds.) (2014). *The New Extractivism. A Post-Neoliberal Development Model or Imperialism of the Twenty-First Century?* London and New York: Zed Books.

# 4 The power politics of agro-extractivism for climate stewardship

*Arturo Ezquerro-Cañete, Alberto Alonso-Fradejas and Ben M. McKay*

Extractivist capitalist agriculture has become the dominant model of the global agro-commodity system under today's environmental, climate, and social crises. This form of production is the basis for 'flex crop' complexes like soybeans, oil palm, and sugarcane that are now championing the current debates on 'sustainable agricultural intensification', 'green commodities', and 'climate-smart agriculture' (World Bank, 2015; UNDP, 2016), despite their reliance on fossil fuels and capital-intensive, external inputs. While contradictions abound, this model has expanded globally, and particularly in Latin America, alongside increased corporate consolidation (Gras and Hernández, 2014), the introduction of agro-biotechnology and transgenic seeds (Otero and Lapegna, 2016), and the growing penetration of extractive and financial capital into the countryside (Gago and Mezzadra, 2015). At the same time, the growing physical trade flows of biomass are exacerbating the climate, environmental, and human health problems associated with extractivism (Gudynas, 2020). Because of its overdependence on fossilised biomass and associated land-use changes, the agricultural and forestry sector account for 45 per cent of the greenhouse gas emissions in Latin America (ECLAC, 2021a). The expansion of large-scale monocrop agriculture and cattle grazing is driving deforestation at an alarming rate: between 1990 and 2020 the total loss of forest cover across the region was 138 million hectares, equivalent to just over the entire area of Peru (ECLAC, 2021b).

Despite the mounting evidence of capitalist agriculture's biophysical contradictions (Weis, 2010)—as well as the escalating social–environmental conflicts linked to the appropriation and dispossession of territories and natural resources (Cáceres, 2015; Svampa, 2019)—the agro-extractivist model continues to be promoted under the guise of sustainable development. The World Bank insists on the need to 'green' capitalist agriculture by introducing 'climate-smart' farming techniques and technologies (World Bank, 2015), in tandem with a reformed market-oriented productive model that incorporates family and petty capitalist farmers into global value chains to reduce rural poverty (World Bank, 2007). The UNDP's 'Green Commodities Programme', launched in 2009, promotes public-private partnerships, private sector-led commitments and international voluntary business initiatives on

DOI: 10.4324/9781003301981-7

high-value agricultural commodities like soy, palm oil, and pineapples, as the best way to reconcile climate mitigation and adaptation with agricultural intensification (UNDP, 2016, 2021).

As Akram-Lodhi (2021: 696) stresses in his critique of the corporate food system, 'the fetishism of technological solutions fails to situate these technologies within the profit-seeking that is at the heart of the social relations of capitalism'. The depoliticised nature of these solutions legitimises the re-articulation of neo-Malthusian assumptions under climate change discourse (Ojeda et al., 2020) and fails to address the deep-rooted structural causes of rural inequalities (Guereña, 2016), as well as diverting attention from the human rights and democratic representation of a diversity of rural working people (UNDROP, 2018).

Combining agrarian political economy and political ecology perspectives, we elaborate on the political dynamics and actors that justify, legitimise, and ultimately allow for heightened resource extractivism in agriculture. In doing so, we challenge the discursive production and legitimacy of the dominant agro-extractivism-for-sustainability models in Bolivia, Guatemala, and Paraguay today. These three countries are among the most agrarian economies in the region with corporate flex crop complexes spreading like wildfire in recent years (McKay et al., 2021). They continue to show persistently high rates of rural poverty and food insecurity, as well as some of the highest levels of land inequality in the world.[1] They also represent, over the past two decades, distinct political regimes ranging from the progressive left in Bolivia under the 13-year rule of Evo Morales (2006–2019), to the conservative right in Guatemala, and the somewhat hybrid case of Paraguay where the brief experience of the centre-left administration under Fernando Lugo (2008–2012) ended in a landlord-led parliamentary coup and return of the hegemonic Colorado Party.

Following this introduction, we present the broad contours of the agro-extractivism-for-sustainability model in Bolivia, Guatemala, and Paraguay through a framework that emphasises seven key extractivist features. Building on these, we then turn to examine the role of diverse state and societal actors in the rise of agrarian extractivism and the use of sustainability narratives for social legitimacy in the three countries. We conclude by stressing that a form of 'power politics' in which transnational agribusinesses are intimately linked to the state and elites is paving the way for enhanced resource extractivism in mainstream sustainability transformations today.

## Agrarian extractivism in Bolivia, Paraguay, and Guatemala

The term 'agro-' or 'agrarian extractivism' has a recent history. It emerged as an analytical category with which to investigate attempts to articulate a new political economy and ecology of agrarian and environmental change in Latin America at the turn of the century (see, for example, Alonso-Fradejas et al., 2008; Teubal, 2009; Gudynas, 2010). Subsequently, it has been used as the foundation for updating the contemporary meaning of the agrarian question (Petras and Veltmeyer, 2014), as a conceptual tool for understanding the rise of flex crop complexes (Alonso-Fradejas, 2015; Ezquerro-Cañete, 2016; McKay, 2017), the gendered effects of violence and natural resource extraction (Leguizamón, 2019; Berman-Arévalo and Ojeda, 2020), the changing contours of power in the global agro-commodity system (Ye et al., 2020), as well as a framework for the analysis of the predatory extractivist dynamics of contemporary capitalist agriculture (McKay et al., 2021).

It is towards this project of the continuing maintenance of the theoretical rigour that underpins empirical analysis in critical studies of agrarian and environmental change (see Akram-Lodhi et al., 2021) that our own research is directed. In the first edited volume on this topic, *Agrarian Extractivism in Latin America* (McKay et al., 2021), we proposed to investigate the extractivist dynamics of dominant forms of biomass production today by inquiring about the following dimensions: (i) sectoral and commodity particularities; (ii) flows of capital; (iii) labour dynamics; (iv) resource access and property dynamics; (v) flows of knowledge; (vi) flows of non-human nature's energy and materials; and (vii) territorial restructuring and developmental effects. This expanded conceptualisation provides a more comprehensive analysis of contemporary capitalist agriculture's extractive features across various crop complexes, modalities, spaces, geographies, and political economies.

In Bolivia and Paraguay, for example, the expansion of agricultural frontiers over the past two decades is part of a larger agro-extractivist imperative that can be seen throughout the Southern Cone region of South America—the so-called 'Soy Republic' (Rulli, 2007). In both countries, the agro-industrial soy complex is largely controlled by foreign capital, with little to none of the value-added components produced in-country. Labour has been rendered surplus to the needs for capital accumulation, resulting in exclusionary dynamics and a re-concentration of landholdings in the countryside. The reliance on genetically modified organisms and their commodified technological packages not only discards Indigenous and peasant ways of working the land but also exhausts external nature by means of soil erosion, agro-chemical contamination, and large-scale deforestation. Combined, these dynamics render the soy complex similar to an extractive enclave—an '*enclave sojero*' in the analysis of Fogel and Riquelme (2005)—as surplus value, rents, and non-human nature are appropriated, or extracted, from the local economies.

In Guatemala, the rise of oligarchy-led flex sugarcane and oil palm complexes involves a predatory form of agrarian extractivism which is driving a process of 'impairing destruction'. This involves a job-poor, culturally insensitive, toilsome, and unpaid labour-based 'productive' economy that leaves behind most local residents. Particularly, it exhausts young and female bodies and erodes the communal fabric and institutions that allow for the reproduction of more culturally and ecologically sound communities and identities, and a degree of local value sharing which is helpful to everyone and vital for the underprivileged. It is also the underprivileged who get the short end of the stick in the environmental and social cost-shifting relations behind the manufacturing of toxic landscapes by cane and palm companies. Thus, the rise of the flex cane and palm complexes both increases and stagnates the reserve army of labour, while simultaneously pushing the relative surplus population to the limits of subsistence (Alonso-Fradejas, 2020: 136–137).

In the following section, we map out the political contours of these rural transformations in each country, paying particular attention to state-society relations. Following Poulantzas (1978), we approach the state as a contradictory space where different political actors pursue their interests and deploy their strategies at multiple levels. Viewing the state in this way—that is, as an arena of contention for diverse fragmented class interests disputing their share of control—facilitates a deeper understanding of the relations of power and changing balance of social forces in the countryside (Wolford et al., 2013; Vergara-Camus and Kay, 2017). In understanding the role of these changing state–society relations in the making of the agro-extractivism-for-sustainability model, we pay special attention to the political agenda of powerful actors behind the major flex crop complexes in Bolivia, Paraguay, and Guatemala.

## The power politics behind the rise of agro-extractivism

### *Bolivia*

The politics of agro-extractivism in Bolivia must be understood in the context of the development and expansion of the soy complex. It was only in 2005 that genetically modified soybean seeds were legalised in Bolivia. The newly commodified seed was accompanied by technological packages and a capital-intensive form of production as farmers became inserted into a corporatised agro-food system. The integration of smallholders into the soy complex, who represent the rural majority, has led to an increased dependence on external inputs—that is, chemical-based pesticides and fertilisers, GM seeds, and heavy machinery—as well as an increasingly monopolised control over the storage (silos), processing and access to external markets necessary for the export-oriented crop.

This transition coincided with the election of Evo Morales and the *Movimiento al Socialismo* (Movement Towards Socialism, MAS) who came to power with overwhelming support from the country's historically marginalised populations, including some of the most influential social movements representing the Indigenous, peasants, women, and the rural and urban working classes (see McKay, 2018a). Morales promised an 'agrarian revolution', which would transform the unequal landholding structure and incorporate concepts such as food sovereignty, rights of mother nature and *vivir bien* into the *New Economic, Social, Communitarian, and Productive Model*. Such reforms would require dismantling the economic and land-based power of the Santa Cruz elite, referred to by some as the 'barons of the east' (Soruco et al., 2008), as Bolivia's agrarian structure remained highly unequal, based on *minifundio* and subsistence agriculture in the western highlands and large-scale, capital-intensive monocultures in the eastern lowlands (Kay and Urioste, 2007: 69). Despite earlier attempts at agrarian reform in 1953 and 1996, Bolivia's agrarian reform was left unfinished and the rise of Evo Morales and the MAS to power came with much anticipation and hope for transformative change.

Promises for a redistributive agrarian reform, however, went unfulfilled. MAS entered into a strategic alliance with the agribusiness sector, shifting its discourse from an 'agrarian' to a 'productive' revolution with the need to expand the agricultural frontier in the name of 'food security' and 'food sovereignty'. The soy complex became central to a newly established alliance among state and agro-capital elites and its expansion was framed as a means to achieve inclusive, sustainable development and as a pathway towards food sovereignty. Rather than democratising and taking control over its food system, Bolivia became more dependent than ever on food imports during the first term of the MAS, with food imports amounting to US$1.1 billion (Urioste, 2011: 31). While important progress was made in terms of formalising land titles for Indigenous territories, there was never a serious attempt at actually reforming the unequal landholding structure (see Urioste, 2012; Colque et al., 2016). Rather, a state-capital alliance was formed which enabled the MAS to gain political support and ease oppositional tensions among economically powerful groups, maintaining its political power and control, while enabling agribusiness and landholding elites to increase their control over land and the soy complex in the eastern lowlands. Such an alliance resulted in many internal frictions within the MAS and among many of its constituents. As Bolivia's former vice minister of land, Alejandro Almaraz (2014: 54), put it after he parted ways and became a critic of the MAS, 'The Indigenous and peasant project… has been defeated, and the dominant interests and power of the business sector, the oligarchs and the latifundistas have been reinstalled'. These power politics of agrarian change have enabled agribusiness and landholding elites to increase their control over Bolivia's land and agricultural complex, extracting surplus value, rents, energy and materials, while rendering smallholder peasants surplus to the requirements for capital accumulation.

At the end of 2018, agribusiness representatives and the government launched the 'biodiesel era'. Fuelled by discourses of 'green energy' and sustainability, the biofuel programme seeks to increase soybean and sugarcane production for biodiesel and anhydrous ethanol, respectively. The public-private investment committed roughly US$2 billion, estimating that it would take at least 250,000 hectares of new land for this project to start and be profitable. Agribusiness lobbyists pressed the government to legalise new varieties of GM crops, while also pushing for flexibility of the norms and regulations on deforestation and burning, something that was granted in the period 2017–2019 (Law 741 and DS 3973 considered as 'legal doors' for forest clearing and burning). The plan is for the state to be the main buyer of the biofuels for use as an additive and partial substitute for imported diesel (McKay and Colque, 2021).

Deregulations on deforestation combined with state discourses to expand the agricultural frontier for biofuels provided favourable conditions for the use of illegal wildfires to open up new areas without consequences. The state's acceptance of biofuels generated great expectations among the landowners of the *Chiquitanía* interested in enabling more farmland. This is in addition to the new trade deal with China to export beef, which certainly provides incentives to open up new lands for livestock grazing. The so-called 'green economy' initiatives continue to depend on and strengthen corporate-led, external-input-dependent, plantation agriculture with all of its extractivist features. These are some of the contradictions, among others, that ultimately led to a crisis of legitimacy as Morales' increasingly authoritarian tendencies, alliances with classes of capital, and dependence on the extractive economy led to his demise as he lost support from his social bases and was not willing to give up power. He was ultimately forced into exile in 2019 (McKay and Colque, 2021).

### *Paraguay*

The expansion of Paraguay's agro-extractivism frontier traces back to the authoritarian agrarian modernisation project of the Stroessner dictatorship (1954–1989). With the transition to democracy in the early 1990s, the dynamics of agrarian change shifted away from the minifundio production of cotton, towards the cultivation of (non-GM) soybeans which limited both land access and employment opportunities for the peasant sector (Carter et al., 1996). The introduction of genetically modified (GM) soy into the Paraguayan countryside—entering first illegally via Argentinian seeds often brought in by Brazilian producers, before being formally legalised in 2004—spurred an agro-export boom which directly favoured large-scale farmers who absorb relatively little labour per hectare. Consequently, this neoliberal soy regime has fostered a highly exclusionary growth trajectory that leaves peasants out as both producers and workers (Ezquerro-Cañete, 2016; Wesz, 2022), while entire rural communities are increasingly becoming isolated islands of poverty surrounded by enormous soybean plantations (see *inter alia*, Fogel and Riquelme, 2005; Palau et al., 2007; Riquelme and Vera, 2013). Beyond its negative socio-economic impacts, the consolidation of this agro-extractive model has had profound political consequences for the Paraguayan state and state-society relations.

The 2008 election of Fernando Lugo, a Catholic bishop influenced by liberation theology with ties to campesino organisations, brought an end to the more than six decades of Colorado Party hegemony and represented the first peaceful handover of power between political parties in Paraguayan history.

Lugo's electoral platform had centred on far-reaching socio-economic reforms to address Paraguay's long-standing issues of poverty, inequality, and corruption. Critically, redistributive land reform was placed squarely back on the political agenda, an issue of particular importance in a country with

> the most unequal land distribution in the world, with a small landowning oligopolistic elite that includes a significant number of foreign landowners concentrating almost the entire agricultural area, while the vast majority of peasant and Indigenous families lack sufficient land to survive.
>
> (Guereña and Rojas, 2016: 14)

However, despite an explicit commitment to agrarian reform and peasant farming, Lugo's government proved too weak to implement substantial agrarian reform and key campaign promises faced deadlock. This was due, in large part, to an anti-reform alliance between the powerful growers' association, *Asociación de Productores de Soja, Oleaginosas y Cereales del Paraguay* (Paraguayan Association of Producers of Soybean, Oilseeds and Cereals, APS) and the cattle-ranchers' association, *Asociación Rural del Paraguay* (Rural Association of Paraguay, ARP).[2] ARP and APS are both members of the *Unión de Gremios de la Producción* (UGP), a powerful umbrella association established in 2005 to defend the interests of producers and exporters of agricultural goods. Through the UGP, *brasiguayo* soybean farmers and cattle-ranchers opposed moves towards a more inclusionary style of development, as expressed through their vehement opposition to land reform and fiscal reform (Ezquerro-Cañete, 2017: 188–189).

Much of the early disputes over agrarian politics and environmental state governance centred around the seemingly obscure phytosanitary regulation agency, SENAVE (National Service for Plant and Seed Health and Quality). Overnight, SENAVE went from being an invisible agency concerned primarily with measuring the purity of plant material and agrochemicals to being the target of a concerted propaganda campaign against Lugo's administration, orchestrated by the UGP. The principal target of the UGP's campaign was Miguel Lovera, a left-wing environmentalist, appointed as the head of SENAVE two years into Lugo's administration, with the mandate to enforce legislative restrictions on soy production (primarily its use of pesticides) (see Hetherington, 2020). Another point of contention resolved around the question of extractive rent. Unlike neo-extractivist policies pursued in other countries in the region, Paraguay has maintained its laissez-faire strategy in the agricultural sector. Between 2003 and 2017, fiscal reform proposals for the introduction of a tax on unprocessed grain and oilseed exports have been presented at least five times by different congressional benches but have failed on every occasion (Fogel et al., 2018).

The fierce rejection of Lugo's tepid attempts to regulate the agribusiness sector culminated in a 'parliamentary coup', orchestrated by the landlord class and preceded by spectacular acts of violence against campesinos.

On June 15, 11 landless farmers and six police were killed in a bloody incident at Marina Cue, Department of Canindeyú (CODEHUPY, 2012). In the immediate aftermath of the 'Curuguaty Massacre', a medley of conservative social forces saw their opportunity and converged around the impeachment and removal of Lugo. Accusations of fomenting the invasion of private property by land-hungry campesino families, spearheaded by highly placed spokespeople for the soy producers (such as Hector Cristaldo, head of the UGP, as well as spokespeople for Cargill and Monsanto), blamed Lugo for the deaths and called for his immediate impeachment (*Ultima Hora*, 2012). Given that Lugo's position vis-à-vis the legislature was never strong, it is no surprise that Congress was able to carry out an express impeachment on 22 June 2012.

In the aftermath of the impeachment and removal of Lugo, there was a fast approval of various other varieties of GM crops: eight new approvals during the 13-month interim presidency of Federico Franco alone. The successive Colorado administrations of Horacio Cartes (2013–2018) and Mario Abdo Benítez (2018–present) have returned Paraguay to the orthodox neo-liberal camp of Latin American power politics and reinforced the predatory and repressive features of an agro-extractive export model characterised by recurring state violence and criminalisation of the campesino movement (Ezquerro-Cañete, 2019).

### *Guatemala*

In Guatemala, the lack of a charismatic political leader is more than compensated by nepotistic and kleptocratic rule combined with impunity and the tight grip of the oligarchy over the national economy and polity. The rise of the flex cane and palm complexes from 2005 onwards aptly showcases the key role of big businesses linked to the state and elites in the power politics of agro-extractivism for climate stewardship (Alonso-Fradejas, 2021: 15).

Particularly, amid negative responses at the grassroots and a related global airing of grievances that seriously threatened their businesses, a new generation of executives within the oligarchy has reframed the flex cane and palm complexes as planetary stewards with the capacity to address global climate, environmental, and social crises. In their efforts to present the flex cane and palm complexes in this light, the new-wave executives and their supporters in the state and the society have developed an authoritarian corporate populist agenda with two main pillars (Alonso-Fradejas, 2021: 15).

One is the authoritarian and violent pillar mobilised through the 'iron-fist-in-a-velvet-glove' strategy. This political strategy is specially reserved for adamant transformative challengers and especially for leftists and/or 'insurrectionary Indian[s]' (Hale, 2004). But the iron fist strikes hard at anyone who dares to contest the dominant agro-extractivist pathway to sustainability and its oligarchic hegemon, whether it be a state or a social actor, national or foreign (Alonso-Fradejas, 2021: 12–13). To this end, this strategy relies on the 'rule of law' and 'jungle-law' tactics.

The rule-of-law tactic mobilises state powers to turn the interest of a few cane and palm tycoons into the 'national interest'. In so doing, flex cane and palm complexes' supporters leverage their trade and political organisations[3] to keep a favourable balance of forces within the state. The rule-of-law tactic serves the iron-fist-in-a-velvet-glove strategy through advocacy, judicial, and violent means of contention, deployed either sequentially or simultaneously. A major example of rule-of-law advocacy is the fast-track approval by the Guatemalan Congress in 2013 of eight new laws on investment protection and labour flexibilisation promoted by the Committee of Agricultural, Commercial, Industrial, and Financial Associations (CACIF). This happened while the Congress froze, once again, the discussion of the *Comprehensive Rural Development Law* (pending since 2008) and promoted by a coalition of agrarian and environmental justice movements. If advocacy fails or the situation calls for an exemplary response, litigation ensues. For instance, the CACIF's lawyers were involved in the arbitration panel to which the Office of the United States Trade Representative brought Guatemala in 2014 for violations of labour rights. Of the 16 companies the US government faulted, four were palm companies (Véliz, 2015). In the end, the two governments agreed on an enforcement plan to resolve the labour concerns raised by the USA and no company was prosecuted. When advocacy and litigation take too long or do not produce the expected outcomes, authoritarian corporate populism mobilises state violence cloaked in the rule of law. A notorious example is the eviction by combined military and police forces of 769 *Maya-Q'eqchi'* families from the cane fields they had been occupying for a year in the Polochic Valley to protest the way in which a cane company was hoarding land (Alonso-Fradejas, 2013).

However, it was not only the military and the police that were involved in the evictions. The cane company´s security chief was in command of some 50 men tasked with burning the crops, harvests, and houses of the evicted families. This taskforce included Maya-Q'eqchi' men—just as landless and jobless as those they were evicting. These ´barefoot thugs´ are in fact the cannon fodder of the 'jungle-law' tactic. This tactic is named for the generalised context of early 21st-century Guatemala, in which it is not the fittest that prevails but the strongest (Alonso-Fradejas, 2021).

The other pillar of the authoritarian corporate populist agenda is the populist one. Initially, this acted to influence the ideological-political debate over the flex cane and palm complexes through the 'Trojan Horse' and 'discursive-flexibility' strategies. The former has a twofold purpose: to build cane and palm companies' legitimacy at the grassroots and to co-opt opposition. On the one hand, 'corporate coyotes' who enjoy local economic, political, and/or symbolic authority broker land and villagers' consent. On the other hand, the cane and palm companies ally themselves with some leaders of labour unions, peasant, and Indigenous peoples' organisations, and NGOs that can claim a civil-society stake in multistakeholder governance initiatives (Alonso-Fradejas, 2021: 7–8). The 'discursive-flexibility' strategy involves framing flex cane and palm complexes as providing extraordinary solutions to the current climate, environmental, and social crises. To this end, the new-wave executives strategically choose among the policy narratives and representations that better suit their audiences in a 'discursive-flexibility' fashion. The usual representations of cane and palm include 'crops', 'plants', and 'manufactured commodities' (Hunsberger and Alonso-Fradejas, 2016).

However, the corporate populist pillar has evolved to include political concessions to the underprivileged through public grants and multistakeholder governance. All political parties except those on the Left are linked in some way—including through funding—to the oligarchy (Palencia Prado, 2014). Regardless of the ruling party, these shadow rulers influence the government and the Congress in a way that, although neither overwhelming nor uncontested, is strategic for their hegemony (Alonso-Fradejas, 2021). But authoritarian corporate populism has gone beyond even this to include meaningful concessions to working people and the environment in the sphere of private relations of production through the 'staying alive strategy'. The new-wave executives are gradually shifting to a stakeholder-centred corporate governance approach that introduces a series of reforms into the labour, land, and knowledge relations of cane and palm commodity production. First, they are increasing wages and to a lesser extent improving working conditions in exchange for a new flex- and piecemeal-based labour regime. This results in heightened labour productivity but also in harder, longer, and more casual workdays (Alonso-Fradejas, 2020). Second, since bloodline, status, power, and revenues no longer have the same ties to land for the young executives as they did for their elders, they are more open to exploring non-freehold property schemes of land control. Thus, although land purchases continue to be predominant, cane and palm companies are introducing long-term land leases and contract-farming arrangements to their inventory of land control mechanisms. This allows them to counter accusations of land grabbing while expanding cane and palm plantations. Third, they are adopting biological pest control, soil conservation, and other sustainable intensification and 'climate-smart' agricultural practices. While partially reducing the burden of waste and contaminants on people and non-human nature, this knowledge 'fix' enhances the yields and resilience of plantations (Alonso-Fradejas, 2020).

Thus, these corporate concessions do not compromise and ultimately strengthen the ability of the flex cane and palm complexes to remain profitable and the hegemony of the national oligarchy (Alonso-Fradejas, 2021: 10–11).

## Agro-extractivism-for climate stewardship or agribusiness as usual?

Climate and environmental governance is largely shaped by pre-existing institutions and power relations, as well as the expansion of agribusiness which has become increasingly influential in political debates around sustainability transformations, bioenergy, and land- and water-use change. In all three countries, national oligarchies retain a stronghold over the national economy and polity. As a result, the expansion of the flex crop complexes has largely traced over long-standing oligarchic property relations. The undisputed advance of agribusiness has replaced the unproductive *latifundio* of the past with large-scale, capital-intensive monocultures, abetted by transitional capital. Left completely unchallenged is the land-based power of elites, be they the 'barons of the East' in Santa Cruz, the beneficiaries of the clientelist *tierras malhabidas* (ill-gotten lands) across Paraguay's Eastern Border Region, or the new generation within the traditional elite groups in Guatemala that have turned their elders' domestic palm oil and sugarcane mills into transnational flex crop complexes that claim to have the ability to harness the worlds' environmental and social crises. In Paraguay, the landlord class was a major instigator of the 'express impeachment' and 'parliamentary coup' that ousted President Lugo, and which sought thereby to ensure the continuation of the oligarchic state and the agro-extractivist development model that it served (Ezquerro-Cañete and Fogel, 2017). Elites in Bolivia and Guatemala play a similar role in national politics, albeit arguably in a less overt manner.

State actors and elites have also formed strategic alliances with the agribusiness sector which have blunted the potential for transformative change of left-wing governments that had promised to carry out land redistribution and improve the living conditions of working people. In Bolivia, despite discourses of an 'agrarian revolution' and a transition towards food sovereignty, a state-capital alliance formed between the MAS government and the agro-industrial elite around 2010 as discourses changed to a 'productive revolution' and the need to expand the agricultural frontier. A mutually beneficial and strategic alliance was formed to maintain political and economic power, yet this marked the beginning of a rupture between the MAS and its main constituents, foreshadowing the political crisis which erupted in 2019 (Webber, 2017; McKay, 2018b; McKay and Colque, 2021). Likewise in Paraguay, Lugo's initial pledge of redistributive land reform was quickly downscaled to a modest reform agenda in acquiesce to the mounting resistance of the powerful APS–ARP alliance. And in Guatemala, the 'rule-of-law' authoritarian corporate populist tactic has been useful to pre-empt any serious redistributive measure in the series of rural development and land policies approved from 2009 on. The case of the 2014 land policy is particularly telling. When questioned by social movement representatives about the reasons for the major differences between the initial and final drafts of the land policy, a sub-secretary of agrarian affairs explained, 'It is not exactly what we aimed at, right, fellas? But as the saying goes, where a captain rules a sailor has no sway!' (quoted in Alonso-Fradejas, 2021: 13).

Other types of strategic alliances take the form of 'multistakeholder governance', as advocated by the UNDP's Green Commodities programme which has been adopted in both Guatemala (cocoa and oil palm) and Paraguay (beef and soy). This approach continues to champion non-binding governance mechanisms and corporate codes of conduct, be they of public nature, like the World Bank's *2010 Principles for Responsible Agricultural Investment* and the biofuels sustainability scorecard introduced by the Inter-American Development Bank in 2008, or developed in private actors-led multistakeholder initiatives such as the *Roundtables on Sustainable Palm Oil* (RSPO) and *Responsible Soy* (RTRS). Beyond their non-binding and voluntary character, many of these 'soft law' corporate governance tools are often riddled with loopholes and ultimately allow for 'changing everything so that everything stays the same' regarding the distribution of ecological, economic, and symbolic benefits and burdens of mainstream sustainability transformations. In practice, the formal state institutions in charge of enforcing environmental, labour, or land laws receive minimal support, as evidenced in Paraguay with the lack of support afforded to SENAVE to carry out their inspections of soybean farms, measuring barriers, and responding to complaints of rural school spraying (see Kretschmer et al., 2020). Similarly, Bolivia's biodiesel program has largely been used to justify the expansion of the agricultural frontier, resulting in widespread deforestation and encroaching into Indigenous peoples' territories in the name of the 'green economy'. And in Guatemala, holding flex cane and palm companies accountable for environmental disruption is constrained because 'Environmental Impact Assessments' are mandatory only for processing plants, but not for cane and palm plantations (Alonso-Fradejas, 2015).

Moreover, through direct political means, corporate actors have taken a prominent role in influencing the regulatory environment towards positions that favour enhanced resource extractivism in mainstream sustainability transitions. These mechanisms include the traditional practice of lobbying, as clearly demonstrated in Paraguay with the UGP's ability to forestall numerous tabled motions to introduce an export tax of a mere six per cent on unprocessed cereals and impede the application of pesticide laws. A more direct way to influence regulatory outcomes in the three countries includes 'revolving door' appointments, wherein individuals from the agribusiness industry are appointed to government regulatory positions and later go back into businesses as lobbyists. In Bolivia, a mutually beneficial alliance between the MAS government and the agribusiness elite emerged as a means to gain and maintain their political and economic power, respectively. And we saw how authoritarian corporate populism in Guatemala strongly relies on advocacy and litigation to turn the interest of selected oil palm and sugarcane tycoons into the national interest.

Finally, we can also identify various sources of corporate influence in the dominant climate stewardship discourse that justify, legitimise, and ultimately allow for the paradox of heightened resource extractivism to save the planet. In Guatemala, the oil palm growers guild promotes their business as highly productive and environmentally sound means of feeding the world, generating renewable energy, and cooling down the planet while simultaneously sponsoring employment, economic growth, and good governance (Hunsberger and Alonso-Fradejas, 2016). In Paraguay, the soy boom is portrayed as the motor that has propelled the country onto the world stage as an 'agro-industrial powerhouse'. According to agribusiness newsletters from the UGP, 'Genetically modified crops make it possible to increase food production and, at the same time, reduce the use of agrochemicals, preserving the land and the environment'. Such claims border on the farcical considering that the quantity of pesticides and agrochemicals being used has increased astronomically with the spread of soy, with most of the importation and distribution happening at the margins of the formal market (see Hetherington, 2020). In Bolivia, both state and agro-capital elites frame extractivist agriculture as a means to achieve food sovereignty, for 'energy sovereignty' via biofuels production, and for 'pro-poor' inclusive growth, despite its glaring contradictions (see ANAPO, 2014).

## Conclusion

Governments across Latin America, from the progressive Left to the conservative Right, and traditional economic and political elites, remain firm in their support of resource extractivism, now especially for green growth purposes. Paradoxically, however, the dominant green growth paradigm seeks to decouple economic growth from resource use to cool down the planet by furthering resource extraction and thus the social metabolism of sustainability transformations. Nonetheless, the agro-for climate stewardship discourse shifts the focus away from this paradox and its underlying ecological and socio-economic contradictions and into the technical-managerial innovations for the reproduction of the fundamental natural and social conditions of agro-commodity production. This ecomodernist turn is facilitated by an alliance of agribusiness, state actors, and elites with the ability to steer ideas, knowledge, and policy on sustainability transformations.

## Notes

1 Rural poverty was over 50 per cent in all three counties (FAO, 2018). Gini coefficient for land distribution was 0.93 in Paraguay (2008), 0.84 in Guatemala (2003), and 0.77 in Bolivia (1984) (Guereña, 2016).
2 The ARP was founded in 1885. Most high-income families residing in Asunción own an *estancia* (cattle ranch) so there is considerable overlap between cattle ranchers and other stakeholders, including the Colorado Party. Founded in 1999, the APS became the mouthpiece for the 30,000 medium- and large-scale commercial farmers, often second-generation immigrants from Brazil of European extraction ('*brasiguayos*'), who account for around 90 per cent of national soybean production (Ezquerro-Cañete, 2017).
3 Especially including the Guatemalan Sugar Producers Association (ASAZGUA) and the Oil Palm Growers Guild (GREPALMA). Both are part of the powerful trade and political organisation of the Guatemalan oligarchy, the Committee of Agricultural, Commercial, Industrial, and Financial Associations (CACIF).

## References


Akram-Lodhi, H. (2021). "The Ties that Bind? Agroecology and the Agrarian Question in the Twenty-First Century." *Journal of Peasant Studies*, 48(4): 687–714.

Akram-Lodhi, H., Dietz, K., Engels, B., and McKay, B. (eds.). (2021). *The Edward Elgar Handbook in Critical Agrarian Studies*. Chelmsford: Edward Elgar.

Almaraz, A. (2014). "Las Luchas Indígenas y Campesinas en los Dos Ciclos de la Reforma Agraria." In Fundación TIERRA (ed.), *Recientes Transformaciones Agrarias en Bolivia: Memoria*, pp. 49–57. La Paz: Fundación TIERRA.

Alonso-Fradejas, A. (2013). "'Sons and Daughters of the Earth': Indigenous Communities and Land Grabs in Guatemala." *Land & Sovereignty in the Americas Series*, Issue Brief 1. Oakland: Food First.

Alonso-Fradejas, A. (2015). "Anything But a Story Foretold: Multiple Politics of Resistance to the Agrarian Extractivist Project in Guatemala." *Journal of Peasant Studies*, 42(3–4): 489–515.

Alonso-Fradejas, A. (2020). "'Leaving No One Unscathed' in Sustainability Transitions: The Life Purging Agro-Extractivism of Corporate Renewables." *Journal of Rural Studies*, 81: 127–138.

Alonso-Fradejas, A. (2021). "The Rise of Authoritarian Corporate Populism." *Latin American Perspectives* (forthcoming).

Alonso-Fradejas, A., Alonzo, F., and Dürr, J. (2008). *Caña de azúcar y Palma Africana: Combustibles para un Nuevo Ciclo de Acumulación y Dominio en Guatemala*. Guatemala: IDEAR.

ANAPO. (2014). "Soya Permite Lograr la Soberanía Alimentaria del País." *ANAPO Noticias*, 105.

Berman-Arévalo, E. and Ojeda, D. (2020). "Ordinary Geographies: Care, Violence, and Agrarian Extractivism in 'Post-Conflict' Colombia." *Antipode*, 52(6): 1583–1602.

Cáceres, D.M. (2015). "Accumulation by Dispossession and Socio-Environmental Conflicts Caused by the Expansion of Agribusiness in Argentina." *Journal of Agrarian Change*, 15(1): 116–147.

Carter, M.R., Barham, B.L., and Mesbah, D. (1996). "Agricultural Export Booms and the Rural Poor in Chile, Guatemala, and Paraguay." *Latin American Research Review*, 31(1): 33–65.

CODEHUPY. (2012). *Informe de Derechos Humanos Sobre el Caso Marina Kue*. Asunción: Coordinadora por los Derechos Humanos del Paraguay.

Colque, G., Tinta, E., and Sanjinés, E. (2016). *Segunda Reforma Agraria: Una Historia que Incomoda*. La Paz: TIERRA.

ECLAC. (2021a). *Economic Survey of Latin America and the Caribbean, 2021*. Santiago: ECLAC.

ECLAC. (2021b). *Forest Loss in Latin America and the Caribbean from 1990 to 2020: The Statistical Evidence*. ECLAC Statistical Briefings 2. Santiago: ECLAC.

Ezquerro-Cañete, A. (2016). "Poisoned, Dispossessed and Excluded: A Critique of the Neoliberal Soy Regime in Paraguay." *Journal of Agrarian Change*, 16(4): 702–710.

Ezquerro-Cañete, A. (2017). "Paraguay: Class Struggle on the Extractive Frontier." In Petras, J. and Veltmeyer, H. (eds.), *The Class Struggle in Latin America*, pp. 182–206. London: Routledge.

Ezquerro-Cañete, A. (2019). Deadly Soy: The Violent Expansion of Paraguay's Agro-Extractive Frontier." In Paley, D. and Granovsky-Larsen, S. (eds.), *Organized*

*Violence: Capitalist Warfare in Latin America*, pp. 78–95. Regina: University of Regina Press.

Ezquerro-Cañete, A. and Fogel, R. (2017). "A Coup Foretold: Fernando Lugo and the Lost Promise of Agrarian Reform in Paraguay." *Journal of Agrarian Change*, 17(2): 279–295.

FAO. (2018). *Panorama de la pobreza rural en América Latina y el Caribe 2018*. Santiago: FAO.

Fogel, R., Costa, S., and Valdez, S. (2018). *Forjando privilegios: Discursos, estrategias y prácticas del empresariado del agronegocio para la incidencia en la política tributaria paraguaya*. Buenos Aires: CLACSO.

Fogel, R. and Riquelme, M. (eds.) (2005). *Enclave Sojero: Merma de Soberanía y Pobreza*. Asunción: Centro de Estudios Rurales Interdisciplinarios.

Gago, V. and Mezzadra, S. (2015). "Para una Crítica de las Operaciones Extractivas del Capital: Patrón de Acumulación y Luchas Sociales en el Tiempo de la Financiarización." *Nueva Sociedad*, 255: 38–52.

Gras, C. and Hernández, V. (2014). "Agribusiness and Large-Scale Farming: Capitalist Globalisation in Argentine Agriculture." *Canadian Journal of Development Studies*, 35(3): 339–357.

Gudynas, E. (2010). "Agropecuaria y Nuevo Extractivismo Bajo los Gobiernos Progresistas de América del Sur." *Territorios*, 5: 37–54.

Gudynas, E. (2020). *Extractivisms: Politics, Economy and Ecology*. Halifax: Fernwood Publishing.

Guereña, A. (2016). *Unearthed: Land, Power and Inequality in Latin America*. Oxford: Oxfam.

Guereña, A. and Rojas, L. (2016). *Yvy Jára: Los Dueños de la Tierra en Paraguay*. Asunción: Oxfam Paraguay.

Hale, C.R. (2004). "Rethinking Indigenous Politics in the Era of the 'Indio Permitido'." *NACLA*, 38(1): 16–20.

Hetherington, K. (2020). *The Government of Beans: Regulating Life in the Age of Monocrops*. Durham: Duke University Press.

Hunsberger, C. and Alonso-Fradejas, A. (2016). "The Discursive Flexibility of 'Flex Crops': Comparing Oil Palm and Jatropha." *Journal of Peasant Studies*, 43(1): 225–250.

Kay, C. and Urioste, M. (2007). "Bolivia's Unfinished Agrarian Reform: Rural Poverty and Development Policies." In Akram-Lodhi, H., Borras, S.M., and Kay, C. (eds.), *Land, Poverty and Livelihoods in the Era of Globalization: Perspectives from Developing and Transition Countries*, pp. 41–79. London: Routledge.

Kretschmer, R., Areco, A., and Palau, M. (2020). *Escuelas Rurales Fumigadas en Paraguay*. Asunción: Base Investigaciones Sociales.

Leguizamón, A. (2019). "The Gendered Dimensions of Resource Extractivism in Argentina's Soy Boom." *Latin American Perspectives*, 46(2): 199–216.

McKay, B.M. (2017). "Agrarian Extractivism in Bolivia." *World Development*, 97: 199–211.

McKay, B.M. (2018a). "The Politics of Convergence in Bolivia: Social Movements and the State." *Third World Quarterly*, 39(7): 1247–1269.

McKay, B.M. (2018b). "The Politics of Agrarian Change in Bolivia's Soy Complex." *Journal of Agrarian Change*, 18(2): 406–424.

McKay, B.M., Alonso-Fradejas, A., and Ezquerro-Cañete, A. (eds.). (2021). *Agrarian Extractivism in Latin America*. London: Routledge.

McKay, B.M. and Colque, G. (2021). "Populism and Its Authoritarian Tendencies: The Politics of Division in Bolivia." *Latin American Perspectives*, (forthcoming).

Ojeda, D., Sasser, J.S., and Lunstrum, E. (2020). "Malthus's Specter and the Anthropocene." *Gender, Place & Culture*, 27(3): 316–332.

Otero, G. and Lapegna, P. (2016). "Transgenic Crops in Latin America: Expropriation, Negative Value and the State." *Journal of Agrarian Change*, 16(4): 665–674.

Palau, T., Cabello, D., Maeyens, A., Rulli, J., and Segovia, D. (2007). *Los Refugiados del Modelo Agroexportador. Impactos del Monocultivo de Soja en las Comunidades Campesinas Paraguayas.* Asunción: BASE Investigaciones Sociales.

Palencia Prado, M. (2014). "Elites y Lógicas de Acumulación en la Modernización Económica Guatemalteca." In Hershberg, E. and Pérez Sáinz, J.P. (eds.), *Ejes de Acumulación Transformados*, pp. 1–34. San José, Costa Rica: FLACSO.

Petras, J. and Veltmeyer, H. (2014). "Agro-Extractivism: The Agrarian Question of the 21st Century." In Petras, J. and Veltmeyer, H. (eds.), *Extractive Imperialism in the Americas: Capitalism's New Frontier*, pp. 62–100. Leiden: Brill.

Poulantzas, N. (1978). *State, Power, Socialism*. London: Verso.

Riquelme, Q. and Vera, E. (2013). *La Otra Cara de la Soja: El Impacto del Agronegocio en la Agricultura Familiar y la Producción de Alimentos*. Asunción: Proyecto Acción Ciudadana contra el Hambre y por el Derecho a la Alimentación.

Rulli, J. (ed.) (2007). *United Soya Republics: The Truth About Soya Production in South America*. Buenos Aires: Grupo de Reflexión Rural.

Soruco, X., Plata, W., and Medeiros, G. (2008). *Los Barones del Oriente: El Poder en Santa Cruz Ayer y Hoy*. La Paz: Fundación TIERRA.

Svampa, M. (2019). *Development in Latin America: Toward a New Future*. Halifax: Fernwood Publishing.

Teubal, M. (2009). "Peasant Struggles for Land and Agrarian Reform in Latin America." in Akram-Lodhi, H. and Kay, C. (eds.), *Peasants and Globalization: Political Economy, Rural Transformation and the Agrarian Question*, pp.148–166. London: Routledge.

*Ultima Hora*. (2012). "Los Agroempresarios Apoyan Proceso de Destitución del Presidente Lugo." *Ultima Hora*, 22 de junio.

UNDP. (2016). *Six Years of Innovation and Impact (2009–2015)*. New York: UNDP.

UNDP. (2021). *Palm Oil, Pineapples and Partnerships: Impact and Lessons from a Decade of Transforming Agricultural Commodities*. New York: UNDP.

UNDROP. (2018). "United Nations Declaration on the Rights of Peasants and Other People Working in Rural Areas A/RES/73/165." https://digitallibrary.un-.org/record/1661560/files/A_RES_73_165-EN.pdf.

Urioste, M. (2011). *Concentracion y Extranjerizacion de la Tierra en Bolivia*. La Paz: Fundación TIERRA.

Urioste, M. (2012). "Concentration and 'Foreignisation' of Land in Bolivia." *Canadian Journal of Development Studies*, 33(4): 439–457.

Véliz, R. (2015). "Denuncias, Demandas y un Estado Sordo." *Plaza Pública*. https://www.plazapublica.com.gt/content/denuncias-demandas-y-un-estado-sordo

Vergara-Camus, L. and Kay, C. (2017). "Agribusiness, Peasants, Left-Wing Governments, and the State in Latin America: An Overview and Theoretical Reflections." *Journal of Agrarian Change*, 17(2): 239–257.

Webber, J.R. (2017). "Evo Morales, *Transformismo*, and the Consolidation of Agrarian Capitalism in Bolivia." *Journal of Agrarian Change*, 17(2): 330–347.

Weis, T. (2010). "The Accelerating Biophysical Contradictions of Industrial Capitalist Agriculture." *Journal of Agrarian Change*, 10(3): 315–341.
Wesz, V.D. (2022). "Soybean Production in Paraguay: Agribusiness, Economic Change and Agrarian Transformations." *Journal of Agrarian Change*, 22(2): 317–340.
Wolford, W., Borras S.M., Hall, R., Scoones, I., and White, B. (2013). "Governing Global Land Deals: The Role of the State in the Rush for Land." *Development and Change*, 44(2): 189–210.
World Bank. (2007). *World Development Report 2008: Agriculture for Development*. Washington, DC: World Bank.
World Bank. (2015). *Future of Food: Shaping a Climate-Smart Global Food System*. Washington, DC: World Bank.
Ye, J., van der Ploeg, J.D., Schneider, S., and Shanin, T. (2020). "The Incursions of Extractivism: Moving from Dispersed Places to Global Capitalism." *Journal of Peasant Studies*, 47(1): 155–183.

# 5 Water, land and gold

## Extractivism and the environment in Colombia

*Carolina Arias Hurtado and León Felipe Cubillos Quintero*

This chapter analyses the dynamics of extractivism as it pertains to water, land and gold, from the theoretical perspective of socio-cultural studies. Within the framework of the geoeconomics and geopolitics of capital, it presents a current overview of three examples of the extractivist model that exists in Colombia (large and 'small' hydroelectrical plants, agricultural monoculture and forest plantations and mega-mining) endorsed as the *driver of development* and key source of funding for work towards peace and for the economic recovery from the crisis generated by the COVID-19 pandemic.

In this context, the article also examines the principal strategies, social agents and class divisions that make up the social arena of 21st-century extractivism in the country and, in turn, embodies the discursive disputes and the work of development with respect to the agency of the private sector, the role of the State and the actions of social movements.

A case study—that of the *Quinchía* municipality—illustrates how the new *environmental situation* manifests in territorial terms, in which old problems and conflicts are aggravated. The main conclusion argues that extractivism is not only environmentally, culturally and socially unsustainable but also one of the key obstacles in the quest for and construction of peace.

### The extractivist model in Colombia today

Latin America contains a third of the planet's fresh water, is home to five of the ten most biodiverse countries and is the region with the most biodiversity by area: the Amazon basin, with fertile soils and climates suitable for many agricultural products, is also rich in precious metals and strategic minerals, as well as the largest oil reserves and vast gas deposits.

In this context, Colombia has been a key country within the political-economic and military reach of the region's hegemonic powers, particularly the United States, and in the extractive sector by Canada and Spain, with their financial institutions, development agencies and transnational corporations.

The first wave of neoliberal reforms marked a decisive moment in the present extractivist surge, coming in the midst of the crisis created by the fall of international prices for oil and coffee; as well as the worsening of the largest

DOI: 10.4324/9781003301981-8

social and armed conflict in the continent, the origins of which recall the fight for land and agrarian reform. While the country succeeded in bringing in a new constitution in 1991, the government of President Cesar Gaviria (1990–1994) sank the CEPAL model; brought in reforms in favour of new strategic sectors: monoculture crops and forestry, mega-mining, energy and hydrocarbons; promoted the idea that at least half of the country's economic growth should be in the form of Foreign Direct Investment (FDI) in those sectors under the principals of equality, universality and automaticity, establishing agreements for the opening of international commerce (FTA) under unequal relations with countries in the Global North.

Under the precepts of the Land Market Policy promoted by the World Bank, during the last decade of the 20th century, the Colombian Institute of Agrarian Reform (INCORA) was reformed and a subsidy for land acquisition was established. The *Peasant Reserve Zones* were created, but encountered financial, administrative and contextual challenges in their implementation, and were supplanted by the *Business Development Zones* prioritised by the government and the development policy of promoting productive chains (Machado, 2017).

The Mining and Energy Planning Unit (UPME) was also created as a dependency attached to the Ministry of Mines and Energy; the foundations of the electricity generation, interconnection, transmission, distribution and marketing regime were laid, a sector in which Spanish companies positioned themselves as major competitors; and under the financing and advice of the Canadian government—through a cooperation agreement with the Canadian International Development Agency (CIDA) and the Canadian Energy Research Institute (CERI)—strategies were established to strengthen the Colombian mining sector.

With the issuance of the Colombian Mining Code (Law 685 of 2001), mining was essentially a public utility and preferred over any other activity; the role of the State in terms of regulation and participation in mining activity through industrial and commercial companies was limited, but its role in promoting the sector to private investment was strengthened, with priority given to transnational capital; and traditional mining was declared illegal due to the lack of a concession title. Additionally, Law 697 of 2001 was approved to promote the rational and efficient use of energy, which laid the foundations for the promotion of so-called alternative energies: solar, wind, geothermal, biomass and small hydro energy uses (less than 10 MW).

With the arrival of Álvaro Uribe Vélez to the presidency (2002–2010) and the famous Law 790 of 2002 that endorsed the Public Administration Renewal Program and granted extraordinary powers to the President, INCORA and other entities dedicated to rural development were abolished, such as the National Land Adaptation Institute (INAT) and the Co-financing Fund for Rural Investment (DRI Fund); and INCODER was created as a dependency attached to the Ministry of Agriculture and Rural Development responsible for promoting the land market policy, the search for competitiveness and greater participation in international markets. They would also pass controversial laws (some declared unconstitutional by the Constitutional Court), such as Law 1152 of 2007 or the Rural Development Statute, which according to various analysts 'left loopholes to legalise land illegally appropriated by paramilitaries, drug traffickers and other social actors' (Machado, 2017: 78), and the Secure Agro Income Law, which led to the prosecution of high-ranking public officials, such as the Minister of Agriculture himself.

Starting in 2004, a new cycle of reforms began of the institutions in charge of regulating mining, under the direction of the Ministry of Mines and Energy. The state-owned industrial and commercial company MINERCOL Ltd., responsible for the country's mining administration, was liquidated. The National Institute of Geological-Mining Research (INGEOMINAS) was transformed into the Colombian Institute of Geology and Mining (under the same acronym) and assumed functions of mining authority, abandoning fundamental areas for the welfare of society such as research on geological threats. At the same time, the Energy Mining Planning Unit (UPME) was reformed to specialise in disseminating the country's mining potential in the context of large private and transnational investors, seen as the only ones with the potential to boost Colombia's economic growth. In 2006, UPME presented the most ambitious and long-term plan that the country had had for the mining sector: *Colombia, mining country*, and the *National Plan for Mining Development—Vision for the Year 2019*, whose main objective was to make Colombia one of the three main Latin American destinations for FDI in mining (Arias Hurtado, 2013).

At the beginning of the second decade of the 21st century, extractivism was declared the engine of Colombia's development under the government of Juan Manuel Santos (2010–2018). In 2011, the National Mining Agency (ANM) was created as the entity responsible for the processes of titling, registration, technical assistance, development, promotion and surveillance of the country's mining resources. The Colombian Institute of Geology and Mining (INGEOMINAS) was transformed into the Colombian Geological Service (SGC), as a technical support unit of the ANM.

The first significant achievement of these institutional efforts was the determination of the Country's Mining Potential, which gave way to the Strategic Mining Reserve Areas (AEM), governed under a new contracting system: special concession contracts on strategic reserves awarded through auction or bidding processes. Soon, more than 20 million hectares divided into 516 mining blocks over 20 departments were declared as AEM, including protected natural areas and collective territories of Indigenous and Afro-descendant communities, without carrying out the prior consultation process (Arias Hurtado, 2020).

Stimuli were also deepened to promote the development of energy projects with non-conventional energy sources (FNCE), such as hydroelectric plants. Through Law 1715 of 2014, the integration of the FNCE into the Colombian energy system was guaranteed, accompanied by tax and tariff incentives, in addition to energy purchase agreements to guarantee participation in the country's electricity market that operates freely in accordance with the conditions of supply and demand, being managed by XM Compañía de Expertos en Mercados, a subsidiary of the ISA Business Group with a wide presence in Latin America in the electrical, road, telecommunications and ICT sectors. In addition, the Colombian National Energy Plan was released: *Energy Ideology 2050*, and in 2015, the *Atlas of the Hydroenergetic Potential of Colombia* was presented, which resulted in more than 570 applications for the establishment of hydroelectric projects in the country.

Under the watershed of what has been called the 'energy transition', in 2016, the *Report on the World Development of Small Hydroelectric Power* issued by the United Nations Organisation for Industrial Development (UNIDO) identified Colombia as the country with the greatest potential for power generation through undeveloped hydroelectric plants in the world, which will inevitably result in the multiplication of these 'small' hydroelectric plants in various territories.

During the government of President Juan Manuel Santos (2010–2018), the existence of an internal armed conflict was recognised; progress was made in the Victims Law (Law 1148 of 2011), with the consequent creation of the Victims Unit and the Land Restitution Unit (URT), attached to the Ministry of Rural Development; and peace negotiations between the Colombian State and the Revolutionary Armed Forces of Colombia-Army (FARC) were pursued, culminating in the signing of the Peace Agreements. Within this framework, the National Land Agency (ANT) was created and charged with the policy of legalising rural property; the Rural Development Agency (ADR) was responsible for the execution of the agricultural and rural development policy within a regional context; and the Territorial Renewal Agency (ART) was a specialised entity for the areas most affected by conflict (ZOMAC).

With the return of the 'iron fist' of Álvaro Uribe Vélez, under the government of President Iván Duque (2018–2020), the neoliberal and conservative agenda intensified; the submission of the country to North American interests deepened, as is well illustrated by the shameful acts of intervention against Venezuela and the progressive governments of the region; and the Peace Agreements have been breached.

This development model has also been accompanied by an international and national security agenda that in recent years has its antecedents in Plan Colombia (1999), which allowed territorial control of areas of agro-industrial and mining-energy importance following the distraction of the war on drugs, through militarisation, selective violence and the internationalisation of the conflict (Arias Hurtado, 2011). Currently, the strategy seems to deepen with a security agenda that implies the militarisation of environmental management, as Eduardo Gudynas (2019: 1) warned: 'Nature is presented as an "asset" that will be protected by the military and police, where the "political" component of an environmental policy remains subdued to its militarization'.

As a result of strategies to promote extractivism in Colombia, at the end of the second decade of the 21st century, the Hidrosogamoso, Valencia Samper 1 and 5, Salto II, Popal and Laguneta hydroelectric megaprojects were in operation; 115 hydroelectric projects in the form of small hydroelectric plants (PCH) (UPME, 2019); and rapidly began producing 17 per cent of the country's energy with the Hidroituango project.

According to the Electricity Information System (SIEL) (UPME, 2021), between 2010 and 2021, 1,700 power generation projects were submitted to the Mining and Energy Planning Unit, mainly of two types: solar (918) and hydraulic (570), although there are also thermal (123), wind (53) and biomass (34) projects, in addition to a geothermal project. In the case of the departments with the most hydraulic power generation projects presented to the UPME, Antioquia stands out with 221 projects and the small department of Risaralda with 57.

In the case of forest extractivism, one of the first examples in Colombia is the pine and eucalyptus plantations of the company Smurfit Kappa Colombia (SKC), a subsidiary of the Irish transnational Smufit Kappa. It currently has 69,500 ha in the departments of Tolima, Cauca, Valle del Cauca, Caldas, Quindío and Risaralda from which it extracts 830,000 tons of wood per year.

For their part, Hass avocado monocultures have become the 'agro-industrial' boom as a result of growing global demand, mainly from US, European and Asian markets and the climatic and agro-ecological characteristics of the country that make their production possible for ten of the 12 months of the year. According to the FAO, Colombia is the world's third largest producer of this variety of avocado. It is estimated that this monoculture is present in at least 70,000 ha of the country, placing it in third place worldwide in cultivated area, and has the potential to cultivate 3.3 million hectares, almost four times the area dedicated to coffee today.

This type of extractivism is in the hands of large companies, some national such as Grupo Cartama, NAF, ALS Inversiones SAS and Vitalway SAS and in most instances of foreign capital such as the Israeli Managro, the American Wakate SAS, the South African Westfalia, the Chilean Altos del Valle and Green SuperFood, the Mexican Michoacán and the Peruvian Camposol and Cerro Prieto.

Regarding mining extractivism, according to the ANM for the year 2020, there were 7,710 valid mining titles registered, covering some 2.7 million hectares, corresponding to 3.2 per cent of the national territory (ANM, 2020). Of the 32 departments, only one does not have concessions: San Andrés and Providencia, an insular territory. Even in the Amazon five mining titles have been awarded.

It is worth emphasising that large-scale mining in Colombia is basically owned and operated by foreign capital in all of its phases, with Canadian capital predominating, and there are no 100 per cent publicly owned mining companies. Among the largest mining transnationals present in the country are the Canadian Grancolombia Gold, Continental Gold Corp, Royal

Road Minerals, Libero Copper Corporation, Newrange Gold Corp, Max Resources, Atico Mining Corporation, Batero Gold Corp, the South African Anglo Gold Ashanti and the Australian Los Cerros.

According to the Ministry of Environment and Sustainable Development (2013), after the boom in international commodity prices in Colombia, 46 mining titles had been granted in 15 National Natural Parks (PNN), corresponding to 45,236 ha; 5 titles in four Regional Natural Parks (PNR) (251 ha), which are also within the *Coffee Cultural Landscape of Colombia*, declared a World Heritage Site; 57 titles in 21 Protected Forest Reserve Zones (ZRFP) (22,103 ha); 790 titles in the 7 Forest Reserve Zones of Law 2 of 1959 (1,016,100 ha); and 391 titles in 22 *paramos* (108,972 ha) that are outside the PNN and PNR. The panorama of current mining applications is even more worrying: 560 applications in 38 PNN, corresponding to 426,457 ha; 46 requests in 6 PNR (17,359 ha); 327 requests in 47 ZRFP (264,140 ha) equivalent to 56 per cent of these zones; 4,225 applications in 7 Forest Reserve Zones of Law 2 (6,685,556 ha); and 1181 requests in 47 *paramos* (555,398 ha), that is, 47 per cent of these ecosystems.

Water is one of the main victims of large-scale mining, forest plantations and Hass avocado monocultures, as well as hydroelectric projects. In all cases, it is essential for the existence of these types of extractivism and competes with other uses of the vital liquid, such as human water supplies.

In the case of hydroelectric projects that are presented under the name of 'clean energy', the environmental authorities themselves recognise the environmental impacts on the territory related to: modification of the organic layer of the soil, compaction, susceptibility to erosion, changes in infiltration capacity and productive capacity; alteration of the properties of surface and groundwater, loss of recharge capacity and decrease in water availability; removal of vegetation cover, fragmentation and deterioration of ecosystems, changes in the composition and distribution of fauna; generation of emissions and noise; landscape changes; among other impacts (Risaralda Regional Autonomous Corporation—CARDER, 2021).

This model of development has also been responsible for the fragmentation, overlapping and loss of control of collective territories. Without any effective participation of the communities for the year 2012 in Colombia, 14 Indigenous reserves were fully titled, 27 were titled in more than 50 per cent of their surface and 17 per cent of the area of the reserves in the country was requested for mining (Fierro, 2012).

In the case of hydroelectric projects, the panorama is no different. Many of the territories identified and prioritised in the *Atlas of Hydroenergy Potential of Colombia* to develop hydroelectric projects (large plants, micro plants, mini plants, small plants and pico plants) overlap with the collective territories of Indigenous and Afro-descendant communities, which is presented by the Mining and Energy Planning Unit 'as a restriction for hydropower use', as well as 'the existence of parks and/or nature reserves and/or protected areas and the moorland, mangrove and wetland areas, archaeological and fishing sites' (UPME, 2015: 126).

Extractivism has also deepened social inequalities, worsening poverty and social inequity. In the mining municipalities, unsatisfied basic needs are worse according to the indicators, in addition to infant mortality, and the population living in misery is the highest in the country (Garay, 2013). Poverty is almost three times greater than at the national level in the municipalities where the large transnationals operate (Pardo, 2017).

Extractivism has reprimaritised our economy and undermined the possibilities for diversifying the productive matrix. In just two years, exports of these commodities almost tripled, going from 7,344 million dollars in 2007 to 18,035.4 million in 2009; and by 2011, they corresponded to 88.5 per cent of the country's total exports (Arias Hurtado, 2020).

Extractivism is synonymous with violence: the war on drugs has played a central role in the militarisation of strategic territories for their natural heritage, and on many occasions, it manifested via paramilitary actions. The Special Jurisdiction for Peace (JEP) has revealed new findings related to the dispossession of land in Colombia by paramilitary groups that are supported by mining companies, such as the South African AngloGold Ashanti (Fundación Forjando Futuros, 2018).

In the municipalities where the extractivist mining model is present, the levels of violence are much higher than the national average: close to 70 per cent of the forced displacements that have occurred in the last three decades in Colombia have occurred in mining areas, 88 per cent of the human rights violations in Colombia occur in the municipalities where large-scale mining is carried out (Garay, 2013). Furthermore, during the period of *Democratic Security* 'in 303 mining-energy municipalities, 26 senators and representatives were elected under pressure from the military-paramilitaries, most of them drafters of laws that ceded national sovereignty over our resources' (Ramírez, 2007: 2).

This is also the case of the territories where hydroelectric projects are located, as evidenced by the municipalities and communities once again displaced from their territories in the area of influence of the infamous Hidroituango megaproject.

The current displacement due to violence is a matter that Isabel Cristina Zuleta, spokeswoman for the *Ríos Vivos Movement*, has been denouncing for more than a decade. The Memory and Conflict Observatory of the National Center for Historical Memory highlighted between 1958 and 2018, 110 massacres and 2,435 victims of the conflicts in the 19 municipalities that, directly and indirectly, have to do with the Hidroituango project. The obstructions presented in the tunnels in April 2018 forced an unscheduled filling of the reservoir that prevented road access to the municipality of Ituango (which continues today), in addition to the partial and anticipated collapse of the town of Orobajo in Sabanalarga and the village of Barbacoas in the municipality of Peque, when in mid-May of that year, the preventive evacuation of 120,000 people from four departments was carried out. Other facts related to the technical failures, political commitments, the arrogance of the large economic sectors but, above all, the suffering of communities and damage to nature, are already known nationally and internationally, thanks, among other reasons, to the courage and *verraquera* of the Ríos Vivos movement (Cubillos Quintero, 2021: 2).

The scenario is so alarming that there is an overlapping of valid mining titles and applications in almost all the municipalities where the victims of the Colombian armed conflict have managed to be included in the land restitution programs (Garay, 2013), as is the case of Quinchia municipality. In other words, the victims of the armed conflict are being re-victimised by the extractivism of the 21st century.

Meanwhile, throughout Colombia, the extractivism of large national and transnational capital is exhibited as the main source of economic reactivation in the face of the crisis generated by the COVID-19 Pandemic and the 2021 Social Unrest; but what we are witnessing is the worsening of conflicts and the violation of environmental rights, since large international and national interests have the Letter of Marque to exploit the heritage of one of the most biodiverse-rich countries (Arias Hurtado and Cubillos Quintero, 2018), as seen in the municipality of Quinchía.

## The social space of extractivism: case study of Quinchía in the Colombian Coffee Region

Located in the northeast of the department of Risaralda, the municipality of Quinchía covers 146 km$^2$, where 145 km$^2$ corresponds to the rural area. This municipality has a population of 27,292 people. In addition, 8,160 people recognise themselves as Indigenous, belonging to the Escopetera and Pirza Reservation, the Emberá Karamba Partiality and the Emberá Chamí Partiality. In Quinchía, socio-cultural relations of peasant and Indigenous communities dedicated to agriculture and traditional mining (undermining, barequeo mining and cubic mining) predominate.

At the departmental level, Quinchía was the municipality with the lowest human development index (0.608) and is currently the fourth with the highest percentage of Unsatisfied Basic Needs in rural areas (19.08 per cent); the second municipality with the most displaced persons due to the armed conflict with 12,996 people between 1984 and 2017 and one of the Areas Most Affected by the Conflict (ZOMAC) in Risaralda (Arias Hurtado and Cubillos Quintero, 2021). In this context, in recent years, an accelerated expansion of the extractivist development model (large gold mining, pine and eucalyptus plantations, Hass avocado monocultures and hydroelectric plants) in the hands of large national and foreign companies has been observed in this municipality.

According to the Colombian Mining Registry, between 1990 and 2021 Quinchía had 35 mining titles that cover an area of 69.04 km$^2$ (6909.83 ha), corresponding to 47 per cent of the land area of the municipality. Currently, 24 titles are active in an area of 57.74 km$^2$ (5774 ha), that is, 39.54 per cent of the municipality is licenced for mining. Of the 24 valid titles, only two are destined for traditional mining, seven titles are in the hands of individuals and small companies and 15 titles are from the Canadian transnational Batero Gold Corp. (Miraflores Compañía Minera SAS), the South African Anglo Gold Ashanti (AngloGold Ashanti Colombia SAS) and the Australian Los Cerros (Sociedad Minera Quinchía SAS).

The municipality has also witnessed the appearance of the 'new green gold' (the avocado crop) and the enormous progress it is having in the region. In Quinchía, the Hass avocado monoculture went from occupying 10 ha in 2007 to 124 ha in 2018, an increase of 1,140 ha, under the control of companies with the participation of national businessmen such as Grupo Cartama, associated with the English transnational Fresca Group in Cartama UK, in a competition that has also attracted Israeli, Spanish, South African and Chilean capital. Another expression of the extractivist model in Quinchía is the forest plantations of the company SKC: more than 500 ha in the municipality of Quinchía are destined for eucalyptus monocultures.

In 2010, the first hydroelectric power generation project for the municipality of Quinchía was presented to SIEL by Universal Stream SAS. By 2014, this company had filed four more projects for the municipality. For its part, the E-LECTRICA SAS Company presented three projects between 2018 and 2020. In parallel, between 2016 and 2021 the department's environmental authority (CARDER) received requests for environmental reviews for six projects, under the name of Small Hydroelectric Power Plants (PCH) for the installed capacity: one project of the company Development of Energy Projects of Colombia SAS (formerly Development of Energy Projects OPIRAMA SAS); four from the company E-LECTRICA SAS; and one from Sociedad Ingeniería y Asesorías Globales SAS.

In Quinchía, the panorama is even more complex if one considers the superimposition of 'small' hydroelectric plants, agricultural monocultures, forest plantations and mega-mining on territories with the presence of Indigenous communities, traditional agriculture and mining, community aqueducts and land restitution processes; not counting the current and future variations in flows as a result of the climate crisis.

Based on the analysis of the *positions, dispositions and position taking* of 45 real *social agents* related to extractivism in the 21st century in the municipality of Quinchía (transnational corporations, national companies, national, departmental and local government agents, political parties, social movements, community organisations and academic agents), we can illustrate in Figure 5.1, the position of said agents in the *social space*,[1] according to the possession of total capital (volume and structure of economic, cultural and social capital).

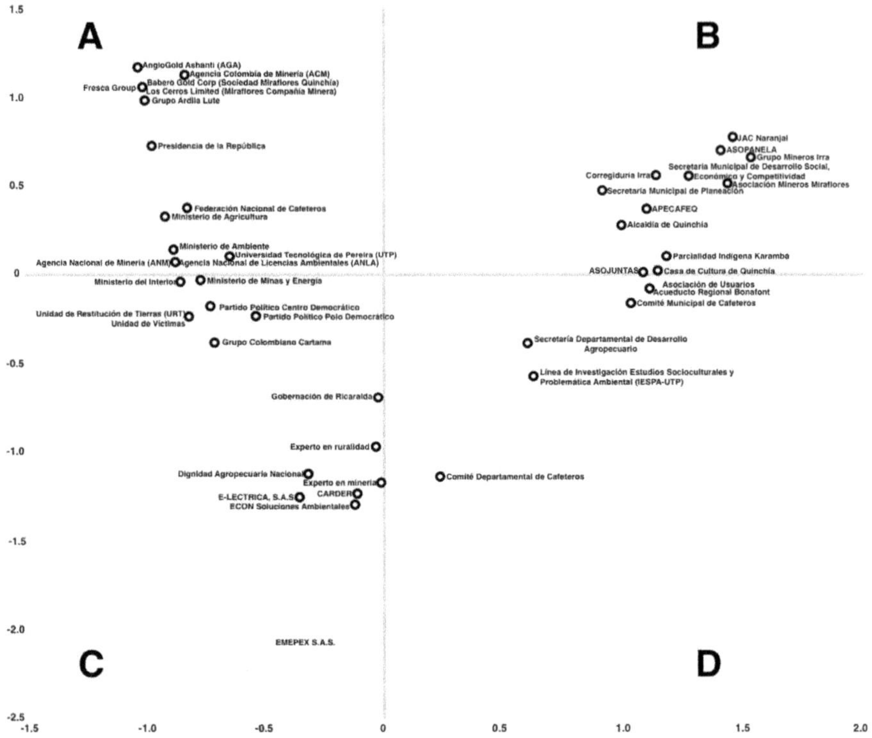


*Figure 5.1* Local social space occupied by 21st-century extractivism in the municipality of Quinchía.
*Source:* Arias Hurtado and Cubillos Quintero (2021).

In this way, the different social agents can be related by proximity and distance, forming *bodies or class fractions* with which four quadrants can be contrasted (A, B, C and D) that will help interpret possible alliances, *oppositions* in real territories and conflicts that are generated in the extractivism of the 21st century, in this case in the *local social space* of the municipality of Quinchía, Colombia (Arias Hurtado and Cubillos Quintero, 2021).

In the social space the following *oppositions* are expressed:

- **First opposition**: Between *volume and capital structure* within **Quadrant C**.
- **Second opposition**: Against the *volume and structure of cultural, social and economic capital* between **Quadrant C** and **Quadrant A**.
- **Third opposition**: Against the *volume and structure of cultural, social and economic capital* between **Quadrant A** and **Quadrant B**.

**The first opposition:** Between *volume and capital structure* within **Quadrant C**.

In this quadrant where public agents predominate, the predominance of the Ministries of the Interior and the Ministry of Mines are at the top as a class fraction; a little lower are two government units of national order (Land Restitution Unit—URT and National Unit of Victims—UNV) close to two Senators of the Republic, one from the ruling Political Party and another from the opposition. By volume of capital, political social agents predominate, while by capital structure, a greater balance between the three capitals is noted. The Ministry of Mines and Energy, like the Ministry of the Interior, have greater economic and social capital, and the two national government units have cultural capital, also lower than the predominance of economic and cultural capital.

For public policy purposes, the Ministry of the Interior, the UNV and the URT are committed to citizen rights (let's not forget that Quinchía has a record of 12,996 displaced persons from the war); in a rural environment that needs the support of the State for its social and economic recovery. However, the presence of the Ministry of Mines and Energy, as well as the Cartama Business Group, shows the willingness to determine development based on mining policies, such as the consolidation of agribusiness, as evidenced by cultivation of the Hass avocado.

In the lower part, a more ambiguous fraction of class agglomerates. An Expert in Rurality appears (Darío Fajardo), below the Dignity Agricultural Social Movement, a National Expert in Mining (Julio Fierro), the departmental environmental authority that is the Regional Autonomous Corporation of Risaralda (CARDER) and the two national companies committed to implement 'small' Hydroelectric Plants: E-LECTRICA SAS and ECON. By volume of capital, the disposition against the public prevails: Dignidad Agropecuaria has a historical presence and political and community leadership both in the resistance of peasant social, cultural and economic activities and in the direction of community aqueducts; like the two national experts, they defend the agreements reached in the 2016 peace process, related to land and the rights of victims.

The two national companies related to power generation break into the Quinchía and Opirama rivers as economic and social capitals prevail. Among this ambiguous class, fraction appears a departmental environmental control entity such as the Regional Autonomous Corporation of Risaralda—CARDER—where social capital predominates over the other two capitals.

Two other particular positions are held by the Government of Risaralda and the marketer of agricultural products IMEPEX SAS, which operates from Valle del Cauca, with the processes of marketing abroad the products of the community organisation ASOPANELA.

The oppositions between the social agents in this **Quadrant C** can be indicated between the mining policies of the Ministry of Mines and Energy, the development of the Hass avocado agroindustry, the national Cartama avocado company and the irruption of the 'small' hydroelectric plants.

This opposition between these national and regional social agents can also be recognised as one of the structural causes of several socio-environmental conflicts in the municipality of Quinchía, since many of the lands to be returned in several of its townships compete with titles or future concessions for mining companies to be awarded. The same can happen with the land that Cartama has been acquiring, without the municipal administration being aware of it.

**Second opposition** Regarding the *volume and structure of cultural, social and economic capital* between **Quadrant C** and **Quadrant A.**

In the 13 *social agents* that are part of **Quadrant A**, private social agents predominate and it is the only Quadrant that has international agents. Because it contains the social agents with the largest volume of capital, and the social agent with the largest presence in the national government (Presidency of the Republic), it can be considered as the quadrant that brings together the most efficient social agents.

In the centre of the upper part is the first class fraction: with the largest volume of capital, the South African mining transnational Anglo Gold Ashanti, accompanied by the Colombian Mining Association, the Canadian mining company Batero Gold Corp, the English transnational products related to the fruits and vegetables Fresca Group and also the Australian mining transnational Los Cerros Limited. The capital structure shows a high predominance of economic and social capital over the cultural capital that is required to know and recognise the mining and agricultural territorialities. We venture to point out that these first six social agents have a homology and the same *illusio*[2] that leads them to justify wanting to set up in our territory, large processes of extractivist development both from transnational mining and from agribusiness.

At the bottom of **Quadrant A** are the National Federation of Coffee Growers and the Ministry of Agriculture. The first with a higher volume of capital and a capital structure divided equally among its three properties. The Ministry of Agriculture maintains constant the social agents of this quadrant, with a predominance of social and economic capitals, while in the National Federation of Coffee Growers there is a greater presence of cultural capital. These two social agents come together with a fraction of the class that borders on **Quadrant C** where the Ministry of Environment and Development, the Technological University of Pereira (UTP), the only regional social agent and the two National Agencies appear: the Mining Agency (ANM) and the National Environmental Licensing Authority (ANLA). It is important to note that being on the border with **Quadrant C**, these four social agents could form a single class fraction also with the Ministries of the Interior and the Ministry of Mines and Energy that are in the upper part of said Quadrant.

More than oppositions, the class fraction located in the lower part of **Quadrant A** maintains a subordinate position vis-à-vis the social agents of the upper part, being prone to the extractivist development model. However, this subordination will depend on the provisions and positions taken by the efficient social agents, given the public and democratic nature of the autonomy of decisions and the social responsibility of a state university, the emphasis on rural development drawn up by a Ministry of Agriculture related to the first point of the Peace Agreement and the decisions to be defined in a Development Plan and an inclusive Public Agenda

However, this understanding that exists in the territory (if we understand it in the light of the *social agents* of **Quadrant A**), becomes much more complex when contrasted with the reading made in **Quadrant C**: Oppositions and conflicts become more acute.

The *illusio* shared by the efficient social agents of **Quadrant A** is a structuring factor that determines the socio-environmental conflicts in the territory that, based on economic ambitions, faces the possible left hands of the State (Bourdieu, 2000), such as the Ministry of the Interior, the Land Restitution Unit and the Victims Unit that have direct responsibilities with the common good, in front of the right hands of the State responsible for economic development, such as the Ministry of Mines and Energy, the National Mining Agency, the National Authority for Environmental Licenses; political movements and national experts on rural and mining issues against transnational companies and national economic emporiums; environmental control entities (CARDER) against licence applications for new hydroelectric projects (E-LECTRICA—ECON).

In both Quadrants, the role of the highest representative of the government at the national level, as the most important public administration position at the departmental level, is located in a strategic place (the centre in each of the two quadrants) evidencing the sensitivity of the dispositions and decision-making regarding the public sphere, which will or will not help widen or narrow the gap between the dominators and the dominated.

The active and latent socio-environmental conflicts will be evidenced in the encounter with the *class fractions* of the *local social agents* typical of **Quadrant B**.

**Third Opposition**: Against the *volume and structure of cultural, social and economic capital* between **Quadrant A** and **Quadrant B**

Of the 12 social agents that appear in **Quadrant B**, all of them have the peculiarity of being part of the municipality of Quinchía: they literally *represent the local social agents.*

By volume and capital structure, they are the social agents with the greatest knowledge, habitus, practices and trajectories in the agricultural and mining territories, however, they possess a low level of economic and social capital compared to that held by the social agents of **Quadrants A**, **C** and **D**. They expose their cultural capital as the main asset, in the power game that is established in this possible field related to the claim of agricultural and mining territorialities in the municipality.

Traditional miners and peasants dedicated to traditional agriculture and the Emberá Karambá Indigenous Partiality are vulnerable to regulatory pressures, where non-formal miners are persecuted by the State, with the ambiguity that places the Municipal Mayor's Office at a regulatory crossroads due to their interest in protecting the historical tradition of small miners. Without taking into account the re-victimisation suffered by peasant and Indigenous communities, the latter face the non-recognition of effective participation in processes related to prior, free and informed consultation and respect for their areas of control that they need to become a Reserve.

The hypothesis pointed out in the second opposition, that the *illusio* shared by the efficient social agents of **Quadrant A** becomes structuring factors that determine socio-environmental conflicts, showing what constitutes a cultural heritage for the mining and agricultural associations, and the Emberá Karamba Indigenous Partiality, where the transnationals, the Presidency of the Republic and the economic groups constitute only an instrumental value where the environment as a right and as a heritage is traded for an economic resource, an asset for the nation or a mining *portfolio*. In this way, *common goods* such as water, land and gold are placed at the service of large energy, agricultural/forestry and mining projects whose direct benefit will remain with Australian, South African, Canadian, British and 'country' companies.

The socio-environmental conflicts of land use arise over conflicts over the land that the Indigenous communities claim to *encompass* the lands necessary to form their Resguardo, in addition to the restitution of lands promised to the 12,996 victims of the conflict, and to the inhabitants of the villages designated as part of the Coffee Cultural Landscape. Hills like Batero, waters like the Opirama River or territories like the Miraflores village are a constitutive part of the cosmovisions on which the Indigenous Partialities and the Escopetera and Pirza Resguardo rely to defend their identity and their rights.

Although **Quadrant D** was not directly mentioned among the quadrants that represent the most direct oppositions in the social space, due to its relative importance compared to its dispositions and future decision-making, among the dominators and dominated of this social space, it is necessary to proceed to the analysis of the five social agents that are part of said quadrant.

These five social agents bring together departmental and local organisations, associations and research lines. It is the most dispersed quadrant compared to the conformation of possible class fractions, where the Association of Users of the Bonafont Regional Aqueduct and the Municipal Committee of Coffee Growers are grouped, who could also be grouped with the Association of Community Action Boards—ASOJUNTAS, the Emberá Karambá Indigenous Partiality and the House of Culture to create a class fraction between Quadrants C and D.

Two strategic positions are held by the Research Line in Sociocultural Studies and Environmental Issues—IESPA—of the Technological University of Pereira and the Departmental Committee of Coffee Growers. The second, insofar as it can serve as direct contact between the *illusios* that can configure the class fractions between Quadrants B, C and D; while the first—IESPA—can serve as a bridge between the Departmental Secretariat of Agricultural Development and the Committee itself. The option to defend and vindicate both mining and traditional agriculture, respectively, has been clear (www.iespautp.tk).

The limits and scope offered by the provisions of the four quadrants resulting from this analysis of multiple correlations can be found in the conclusion of the book: *Water, Land and Gold: the urgent environmental situation in the face of extractivism in the 21st century* (Arias Hurtado and Cubillos Quintero, 2021).

## Conclusions

From the work carried out by the Programme of Research in Sociocultural Studies and Environmental Problems (Cubillos Quintero, 2006; Arias Hurtado, 2013; Cubillos, 2020; Arias Hurtado and Cubillos Quintero, 2021) in municipalities of the Colombian Coffee Region such as Pereira, Calarcá, Marmato and Quinchía, three ideal types of class fractions are identified that compete and struggle within the social space of 21st-century extractivism.

The ideal-type approach (Weber, 2008) understands the particularities of social agents from their distinctive features according to the relative value of each environmental situation. The first ideal type shows a collusion between the social agents represented by the transnationals with the social agents of the High State Management and the interests of the large national economic groups. These agents come together in a class fraction that is distinguished by its great economic resources, high social capital and specialised and technical knowledge put to the service of the justification and application of extractivism.

Their strategies operate in the transformation of normative impediments, intervention in land planning decisions, as well as departmental and municipal development plans, in the symbolic violence spread by the media, in their promotion and participation in social projects that compensate and mitigate the social groups harmed by their projects.

Their ideological matrix is in accordance with globalisation, neoliberal economics and development. Their promises declare corporate social responsibility, better material living conditions such as new and better jobs, as well as training offered for the retraining of former farmers or miners.

It is necessary to point out that the High Command of the State represents only *the right hand* of the State (Bourdieu, 2000), while there is a second hand, the left hand, committed to health, education, work, housing, culture, etc., as common goods of society.

This left hand of the State, along with some academics and researchers, in addition to some economic groups and representatives of regional political power, may represent the second ideal type in which they broker interests related to the construction of public policies linked to a Welfare State, where the markets are at the service of the State to generate sustainability policies in the regions and localities.

The Ministries of Education, or Health, or Labour, etc., have neither the economic resources nor the social capital nor the technical knowledge (cultural capital) that can impose development; nevertheless, they put their respective experiences to work on substantive issues. Its provisions and oppositions are based on the environment as a right, to promote its neostructuralist prerogatives in the face of the neoliberal attacks of the first developmentalist faction.

The creation of the Land Restitution Unit and the Victims Unit is framed in the Peace Agreement between the Colombian State and the Revolutionary Armed Forces of Colombia (FARC), which channel country projects aimed at consolidating rural development for the benefit of Colombians.

The third ideal type includes the class fraction that is part of the local territories. Grassroots social organisations, committed to agricultural and mining production processes, in addition to environmental groups or community aqueduct associations, put pressure on municipal institutions to champion purposes committed to the economic, social and environmental sustainability of the territories as *resistances* that seek socio-cultural alternatives to developing.

They have greater knowledge of the territory, a patented cultural heritage in worldviews and traditional practices when native peoples live there. They tend to have a high sense of commitment and social organisation that allows them to generate support networks to oppose development projects. Examples of *resistance* from black, peasant and Indigenous communities abound in the Latin American context.

Each confrontation with extractivism in the 21st century is giving an account of social agents that make up a field from which it is possible to understand the positions and taking of positions and neoliberal, neostructural and social resistance interests that are played in all territorial social space.

In this context, the importance of territory is relocated in its multiple levels, the reconstruction of the public conception of the State, the processes of appropriation and territorial defense and the proposals of social and solidarity economy. This overwhelming action of the extractivist development model also forces, in the epistemological and methodological field of militant research, to move from an explanatory model to a model committed to *Praxis*, not only to try to understand comprehensively and with an interdisciplinary lens the urgent environmental situations but also mainly to assume a confrontational role against the power asymmetries that configure the development strategies of the extractivist model in Latin America.

## Notes

1 What we call 'the local social space of 21st Century extractivism' in the municipality of Quinchía is inspired by the research approach of the Theory of Fields used by the French sociologist Pierre Bourdieu. The theoretical-methodological details and empirical results for the case in question can be found in Arias Hurtado & Cubillos Quintero (2021).

2 The term 'ilusio', as understood and used by the sociologist Bourdieu, refers to the belief in the validity and legitimacy of the 'state of things' as a specific form of interest that calls for a particular field in which each social agent has a specific intention and purpose that can only be known through historical analysis.

## References

ANM – Agencia Nacional de Minería (ANM). (2020). *Estado de la titulación minera en Colombia.* Bogota: ANM.

Arias Hurtado, C. (2011). Gestión pública desde la gestión comunitaria como alternativa local al desarrollo rural. *Scientia Et Technica*, 2, 293–298.

Arias Hurtado, C. (2013). ¿Neo-extractivismo o desarrollo local? Conflictos territoriales y patrimoniales en el pueblo minero de Marmato. Cochabamba: Universidad Mayor de San Simón.

Arias Hurtado, C. (2020). *Extractivismo del siglo XXI. Un análisis desde las luchas sociales en los Potosís mexicano y colombiano.* Zacatecas: Universidad Autónoma de Zacatecass.

Arias Hurtado, C. & Cubillos Quintero L.F. (2021). *Agua, Tierra y oro: la situación ambiental del extractivismo del siglo XXI. Caso, Quinchía, Colombia.* Pereira: Editorial Universidad Tecnológica de Pereira.

Arias Hurtado, C. & Cubillos Quintero, L.F. (2018). Análisis de la jurisprudencia de la Corte Ambiental en la SU 133/17: La protección de los derechos constitucionales en Marmato frente a la gran minería. In Orduz, N. (Ed.), *La Corte Ambiental. Expresiones ciudadanas sobre los avances constitucionales* (pp. 115–139). Bogota: Fundación Heinrich Böll. Bogotá.

Bourdieu, P. (2000). *Contrafuegos. Reflexiones Para servir a la resistencia contra la invasión neoliberal.* Barcelona: Anagrama. Barcelona.

CARDER – Corporación Autónoma Regional de Risaralda (CARDER). (2021). *Estados de las solicitudes de los trámites ambientales para pequeñas centrales hidroeléctricas en el departamento de Risaralda.* Autor. Pereira: CARDER.

Colombia – Ministerio de Ambiente y Desarrollo Sostenible. (2013). *Minería en zonas de protección ambiental.* Autor. Bogotá: MADS.

Cubillos Quintero, L.F. (2006) La *Legitimidad social del proceso de reconstrucción del Eje Cafetero Colombiano.* Berlin: Freie Universitaet Berlin. Berlin.

Cubillos Quintero, L.F. (2020). *La interdisciplinariedad en las ciencias ambientales: la problemática ambiental del territorio como categoría de investigación para los estudios ambientales.* Pereira: Universidad Tecnológica de Pereira y RCFA. Pereira.

Cubillos Quintero, L.F. (2021). ¿Aguas para producir energía o aguas para la defensa de la vida? *El Opinadero*, Agosto 16. https://elopinadero.com.co.

Fierro, J. (2012). *Políticas mineras en Colombia.* Bogotá: ILSA.

Fundación Forjando Futuros. (2018). *Informe elaborado para la JEP: Empresa, desplazamiento y despojo de tierras en Colombia.* Bogota: Jurisdicción Especial para la Paz.

Garay, L. (Ed.). (2013). *Minería en Colombia. Fundamentos para superar el modelo extractivista* (Vol. 1). Bogota: Contraloría General de la República.

Gudynas, E. (2019). ¿Se militariza la gestión ambiental y territorial? *El Espectador*, 11 (1), enero- Junio, pp. 9–16.

Machado, A. (2017). *El problema de la tierra. Conflicto y desarrollo en Colombia.* Bogota: Debate.

Organización de las Naciones Unidas para el Desarrollo Industrial (ONUDI). (2016). *The World Small Hydropower Development Report 2016.* Autor. Viena: ONUDI.

Pardo, L.Á. (2017). *Los quince mitos de la gran minería en Colombia.* Bogota: Heinrich-Böll-Stiftung.

Ramírez, F. (2007). Tierra y minería, el conflicto en Colombia. *Grupo Semillas*, Julio 3, pp. 32–36.

UPME-- Unidad de Planeación Minero Energética (2015). *Informe de Gestion 2014 – 2015.* Bogota: UPME.

UPME (2021). *Sistema de Información Eléctrico (SIEL) Estado 2021.* Bogota: UPME.

UPME (2019). Plan Energético Nacional 2020-2050. Bogota: UPME.

Weber, M. (2008). *Economía y Sociedad.* Mexico: Fondo de Cultura Económica.

# Part III

# Towards a Sustainable Development Pathway

## A New Industrial Policy for Natural Resource Extraction

# 6 Is there a role for extractivism in a post-development transition towards sustainability?

*Juan Carlos Moreno-Brid, Alicia Puyana Mutis and Stefanie Garry*

At the outbreak of the global pandemic in 2020, Latin America's economy was already immersed in a marked slowdown of its long-term growth rate: a slowdown that had started many years before. The average annual rates of increase in its real GDP of six to seven per cent that marked the 1960s and 1970s were seen in the last three decades—since 1990—only sporadically, and this in very few countries. The closest thing to a generalised boom of the region in the 21st century, albeit very brief, was recorded in 2003–2008 when, driven by demand from China and some other Asian nations, a number of South American economies saw their activity levels expand substantially. A process of re-primarisation of their exports took place, accompanied by an acute expansion in their sales in a context of escalating prices of raw materials and agricultural products (commodities) in world markets

This boom that greatly stimulated the dynamism of extractive economies was short-lived. It was radically truncated in 2009 by the international financial crisis, which originated in the *sub-prime mortgage* markets of the United States. The crisis ultimately led to the collapse of global trade and financing, as well as of production and employment practically worldwide. The global and regional recovery did not take long to manifest. By 2010, GDP and employment were already in full rebound. However, in what came to be called the 'Great Moderation' or the 'New Normality', the post-2009 world economy and international trade no longer had the momentum of previous years. In Latin America, the boom of 2003–2008 remained a noteworthy anecdote, as the region soon showed again poor dynamism, as key constraints linked to the balance of payments and a poor investment performance still bound its long-term economic growth (CEPAL, 2021a; Moreno-Brid and Gary, 2016).

In short, even before the SARS-COVID pandemic, Latin America was stuck in a path of slow growth, stark inequalities and poverty (ECLAC, 2018). The pandemic came to exacerbate the cutting failures in its development pattern. The region's real GDP fell almost seven per cent in 2020, and the closure of millions of companies across the subcontinent led to the destruction of millions of jobs. Long-standing deficiencies in health and nutrition, the absence of adequate systems of social protection including unemployment benefits—in short, the lack of a Welfare State—were decisive for the

DOI: 10.4324/9781003301981-10

pandemic to translate into millions of excess deaths, in addition to the deterioration of labour markets and the further exacerbation of poverty. Inequalities were accentuated, in a particularly alarming manner, in gender-based issues and in many other economic and social aspects (CEPAL, 2020a).

The economic recovery in 2021 did not have the strength to compensate for the collapse that took place in 2020. Troublingly, it will take years until Latin America recovers the maximum levels of GDP per capita registered before the pandemic (CEPAL, 2020b). And the same is true for the incidence of poverty. Indeed, back-of-the-envelope estimates suggest that the average annual rate of growth of Latin American from 2014 to 2023 may be less than one per cent; a result lower than the 1.4 per cent that was registered in the 1980s (Ocampo, 2021). In fact, it is the region with the worst economic and social performance in the face of the pandemic in the developing world. Reference to the current times as a new 'lost decade' in the region is becoming commonplace (Ocampo, 2021).

It is therefore urgent, beyond the short run, to identify the main restrictions that Latin America is facing in its unsuccessful search for robust and sustainable development, a problem greatly exacerbated by the spread and virulence of the coronavirus. This identification is vital for the design of what should be a new agenda of public policies to ensure sustained and sustainable development of our peoples in the new post-pandemic normality or with COVID-19 as an endemic virus (Rawal, Ghosh and Chandrasekhar, 2021). As a starting point for this reflection, recall that on the aftermath of the lost decade in the 1980s, several governments in the region turned their development agenda in favour of neoliberalism and rejected their long-standing strategy of state-led industrialisation (Furtado, 2002). In this endeavour, they proceeded to take low inflation and small fiscal deficits as the priority of macroeconomic policy, coupled with the dismantling of industrial policies, the drastic opening of domestic markets to foreign competition and the adoption of conditional cash transfers as the main tool for poverty alleviation (CEPAL, 2021). Thus, with the adoption of neoliberalism, the quest for universal social protection was abandoned and substituted by targeted programs aimed at the poorest families. These conditional transfers were able to temporarily and partially alleviate precarious conditions but were unable to drive job creation and decent wages in a long-term fashion (ILO, 2015). In fact, high percentages of the population in the region remained mired in precariousness, with incomes below subsistence levels, and vast contingents suffered severe deficiencies in food, health, education, housing and basic services. Although inequality—as measured in terms of the GINI coefficient—fell in some countries, Latin America continued to be the most unequal region in the world. Moreover, despite (or because of?) these neoliberal reforms, the region failed to register high and sustained rates of economic expansion.

The previous diagnosis, with some nuances, is common for all Latin American nations during the long decades that stretch from the 1980s to the present. And what happened to the extractive economies? It is not an exaggeration to argue that, with a few exceptions, the region's economies are largely extractive in nature; with a development pattern based to a significant extent on the exploitation of natural resources. The few exceptions have based their competitiveness on low labour costs, mainly linked to a scantly qualified and under-remunerated workforce, plagued by poor levels of productivity. In some Latin American economies, the whole export structure is marked by its extractivist character. In others, this character is confined to specific industries, for example, those linked to energy, transportation or agricultural systems.

As shown in Figure 6.1, from the 1960s to 2020, in Latin America, only Peru and Chile—exporters of minerals and metals—together with Uruguay

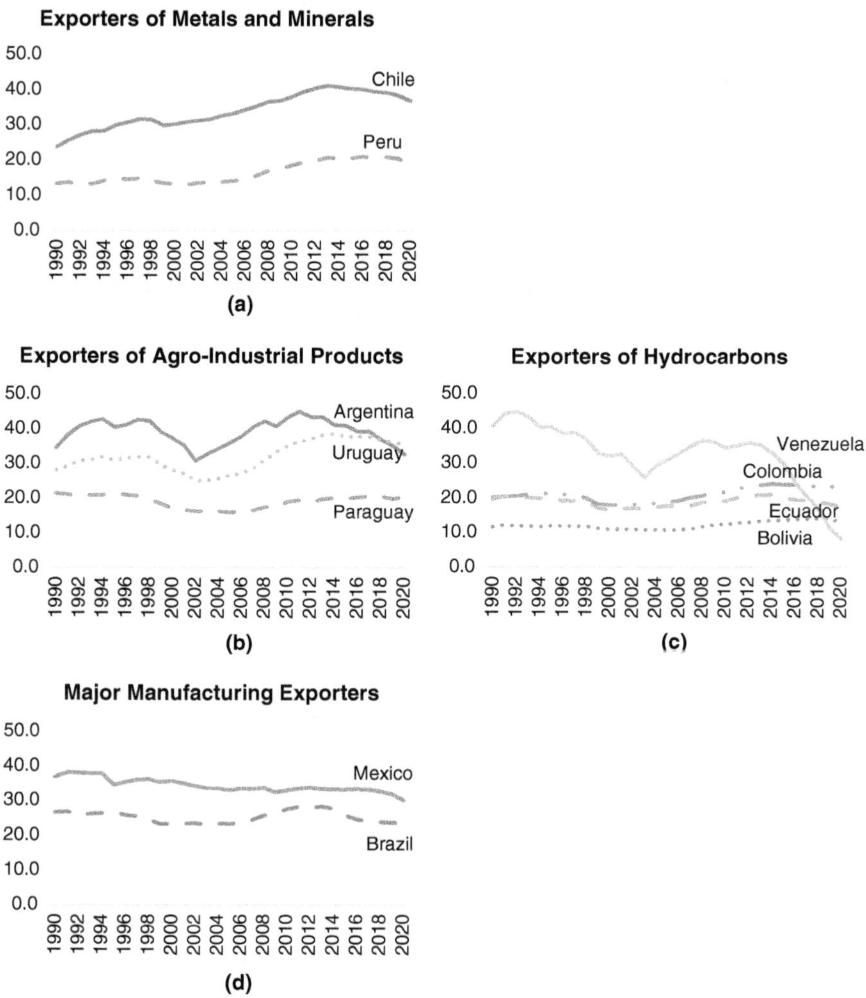


*Figure 6.1* Latin America: Real GDP per capita as a percentage of that of the United States, 1990–2020. Countries selected based on their export orientation.

*Source:* IMF WEO April 2021. Data for 2020 are based on IMF estimates except for Mexico, Bolivia since 2017, Peru since 2018 and Uruguay since 2015.

(an essentially agricultural exporter) managed to somewhat reverse their lag relative to the United States in terms of real GDP per capita. These three economies, however, once again have fallen behind the United States in recent years.

The other economies on the subcontinent performed much worse. The hydrocarbon exporters—neither Venezuela, a rather alarming case, or Colombia, Ecuador and Bolivia—did not register any progress in catching-up with the United States in this long period. The manufacturing exporters, Brazil and Mexico, fared worse, experiencing a significant setback. They closed this period with a gap compared to the United States, in terms of real GDP per capita, greater than the one prevailing at the beginning of the period. Argentina and Paraguay—agribusiness exporters—in a context of sharp fluctuations in their economic and commercial activity, did not experience any comparative improvement in this matter. In brief, over this entire period, the two Latin American mineral and metal exporting economies displayed certain catch-up convergence towards the United States, quite a contrast with the orthodox economists' expected outcomes of the neoliberal reforms (Puyana et al., 2018).

The scant dynamism of Latin America is linked to the quasi-chronic weakness of the engines of growth of its domestic production and employment. Among them stands out the weak performance of gross fixed capital formation. Without it, there simply can be no significant long-term growth (see Table 6.1).

As Table 6.1 shows, investment in general had been losing its weight in GDP for some time, associated with a decline in its contribution to long-term economic growth. Since 2015, the investment-to-GDP ratio was less than 20 per cent. It has shrunk further since then; instead of approaching the 25 per cent essential to cement a long-term persistent annual expansion rate of five per cent of real GDP.

There are strong disparities in the investment ratios across the region; disparities partly related to the export orientation of the economies. Exporters of metals and minerals, as well as those of hydrocarbons, almost systematically report ratios above 20 per cent. Agro-industrial economies, in contrast, register investment ratios several points lower as a proportion of GDP. This pattern is also common to manufacturing exporters, especially for Brazil. Regarding recent trends, only Bolivia and Colombia—exporters of hydrocarbons—managed to maintain the share of investment in GDP since 2015. Ecuador, although it is the economy that shows the best investment figures, also experienced a fall in its ratio in almost five percentage points compared to its peak in 2013.

The pandemic hit private investment brutally, as it abruptly brought about enormous uncertainties and new risks that deteriorated the prospects for businesses over the short and long runs. The contraction of investment hit infrastructure as well as capital formation in machinery and equipment. The failure to modernise and in some cases even to maintain the capital stock

*Table 6.1* Latin America Gross fixed capital formation, selected countries by export specialisation: 1990–2019 (share of real GDP, in percentages)

| | *1990s* | *2000–2008* | *2009* | *2010* | *2011* | *2012* | *2013* | *2014* | *2015* | *2016* | *2017* | *2018* | *2019* |
|---|---|---|---|---|---|---|---|---|---|---|---|---|---|
| Export orientation | 18.6 | 18.2 | 19.9 | 21 | 21.7 | 22 | 22 | 21.3 | 20 | 18.7 | 18.1 | 18.3 | 18.2 |
| Metals and minerals | | | | | | | | | | | | | |
| Chile | 14.4 | 17.5 | 20.2 | 21.6 | 23.6 | 24.9 | 24.8 | 23.1 | 22.6 | 21.9 | 21 | 21.1 | 21.8 |
| Perú | 16.6 | 16 | 20.9 | 23.5 | 24.3 | 26.3 | 26.2 | 25.1 | 22.5 | 20.7 | 20.5 | 20.6 | 21 |
| Agro-industrial | | | | | | | | | | | | | |
| Argentina | 13.9 | 13.7 | 14.5 | 16.6 | 18.4 | 17.3 | 17.3 | 16.5 | 16.7 | 16 | 17.7 | 17.1 | 14.6 |
| Paraguay | 21.3 | 17.3 | 18.6 | 21.3 | 21 | 19.3 | 19.2 | 19.6 | 18.7 | 18.3 | 18.4 | 19.1 | 17.8 |
| Uruguay | 16.3 | 15.6 | 17.7 | 19.1 | 19.4 | 22.1 | 22 | 21.8 | 19.7 | 19.1 | 15.7 | 15 | 15.2 |
| Hydrocarbons | | | | | | | | | | | | | |
| Bolivia | 16 | 14.2 | 16.1 | 16.6 | 19.5 | 19 | 19.9 | 20.7 | 20.7 | 20.6 | 22.1 | 21.9 | 20.7 |
| Colombia | 19.2 | 16.9 | 21.5 | 22 | 23.1 | 23 | 23.7 | 24.8 | 24.8 | 23.6 | 23.7 | 23.4 | 23.7 |
| Ecuador | 18.7 | 21 | 23.1 | 24.6 | 26.1 | 27.3 | 28.7 | 28.3 | 26.5 | 24.5 | 25.2 | 25.3 | 24.5 |
| Manufactures | | | | | | | | | | | | | |
| Brazil | 18.5 | 17.4 | 18.7 | 20.5 | 21.1 | 20.9 | 21.4 | 20.4 | 18.2 | 16.6 | 15.9 | 16.3 | 16.5 |
| Mexico | 20.3 | 20.6 | 21.7 | 21.6 | 22.5 | 22.7 | 21.7 | 21.7 | 22 | 21.6 | 20.9 | 20.7 | 19.7 |

*Source:* Own elaboration based on official ECLAC data.

undermined the region's capacity and potential to achieve high and persistent economic growth.

In addition, the COVID-19 crisis brutally pressured public finances to face the social costs; a pressure that in many cases led to cuts in public investment and, thus, to a deterioration of infrastructure. The region's lag in infrastructure was already worrying before the pandemic. Indeed, in general, the economies—extractive or not—of Latin America did not take advantage of the 2003–2008 commodities boom to implement massive investment projects neither to modernise their infrastructure nor to reverse the re-primarisation of their productive structures. On the contrary, in many of them, the improvement of the terms of trade—in tandem with real appreciations of the exchange rates and the absence of industrial policies—pushed towards premature deindustrialisation. This absence of a structural transformation was particularly costly as the reversal of the terms of trade from 2009 made it more difficult to get out of the trap of slow growth and inequality.

Another key feature of the Latin American economies, pre-pandemic—and exacerbated by it—are the weaknesses and inadequacies in fiscal matters. The effective tax burden is low in almost all countries, although with differences. And its impact on achieving a more equitable distribution of income is very limited, in fact, almost nil in most countries of the region. The Gini index corresponding to the distribution in the vast majority of economies, calculated with income data, is very similar before and after taxes and transfers. This weak distributional effect of Latin America's tax system contrasts strongly with the experience of the OECD, in which the GINI after taxes and transfers is 20–30 per cent lower than before these operations.

The structural fiscal weakness has deep roots in the political economy and is also manifested in the region's inability to apply countercyclical macroeconomic policies, In fact, for a large number of nations in the region, government income is tightly linked to the evolution of foreign trade. Thus, adverse external shocks translate automatically into fiscal shocks; a twin deficit type of phenomenon. In addition, such fiscal weakness undermines the region's long-term development prospects to the extent that public investment becomes the variable of adjustment, in times of fiscal pressure. If to these flaws we add the absence of robust institutional systems for the design, approval, monitoring and evaluation of public sector investment projects, the need for a fiscal reform is a pressing issue.

Fiscal fragility has an additional twist in extractive economies because natural and mineral resources are, if not the most important, a major source of public sector revenues. Such dependence on the external sector for fiscal matters makes these economies highly vulnerable to adverse external shocks, in particular to fluctuations in commodity prices on world markets and in export flows. As Table 6.2 shows, the trajectories of the terms of trade are not necessarily homogenous in the region, and they strongly depend on their pattern of export specialisation.

*Table 6.2* Selected countries of Latin America. Terms of trade, 1990–2019 (2010 = 100.0)

| | *1990* | *1995* | *2000* | *2008* | *2009* | *2019* |
|---|---|---|---|---|---|---|
| Latin America | 67.7 | 70.9 | 76.5 | 97.4 | 90.1 | 91.1 |
| South America | 52.3 | 59.5 | 64.5 | 93.5 | 87.5 | 92.0 |
| Exporters of metals and minerals | 49.5 | 55.1 | 50.1 | 81.2 | 82.4 | 93.8 |
| Exporters of hydrocarbons | 39.4 | 34.3 | 53.2 | 109.4 | 87.8 | 82.6 |
| Central America, Haiti and Dominican Republic | 109.3 | 123.9 | 115.8 | 94.7 | 102.0 | 91.5 |
| Exporters of agro-industrial products | 74.2 | 77.1 | 73.3 | 96.3 | 97.5 | 103.6 |

*Source:* Authors' own elaborations based on ECLAC data.

According to figures from ECLAC based on official data (CEPALStat, n.d.), in the middle of the previous decade (circa 2015), the proportion of fiscal income coming directly from the exploitation of natural resources ranged from a maximum of 14.2 per cent of GDP in Bolivia, 12 per cent Venezuela and Ecuador, followed by Mexico with eight per cent and Colombia with 5.1 per cent. On the other hand, it was quite low in Peru, Brazil and Chile with records between two and three per cent and Argentina with 1.8 per cent.

The COVID-19 pandemic has dramatically set the vital challenge—in the strict sense of this word—to the region and the world of reorienting its short- and long-term development agenda as soon as possible. In addition to addressing the economic and social emergency that is still present with successive waves of contagion and the appearance of new strains of the virus, Latin America must redefine the priorities of its development agenda, redesign accordingly its policy instruments to achieve them and—most importantly—create the political consensus for it. Puyana and García (2021) argue that one of the biggest failures of the current administration headed by Lopez Obrador is the failure to make this adjustment to both a post-COVID world and the policy requirements of a 'green new deal' and a post-extractive transition that takes into account and seeks to reconcile the conflicting demands of the biosphere and development, as Prebisch (1980) understood them. Taking ECLAC data (2020b) as a reference, we share a reflection on this matter that is valid for all the region—regardless of the degree of their extractivist orientation. This reflection covers three major dimensions: (i) economic, (ii) social and (iii) environmental.

On economic matters, Latin America—and perhaps more so its extractivist economies—is urged to substantially increase private and public investment, in modern and innovative machinery and equipment as well as in state-of-the-art infrastructure in accordance with new technologies, telecommunications and artificial intelligence. This investment is a prerequisite for transforming its economic structure in order to densify its production chains—Hirschman-style, backward and forward linkages—and thereby raise the Keynesian income multiplier of its exports in terms of domestic value added and the creation of decent jobs.

Such a surge in fixed capital formation must be promoted within the framework of a New Pact for Social and Economic Development. All this must be combined with an active industrial policy that reduces the income elasticity of imports and increases that of exports, to alleviate the balance-of-payments constraint on the region's long-term economic growth. This is the only way to ensure that export dynamism underpins a substantial wave of fixed capital investment to transform and modernise the industrial structure, the productive matrix of the region and its more positive insertion into international markets and global value chains. It is crucial that the new investment is geared towards modifying the core of the region's competitive advantages in global markets, away from its base in either low-skilled labour, low labour costs or negligence—not to mention destruction—in the irresponsible management of natural resources to gravitate firmly and persistently to innovation, added value and decent work in a context of environmental sustainability. This is linked to the second dimension, the social one.

Given the vast levels of poverty and job insecurity, the region needs to accelerate growth in productive activities with increasing returns to scale and a progressive use of increasingly skilled labour. In a special call to extractive economies, extractive industries based on exploitation of the region's wealth of natural resources, and the processing of these resources to add value to the exported commodities, must become a robust engine of economic expansion and job creation, although at the same time care must be taken to ensure a more equitable social distribution of the fruits of economic growth—that is, resource rents—which can be achieved by means of a neodevelopmental and neoextractivist policy of poverty reduction (channelling some of the fiscal resources derived from the export sale of the region's natural resources). The absence of a universal social protection system must be faced, including guaranteeing universal access to clean water and sanitation, a problem for many extractive economies. Addressing this challenge must take place without any excuse and requires a deep fiscal reform to strengthen public revenues and reduce their dependence on natural resources. The reform must aim to enhance the fiscal impact on reducing inequality and the possibilities for the application of countercyclical policies. Such a reform must guarantee resources for the expansion and modernisation of infrastructure, accompanied by corresponding changes in the patterns of public spending to ensure that resources are used with efficiency, transparency and accountability. From our point of view, a legitimate and powerful instrument for this to happen, would be to establish a Fiscal Council dependent on the Legislature, similar in form and function to the United States Congressional Budget Office.[1]

The third dimension is the environment. Given the climate change emergency, if the region seeks to fulfil its international commitments and ensure equity for future generations, it must dedicate massive resources—real, financial and political capital—to redesign its productive structure and growth pattern to guarantee a swift and significant reduction in Latin America's carbon footprint. Sustainable development requires minimising environmental liabilities. In this regard, a change in the institutional and legal context is crucial to build effective regulatory structures and processes based on international regulations of the extractive sector. This must be done with a full commitment to environmental sustainability, with accountability and legally binding responsibilities for all actors involved, including the Indigenous communities on the extractive frontier. This requires monitoring and oversight mechanisms with timely, relevant and reliable information. An alternative that gains strength in the context of the current climate catastrophe is the so-called circular economy. It proposes to conceive the dynamics of economic growth as a cycle of sustainable production, distribution and consumption; all this with an industrial policy that prioritises the extraction and exploitation of renewable resources and incorporates modern green technologies (Gallagher and Kozul-Wright, 2019; UNCTAD, 2019).

The three dimensions assessed above are interdependent. Either progress is made in each of them, or no progress can be made in any of them. Neglecting the environment is not an option. Continuing to disregard inequality and poverty for the sake of a future trickle-down effect, of automatically spilling the benefits of growth to the poor, is a reckless chimaera that risks setting the landscape of political and social stability on fire. Predicting zero-growth, de-growth, is irresponsible in a region that lacks a minimal social protection network, especially given its characteristically precarious labour market, plagued by informality, weak productivity and low wages that affect vast contingents of the population.

## Final reflections and conclusions

The pandemic brought about overwhelming evidence that the traditional agendas of first growing, then distributing and then caring for the environment are criminally irresponsible and inefficient. Reconciling the three dimensions in a new agenda becomes more difficult for extractive economies, since their traditional engine—and in many cases their only engine—of growth has strong negative environmental externalities. Likewise, their employment and income multipliers are low due to the weak backward and forward linkages of its extractive and mining industries. To a large extent, implementing a different development agenda depends on the political economy, in particular on the strength of public finances to capture the extraordinary income from commodity booms and to redistribute them to cement a new non-extractivist development pattern. Politically this is not for the faint of heart.

Macro policy also needs to be thoroughly reviewed. Monetary and fiscal instruments must be coordinated to promote inclusive and sustainable development while maintaining stable inflation, and public finances and debt on a sustainable path. Likewise, macroeconomic policies must aim—in a similar line to the orientation of the US FED—not only to contain inflation but also to keep employment close to its level of full use. In this process, the health of public finances must be commensurate from a holistic developmental perspective, and not merely be measured by the magnitude of the fiscal balance. For this reason, its priority must be on how to strengthen and how to better coordinate the public sector's income, expenditure and financing to build an economy marked by high and persistent growth, committed to equality and to environmental sustainability with financial robustness.

Putting this agenda in motion, beyond the pandemic, is a political challenge. Solving the technical complexity of the public policies required to promote and guarantee this agenda is undoubtedly important. But the crucial problem is the reshaping of a New Social Contract committed to a robust, inclusive and sustainable development agenda. Without this New Social Contract there is no future for the region's development.

The political task ahead is arduous. Overcoming inertia, resistance and obstacles rooted in political economy is perhaps more difficult in extractive economies. Their institutional frameworks and systems of economic and political power developed around how and by whom extractive income is appropriated and how it is distributed can be the cause of violent conflict, of epic economic, social and political rift. In situations of fiscal and balance-of-payments crises, this dispute may well explode into violence around the question of which groups pay what costs, when and how?

In good times, it is perhaps more likely to occur that an improvement in the economic and social welfare of the many does not have to come at the cost of a decrease in the income, assets or wealth of the few. It only implies a more equitable distribution of the increase in national income. That is to say, a priori—in theory, but perhaps not in practice as shown by various experiences in the Southern Cone—it is conceivable to negotiate a more equitable distribution of the surplus generated by, say, an improvement in the terms of trade. In this endeavour, with an ad hoc political pact, the questions to be answered are: Is the source of the extractive surplus to be nationalised? Are private profits to be taxed more? How should the additional windfall income of the extractive sectors be significantly appropriated to benefit the population? How should the government do it without disrupting exports or discouraging investment? How to implement a political pact that, on the one hand, encourages investment and sustainable production and, on the other hand, increases fiscal revenues?

Addressing the above challenges requires correcting the inertial dynamics in the region's economic and social spheres. The checks and balances of political and economic power must recognise and must internalise that the old path of development no longer holds. Pervasive inequality, job precariousness and irresponsible management of natural resources does not work for the many tomorrows, however profitable it may be or seem for the few today. Post-pandemic development must be inclusive and environmentally sustainable, or it will not be development at all.

To get out of the crisis, as we never tire of repeating, Latin America requires a New Social Contract to face the long-standing and recent challenges evidenced by the pandemic. The international financial crisis of 2009 gave rise to the Global Green New Deal initiative as a global agreement for sustainable development. That agreement seemed imminent at the time, but it did not materialise into operational initiatives. Hopefully, the crisis triggered by the COVID-19 pandemic lays the foundations and political conviction urbi et orbi in favour of a New Sustainable and Inclusive Agreement in all economies—extractive or not.[2]

## Notes

1 See http: //www.cbo.gov.
2 For a very recent and most interesting alternative, see UNCTAD (2019), Towards a Global Green New Deal, https://unctad.org/en/node/2118; and the range of proposals of the group New Development Course of the UNAM; http://www.nuevocursodedesarrollo.unam.mx/.

## References

CEPAL – Comisión Económica para América Latina y el Caribe (2021a). *Estudio Económico de América Latina y el Caribe 2021: dinámica laboral y políticas de empleo para una recuperación sostenible e inclusiva más allá de la crisis del COVID-19.* United Nations: Santiago. Available at: https://cepal.org/es/publicaciones/47192-estudio-economico-america-latina-caribe-2021-dinamica-laboral-politicas-empleo.

CEPAL (2021b). *Panorama Fiscal de América Latina y el Caribe 2021: los desafíos de la política fiscal en la recuperación transformadora pos-COVID-19.* United Nations: Santiago. Available at: https://www.cepal.org/es/publicaciones/46808-panorama-fiscal-america-latina-caribe-2021-desafios-la-politica-fiscal-la.

CEPAL (2020a). *Estudio Económico de América Latina y el Caribe 2020: principales condicionantes de las políticas fiscal y monetaria en la era pospandemia de COVID-19.* United Nations: Santiago. Available at: https://cepal.org/es/publicaciones/46070-estudio-economico-america-latina-caribe-2020-principales-condicionantes.

CEPAL (2020b). *Informe sobre el impacto económico en América Latina y el Caribe de la enfermedad por coronavirus (COVID-19).* United Nations: Santiago. Available at: https://repositorio.cepal.org/handle/11362/45602.

CEPALStat (n.d.). *Bases de Datos y Publicaciones Estadísticas.* Available at: https://statistics.cepal.org/portal/cepalstat/open-data-api.html?lang=es.

Furtado, C. (2002). *En busca de un nuevo modelo, reflexiones sobre la crisis contemporánea (2002).* Buenos Aires: F.C.E.

Gallagher, K. and R. Kozul-Wright (2019). *A New Multilateralism for Shared Prosperity: Geneva Principles for a Global Green New Deal.* Available at: https://www.bu.edu/gdp/files/2019/05/Updated-New-Graphics-New-Multilateralism-May-8-2019.pdf.

ILO – International Labour Organization (2015). The ILO Decent Work Agenda. http://www.oit.org/global/topics/decent-work/lang--es/index.htm.

Moreno-Brid, J.C. and S. Garry (2016). "Economic performance in Latin America in the 2000s: Recession, recovery, and resilience?" *Oxford Development Studies,* 44(4): 384–400. DOI: 10.1080/13600818.2015.1127907.

Ocampo, J.A. (2021). "Latin America's New Lost Decade." Project Syndicate, 20 December 2021. Available at: https://www.project-syndicate.org/commentary/latin-america-slow-economic-recovery-raises-lost-decade-worries-by-jose-antonio-ocampo-2021-12?barrier=accesspaylog. Accessed 16 March 2022.

Prebisch, R. (1980). "Biosphere and Development." *CEPAL Review No. 12*, December. https://repositorio.cepal.org/bitstream/handle/11362/10453/269_en.pdf?sequence=1&is Allowed=y.

Puyana, A. and D. García (2021). "Mexico: Confronting the Pandemic while Transforming the Political Landscape." In Rawal, V., Ghosh, J. and Chandrasekhar, C. P. Editors, *When Governments Fail. When Governments Fail. A Pandemic and Its Aftermath*, pp. 209–236. New Delhi: Tulika Books.

Rawal, V., J. Ghosh, and C.P. Chandrasekhar (Eds.) (2021). *When Governments Fail. A Pandemic and Its Aftermath*. New Delhi: Tulika Books.

UNCTAD—United Nations Conference on Trade and Development (2019). Towards a Global Green New Deal. Available at: https://unctad.org/news/toward-global-green-new-deal.

# 7 The green energy transition

## Expansion and deepening of extractivism

*Alicia Puyana Mutis and Isabel Rodríguez Peña*

This chapter argues that substituting coal, oil and gas as energy sources with wind, sun, water and land extends and prolongs rather than reduces extractivism. It does so firstly by privatising these public goods to transform them into electricity and generate income from their sale on domestic and foreign markets and secondly by increasing the production and consumption of strategic metals and minerals. This chapter points to the little progress made by green energies in Canada, the USA and Mexico, according to purpose-designed indexes. Achieving energy security goals implies greater extractivism. Finally, it presents some options to reduce the effects of energy extractivism and transition towards safe and equitable energy from an environmental and social point of view.

For a number of reasons, energy security and energy transition policies amplify and perpetuate extractivism. Eliminating $CO_2$ emissions by substituting energy from coal, oil and gas for wind, solar, hydroelectric, nuclear and other energy sources of agricultural origin, leads to the privatisation of public goods: sun, wind, water and land, transforming them into so-called 'natural capital' to be commercialised as electricity or fuel, and to reap rents from their sale on domestic and foreign markets. Additionally, low-emission technologies will multiply the demand for the required critical minerals and metals. Thus, the mobilisation of financial capital in the commodification of natural resources and the ecosystem is the newest form of the expropriation and privatisation of nature, a process legitimised as the only way to combat climate change and preserve life on earth (Foster, 2022). Energy security and energy transition policies as predicated today constitute the only alternative to curbing climate change and avoid a global catastrophe. Formulated in this way, they constitute a categorical imperative of an obligatory character. As the Intrinsic Exchange Group IEG told its investors, 'while the asset value of the world economy is $512 trillion, the asset value of the earth's natural capital is estimated at $4 quadrillion ($4,000 trillion), all potentially for the taking' (cited by Foster, op cit: 1).

It is a central task of every government to guarantee access to energy in a sustained manner and at affordable prices for their populations. This is an indispensable basis for the development and stability of the social and economic life of every nation, as evidenced by the cut in oil production by OPEC in 1973 as well as by the current rise in electricity prices in Europe,

DOI: 10.4324/9781003301981-11

which represents a large proportion of household spending. Both represented a serious blow to society. The price shock of 1973 led to the formulation of intergovernmental agreements to guarantee access to energy for industrialised countries, large consumers and oil importers at prices that did not affect their economy. Today, there is a demand to accelerate the shift of sources of energy towards wind, solar, hydroelectric, plant-based and nuclear, without considering the costs that this change implies.

When energy security in 1974 became a global concern, oil was the most important source of energy, to the degree that the 20th century would be known as the oil civilisation (Lord, 2010). Reducing the burden of crude oil in the economy involved implementing a wide range of policies that, agreed internationally, had to be translated into national plans, programs and measures, in a long and complex process of negotiation and implementation of the agreements, slow to come to fruition and difficult to assess, affecting multiple spheres of a country's economy and the livelihoods and interests of its inhabitants. Continuous and unpredictable technological change and concerns about climate change add further complications and reasons to conceptualise energy security more holistically and to question the positive and negative effects of green energies and how 'green' they really are.

No less complex is extractivism itself, which evolves with technological change, economic growth, productive social structures and intermediate and final levels of demand. In this chapter, extractivism means the exploitation and intensive use of raw materials either for export with little or no transformation, or for consumption by the domestic market, and the extraction of profits from the use of that resource. As such, the use of the air, sun or water for power generation and as an input in the entire domestic or foreign production chain is considered extractivist. This extractivist category further includes tourism, agricultural plantations of coffee, sugar cane, tea and forestry, among others (Myint, 1958; Puyana, 2017).

The energy transition, as a route to energy security, creates a new form of extractivism and new sources of income, by privatising the sun, the air, the water and areas of land that are public goods, not created by human agency and previously not treated as commodities, to convert them into electricity for the domestic electricity market created for that purpose. The resulting profits are captured by the owners of the capital, which itself is highly concentrated. The concentration of capital in a profit-seeking activity implies the same concentration of income and raises social inequality (Watkins, 1963). The new energies are as, or more, intensive than the traditional ones, in terms of technology and foreign investments, from which they earn profits that absorb practically all the income produced. In the case of fossil fuels and hydroelectricity, profits are captured by the governments of the producing countries and the multinational oil companies and in the case of new energies, the private sector, domestic and foreign. The close connection between the economic cycles of countries specialising in raw materials and energy and the prices of these leads to economic instability and political conflicts over the distribution of the benefits and costs of the transition.

Despite the push towards an energy transition, by the 2050s, oil and hydrocarbons are still expected to contribute a majority proportion of the energy mix, due to their lower relative costs and higher energy content compared to green energies. This is why they continue to compete with hydroelectric, wind, solar, nuclear and plant-based energy, despite the great reduction in production costs achieved by the latter in the past two decades. Another aspect to consider is the political character of energy security and the energy transition, as shown by the turnaround in President Obama's environmental policies, President Trump's denial of climate change and Biden's reassertion of the US commitment to the Kyoto protocol, swings that occur when the party in power is replaced. Indeed, since 1974, the incentives to substitute oil suggest that domestic, partisan and personal interests set the tone for the energy policy of the USA and in general, of any country, as may be deduced from the environmentalist and productive policy of President Biden (Parshley, 2022; Puyana and Romero 2022). Energy security involves growing tensions between domestic and international interest groups, involving hegemony and geopolitics, which are not always made explicit in negotiations or debates (Puyana and Rodríguez, 2020).

This chapter is organised as follows: the first section deals with the relationship that energy security and the energy transition maintain with extractivism and the implications for North America. It begins with the definitions of extractivism and points to the variables shared by the generation of wind, solar and hydroelectric energy, suggesting that in the primary and global energy mix, even considering the rise of the new and green ones, fossil fuel is dominant and will continue to be so until 2050. Thus, it is worth asking about the reasons for their slow decline. The second section analyses the trajectory from energy security to the energy transition and proposes that there are several different transitions, all of them complex and difficult to solve. It explores the characteristics of extractivism and suggests that the energy transition opens up new sites of extractivism and sources of rent extraction. The third section explores the trajectory of energy security and the energy transition in North America, as it transitioned from rent extraction from oil, coal and gas, to rent extraction from the sun, air, water and land. It measures the progress of energy security through four indices purpose-designed for this chapter and describes the factors that explain the evolution of each. The fifth section presents the conclusions.

## Security and energy transition and extractivism

The connection between oil, energy security and the energy transition and extractivism lies with the exploitation of natural resources such as coal, gas and oil and the resources used in transition energy sources: water, sun, wind and land. These natural resources are privatised and transformed into fuels and electricity for sale on foreign and domestic markets. Converting corn and other agricultural products into ethane implies switching agricultural production from food to fuel, a transformation of questionable ethics, since it pits the population in competition with cars, at a time when two billion people around the world suffer from acute and severe malnutrition. These extractivisms, extractions and 'extrahections' (Gudynas, 2013) involve the sometimes-violent appropriation of natural resources owned by the nation and deny the rights of whole populations (over generations) and of nature, in low-, medium- or high-intensity exploitation, destined for the local, national or foreign markets (Gudynas, 2013). Due to its low intensity, the cultivation of food for self-consumption is not extractivist; nor is its final destination the market. On the other hand, the medium-scale production of fruits and vegetables and the large-scale production of certain gravels and sands for construction, for the regional and national markets and greenhouse flowers, are extractivist. In general, these commercial activities refuse to recognise that nature is the basic sustenance of human life, which is why the constitutions of Ecuador and Bolivia enshrine these rights, integrating them with human rights. Article 71 of the Ecuadorian Charter of 2008 establishes that nature (Pacha Mama) allows the '...realization and reproduction of life and has the right to full respect for its existence and the maintenance and regeneration of its vital cycles, structure, functions and evolutionary processes' (Bagni, 2018: 3).

The exploitation of land—a good not produced by human agency—generates rents that grow *pari passu* with the population, food demand, economic development and changes in consumption patterns due to higher GDP per capita. The interest in maintaining this rent induces dependence of the economy on price cycles and perpetuates the pattern of development and the rent-seeking structures of the state and society (Karl, 1999).

Oil revenues are very high, a result of the diversity of oil wells in terms of both size and qualities of crude oil, the concentration of reserves and production and the strategic nature of crude oil, resulting in a non-competitive international market.[1] Agricultural land is less concentrated than oil, but not so agricultural technology, or productive and commercial capital, which leads to similar patterns in production and the distribution and appropriation of rent, creating costly barriers to entry. On the other hand, the land differs in physical and chemical qualities and in yields, giving rise to agricultural rents. In short, the link between extraordinary income from raw materials and the economies of exporting countries is direct and mediated by various political and social factors (Karl, 1997; Puyana, 2015; Puyana and Rodríguez, 2020).

Economic shocks due to price increases of raw materials and the concomitant increases in income are one of the well-known effects of extractivism, leading to the premature decline in agriculture and manufacturing in terms of GDP and employment; slow growth in labour productivity; increased precariousness of jobs; and remuneration (Furtado, 1973; Prebisch, 1948; Puyana, 2015). Out of this emerges, on the one hand, elites who benefit from the dynamism of the booming energy sector and, on the other hand, masses of underemployed, unskilled workers (Svampa, 2019). It is possible that the dependence of the exporting countries on agricultural raw materials is less than that of the oil producers and that their economies, foreign investment flows and inflation are less exposed to price variations, but the effects indicated do occur (Karl, 1997; Furtado, 1982; Puyana, 2015, 2017).

The effects of the energy transition are multiple. It reduces the production and sale of oil, the income of the oil companies and of the governments whose treasuries depend on them to a greater or lesser extent. It creates macro- and micro-economic imbalances that require mediating policies. It contracts oil tax revenues, making it necessary either to reduce spending, raise taxes or create new sources of revenue. The contraction of public income raises complex questions: how to finance the transition? What strategies will oil companies pursue? How will private companies use the income from green energy? It is necessary to consider that while governments offer incentives for new energies, subsidies for consumers and restructure spending and income policies, multinationals are attempting strategic changes. Aramco, the Saudi Arabian oil company, for example, has begun a discreet strategy of diversifying its energy supply with external sales of electricity, building solar parks, while British Petroleum and Shell venture into biomass and wind power and several others announce targets of zero carbon emissions by 2050. Latin American oil companies, focused on improving oil production technology, are making little progress in the energy transition.

While the impact of fossil fuels on global warming is clear, the path to de-fossilisation of economies is hazy, with no consensus on whether the correct path is to reduce emissions or leave fossil fuels in the ground, whether to slow down economies and questioning whether gas counts as a transition energy for the short or long term or as a green energy. In this line, the French Commissioner to the European Union, T. Breton, has argued: 'Gas is not the best way to achieve our goals (reducing emissions and preventing global warming) because it generates $CO_2$, but as a transition energy it is better than coal. It is necessary' he adds, 'to have the financial resources to decarbonise the economy and a more scientific taxonomy of energy sources, including nuclear' (Khan, 2022: 3). But with what appears to be a clear disqualification of the European Union's classification of gas as a form of green energy (European Union, 2022),[2] Breton's strategy would impose heavy costs on the global and North American energy system, which is heavily dependent on oil and gas (see Tables 7.1 and 7.2). On the other hand, by 2050 one-third of the amount of fossil fuels will be consumed compared to 2019.

*Table 7.1* Global demand for primary energy. 1949–2050. Percent share

| *Energy source* | *1950* | *1970* | *1980* | *1990* | *2010* | *2020* | *2030* | *2040* | *2050* | *1950–2020* |
|---|---|---|---|---|---|---|---|---|---|---|
| Oil | 38.5 | 47.01 | 45.1 | 38.5 | 33.7 | 30.3 | 30.6 | 29.1 | 28.1 | −0.2 |
| Gas | 17.2 | 16.96 | 18.4 | 21.2 | 22.6 | 24.5 | 23.6 | 22.4 | 21.8 | 0.4 |
| Coal | 35.7 | 30.1 | 26.9 | 27.1 | 29.9 | 25.9 | 22.1 | 21.2 | 19.9 | −0.3 |
| Fossils total | 91.4 | 94.07 | 90.4 | 86.8 | 86.2 | 80.7 | 76.3 | 72.7 | 69.8 | −0.1 |
| Nuclear | 0 | 0.36 | 2.5 | 5.8 | 5.2 | 4.6 | 4.5 | 4.2 | 3.7 | 4.6 |
| Other renewable | 8.6 | 5.54 | 7.1 | 7.4 | 8.6 | 14.7 | 19.2 | 23.1 | 26.5 | 0.7 |
| Total renewable | 8.6 | 5.9 | 9.6 | 13.2 | 13.8 | 19.3 | 23.7 | 27.3 | 30.2 | 1.2 |
| Total | 100 | 100 | 100 | 100 | 100 | 100 | 100 | 100 | 100 | 0.0 |

*Source*: Prepared by the author, based on: International Energy Outlook 2021, EIA and https://www.eia.gov/international/data/world/total-energy/total-energy-consumption?

*Table 7.2* Demand for primary energy in North America. 1975–2020 (percent share)

| | | | | | | | | | | 2050 | TCPA | |
|---|---|---|---|---|---|---|---|---|---|---|---|---|
| | | *1980* | *1990* | *2000* | *2005* | *2010* | *2015* | *2020* | *2030* | *1980–2020* | *2020–2050* | |
| USA | Oil | 43.8 | 39.7 | 38.8 | 40.4 | 37.0 | 37.3 | 38.9 | 40.6 | 39.3 | −0.30 | 0.04 |
| | Gas | 25.9 | 23.2 | 24.1 | 22.5 | 24.9 | 28.6 | 33.0 | 31.0 | 32.1 | 0.60 | −0.09 |
| | Coal | 19.8 | 22.7 | 22.9 | 22.7 | 21.1 | 15.8 | 9.0 | 7.2 | 5.5 | −1.95 | −1.62 |
| | Fossil total | 89.5 | 85.6 | 85.8 | 85.7 | 83.1 | 81.7 | 80.9 | 78.8 | 77.0 | −0.25 | −0.16 |
| | Nuclear | 3.5 | 7.2 | 8.0 | 8.1 | 8.6 | 8.5 | 8.5 | 6.4 | 5.4 | 2.23 | −1.48 |
| | Renewables | 7.0 | 7.1 | 6.2 | 6.2 | 8.4 | 9.9 | 10.7 | 14.8 | 17.6 | 1.07 | 1.69 |
| | Total renewables | 10.5 | 14.4 | 14.2 | 14.3 | 16.9 | 18.3 | 19.1 | 21.2 | 23.0 | 1.52 | 0.62 |
| Canada | Oil | 40.8 | 31.6 | 31.3 | 34.4 | 34.8 | 33.7 | 29.9 | 31.3 | 28.7 | −0.77 | −0.14 |
| | Gas | 20.1 | 22.7 | 24.4 | 23.5 | 25.8 | 28.9 | 30.6 | 31.9 | 36.2 | 1.06 | 0.56 |
| | Coal | 8.2 | 9.2 | 9.4 | 8.7 | 6.9 | 4.8 | 3.4 | 1.3 | 0.5 | −2.18 | −6.00 |
| | Fossil total | 69.1 | 63.4 | 65.1 | 66.6 | 67.5 | 67.4 | 63.9 | 64.4 | 65.4 | −0.19 | 0.08 |
| | Nuclear | 4.4 | 7.5 | 6.2 | 7.1 | 7.0 | 7.4 | 6.1 | 5.0 | 1.6 | 0.85 | −4.38 |
| | Renewables | 26.6 | 29.1 | 28.7 | 26.3 | 25.5 | 25.2 | 29.9 | 30.6 | 33.0 | 0.30 | 0.32 |
| | Total renewables | 30.9 | 36.6 | 34.9 | 33.4 | 32.5 | 32.6 | 36.1 | 35.6 | 34.6 | 0.39 | −0.14 |
| Mexico | Oil | 70.5 | 68.3 | 64.0 | 58.0 | 54.9 | 50.4 | 44.4 | 41.8 | 39.2 | −1.15 | −0.42 |
| | Gas | 22.2 | 21.6 | 23.8 | 28.2 | 31.2 | 35.1 | 32.4 | 35.1 | 30.9 | 0.95 | −0.15 |
| | Coal | 2.3 | 3.3 | 4.3 | 7.0 | 7.2 | 7.2 | 5.6 | 3.7 | 3.3 | 2.20 | −1.71 |
| | Fossil total | 95.0 | 93.2 | 92.1 | 93.1 | 93.3 | 92.7 | 82.4 | 80.6 | 73.5 | −0.36 | −0.38 |
| | Nuclear | 0.0 | 0.6 | 1.2 | 1.5 | 0.7 | 1.4 | 0.9 | 1.5 | 0.6 | 1.41 | −1.71 |
| | Renewables | 5.0 | 6.2 | 6.7 | 5.4 | 6.0 | 5.9 | 16.7 | 17.9 | 26.0 | 3.08 | 1.49 |
| | Total renewables | 5.0 | 6.8 | 7.9 | 6.9 | 6.7 | 7.3 | 17.6 | 19.4 | 26.6 | 3.22 | 1.38 |
| North America | Oil | 44.6 | 40.2 | 39.4 | 40.8 | 37.9 | 37.7 | 38.3 | 39.6 | 38.0 | −0.38 | −0.03 |
| | Gas | 25.2 | 23.1 | 24.2 | 22.9 | 25.4 | 29.1 | 32.7 | 31.5 | 32.5 | 0.65 | −0.02 |
| | Coal | 17.8 | 20.3 | 20.4 | 20.2 | 18.6 | 13.9 | 8.0 | 6.2 | 4.6 | −1.98 | −1.81 |
| | Fossil total | 87.6 | 83.6 | 84.0 | 83.9 | 81.9 | 80.6 | 79.0 | 77.3 | 75.1 | −0.26 | −0.17 |
| | Nuclear | 3.5 | 6.9 | 7.4 | 7.6 | 7.9 | 7.9 | 7.5 | 5.7 | 4.4 | 1.97 | −1.80 |
| | Renewables | 8.9 | 9.4 | 8.6 | 8.4 | 10.2 | 11.5 | 13.5 | 17.0 | 20.5 | 1.04 | 1.40 |
| | Total renewables | 12.4 | 16.4 | 16.0 | 16.1 | 18.1 | 19.4 | 21.0 | 22.7 | 24.9 | 1.33 | 0.56 |

*Source*: Our own elaboration, based on BP (2021).

The situation in the North America region is no better. Indeed, in 2020, the share of fossil fuels ranged between 89.3 per cent in Mexico and 67.65 per cent in Canada and it is estimated that by 2050 the structure will be similar to world averages.

## Permutations of the energy transition

Over the past five years, the energy transition has gained political and academic prominence, subsuming that of energy security and renewing the classic analyses of extractivism. It now includes the goals of environmental sustainability and social justice and involves various transitions in successive stages that began in February 1974. Each of these merits joint and individual analysis (Puyana et al., 2021).

The first phase of energy security and energy transition policies, adopted in February 1974, mandated the following: (1) diversify the oil markets with new suppliers, domestic and foreign, to limit imports from OPEC; (2) promote other sources of energy: coal, gas and nuclear energy; (3) reduce energy consumption and the energy intensity of the national economy; and (4) beginning in the 1990s, promote renewable energies: mainly wind, solar and hydroelectric.

Wind, solar, hydroelectric and plant-based power generation have the same political, economic and social effects as mining and fossil fuel extractivism: price instability; high technological intensity; deindustrialisation and deagriculturalisation; income generation; and concentration of capital and inequitable distribution of income; they are *focal points* for social and political conflicts, land dispossession and violation of the human rights of Indigenous and peasant communities (Gudynas, 2009; Pineault, 2020; Puyana, 2015, 2019; Svampa, 2012).

In energy security and the energy transition, several transitions converge, each of which generates new and unprecedented mismatches, when transiting: (i) from exporter extractivism to the extractivism of the internal market; (ii) from non-renewable to renewable energy sources; (iii) from the balance of the energy market: due to the differences in the income and price elasticities of the supply and consumption of non-renewable to renewable energies; (iv) from existing to new producers of energy; (v) from old to new recipients of rent: the public sector in the case of fossil fuels to the private sector in the case of new energies; and (vi) from distribution patterns and channelling income to the economy. These shifts illustrate the political and economic complexity of energy security and energy transition policies, since they constitute models of political economy and national consensus different from those institutionalised in the past six to eight decades.

Notwithstanding the international agreements put in place, in the years from 1974 to 2020, few achievements have been recorded in the energy transition, with hydrocarbons still contributing 80.7 per cent of the world's primary energy. This represents a decrease of 13.4 percentage points over

50 years, and a further decrease of 11 points is expected by 2050, with oil providing about 30 per cent of the world's primary energy at that point (see Table 7.1). The transformation of the energy mix is far from the goals suggested by the most recent report of the Intergovernmental Panel on Climate Change (IPCC), which states that only one of the five feasible strategies would succeed in containing global warming below 1.5°C (IPCC, 2021). This route implies abandoning the growth model based on fossil fuels, the intensive use of raw materials and extractivism. Latin America is far from taking this route, as can be deduced from Table 7.2.

## The North America region from the perspective of energy security

Two characteristics distinguish North America: its relative wealth in oil and other energy sources and the integration of its economies to the energy sector. Each country in the region has developed its potential according to national strategies and according to its perception of the value of these resources in terms of their security and according to the economic model that each one has implemented, even if they do not fully coincide with the reasons that encouraged the signing and institutionalisation of regional economic integration agreements. In the three countries, and around the world, energy policies have been a key issue for the development and health of the national economy (Puyana, 2015). In summary, the region revolves around the energy axis of the USA due to its high consumption and production of oil, gas and even coal, and to a large extent the trajectory of energy security and the energy transition, are spokes connected to the US political and economic axis.[3]

Mexico went from having oil reserves higher than the USA and being a net exporter, selling over 50 per cent of its production, to restricting foreign sales due to the depletion of the Cantarell field. The USA now dominates the energy landscape as the largest oil and second-largest gas producer, whereas 15 years ago it was only the largest in terms of consumption. Canada commenced external sales of crude oil in the 1970s under the OPEC policies mentioned above (Puyana and Rodríguez, 2020). Energy consumption and $CO_2$ emissions are also dissimilar, in per capita terms, as indicated in Table 3. The USA is the largest producer and consumer of fossil fuels in the region, representing 70 per cent of the former and 80 per cent of the latter in 2020. It emits less $CO_2$ per person and in GDP terms than Canada, but more than Mexico, and in 2020, represented 83, 82 and 93 per cent of the demand for oil, gas and coal, respectively.

The difference between the regional weight of the USA in terms of reserves (28.3 per cent) and in oil consumption (8.7 per cent) means that the remaining demand is met by imported oil. It also indicates a distinct management of its resources leading to this higher consumption, as reflected in the trajectory of energy security and the energy transition in the region. Indeed, in 2020, imports from Canada and Mexico supplied nearly 25 per cent of US

*Table 7.3* North America: Production and consumption of fossil energy and $CO_2$ emissions 2000–2050

| *USA* | | *2000* | | | *2010* | | | *2020* | | | *2030** | | *2050** | |
|---|---|---|---|---|---|---|---|---|---|---|---|---|---|---|
| | | *Can* | *Mex* | *USA* | *Can* | *Mex* | *USA* | *Can* | *Mex* | *USA* | *Can–Mex* | *USA* | *Can–Mex* | |
| Oil | Reserves | 12.8 | 76.7 | 10.4 | 15.9 | 79.4 | 4.7 | 28.3 | 68.2 | 2.5 | n/d | n/d | n/d | n/d |
| | Production | 55.7 | 19.5 | 24.9 | 54.6 | 24.1 | 21.4 | 70.0 | 21.8 | 8.1 | 71.4 | 28.6 | 73.7 | 26.3 |
| | Consumption | 83.0 | 8.7 | 8.3 | 80.5 | 10.5 | 9.0 | 82.7 | 11.0 | 6.3 | 81.8 | 18.2 | 82.4 | 17.6 |
| Gas | Reserves | 66.2 | 22.6 | 11.2 | 78.7 | 17.9 | 3.3 | 83.3 | 15.5 | 1.2 | n/d | n/d | n/d | n/d |
| | Production | 71.2 | 24.2 | 4.6 | 74.1 | 19.3 | 6.6 | 82.4 | 14.9 | 2.7 | 78.7 | 21.3 | 79.2 | 20.8 |
| | Consumption | 83.4 | 11.8 | 4.8 | 80.4 | 11.4 | 8.2 | 80.7 | 10.9 | 8.4 | 80.0 | 20.0 | 77.3 | 22.7 |
| Coal | Reserves | n/d | n/d | n/d | 96.8 | 2.7 | 0.5 | 97.0 | 2.6 | 0.5 | n/d | n/d | n/d | n/d |
| | Production | 92.4 | 6.6 | 0.9 | 92.5 | 6.2 | 1.3 | 91.1 | 7.6 | 1.3 | 92.3 | 7.7 | 99.8 | 0.2 |
| | Consumption | 93.6 | 5.3 | 1.1 | 93.0 | 4.6 | 2.4 | 92.9 | 5.0 | 2.1 | 87.5 | 12.5 | 99.7 | 0.3 |
| CO2 | CO2/GDP | 39.54 | 40.02 | 20.45 | 35.51 | 39.74 | 24.75 | 31.08 | 44.61 | 24.31 | n/d | n/d | n/d | n/d |
| | $CO_2$/per capita | 50.38 | 40.75 | 8.87 | 47.20 | 42.26 | 10.54 | 43.63 | 46.29 | 10.08 | n/d | n/d | n/d | n/d |
| $CO_2$/GDP USA/Can USA/Mex | | 1.0 | 1.0 | 1.9 | 1.1 | 1.0 | 1.6 | 1.3 | 0.9 | 1.6 | X | X | X | X |
| $CO_2$/Cap. USA/Can USA/Mex | | 1.0 | 1.2 | 5.7 | 1.1 | 1.2 | 4.8 | 1.2 | 1.1 | 5.0 | X | X | X | X |

*Sources*: prepared by the author, based on BP, Statistical Energy Review, July 2021; EIA at eia.gov/international/data/coal; * BP's business-as-usual scenario. The 'fast' scenario projects lower production and consumption of fossil sources. * 'net zero': accelerated reductions.

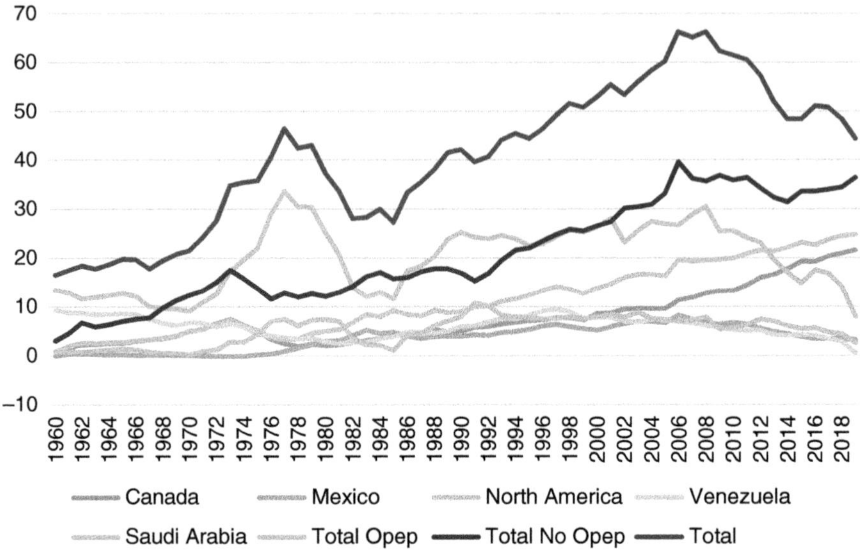


*Figure 7.1* US: Oil imports from Canada and Mexico as percentages of total US consumption. 1960–2020

oil consumption (Graph 7.1). The countries displaced from this major market are OPEC, among them Saudi Arabia, Iran and Venezuela, the latter for political reasons rather than prices, falling production or depletion of wells, as in Mexico. While the imported supply of total consumption fell from the peak recorded in 2005–2007, those in North America climbed due to growth in Canada, while Mexico lost ground. Mexico and Canada accelerated their exports in the early 1980s, attributable to energy security policies after 1974.

The USA is the main importer of oil from Canada and Mexico, accounting for nearly 80 per cent of crude oil exports and supplying a higher proportion of gasoline, particularly to Mexico (Puyana, 2015). The discovery of the mega field in Alberta allowed Canada to become a net exporter of crude oil, meaning that Canada and Mexico provide about 30 per cent of total crude oil imports which cover approximately 17 per cent of total US oil consumption. Fracking production made the USA the world's largest producer of crude and refined oil and for the first time in history, the US energy trade surplus fell by 27 billion pesos, contributing to a large extent to reducing the country's total trade deficit. Since oil represents 92 per cent of the value of imports and 74 per cent of the value of energy exports, its trajectory impacts on the trade balance of the USA.[4]

The intra-regional gas trade presents a different picture to oil intra-regional trade, with similar prices, and supply and demand relationships, but with dissimilar geographical patterns since the gas trade is regional rather than global, like oil (Baldwin and Lopez-Gonzalez, 2012). The USA and Canada, respectively, provide 47 per cent and 53 per cent of the 145 billion cubic feet of gas exchanged in the region in 2018, a cross-exchange in which one or the other country are exclusive suppliers in certain regions. The USA is the only supplier of gas and gasoline to Mexico (BP, 2021). As with crude oil, the production of shale oil and gas since the beginning of the new century positioned the USA as the world's leading gas producer.[5]

According to Gudynas (2013), the energy industry in Canada, the USA and Mexico is an extractivist activity of intensive exploitation of natural resources, for the domestic and foreign markets. Canada is a net exporter of energy, the US exports gas and coal, and Mexico oil, and at one time or another, all three countries export or have exported, a considerable proportion of their production, while supplying their relatively high domestic consumption. In any case, the engine driving the exploitation of natural resources to produce energy is the appropriation of the high rents these generate, regardless of the market in which the production is sold.

The US policy to achieve energy self-sufficiency and the industrialising plans of the Biden administration (the Democrat version of Trump's *Make America Great Again*) could unleash a kind of demand extractivism, since the US extractivist demand feeds off and requires the existence of extractivist activities in Latin America and the Global South, applicable to relations between developed and developing countries (Hickel, 2022). Ensuring the energy security of the USA and providing the energy required by the plan to rebuild the national economy and counter Chinese competition will demand raw materials for the production of electric vehicles and high-tech industries for the production of microchips and the digital economy. In this context, it is in the national interest of each of the members of the United States–Mexico–Canada Agreement (USMCA) that their governments ensure the supply of oil in the quantities required by their economies.

Although it is the responsibility of humanity to act on the causes of climate change, this responsibility is not distributed equally among all the countries of the world, or according to the population or economy of each one. It is greater in developed countries that were pioneers in industrialisation and that were most responsible for the production and consumption of fossil fuels, even if they did not have reserves, since until 1973 they had advantageous concessions with taxes lower than eight per cent of the extracted value. Their responsibility dates back to the beginning of the 20th century and covers the entire period since oil replaced coal as the main fuel, the period of integration of the national and international markets and industrialisation, particularly after World War II, when the so-called oil civilisation was consolidated, due to its role in practically the entire economic structure: production, transportation and services. Indeed, the USA, Canada, Europe, Israel, Australia and Japan between them are responsible for 92 per cent of excess emissions that will lead the global temperature to exceed 1.5°C over the pre-industrial period; hence, the majority of the population of developing countries are responsible for hardly any of the climate crisis (Hickel, 2022). The per capita consumption of raw materials in developed countries is four times greater than in the Global South (ibid.). The consumerism of the most developed countries coexists with the low consumption levels of poor countries that supply raw materials. This issue of equity has not been fully explored, while equity within countries is emphasised, leaving out the disparity between countries in terms of consumption and $CO_2$ emissions. The success of energy security and energy transition policies depends on the extent to which they respond to national contexts and how, based on these, responsibilities are taken to remedy the environmental damage and the effects of both current energy extractivism and those arising from strategies for energy security and the energy transition.

## Is environmentally and socially sustainable energy progressing in North America?

In this chapter, the trajectory of energy security and the energy transition in North America marks the passage from energies based on fossil resources (coal, oil and gas) to hydroelectric, wind, solar and nuclear energies. In terms of extractivism, both involve the extraction and intensive use of natural resources, leading to environmental damage and complex social effects, which current energy security policies ignore, hide or accept.

To measure the trajectory of energy security, constructed according to the rules described above, four indices were designed on the basis of two axes: availability and sustainability, the first associated with availability of reserves and the second with the volume of production and imports of fossil fuels. Reserves and production have a positive relation to energy security and import a negative one. Since the axis of the energy transition is to diversify the primary supply with non-fossil fuels that are supposed to be less $CO_2$ intensive, any increase in their participation represents progress towards energy security, which deepens extractivism, as argued in the first section of this study which holds that the production of electricity, wind, solar, nuclear and hydroelectric energies should be added to the category of extractivist activities, a conclusion that agrees with Puyana et al. (2021).[6] The value of the indexes oscillates between zero and one; values closer to one indicate improvements in the indicator, while values approaching zero indicate the opposite. Next, the construction of the indexes is described and the results are discussed.

## Oil Security Index (OSI)

Three composite variables make up the OSI[7]: (1) oil intensity calculated on the basis of the ratio of apparent consumption to GDP, where apparent consumption is calculated from the sum of production plus imports minus exports. This variable is inversely related to energy efficiency, in the sense that a reduction in the ratio indicates lower oil consumption per unit of GDP, due to changes in the productive structure towards more capital-intensive activities; (2) useful life of the reserves, which is calculated from the quotient of the volume of reserves and annual production, is positively related to energy security and inversely to annual production and indicates greater extractivist activity, meaning greater intensity of exploitation of non-renewable natural

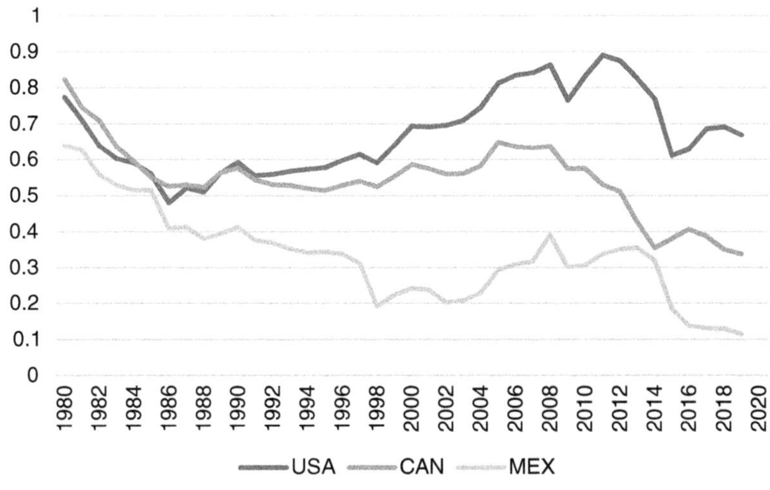


*Figure 7.2* Evolution of the oil security index

resources; (3) dependence on imports measured by the ratio of imports and apparent consumption. The growth of the ratio suggests greater dependence on imports and lower energy security. However, if the growth comes from substituting oil for green energy, there would be greater energy security, and this could maintain or expand the extractivist energy model.

Graph 7.2 suggests a turning point in the evolution of the OSI of Canada, the USA and Mexico occurred in the mid-1980s, with the beginning of the liberal model and structural reforms and the return to extractivism (Puyana, 2017). In Mexico, the OSI reaches its lowest level in 2020, due to the decline in oil reserves and production. Canada and the USA follow the opposite trajectory due to the expansion of the ratio thanks to increased reserves, which prolongs their useful life. These gains in the OSI slowed and regressed at the end of the first decade of this century, especially the expansion of production and exports, higher than that of GDP, increasing the apparent consumption of coal, that is, extractivism and possibly environmental damage.

## GAS Security Index (GSI)

The GSI comprises the same variables as the OSI, with crude oil replaced by gas. The evolution in each country is explained by the increase in gas reserves and production. The greater importance of this index arises from the fact that gas has become the main alternative source to coal in the generation of electricity, and the basis of the energy transition in the medium term (EU, 2022). Despite its current significance in the energy mix, it continues to be criticised due to a lack of clarity about whether it emits less $CO_2$ than coal, since it is still a fossil fuel and a strong emitter of greenhouse gases (Khan, 2022), especially shale gas whose production and use delays energy security, due to $CO_2$ emissions, water contamination and other problems, which have led to the total rejection of this activity. See Graph 7.3 on these trends.

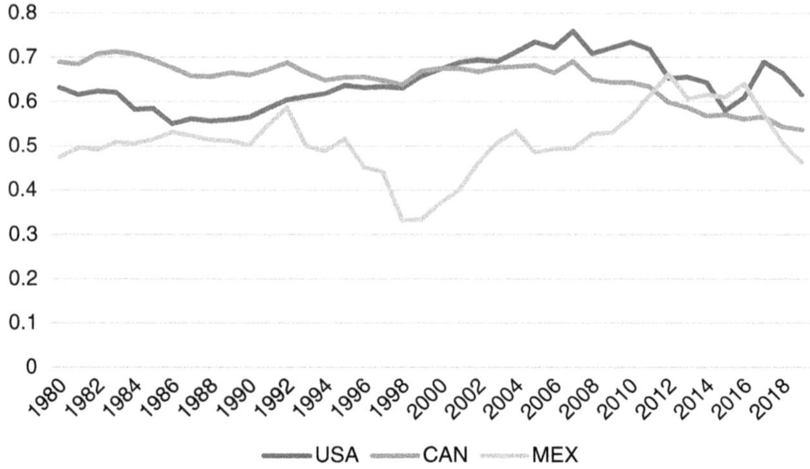


*Figure 7.3* Gas security index

## Energy Diversification Index (EDI)

This index contains two variables: (1) the consumption ratio between oil production (crude oil), gas and coal, where the value is greater than one it indicates losses in energy security due to the fact that consumption would be guaranteed through imports, which is linked to dependence, and (2) the consumption of nuclear and hydroelectric energy and the total consumption of renewables. For the calculation of the index, oil and coal are marked with a negative sign, to indicate the negative relationship with diversification and, consequently, energy security is negatively affected. On the other hand, gas together with renewables enters with a positive value since they are considered central to the energy transition (Aguilera and Aguilera, 2020; EU, 2022; Puyana et al., 2021).

It is worth noting the particularity of the EDI in terms of extractivism, arising from the emphasis given in energy security policies to the diversification of renewable energy sources, without sufficiently weighing aspects such as social conflicts, due to sometimes-violent dispossession of land; changes in land use (Hickel, 2022); weakening of pollination caused by wind turbines; and greater consumption of non-renewable mining resources for their operation. Therefore, any increase in the share of new energies is positive in terms of energy security because diversification increases and, depending on the case of each country, dependence on fossil fuels is reduced. However, these new energies are based on the same extractivist logic of the intensive use of non-renewable resources. From the foregoing, it follows that guaranteeing energy security and the energy transition, either through a greater share of gas or renewable energies, deepens and broadens extractivism. Gas, identified as a new energy substitute for oil and coal, is a fossil fuel and its exploitation is extractivist in nature. Therefore, its higher consumption for electricity production increases both energy security and extractivism.

In the last decade, the supply of renewable energies grew, but its share of total consumption is still low and the reduction in the consumption of coal and oil is slow, since in the generation of electricity these are replaced with gas. It is worth asking whether gas deserves to be classified as an alternative energy, ignoring the fact that it is a source of greenhouse gases. Table 7.4 provides information to exemplify the two arguments. When considering gas as a fossil resource, participation by fossil fuels dominated the mix in 2020 and will continue to do so until 2050. In each of the three countries and in the region, it will predominate despite the implementation of the energy transition,

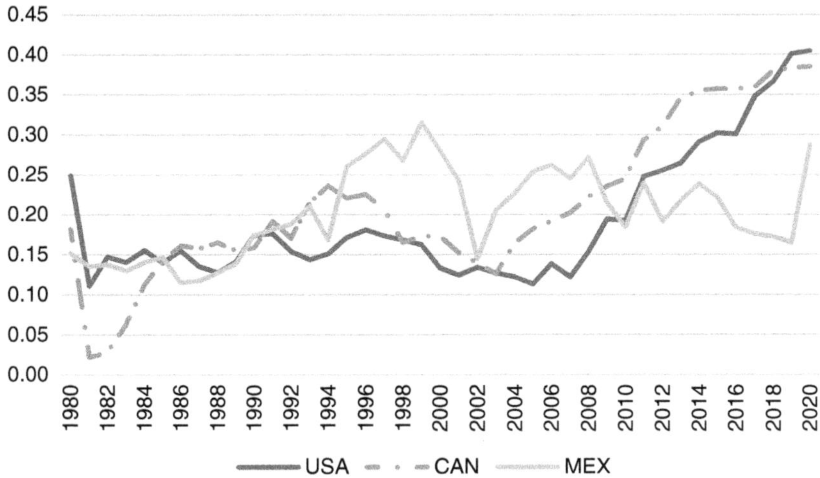


*Figure 7.4* Evolution of the energy diversification index

*Table 7.4* Primary energy consumption in Canada, Mexico and the USA, by resource. Percentage share 1980–2020[8]

| | *Canada* | | *Mexico* | | *USA* | |
|---|---|---|---|---|---|---|
| *Years* | *Fossil* | *Renewable* | *Fossil* | *Renewable* | *Fossil* | *Renewable* |
| 1980 | 69.7 | 30.3 | 94.5 | 5.5 | 73.8 | 7.7 |
| 1985 | 63.7 | 36.3 | 92.6 | 7.4 | 76.3 | 10.1 |
| 1990 | 64.9 | 35.1 | 92.9 | 7.1 | 76.2 | 11.9 |
| 1995 | 63.2 | 36.8 | 91.6 | 8.4 | 74.4 | 12.6 |
| 2000 | 66 | 34.1 | 91.8 | 8.1 | 75.3 | 12.1 |
| 2005 | 66.5 | 33.5 | 93.3 | 6.7 | 76.5 | 12.2 |
| 2010 | 67.2 | 32.8 | 93.3 | 6.7 | 72 | 14.1 |
| 2015 | 66.1 | 34 | 92.9 | 7.1 | 66.3 | 15.2 |
| 2020 | 64.7 | 35.3 | 89.3 | 10.7 | 58.8 | 18.3 |

*Source:* Prepared by the authors, based on British Petroleum, Statistical Review of World Energy (2021), at: https://www.bp.com/en/global/corporate/energy-economics/statistical-review-of-world-energy.html.

while renewable energies remain a low proportion of total consumption and hydro and nuclear energy are a stable proportion.

The increase in the share of renewable energies indicated in the table implies that they grew at rates higher than those of total energy production and fossil fuels, which fell by five percentage points in Canada and Mexico and by 15 points in the USA, the country with the fastest progress in renewables with 18.3 per cent of the total. As of 1974, the market is seen as responsible for climate change yet, in a logical inconsistency, reversing this phenomenon is left to the market. Several reasons could be offered in this regard. One is that energy security gave rise to the

> …historic process of fetishizing $CO^2$ emissions (carbon fetishization), that is, reorienting capital and its relations with the natural world towards the elimination of $CO^2$, a process accepted even by progressive forces, as a reformist agenda, in what Peter Newell and Matthew Paterson call "climate capitalism".
>
> (Merrick, 2015: 2)

If the real purpose is to contain climate change and energy inequality, it is essential to question the logic behind the mercantile strategy of energy security and carbon fetishism, which imply privatising and commodifying natural resources and transforming the natural world into a capital stock for a few, as suggested by Böhm and Dabni (2009).

## Energy Transition Index (ETI)

The ETI includes, with a negative sign, the value of the total consumption of fossil fuels and the generation of $CO_2$; with a positive sign for gas, renewable energies. As in the previous index, improvements in energy security are based on an increase in the consumption of gas and renewable energies and a decrease in $CO_2$ emissions. In this last variable, Mexico has a better position than Canada and the USA.

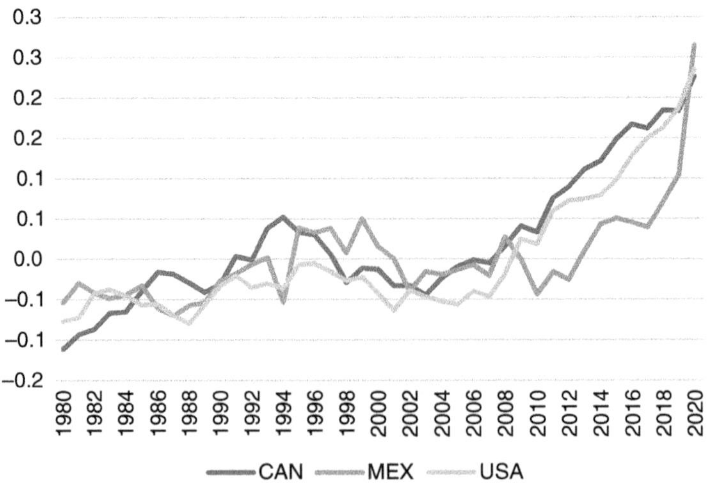


*Figure 7.5* Energy transition index

In summary, the indexes indicate a lower weight of fossil fuels and a greater weight of new energies. This change in the structure of primary energy supply and consumption is based on the exploitation of other natural resources, some renewable, such as wind, water and land, and others non-renewable, such as uranium, lithium, various metals, minerals and rare earths.

The limited decrease in the weight of fossil fuels in the energy mix arises from offsetting this decrease with greater consumption of gas, a fossil fuel and significant emitter of $CO_2$. The slow growth of renewable energies, in the face of a high expansion in demand, opens up spaces for fossil fuels, whose lower production costs and higher energy content per unit of weight are strong competitive advantages. This factor has led to the search for technologies to reduce $CO_2$ emissions from coal, oil and gas, such as carbon capture, the carbon credit market or electric cars, microchips and other intermediate and final goods, the production of which, in the scenario that the International Energy Agency (IEA) calls sustainable, would raise the demand for various metals, minerals and rare earths by more than 200 per cent. All of these are non-renewable resources, whose reserves are either equally or more concentrated than oil and whose environmental, climatic or sociopolitical effects are not yet known (IEA, 2021c). The growth in demand summarised in Table 7.5 is conceived for the Sustainable Development Scenario (SDS) of the Paris Agreement, to keep the increase in global temperature below 1.5C by 2050, improve air quality and guarantee universal access to energy, objectives 3.9 and 7 of the Sustainable Development Goals (IEA, 2021b). This scenario, together with that Net Zero Emissions by 2050 (NZE), assumes strong political support, extensive international cooperation and increased investment. It is based on a series of assumptions about cross-cutting policies, and policies pertaining to the energy sector, the construction sector, the transport sector and the industrial sector.[9] This scenario sheds light on the extractivism inherent in the energy transition as the path towards energy security, showing that new energies and new technologies almost triple the demand for natural resources by 2020, a year of great contraction in economic activity due to the pandemic. In short, the SDS presupposes an increase in the demand for critical minerals to achieve its objectives. That is, keeping the global temperature around 1.5°C above pre-industrial levels intensifies and perpetuates extractivism by establishing the dichotomy of either extractivism or climate change.

These forecasts make it possible to suggest new sources of energy to combat climate change by reducing $CO_2$ emissions, intensifying and perpetuating extractivism as they consecrate these new sources of extractivism as the only way to control climate change. If so, only the economic, political and social effects of extractivism can be controlled and mitigated. There are several policy measures and actions to take, most of them involve reorienting fiscal policies, with regard to the control of extractivism, without annulling those that stimulate the energy transition.

Policies to mitigate the effects of the new extractivism are based on what has been set out in this chapter and in many other findings, on the effects of the exploitation of oil and other raw materials, within the framework of the theories of Dutch disease, the curse of natural resources and neoextractivism.

*Table 7.5* Growth in world demand for metals and minerals from clean energies. 2020–2040 sustainable development scenario

| Mineral demand (thousands of tons) | *Electricity generation: solar* | | | *Electricity generation: wind* | | | *Electric vehicles and storage batteries* | | | *Electrical networks (transmission, distribution and transformation)* | | | *Totals by mineral* | | |
|---|---|---|---|---|---|---|---|---|---|---|---|---|---|---|---|
| | *2020* | *2040* | *The demand is multiplied by…* | *2020* | *2040* | *The demand is multiplied by…* | *2020* | *2040* | *The demand is multiplied by…* | *2020* | *2040* | *The demand is multiplied by…* | *2020* | *2040* | *The demand is multiplied by…* |
| Aluminium | | | | | | | | | | 9104 | 16,327 | 1.8 | 9104 | 16,327 | 1.8 |
| Arsenic | 0.1 | 6.9 | 69 | | | | | | | | | | 0.1 | 6.9 | 69 |
| Cobalt | | | | | | | 21 | 455 | 21 | | | | 21 | 455 | 21.3 |
| Copper | 346 | 989 | 2.8 | 217 | 610 | 2.8 | 119 | 3,330 | 28 | 4,975 | 10,007 | 2.0 | 5,656 | 14,936 | 2.6 |
| Chrome | | | | 29 | 75 | 2.6 | | | | | | | 29 | 75 | 2.6 |
| Tin | 0.6 | 1.8 | 3.0 | | | | | | | | | | 0.6 | 2 | 3.0 |
| Gallium | 0.004 | 2.8 | 672 | | | | | | | | | | 0.004 | 2.8 | 672 |
| Graphite | | | | | | | 155.669 | 3,849 | 25 | | | | 156 | 3,849 | 24.7 |
| Lithium | | | | | | | 22 | 904 | 42 | | | | 22 | 904 | 41.9 |
| Manganese | | | | 46 | 117 | 2.6 | 26 | 418 | 16 | | | | 71 | 535 | 7.5 |
| Molybdenum | | | | 6.0 | 16 | 2.6 | | | | | | | 6.0 | 16 | 2.6 |
| Nickel | | | | 21 | 52 | 2.5 | 81 | 3,344 | 41 | | | | 102 | 3,396 | 33 |
| Silver | 2.0 | 2.3 | 1.15 | | | | | | | | | | 2.0 | 2 | 1.2 |
| Lead | 0.6 | 1.7 | 2.8 | | | | | | | | | | 0.6 | 2 | 2.8 |
| Silicon | 390 | 808 | 2.1 | | | | 0.2 | 97 | 450 | | | | 390 | 905 | 2.3 |
| Zinc | 3.2 | 9 | 2.8 | 321 | 822 | 2.6 | | | | | | | 324 | 831 | 2.6 |
| Vanadium | | | | | | | 0.1 | 219 | 2190 | | | | 0.1 | 219 | 2190 |
| Dysprosium* | | | | 0.3 | 1.0 | 2.8 | | | | | | | 0.3 | 1.0 | 2.8 |
| Neodymium* | | | | 3.1 | 9.0 | 2.9 | 1.8 | 28 | 15 | | | | 4.9 | 37 | 7.4 |
| Praseodymium* | | | | 0.5 | 1.6 | 3.2 | | | | | | | 0.5 | 1.6 | 3.2 |
| Totals by sector | 742 | 1,822 | 2.5 | 644 | 1,704 | 2.6 | 426 | 12,643 | 30 | 14,079 | 26,334 | 1.9 | 15,891 | 42,502 | 2.7 |

*Rare Earth.

*Source:* Own elaboration based on: International Energy Outlook (IEA, 2021a) and IEA (2021c).

Defining extractivism by its effects on the structures of a country, and not by the characteristics of the products, their production and sale, has led to a focus on the backward and forward linkages of the exploitation of resources, those of demand and those of income and emphasising the instability of prices, technological intensity, the concentration of capital and production, the predominance of foreign investments that transfer part of the income abroad, aspects that generate economic crises, displacement and backwardness of other productive sectors and concentration of income from the production and exports of labour-intensive goods and national inputs and derived from the above, deterioration of employment and intensification of inequality (Hirschmann, 1970: Karl 1997, 1999; Puyana, 2015, 2017). Solving these problems requires adjusting the role of the state, which has generally sponsored extractivism, with a view to capturing rent and securing fiscal resources with little or no fiscal cost, providing it with a large margin of discretionary public spending. The state is primarily responsible for extractivist activities benefiting the public interest, the national economy and the majority of the population that does not bow to the demands or lobbying of vested interests, eliminate measures and incentives adapted to the interests of capital. The foregoing entails government actions with a view to designing, among others:

***Tax rules*** to, on the one hand, socialise private income, the new sources of extractivist income, generated by the privatisation of common goods, such as the sun, the wind and the tide, in addition to the land, which differs from taxes to prevent negative social and environmental externalities such as greenhouse gas emissions, and on the other hand, to ensure that most of this income is captured by the public sector and channels its monetisation and direct investments towards work-intensive and low-energy-intensive activities and towards distributive plans. This socialisation of income would make it possible to couple the restructuring of the economy with the generation of formal employment, wage growth and internal demand.

***Productive policies*** that stimulate activities with the largest and most dynamic backward and forward linkages and the most labour-intensive products with low and medium qualifications, little $CO_2$ intensity and sophisticated technologies and other scarce non-renewable natural resources. An example is the cultivation of asparagus and other agricultural products for export that are highly demanding in terms of water and electricity. This and others occupy land previously devoted to staple foods.

***Redistributive measures*** that manage the effects of property concentration, the pre-eminence of foreign investment and of new energy sources. A large part of the profits and income go abroad and are not reinvested in the same activity or in the domestic and local economy. Due to the high level of imported technology and the concentration of production, the distribution of income that remains in the country and that of domestic capital deepen the widespread inequality. The socialisation of income and the productive policies mentioned can mitigate these two concentrating tendencies. As a result, it is appropriate, as Gunton (2020) suggests, to limit and regulate foreign investment and strengthen national property in extractivist activities.

***Distributive actions and training*** to level up labour income, preventing the displacement of fossil fuels by new sources of energy from creating new sectors of the working population that are impoverished and excluded from the labour market. As with any technological change, it is necessary to invest in the training of the outgoing workforce in new technologies or in those used in other activities, as well as to prepare the new generations for the economic conditions and new technologies to come.

## Conclusions

The journey through the themes proposed as exploratory purposes of this chapter show the difficulties and contradictory processes to achieve, despite its urgent and immediate need, the purpose of transforming extractivism into a development strategy that simultaneously stimulates industrialisation, generates more and better jobs, halts the deterioration of the income share of wages for work, reduce inequality, poverty and environmental damage. The urgency is even more vital and of greater complexity given that achieving energy security and the energy transition expands and extends the extractivism of the economy.

Replacing fossil fuels with wind, solar, hydraulic and nuclear energy, which, while they emit $CO_2$, are extractive, privatise and commodify the wind, ocean waves, water and land, which are transformed into merchandise and large sources of capital accumulation, by opening these resources to capital under conditions that guarantee the maximum profitability of investments. These are profits from the exploitation of assets not produced by human agency. This transformation is inherent in all proposals on energy security and transition, while often staying silent on the enormous costs of these policies.

The experiences of Canada, Mexico and the USA in energy security and the energy transition and in the reconstruction of the post-COVID-19 economy show both the importance of oil and the difficulties of moving towards economies that emit less $CO_2$ and methane gas, with a secure supply based on clean energy.

North America constitutes a diverse, historical, social and political region, in terms of resource endowment and economic development, in which the USA leads in practically all areas, particularly in resources, development and energy generation and consumption. With the exploitation of shale oil and gas, the USA rose to first place in crude oil reserves and production, displacing Mexico in terms of reserves.

The values obtained from the calculations of the oil security, energy diversity and energy transition indexes show the relatively meagre progress made in energy security and the energy transition since 1974 and identify which of the variables that make up each of the three indexes present the least satisfactory results and therefore the most significant tasks to be carried out. All the indexes show the contradictions of the strategies, since the gains in energy security imply negative effects by increasing extractivism, forming a balance that is still pending urgent quantification. The positive balance in energy security can decrease and even turn negative when adding the high growth of the exploitation of minerals and rare earths, which demand energy substitution and the new technologies involved, which enhances extractivism and can even perpetuate it.

## Notes

1 Even if the quality and production costs of oil from Cantarell in Mexico and from Cusiana and Cupiagua in Colombia were identical, the transportation costs vary greatly: While Cantarell is adjacent to a port, the Colombian fields are more than 4,000 kilometers away, through mountainous terrain.
2 The EU's taxonomy refers to the classification of economic activities according to environmental sustainability criteria to guide investments, according to the European Green Deal, see European Union (2022).
3 Regional commercial integration in agricultural and manufacturing goods and in trade flows is similarly significant and asymmetric (Puyana, 2015).
4 https://www.eia.gov/todayinenergy/detail.php?id=49656.
5 The energy capacity that the United States has achieved in recent decades has led some authors to call it the United States energy revolution.
6 Puyana and Rodríguez (2020) raised this discussion.
7 The Oil Security Index considers only crude oil and excludes its derivatives.
8 The IEA (2021b) presents four development scenarios for the energy sector by 2025, two normative: Net Zero Emissions by 2050 (NZE) and Sustainable Development Scenario (SDS), and two exploratory: Announced Pledges Scenario (APS), and Stated Policies Scenario (STEPS).
9 The total was calculated from the consumption reported by energy source in the BP stat review (2021) in exajoules.

## References

Aguilera, R.F. and R. Aguilera. (2020). "Revisiting the role of natural gas as a transition fuel," *Mineral Economics* 33: 73–80. https://doi.org/10.1007/s13563-019-00192-5.

Bagni, S. (2018). "Los derechos de la naturaleza en la jurisprudencia Colombiana e Indiana," *Revista Jurídica de Derecho* 7(9), July: 33–53. ISSN 2413-2810.

Baldwin, R. and J. Lopez-Gonzalez. (2012). "Supply-chain trade: a portrait of global patterns and several testable hypotheses," *Working Paper 18957*. National Bureau of Economic Research. Available at: http://www.nber.org/papers/w18957.

Böhm, S. and S. Dabni (Eds.). (2009). *Upsetting the Offset: The Political Economy of Carbon Markets*. UK: MayFlyBooks. Available at http://mayflybooks.org/?p=206.

BP—British Petroleum. (2021). *Statistical Review of World Energy*. Available at: https://www.bp.com/en/global/corporate/energy-economics/statistical-review-of-world-energy.html.

EIA. (2021). *International Energy Outlook 2021*. Available at: https://www.eia.gov/outlooks/ieo/.

EU—European Union. (2022). "EU Taxonomy for Sustainable Activities." Available at: https://ec.europa.eu/info/business-economy-euro/banking-and-finance/sustainable-finance/eu-taxonomy-sustainable-activities.

Foster, B. (2022). "Nature as a mode of accumulation: Capitalism and the financialization of the earth," *Monthly Review* 73(10), March. Available at: https://doi.org/10.14452/MR-073-10-2022-03.

Furtado, C. (1973). *Desarrollo y Subdesarrollo.* Buenos Aires: Editorial Universitaria de Argentina.

Furtado, C. (1982). *Economic Development of Latin America. Historical Background and Contemporary Problems, CUP.* Available at: https://www.todostuslibros.com/libros/economic-development-of-latin-america_978-0-521-29070-8.

Gudynas, E. (2009). "Diez tesis urgentes sobre el nuevo extractivismo," in *Extractivismo, política y sociedad*, pp. 187–225. Montevideo: Centro Andino de Acción Popular (CAAP) de Ecuador y el Centro Latino Americano de Ecología Social (CLAES). Available at: http://extractivismo.com/2009/11/extractivismo-politica-y-sociedad/.

Gudynas, E. (2013). "Extracciones, extractivismos y extrahecciones". *Observatorio del Desarrollo* 18: 1–18.

Gunton, T. (2020). "Staple theory and the new staple boom." In Stanford, J., ed. *The Staple Theory @ 50*, pp. 43–52. Ottawa: Canadian Centre for Policy Alternatives.

Hickel, J. (2022). "De-growth is about global justice," *European Green Journal* 5 January. Available at: https://www.greeneuropeanjournal.eu/degrowth-is-about-global-justice/.

Hirschmann, A.O. (1970). *The Strategy of Economic Development.* New Haven CT: Yale University Press.

IEA. (2021a). *International Energy Outlook 2021, EIA.* Available at: https://www.eia.gov/international/data/world/total-energy/total-energy-consumption?.

IEA. (2021b). "Energy Models," https://www.iea.org/reports/world-energy-model/policies#sustainable-development-scenario-assumptions.

IEA. (2021c). "The role of critical minerals in clean energy transitions," *World Energy Outlook Special Report.* Available at https://www.iea.org/reports/the-role-of-critical-minerals-in-clean-energy-transitions.

IPCC. (2021). *Sixth Assessment Report, Climate Change 2021: The Physical Science Basis.* Available at: https://www.ipcc.ch/report/sixth-assessment-report-working-group-i/.

Karl, T.L. (1997). *The Paradox of Plenty: Oil Booms and Petro-States.* Oakland, CA: University of California Press.

Karl, T.L. (1999). "The Perils of the Petro-State: Reflections on the Paradox of Plenty," *Journal of International Affairs*, 53(1): 31–48.

Khan; M. (2022). "Brussels proposes green label for nuclear and natural gas," *The Financial Times*, January 4, 2022. Available at: https://www.ft.com/content/7872a05f-9e38-4740-9b1b-4efc69ca316c.

Lord, D. (2010). "Playing with oil: Putting performativity at the center of oil civilization," in Denzin, N.K. (Ed.), *Studies in Symbolic Interaction*, 34, pp. 285–293. Available at: https://doi.org/10.1108/S0163-2396(2010)0000034019.

Merrick, J. (2015). "The Paris climate talks and other events of carbon fetishism," *Verso.* Available at: https://www.versobooks.com/blogs/2372-steffen-bohm-the-paris-climate-talks-and-other-events-of-carbon-fetishism.

Myint, H. (1958)." Classical theory of international trade and the underdeveloped countries," *The Economic Journal* 68(270), June: 317–337. Blackwell Publishing for the Royal Economic Society. Available at: http://www.jstor.org/stable/2227598.

Parshley, J. (2022). "Predictions favored solar over wind power. What happened?," *The New York Times,* January 21.

Pineault, E. (2020). "The Panacea: Panax Quinquefolius and the mirage of the extractive economy." In J. Stanford, (Ed.), *A Staple Theory of Economic Growth*, pp. 84–90. Ottawa: The Canadian Centre for Policy Alternatives.

Prebisch, R. (1948). *El desarrollo económico de la América Latina y algunos de sus principales problemas.* Repositorio CEPAL. Available at: https://repositorio.cepal.org/handle/11362/40010.

Puyana A. and J. Romero. (2022). "Does the current political environment open promising directions in the complex Mexico-United States economic integration?," *IDEAS*, February. Available at: https://www.networkideas.org/featured-articles/2022/02/does-the-current-political-environment-open-promising-directions-in-the-complex-mexico-united-states-economic-integration/.

Puyana, A. (2015). *La economía petrolera en un mercado politizado y global. México y Colombia.* Mexico City: FLACSO, México.

Puyana, A. (2017). "El retorno al extractivismo en América Latina. ¿Ruptura o profundización del modelo de economía liberal y por qué ahora?" *Espiral* 24(69): 73–112.

Puyana, A. (2019). "El retorno al extractivismo en América Latina. Su impacto en la desigualdad y el trabajo," in A. Puyana Mutis and M. Rojas (Eds.), *Desigualdad y deterioro de las condiciones labourales Un círculo vicioso en América Latina.* Mexico City: FLACSO México.

Puyana, A. and I. Rodríguez. (2020). "Seguridad energética en México, Estados Unidos y Canadá de 1980 al 2016: centralidad del petróleo y la incorporación de temas ambientales," *Norteamérica* 15(2): 9–37.

Puyana, A., I. Rodríguez Peña, and L. García Manrique. (2021). "Factores relevantes de la inestabilidad del mercado petrolero," *Revista de Economía Institucional* 23(45), June: 227–256. https://doi.org/10.18601/01245996.v23n45.11.

Svampa, M.S. (2019). *Las fronteras del neoextractivismo en América Latina: Conflictos socioambientales, giro ecoterritorial y nuevas dependencias.* Guadalajara: University of Guadalajara/CALAS. Available at: http://calas.lat/sites/default/files/svampa_neoextractivismo.pdf.

Svampa, M. (2012). "Consenso de los commodities, giro ecoterritorial y pensamiento crítico en América Latina," *CLACSO*. Available at: http://biblioteca.clacso.edu.ar/clacso/osal/201209271036 42/OSAL32.pdf.

Watkins, A. (1963). "Staple theory of economic growth," *The Canadian Journal of Economics and Political Science* 29(2): 141–158.

# 8 The new geographies of an energy transition

## A challenge or a developmental opportunity?

*Jewellord Nem Singh*

Although it failed to resolve a number of contentious issues, the COP26 meeting in Glasgow solidified a consensus around the need for a global transition towards clean energy. Implicated in this transition is the widescale adoption of renewables—we must build larger wind turbines, produce more electric vehicles, and phase down coal factories in electrifying rapidly urbanising cities. Climate negotiations often refer to countries' *common but differentiated responsibility* in dealing with the coming planetary crisis. But in reality, the protagonists of such a transformation are European governments and high-tech manufacturing companies involved in the production of wind turbines, hybrid and electric vehicles, fuel cells, and ion batteries. And their policies have a cost—if the world meets the targets of the Paris Agreement, demand is likely to increase by 40 per cent for copper and rare earth elements (REEs), 60–70 per cent for cobalt and nickel, and almost 90 per cent for lithium in the next two decades (International Energy Agency 2021: 5).

In this context, Latin America is increasingly repositioning itself as a supplier of 'critical raw materials' (CRMs). Lithium, graphite, and niobium are key inputs for batteries powering electric vehicle cars and for storage systems for photovoltaic panels and wind generators. Beyond new demands for rare metals to power the energy transition, demand for copper, nickel, manganese, aluminium, and other base metals are increasing in response to the need for new infrastructures for clean energy. However, mining has an intrinsically complex and historically problematic record in the region. For centuries, primary commodities served to insert Latin America in the global economy. Between the 1500s and 1800s, the region was relegated to the periphery, partly a function of the colonial project but also due to the immutable force of extractivist institutions after independence. Through concerted attempts at import substitution industrialisation (ISI) in the 20th century, the region gradually sought to 'catch up' in the development race.

To unpack the possibilities in the 21st century, the chapter returns to the mining-industrialisation nexus. First, I examine the comparative and historical evidence of resource-based industrialisation in Latin America, thereby identifying the limitations of mineral-based development in the 20th century. Second, I argue that the clean energy transition is creating new possibilities

DOI: 10.4324/9781003301981-12

for Latin America to promote industrialisation. Yet, resource-intensive industrial policy requires fundamental rethinking to overcome dependent and unequal development. Finally, I want to reintroduce the literature on East Asian experiences as regards industrial policy to outline the key principles on 'how to do industrial policy' in the 21st century.

## Revisiting Latin America's Economic Performance in the 20th Century

That Latin America was incorporated into the international economic system throughout the 16th and 19th centuries by way of the region's role as commodity producers is indisputable. Yet, the fundamental question is why commodity production failed at achieving industrial catch-up, and whether natural resources are a curse for poorer countries. Looking at cursory evidence, there is undoubtedly sufficient empirical evidence about the failure of mining-based development. Indeed, a long history of critical scholarship questioned whether primary commodity production could lead to industrial catch-up, and if not, alternatives based on manufacturing ought to be pursued to change the position of Latin American economies in the world system (Cardoso and Faletto, 1979; Furtado, 1970). Without revisiting these arguments here (see Nem Singh, 2018; Nem Singh and Bourgouin, 2013), two mechanisms explain the limits of exports-based growth models. First, sector-specific features of the extractive industry. During a resource boom, producers are encouraged to invest in oil and mining and thus leave the non-oil tradeable goods sector with limited capital and labour. Once the export boom is finished, producers are unable to switch back to manufacturing. Apart from these dynamics, price increases also negatively affect currency exchange rates, making manufactured goods and agricultural exports less competitive vis-à-vis mining (Auty, 2001; Di John, 2011). This so-called 'Dutch disease' phenomenon underlines the failure of natural resource specialisation in competing with manufacturing-based development strategies.

Second, a version of the political resource curse has influenced debates on the political economy of Latin American development. This is articulated well by Jonathan Di John (2009; 2014): the enormous amount of mineral rents generated by a resource boom leads to competition among rent-seeking groups to gain access to the oil largesse. As oil, gas and mining become entrenched in the national economy, various social and economic groups bear strong incentives to influence the national state to receive some of these revenues. There are distributional pressures upon which states are socialised to respond. In Latin America, coalition-building was often struck not just between urbanised industrial groups and political elites, but also with agricultural exporters that held political power in the countryside, labour leaders who mobilised workers in defense of corporatism, and in some cases, domestic mining capitalists who argue that mineral revenues ought to be reinvested back into the sector. The decision on who to support and how far (or how long) to extend state resources ultimately depends on the nature of the development strategy of the government in power. Historically, Brazil under Getúlio Vargas (1930–1945) sought a political pact with industrialists from the South while maintaining strong ties with the coffee elites in order to transition towards an industrialised economy. By contrast, Peru had strong ties with private mineral exporters, leading to limited industrialisation efforts even under General Velasco. The general point is that a country's development strategy shapes the balance of power among contending groups within society. In many Latin American societies, extractive capital holds very strong veto power; this had decisive impacts on the industrialisation efforts and the limited developmental outcomes in the region.

According to these theories, increasing dependence on natural resources for exports and revenues will lead to slower economic growth, higher propensity for corruption and rent-seeking, and makes resource economies more prone to political violence (Beblawi and Luciani, 2016; Collier and Hoeffler, 2004). While there is wide-ranging evidence against its theoretical and methodological consistency (see Di John, 2011; 2014), the resource curse holds very strong persuasive powers especially among donor agencies in Africa who continuously associate corruption, economic mismanagement and predatory behaviour as intrinsically linked with the nation-state and its point resources. Relatedly, resource-rich countries suffer from commodity specialisation due to their inability to develop Indigenous technology, build inter-sectoral linkages to counter the enclave nature of mining, and mitigate the social conflicts arising from unchecked exploitation of resources. Some have attributed this development malaise to the detrimental effects of external linkages with advanced industrialised countries: as long as resource producers remain commodity exporters, there are very few incentives to promote export diversification and to craft ambitious industrial plans that would break the cycle of extractivist growth (Burchardt and Dietz, 2014; Veltmeyer, 2013). These arguments powerfully frame contemporary discourses on the developmental challenges among resource-rich countries. As Thorpe et al. (2012) suggest the historical legacies of extractive-led growth heavily weigh upon the politics, institutions, and interests in these countries, such that it is almost impossible to move away from extractivism.

Despite evidence on lacklustre economic performance in Latin America, their natural resource-based development strategies remain in place, and arguably, still maintain legitimacy as a development paradigm.[1] Without dismissing the attendant socio-environmental conflicts intrinsic to resource extraction that leads to legitimate concerns about the validity of the economic model itself (Gudynas, 2016; 2020; Svampa, 2019a), my argument aims to explain how opportunities emerging from the renewable energy transition can be harnessed through progressive politics.

## Critical raw materials and the clean energy transition

The clean energy transition is a historically significant moment for resource producers. It involves the intensive and extensive extraction of 'rare metals'—metal minerals produced in low quantities and utilised as intermediate inputs in the manufacturing of digital, renewable, and energy technologies. These have also been identified by the USA and EU as CRMs, which are both strategically important for industrial competitiveness and at high risk due to possible supply gluts and changes in world markets. The USA lists 35 critical minerals in order of their importance for national security and wider supply chain vulnerabilities (US White House, 2017). The EU Commission report identifies 30 CRMs (European Commission, 2020a; 2020b). In this ordering, critical minerals are grouped into three major categories: heavy rare earths (HREEs), light rare earths (LREEs), platinum group metals (PGMS). The list also includes various ferrous and non-ferrous metals.

Among the minerals listed above, the most significant are REEs. Table 8.1 summarises these 17 chemically similar metals and their applications across various industries. These metals share a strategic importance due to their numerous industrial applications, mostly as intermediate outputs like alloys and components which are then assembled into higher value-added industrial goods such as electric motors and drones (European Commission, 2020a). Rare metals are essential inputs for clean technologies, notably in the mass production of wind turbines, photovoltaic panels, as well as hybrid and electric vehicles (Alves Dias et al., 2020; Nakano, 2021).

The green transition is creating a worldwide demand for critical minerals. As a starting point, we need to identify the distribution of market power, the ways in which industrial policies are linked with mineral extraction, and an evaluation of the potential winners and losers in the 21st century. Table 8.1 already outlined the critical minerals needed by industrialised countries, notably the EU and US governments. Mineral extraction for renewable energy has generated new patterns of trade in the energy sector. On the one hand, resource-poor, industrialised East Asian countries—Japan, Korea, and Taiwan—compete directly with Western capital in various high-end manufacturing sectors, notably automobile, digital and ICT, and intermediate inputs like permanent magnets and semi-conductors. To secure access to minerals, East Asia remains committed to engage with China in regional forums and through bilateral investment agreements with the rest of the developing world. On the other hand, the EU and US governments have been principally concerned with the fact that non-democratic regimes like China and Russia hold so much market power in controlling CRM reserves and production.

The EU has framed increasing insecurity in global resource markets as an indicator of risk and vulnerability. CRM scarcity is perceived as a medium- and long-term challenge for the EU in maintaining its industrial strength and technological competitiveness. Energy transition minerals are highly concentrated in a few countries (see Figures 8.1 and 8.2). For cobalt, lithium, and REEs, the top three producing countries control about three-quarters of current global outputs. The costs of extracting transition minerals have likewise increased in economic and socio-environmental terms. For example, Chilean copper ore quality has declined by 30 per cent over the past 15 years.

*Table 8.1* Rare earths elements and their industrial applications

| *Name* | *Symbol* | *Atomic #* | *Applications and products* |
|---|---|---|---|
| Scandium | Sc | 21 | Aerospace materials, consumer electronics, lasers, magnets, lighting, sporting goods |
| Yttrium | Y | 39 | Ceramics, communications systems, lighting, frequency meters, fuels additive, jet engine turbines, televisions, microwave communications, satellites, vehicle oxygen sensors |
| Lanthanum | La | 57 | Catalyst in petroleum refining, television, energy storage, fuel cells, night vision instruments, rechargeable batteries |
| Cerium | Ce | 58 | Catalytic converters, catalyst in petroleum refining, glass, diesel fuel additive, polishing agent, pollution control systems |
| Praseodymium | Pr | 59 | Aircraft engine alloy, airport signal lenses, catalyst, ceramics, colouring pigment, electric vehicles, fibre optic cables, lighter flint, magnets, wind turbines, photographic filters, welder's glasses |
| Neodymium | Nd | 60 | Anti-lock brakes, air bags, anti-glare glass, cellphones, computers, electric vehicles, lasers, MRI machines, magnets, wind turbines |
| Promethium | Pm | 61 | Beta source for thickness gages, lasers for submarines, nuclear powered battery |
| Samarium | Sm | 62 | Aircraft electrical systems, electronic counter measure equipment, electric vehicles, flight control surfaces, missile and radar systems, optical glass, permanent magnets, precision guided munitions, stealth technology, wind turbine |
| Europium | Eu | 63 | CFL, lasers, televisions, tag complex for the medical field |
| Gadolinium | Gd | 64 | Computer data technology, magneto-optic recording technology, microwave applications, MRI machines, power plant radiation leaks detector |
| Terbium | Tb | 65 | CFL, electric vehicles, fuel cells, televisions, optic data recording, permanent magnets, wind turbines |
| Dysprosium | Dy | 66 | Electric vehicles, home electronics, lasers, permanent magnets, wind turbines |
| Holmium | Ho | 67 | Microwave equipment, colour glass |
| Erbium | Er | 68 | Colour glass, fibre optic data transmission, lasers |
| Thulium | Tm | 69 | X-ray phosphors |
| Ytterbium | Yb | 70 | Improving stainless steel properties, stress gages |
| Lutetium | Lu | 71 | Catalysts, positron emission tomography detectors |

*Source:* Navarro and Zhao (2014: 2) in Nem Singh (2021).

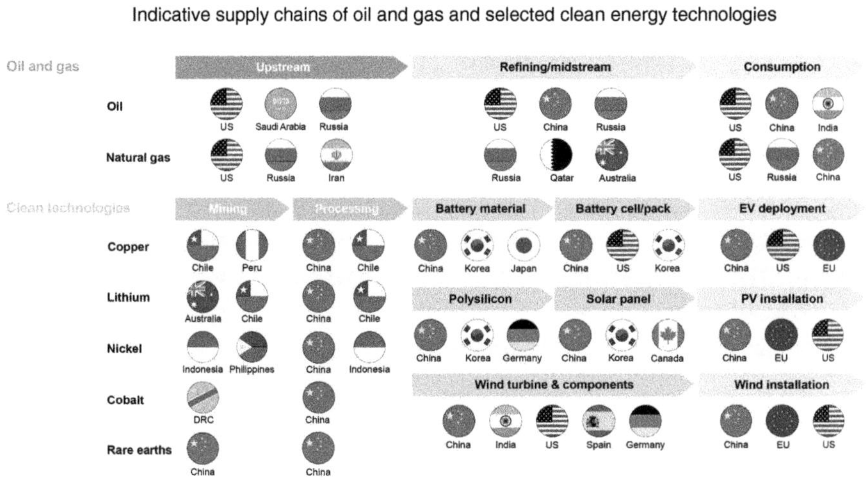




Notes: DRC = Democratic Republic of the Congo; EU = European Union; US = United States; Russia = Russian Federation; China = People's Republic of China.
Largest producers and consumers are noted in each case to provide an indication, rather than a complete account.

*Figure 8.1* The global value chains of energy—a comparison.

Since the 2010s, the vulnerability perspective has been articulated in the EU's major documents. In a recent *Strategic Foresight Report*, the EU outlined key global trends that could impact on the region's position in the world economy, which includes not simply the climate change and environmental challenge but also the increasing redistribution of global power as the geo-economic centre of gravity moves definitively eastwards. China's peaceful rise over the past two decades is over; Western countries now perceive Chinese economic power—and increasingly its military strength—as a medium-term challenge. With COVID-19 activating initiatives to regionalise or domesticate supply chains, policy concerns about balance of power with China has become commonplace in political discourses. China is considered both a geopolitical rival and a business opportunity for Europe. For the EU, protecting their strategic interests requires clearly delineating economic diplomacy with China's geo-strategic and political interests—a precondition that is increasingly difficult to achieve given the growing assertion of Chinese power across policy fields.[2]

Resource producers in Africa, Latin America, and Southeast Asia are well-positioned to take advantage of soaring demands for CRMs. For instance, Mongolia, The Philippines, and Indonesia hold significant nickel and copper reserves which can complement the contribution of Latin American producers such as Bolivia, Peru, and Chile. Yet, evidence for resource-based

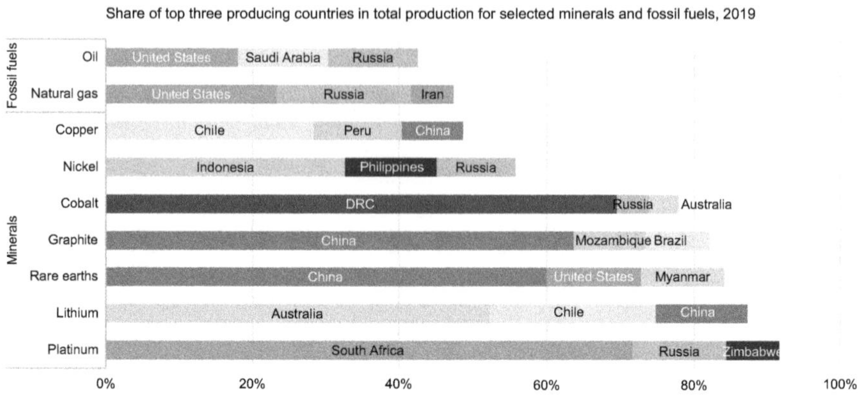


*Figure 8.2* New geographies of energy transition.

in Latin America raises more scepticism that there exists more cautious assessments of the developmental impacts of CRMs (Barandiarán, 2019; Bustos-Gallardo, Bridge and Prieto, 2021; Obaya, López and Pascuini, 2021).

## Reframing Latin America's pessimism on resource-led growth

Without reducing the significance of the arguments against resource extraction, I make some important theoretical and empirical arguments in support of mining-based development. First, demands for base metals like nickel, copper, and iron are expected to steadily increase (International Energy Agency 2021: 5), and with such anticipated rise in mineral use, governments can better prepare against the deleterious effects of cyclical boom and busts, lack of fiscal discipline on how to maximise mineral rents, and investment towards communities at the frontiers of extraction facing grave socio-ecological consequences. There exist some notable examples of institutional innovation despite the preponderance of weak states in the Global South. For example, Peru has implemented the most comprehensive mining reforms towards better revenue distribution between central and regional governments, alleviating the distributional pressures and socio-environmental consequences of localised resource curse (Gustafsson and Scurrah, 2019; Orihuela, 2018). Brazil, with its long history of institution building, was able to promote renewable energy, imposed flexible local content requirements to support Brazilian industrialists, and established strict environmental licencing procedures in the oil and gas sectors (Hochstetler and Kostka, 2015; Massi and Nem Singh, 2020; 2018).

Second, there is growing evidence on 'resource-based industrialisation' strategies, which expands the possibilities for resource producers to maximise gains from resource endowments. For example, Brazil's Petrobras,

Norway's Statoil, and Venezuela's PDVSA (prior to Chávez) were exemplars of how state enterprises have been utilised to achieve the 'big push', natural resources-intensive industrialisation strategy (Di John, 2014; Massi and Nem Singh, 2018, 2020; Thurber and Istad, 2012). Their emphasis was on developing Indigenous technology to create a niche market and to obtain access to downstream networks of consumers, thereby creating vertically integrated firms capable of competing against international oil companies. Within business studies, mining has been treated as a knowledge-intensive economic activity, through which technological learning and targeted R&D spending can generate notable spill-over effects beyond the mining sector (Atienza, Lufin and Soto, 2018; Stubrin, 2017). These studies highlight not just the sectoral linkages and acquisition of technical know-how, but also challenge the basic idea that mining cannot become a source of innovation and growth.

That the world economy remains hierarchical and unequal is indisputable—the hegemony of industrialised countries recognisably stems from unequal terms of trade and disproportionate sharing of socio-ecological damages. As one of my interviewees boldly suggests, 'the EU's lack of geological knowledge today of what minerals exist in its own borders is a direct consequence of its colonial past'. By being reluctant at embracing mineral production in their own territories, the responsibility of sourcing primary materials for the renewable energy revolution is pushed towards poor, resource-rich countries. Without investing in technological know-how and innovation policies, resource-rich countries might miss this opportunity for industrialisation.

But with preparation, this burden, and its harmful effects, can be managed. This can be done by focusing on how mineral states can promote industrial policies aimed at processing critical minerals within their domestic markets. Indonesia's ban on exporting raw nickel and compelling international companies to refine and process mineral ores inside the country is one example. Another method has been the strategic deployment of state-owned enterprises (SOEs) in managing natural resource assets—a policy often adopted by countries with limited production capacity. In the best possible conditions, states might also encourage domestic companies to directly compete with international mining companies in the exploration and production stages, as in the example of Brazil's national oil company Petrobras and regional SOE Codemge. However, this approach requires sophisticated industrial strategies that only countries with sufficient planning and coordination capabilities can implement. Irrespective of the policy choice, the fundamental logic remains: mining is a high-risk industry, requiring enormous capital investments and are regularly subject to market failures. The state, taking a developmental longer-term view, must accept these risks to promote sectoral development. Without undertaking risks and taking a longer-term perspective on development, markets—especially private capital—cannot and are not willing to make these investments. In the age of state capitalism, critical minerals are not simply about efficiency in production. As the Russian invasion in Ukraine attests, geopolitical orders are now being remade and alliances around access to critical minerals are redrawn. The global restructuring of the value chains based on the logic of the market is over. Instead, political and military considerations have begun to guide economic policies. For developing countries, the logic of market liberalism and inter-state cooperation is increasingly becoming incompatible with a development imperative.

### *Lessons from the last commodity boom*

In the 2000s, oil, minerals, and export agriculture experienced soaring commodity prices which enabled commodity-based growth to take place in Latin America and other resource-rich, poor regions. In Latin America, the commodity boom coincided with the election of political parties both Left and Centre along the political spectrum, leading to a golden age of poverty reduction policies. Driven by Chinese demands for natural resources, Latin American elites, social movements, and the public converged towards what Arsel et al. (2016) aptly labelled as the 'extractive imperative' (Svampa, 2019a; 2019b).[3] Natural resource extraction has been (re)imagined as central to Latin America's economic prosperity and is likely to remain the region's central model for economic growth. Despite varying policy orientations across the continent, the majority of elites and social forces consider future economic growth to be based on extraction of mineral resources, although some social movements have advocated for a radical rethinking of the growth model (Gudynas, 2020; Svampa, 2019a).

Latin America is likely to remain a producer of raw materials for commodities both for the Western economies and the emerging economies of Asia, which are increasingly dominating the sector's world trade, finance, and investment. When comparing the producers of raw materials, China, Latin America, and Africa are the main sources of critical minerals for the green transition. However, the assembly of inputs for high technology sectors is predominantly occupied by China, the EU, the USA, and the rest of Asia (see Figures 8.3 and 8.4).

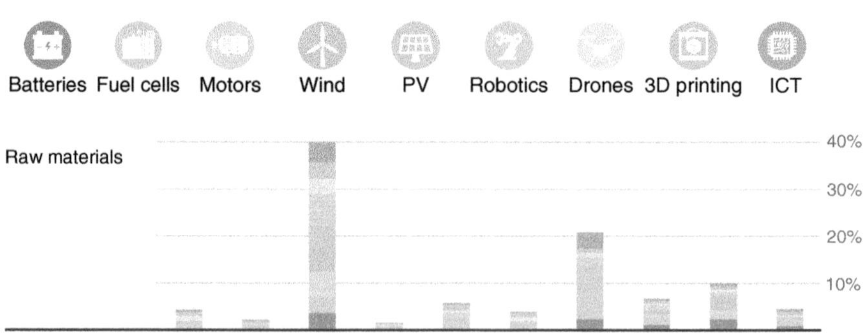


*Figure 8.3* Regional shares in raw materials stages in high technology sectors.

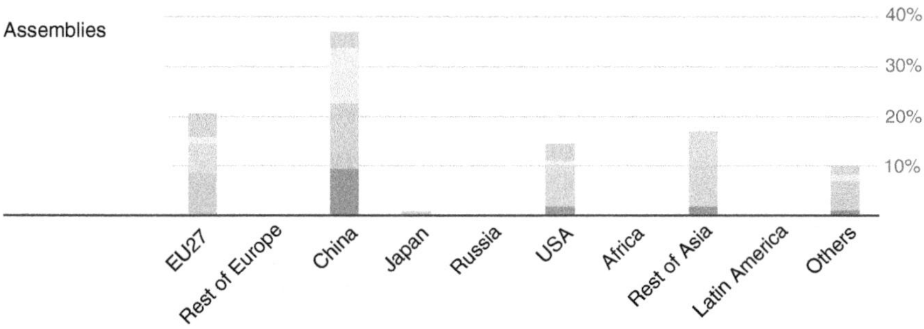


*Figure 8.4* Regional shares in assemblies stages of high-tech manufacturing.

Within the region, Chile and Brazil stand out as potential winners in a race to secure critical minerals for broad-based development, due in large part to their policy initiatives in recent years.[4] In Chile, amidst growing public dissatisfaction with the neoliberal policy regime imposed by the dictator Augusto Pinochet (1973–1989), Socialist President Michelle Bachelet sought a review of the lithium policy by creating the National Lithium Commission. The Commission launched an extensive consultation process throughout the second half of 2014 which highlighted several issues related to the need for Chile to benefit more from lithium extraction:

1 the recognition of the environmental fragility of the salt flats from where lithium is extracted.
2 the maintenance of lithium as a non-concessionable metal which would fall under the purview of the Chilean Nuclear Energy Commission to carefully regulate and control the exploitation, commercialisation, and trade of lithium and its derivatives;
3 strong institutional oversight in managing the salt flats.
4 a SOE to exploit these reserves consistent with the leading role of the Chilean Nuclear Energy Commission in lithium management.
5 the creation and strengthening of a sectoral lithium cluster, which would expand the participation of Chilean firms from upstream to midstream and downstream segments of the value chain.

In January 2016, Bachelet accepted the Commission's main recommendations and used the findings to formulate a national lithium strategy. The state agency CORFO sued the biggest lithium producer, SQM, for breach of contract to expand the company's refining facilities. A taxation-related controversy also came to light in this process. Producers of high-grade lithium carbonates at the largest Chilean salt flat, the *Salar de Atacama*, were paying less than other sites (US$3 per kilogram while other deposits cost between US$4 and US$4.7 per kilogram) but the companies were not paying all the taxes they were required for their high profit margins (Maxwell and Mora, 2020: 67). In the context of growing public demand for state regulation in the sector, the state-owned copper enterprise Codelco also formed a subsidiary in the lithium sector in early 2017 to develop and extract new lithium production facilities. Codelco entered joint ventures with private firms to operate in several salt flats.

These are positive steps for Chile in extending control of the downstream segments of lithium production. These downstream efforts complement attempts to extend state control in the upstream segment of the supply chain, i.e., into the processes that add value to lithium manufacturing and create sectoral linkages (Bustos-Gallardo et al., 2021; Obaya et al., 2021). These regulatory changes are vital steps towards improving the material conditions of those impacted by lithium extraction and enhancing the share of national income of Chileans as they participate in the value chain of clean technology. Still, more is needed to fully embrace a social justice perspective for the development possibilities of rare metals exploitation and commercialisation.

In Brazil, industrial policy disappeared from public discourses over the past six years. Historically, Brazilian growth strategies have been managed through a developmentalist model, whereby combinations of state involvement and market incentives were initiated to pursue ambitious development plans (Limoeiro and Schneider, 2019; Massi and Nem Singh, 2018; 2020). It remains to be seen whether the Brazilian federal government can promote sectoral linkages between REEs and wind power (or whether the unpopularity of President Jaír Bolsonaro will lead to a change in government in favour of the Workers' Party in the upcoming elections). Currently, neither a national industrial strategy nor state-led financing has been utilised under the Bolsonaro government.

However, the State of Minas Gerais holds the most important critical minerals that have the potential to be linked with clean energy sectors, notably in offshore wind turbines, electric vehicles, and photovoltaic solar panels. Through the domestic company *Companhia Brasileira de Metalurgia e Mineração* (CBMM), Brazil developed a chain of user-applications for niobium. By dividing the mineral rights between CBMM and the State of Minas Gerais, the company was able to develop mineral technologies while the state receives mining income through its SOE, *Companhia de Desenvolvimento Econômico de Minas Gerais* (Codemig). There is significant potential in developing the downstream segment of the value chain, linking mineral extraction and production with various phases of production in the clean energy sector. Brazil also holds the world's second-largest known reserves of REEs, although production levels are low. With the advancement of renewable energy, in particular wind turbines, markets might provide new sources of economic dynamism to reinvigorate Brazil's economy. The world's top five markets for wind power installation in 2020 were China, USA, Brazil, the Netherlands, and Germany (Global Wind Energy Council, 2021: 44). Further, no significant slowdown has been reported in project construction during the pandemic in Brazil. New installations in 2020 were developed through private Power Purchase Agreements, which are rapidly growing in Brazil due to wind power's competitive prices. Still, we need a developmental vision both from the Federal and State governments. Without the political will to pursue risky investments and a comprehensive development plan to link the mining and industrial sectors, it would be difficult for Brazil to catch up and achieve its potential as an economic powerhouse in the 21st century.

## What can East Asia teach Latin America?

The laggard economic performance of Latin America vis-à-vis other middle-income countries—East and Southeast Asia being the most important region of comparison—stems from the particular balance of mineral extraction and primary commodity production on the one hand, and the pursuit of risky manufacturing-based development on the other hand. Several observations can be made on why East Asia—followed by Southeast Asia—had more success in attracting foreign investment, developing Indigenous technology, and sustaining a coherent social pact with business groups. First, the organisational structures of their markets shaped the policy choice of abandoning the ISI model in favour of export-oriented manufacturing. Although both East Asia and Latin America adopted ISI strategies in the early 1950s, resource-poor East Asian countries designed their industrial policies towards exports for global markets as the limitation of their domestic markets made the ISI model untenable. By contrast, Latin American states focused on self-sufficiency due to their large domestic markets.

Second, Latin American states during the 20th century faced very little systemic threats, and without an existential challenge to the nation-state, political leaders failed to make difficult and high-risk choices to sustain their growth strategy. In East Asia, Taiwan, South Korea, and Japan simultaneously faced a communist threat that could lead to social instability and geopolitical tensions as a result of Cold War politics. Hence, economic development was paramount to state survival, making rapid industrialisation the overwhelming policy objective of conservative military regimes. Without natural resource rents, financing their industrial strategy required high levels of domestic savings and disciplined use of state subsidies. For this reason, Amsden (2007) refers to the embedding of the *principle of reciprocity* in constructing state-business alliances. By comparison, only Brazil had the drive to industrialise in the absence of large oil reserves, though its strategy depended on a combination of huge SOEs and large business groups based in the South. The outcome of resource-financed industrialisation is best exemplified in Venezuela and Mexico, both of which relied heavily on oil revenues to finance their industrial policy. In Di John's (2014) modest assessment, Venezuela's 'big push' industrialisation financed by the 1970s oil boom was far less cohesive, mired by institutional weakness and limited coordination among state agencies. Car manufacturing and other industrial sectors expanded thanks to oil revenues, but their lack of technological capacity to compete with American capital led to a growth collapse as soon as the oil boom was over in 1986.

Finally, some comparison with Southeast Asia is worth mentioning, especially given that this region is resource intensive. That region was only partially successful in achieving structural transformation, and shares similar political economy features with Latin America. The growth strategy relied on the acquisition of foreign direct investment (FDI) from Japan through the 1980s and then China from 2000 onwards. Unlike East Asia, domestic business groups had far more conflictual ties with the government and their interests aligned more closely with foreign capital (Lim, Gomez and Wong, 2021). To this extent, their industrial strategy concentrated far less on manufacturing than on natural resource extraction, including mining, palm oil, rubber, petroleum, and export agriculture.

## Conclusions

The tide is shifting away from fossil fuel dependency in favour of clean technologies. However, an uncritical embrace of clean technology may also lead to greater inequalities and uneven development. Latin America and Africa will be the new battlefield for resource extraction between China and the West. But these regions can also become a source of new political ideas on how to strike a balance between our insatiable demands for critical minerals and a new resource governance model.

To deal with the complex challenges associated with the transition to green technology, growing demands for critical minerals, and unequal burdens placed on the developing world, we need to incorporate *a social justice perspective*. For some, blame lies with the industrialised world which owes an ecological debt, thereby justifying carbon-based growth in middle- and low-income countries. Other radical calls seek *degrowth*, a reversal of humanity's pursuit of unfettered consumption and production (Kallis, 2018; Kallis et al., 2020). A nuanced position demands *common but differentiated responsibilities*. The basic principle is that because industrialised countries had decades to develop with unrestrained carbon emissions, they are now obligated to reduce emissions and contribute more financial assistance for developing nations to support their energy growth and transition to clean technologies (Gallagher and Xiaowei, 2018: 6).

These debates on how to deal with the uneven costs and burdens of the green transition pose difficult but fundamental questions. Are industrialised countries now more willing to accept the costs of climate change and do more on behalf of the developing world? To what extent can the rapid deployment of clean technologies achieve global targets, given how China's economic development model is based on high energy consumption, much of it with coal (Lewis, 2013: 10–11)? If China does move towards a renewable energy strategy, will the country merely shift the costs and externalities of the transition from the national government and urban China to rural China, Latin America, and other resource-rich regions, making them even more vulnerable to the negative effects of mineral extraction?

This chapter returns to the mining-industrial policy question to explore how new policy ideas can be crafted to address the question of development for mineral-rich states. There are opportunities for mining-based development strategies to be implemented in resource-rich countries. The worldwide shift towards clean technology can offer a window of opportunity for more equitable growth. However, the challenges are undoubtedly formidable. It is important that we draw out the lessons from Latin America's experience of export specialisation and import substitution to enhance policy learning. We should also draw out some important discussions from East Asia's successes—if there is a region to learn 'how to do industrial policy', it should emanate from their experience, not from the lessons of the European industrial revolution in the 18th and 19th centuries.

## Notes

1 For example, neoextractivism models have generated critical discussions on the degree of its political inclusivity and capacity to address environmental consequences. However, it did not fully negate the possibilities for resource-based industrialisation. See Gudynas (2020) and Nem Singh (2018).
2 Author interview with Senior Official, European Commission, November 2022.
3 The term is commonly referred to as the commodity consensus.
4 The discussion here is based on the author's forthcoming monograph (see Nem Singh, Forthcoming).

## References

Alves Dias, P., S. Bobba, S. Carrara and B. Plazzotta. (2020). *"The Role of Rare Earth Elements in Wind Energy and Electric Mobility," EUR 30488*. Luxembourg: Publication Office of the European Union. https://doi.org/10.2760/303258.

Amsden, A. (2007). *Escape from Empire: The Developing World's Journey through Heaven and Hell*. Cambridge, MA: MIT Press.

Arsel, M., B. Hogenboom and L. Pellegrini. (2016). "The Extractive Imperative in Latin America," *The Extractive Industries and Society* 3 (4): 880–887. https://doi.org/10.1016/j.exis.2016.10.014.

Atienza, M., M. Lufin and J. Soto. (2018). "Mining Linkages in the Chilean Copper Supply Network and Regional Economic Development," *Resources Policy*, March. https://doi.org/10.1016/j.resourpol.2018.02.013.

Auty, R.M. (Ed.). (2001). *Resource Abundance and Economic Development*. Oxford: Oxford University Press.

Barandiarán, J. (2019). "Lithium and Development Imaginaries in Chile, Argentina and Bolivia," *World Development* 113 (January): 381–391. https://doi.org/10.1016/j.worlddev.2018.09.019.

Beblawi, H. and G. Luciani (Eds.). (2016). *The Rentier State*. London and New York: Routledge.

Burchardt, H-J. and K. Dietz. (2014). "(Neo-)Extractivism – A New Challenge for Development Theory from Latin America," *Third World Quarterly* 35 (3): 468–486. https://doi.org/10.1080/01436597.2014.893488.

Bustos-Gallardo, B., G. Bridge and M. Prieto. (2021). "Harvesting Lithium: Water, Brine and the Industrial Dynamics of Production in the Salar de Atacama," *Geoforum* 119 (February): 177–189. https://doi.org/10.1016/j.geoforum.2021.01.001.

Cardoso, F.H. and E. Faletto. (1979). *Dependency and Development in Latin America.* Berkeley: University of California Press.

Collier, P. and A. Hoeffler. (2004). "Greed and Grievance in Civil War," *Oxford Economic Papers* 56: 563–595.

Di John, J. (2009). *From Windfall to Curse? Oil and Industrialization in Venezuela, 1920 to the Present.* Pennsylvania: Penn State University Press.

Di John, J. (2011). "Is There Really a Resource Curse? A Critical Survey of Theory and Evidence," *Global Governance* 17 (2): 167–184.

Di John, J. (2014). "The Political Economy of Industrial Policy in Venezuela," In *Venezuela Before Châvez: Anatomy of an Economic Collapse*, edited by R. Hausmann and F. Rodríguez, 321–370. University Park: Pennsylvania State University Press.

European Commission. (2020a). *Critical Materials for Strategic Technologies and Sectors in the EU – A Foresight Study.* Luxembourg: Publication Office of the European Union.

European Commission. (2020b). *Study on the EU's List of Critical Raw Materials – Final Report.* Luxembourg: European Commission.

Furtado, C. (1970). *Economic Development of Latin America: A Survey from Colonial Times to the Cuban Revolution.* Cambridge, UK: Cambridge University Press.

Gallagher, K-S. and X. Xiaowei. (2018). *Titans of the Climate: Explaining Policy Process in the United States and China.* Cambridge, MA: MIT Press.

Global Wind Energy Council. (2021). *Global Wind Report 2021.* Brussels: Global Wind Energy Council.

Gudynas, E. (2016). "Beyond Varieties of Development: Disputes and Alternatives," *Third World Quarterly* 37 (4): 721–732. https://doi.org/10.1080/01436597.2015.1126504.

Gudynas, E. (2020). *Extractivisms: Politics, Economy and Ecology.* Fernwood Publishing Company, Limited. https://books.google.nl/books?id=z-V0zQEACAAJ.

Gustafsson, M.-T. and M. Scurrah. (2019). "Strengthening Subnational Institutions for Sustainable Development in Resource-Rich States: Decentralized Land-Use Planning in Peru," *World Development* 119 (July): 133–144. https://doi.org/10.1016/j.worlddev.2019.03.002.

Hochstetler, K. and G. Kostka. (2015). "Wind and Solar Power in Brazil and China: Interests, State–Business Relations, and Policy Outcomes," *Global Environmental Politics* 15 (3): 74–94. https://doi.org/10.1162/GLEP_a_00312.

International Energy Agency. (2021). "The Role of Critical Minerals in Clean Energy Transitions," *World Energy Outlook Special Report.* Paris: IEA. https://www.iea.org/reports/the-role-of-critical-minerals-in-clean-energy-transitions.

Kallis, G. (2018). *Degrowth.* Agenda Publishing. https://doi.org/10.2307/j.ctv5cg82g.

Kallis, G., S. Paulson, G. D'Alisa and F. Demaria. (2020). *The Case for Degrowth.* Cambridge, UK: Polity Press.

Lewis, J. (2013). *Green Innovation in China: China's Wind Power Industry and the Global Transition to a Low-Carbon Economy.* New York and Chichester: Columbia University Press.

Lim, G., T. Gomez and C.-Y. Wong. (2021). "Evolving State–Business Relations in an Age of Globalisation: An Introduction," *Journal of Contemporary Asia* June: 1–16. https://doi.org/10.1080/00472336.2021.1934720.

Limoeiro, D. and B.R. Schneider. (2019). "Institutions, Politics and State-Led Innovation," In *Innovation in Brazil: Advancing Development in the 21st Century*, edited by E. Reynolds, B.R. Schneider and E. Zylberberg, 23–44. London: Routledge.

Massi, E. and J. Nem Singh. (2018). "Industrial Policy and State-Making: Brazil's Attempt at Oil-Based Industrial Development," *Third World Quarterly* 39 (6): 1133–1150. https://doi.org/10.1080/01436597.2018.1455144.

Massi, E. and J. Nem Singh. (2020). *The Energy Politics of Brazil*. Edited by K. J. Hancock and J.E. Allison, February. https://doi.org/10.1093/oxfordhb/9780190861360.013.22.

Maxwell, P. and M. Mora. (2020). "Lithium and Chile: Looking Back and Looking Forward," *Mineral Economics* 33 (1): 57–71. https://doi.org/10.1007/s13563-019-00181-8.

Nakano, J. (2021). *The Geopolitics of Critical Minerals Supply Chain*. Washington, DC: Center for Strategic and International Studies.

Navarro, J. and F. Zhao. (2014). "Life-Cycle Assessment of the Production of Rare-Earth Elements for Energy Applications: A Review," *Frontiers in Energy Research* 2: 45. https://doi.org/10.3389/fenrg.2014.00045.

Nem Singh, J. (2018). *Governing Natural Resources*. 1st ed. London: Routledge. https://doi.org/10.4324/9781315661162-28.

Nem Singh, J. (2021). *Mining Our Way out of the Climate Change Conundrum? The Power of a Social Justice Perspective. Latin America's Environmental Policies in Global Perspective*. Washington, DC: The Wilson Center.

Nem Singh, J. (Forthcoming). "Business of the State: Why State Ownership Matters for Resource Governance," *Mimeograph*.

Nem Singh, J. and F. Bourgouin (Eds.) (2013). *Resource Governance and Developmental States in the Global South: Critical International Political Economy Perspectives*. International Political Economy. Basingstoke: Palgrave Macmillan.

Obaya, M., A. López and P. Pascuini. (2021). "Curb Your Enthusiasm. Challenges to the Development of Lithium-Based Linkages in Argentina," *Resources Policy* 70 (March): 101912. https://doi.org/10.1016/j.resourpol.2020.101912.

Orihuela, J.C. (2018). "Institutions and Place: Bringing Context Back into the Study of the Resource Curse," *Journal of Institutional Economics* 14 (1): 157–180. https://doi.org/10.1017/S1744137417000236.

Stubrin, L. (2017). "Innovation, Learning and Competence Building in the Mining Industry. The Case of Knowledge Intensive Mining Suppliers (KIMS) in Chile," *Resources Policy* 54 (December): 167–175. https://doi.org/10.1016/j.resourpol.2017.10.009.

Svampa, M. (2019a). *Development in Latin America: Toward a New Future*. Critical Development Studies. Fernwood Publishing. https://books.google.nl/books?id=7Q6WxQEACAAJ.

Svampa, M. (2019b). *Neo-Extractivism in Latin America: Socio-Environmental Conflicts, the Territorial Turn, and New Political Narratives*. Elements in Politics and Society in Latin America. Cambridge: Cambridge University Press. https://doi.org/10.1017/9781108752589.

Thorpe, R., S. Battistelli, Y. Guichaoua, J.C. Orihuela and M. Paredes. (2012). *The Developmental Challenges of Mining and Oil: Lessons from Africa and Latin America*. Basingstoke: Palgrave Macmillan.

Thurber, M. and B.T. Istad. (2012). "Norway's Evolving Champion: Statoil and the Politics of State Enterprise," In *Oil and Governance: State-Owned Enterprises and the World Energy Supply*, edited by D.G. Victor, D.R. Hults and M. Thurber, 599–654. Cambridge, UK: Cambridge University Press.

U.S. White House. (2017). "Executive Order 13817 of December 20, 2017—A Federal Strategy to Ensure Secure and Reliable Supplies of Critical Minerals, 60835". https://www.whitehouse.gov

Veltmeyer, H. (2013). "The Political Economy of Natural Resource Extraction: A New Model or Extractive Imperialism?" *Canadian Journal of Development Studies/ Revue Canadienne d'études Du Développement* 34 (1): 79–95. https://doi.org/10.1080/02255189.2013.764850.

Part IV

# Resistance on the Extractive Frontier

# 9 Reloaded neoextractivism, multi-actor conflicts and alternative horizons

## Keys to the socio-ecological crisis

*Pabel Camilo López Flores and Anna Preiser*

Since the beginning of the millennium, a rising number of socio-ecological conflicts have been registered in Latin America.[1] Often, those are in direct connection with extractivist activities: Latin American countries, despite different political orientations, be they of neoliberal or progressive profile, have been led by neoextractivist development models, based on the exploitation and export of large amounts of natural resources such as metals, fossil fuels and large-scale monoculture and food production. Even though this development model has caused political contestations and exacerbates the socio-ecological crisis with irreversible consequences, such as on climate, the loss of food sovereignty, the degradation of environment and deforestation, in times of an immense economic recession in times of the COVID-19 pandemic, once again the role of natural resources is presented as central to reduce the socio-economic crisis (Benites and Bebbington, 2020). At the same time, the dependence on the world market, the vulnerability of the system and the need for more autonomy and food sovereignty, especially on a local level, become evident.

This prevalent model of development is based on structural inequalities derived from processes of recolonisation (Makaran and López, 2018) and a pattern known as coloniality of power, understood as a pattern based on a racial, epistemological and cultural hierarchy and domination (Quijano, 2000). It is reproduced in the current structure and functioning of the capitalist world-system (Wallerstein, 2005) and/or world-ecology (Moore, 2016). Based on a consolidated asymmetrical international and territorial division of labour, the role of Latin America as a site of continuous and expanding exploitation of natural resources is constituent to global capitalist accumulation (Luxemburg, 2007 [1913]). This has been accompanied by environmental destruction or degradation, affecting people's livelihoods, cultures, social structures, modes of living and understandings of development. Latin America became an important site of socio-ecological movements, ontological and epistemological struggle as well as a site of propositions of various alternatives to the logic of capital, other possible ways of existing and processes of *r-existence* (Porto-Gonçalves and Leff, 2015), reaching from local understandings of *Buen Vivir* to more generalised alternatives such as post-extractivism.

DOI: 10.4324/9781003301981-14

Nevertheless, the reach of socio-ecological movements and realisation of those alternatives—which seem urgent to confront the multiple crisis with its ecological, social, economic and political dimensions—are limited by development projects of the states, international development visions and interests of companies. Therefore, especially in times of a deep global crisis and uncertainties, which can also offer a window of opportunity to imagine and promote alternatives, this model of development and deeply inscribed extractivist structures, should be critically examined.

In this chapter, we seek to contribute to a better understanding of the role of different important actors regarding the conflicts that neoextractivism generates. This relates to their interests, alliances, answers to confront the multiple crises and limitations in fulfilling their objectives: social-territorial movements, the state and companies representing (inter)national capital. We argue that conflicts and social movements are essential in making injustices visible and in challenging prevalent unsustainable structures which have led to the multiple crises; however, propositions for post-extractivist horizons find their limits in the development vision and constitution of powerful actors such as the state and companies. Nevertheless, there are spaces of resistance with re-existence processes with counter-hegemonic possibility and alternative societal potentiality.

## Neoextractivisms and socio-ecological crisis: theoretical considerations

Latin America is currently confronting different crises at the economic, social, ecological, migratory and democratic levels. This can be attributed to global conditions such as climate change or the international and territorial division of labour. Also, the situations on a regional, national or local scale play a role, such as economic and territorial transformations, as well as political changes, orientations on development, geopolitical reconfigurations and its relationship with international and national environmental policies.

In Latin America, with development models based on extractive activities, the main dimensions of this crisis have been deepened during the last three decades—a period marked by a process of deepening the commodification and submission of natural dynamics, reproduction of life, cultural practices and ontologies of different peoples in accordance to demands of capitalist accumulation (Lander and Arconada, 2019). As Burchardt (2018) points out, social and ecological issues emerge as two central problems. It proves to be problematic that until today, almost all the answers to social questions are oriented towards economic growth promoted by the prevailing extractive development model, a model that undeniably contributes to the ecological collapse (Burchardt, 2018). Thus, it is not surprising that the character of neoextractivism as an old as well as current pattern of capitalist accumulation in the periphery of the world system has been widely discussed. From a critical perspective, the term *neoextractivism* criticises and problematises patterns of unsustainable development and the logic of an expanding dispossession, combining multiscalar problems and different dimensions of the current crisis (Svampa, 2019: 14). Nowadays, extractivisms are considered the gravest ecological problems of Latin America (Gudynas, 2018). However, due to politicisation of the ecological crisis and climate change, and the environmental destruction wrought through extractivist activities, valorisation of nature remains at the core of global dynamics (Brand and Dietz, 2014). It is directly related to the predominant global development paradigm, as well as what Brand and Wissen (2021) refer to as the globally expanding Imperial Mode of Living: It is based on unsustainable patterns of production and consumption, that presuppose unlimited access to natural resources, cheap labour and capacities to absorb pollution; ecological and social costs with direct effects on ecosystems and life forms on the planet are externalised. It is also the basis of national development models, based on the intensive exploitation and export of large amounts of nature as a commodity (Gudynas, 2018), leading to the re-primarisation of economies (Svampa, 2019). (Neo)extractivism(s) can thus be considered as *glocal*: they are strongly conditioned by globalisation, as international factors such as demand, prices or investments are important determinants in its expansion and contraction, and they are always locally anchored (Gudynas, 2018). As a constitutive part of capitalism with its compulsion of accumulation, in need of an extra-economic exterior, it constantly integrates new territories, fields, social relations and future markets (Composto and Navarro, 2014) and materialises in the expansion of commodity frontiers into territories previously considered unproductive (Svampa, 2015). This process is considered as accumulation by dispossession (Harvey, 2004), which is a central aspect of the continuing process of colonisation, decolonisation and recolonisation (Makaran and Lopez, 2018). Its ongoing expansion based on exclusion and multiple dispossession processes generates social and territorial transformations of great magnitude (Navarro, 2018). In that sense, from a critical perspective, the term neoextractivism renders a helpful category to explain and analyse underlying power relations, disputes between different actors, as well as shared responsibilities on a global scale between the Global North and South (Svampa, 2019).

At least in the last two decades, the South American context was marked by favourable terms of trade and comparative advantages, known as the super cycle of the resource boom due to the rapid growth and consumption of raw material of emerging countries, especially China, leading to high demand and high prices of various commodities as well as 'a wave of resource-seeking foreign direct investment' into the extractive sector (Veltmeyer, 2016: 32). Also, the financialisation of nature as a new field of investment as capital-securing alternative to falling profit rates on the markets and speculation—also influenced by the expanding green economy—pushed this trend. (Brand and Dietz, 2014; Composto and Navarro, 2014; Kaltmeier, 2020; Svampa, 2019). This favourable constellation of the world market led to the 'commodity consensus' with all governments pushing the expansion of extractivist activities (Svampa, 2015).

After a 'positivity phase', with increased social spending, reduction of poverty and 'the expansion of the participation of the population' (Teran Mantovani and Svampa, 2019: 178), a phase characterised by a 'multiplication of (extractive) megaprojects' (2008–2013/2015) and large infrastructure projects started, and the former extension of collective, territorial and environmental rights found limits in the extension of capitalist exploitation. This led to a rising number of socio-environmental conflicts with national visibility, such as TIPNIS in Bolivia, Baguazo and the Conga in Peru, Belo Monte in Brazil and Yasuní in Ecuador, etc. (Teran Mantovani and Svampa, 2019: 180). The third phase, which lasted at least until the outbreak of COVID-19, was marked by the end of the supercycle of the commodity boom, leading to an increase in extractive projects to compensate for reduced income and growing commercial deficits (de Echave, 2018), to aggravating violent dispossession and breaching of rights of the population and nature, accompanied by criminalisation of protest and a worrying number of assassinations of environmental activists (Teran Mantovani and Svampa, 2019). Gudynas (2018) characterises these violent dynamics, which he terms 'extraheccíon' (Gudynas, 2018: 29), as a precondition and a move to 'hyper-extractivism' (Gudynas, 2018: 28).

Apart from differences between progressive and conservative governments such as the more active role of the state, the nationalisations of strategic sectors and the higher appropriation of rents and socialisation of wealth through social programmes in the former (Gudynas, 2015; Svampa, 2019), all governments assimilated their relation to (neo)extractivism (Brand and Dietz, 2014; Composto and Navarro, 2014); deepening 'the dynamic of dispossession [...] accumulation of land, resources, and territories, principally by large corporations, in multiscalar alliances with different governments' (Svampa, 2015: 66).

Those dynamics were accompanied by the strengthening of extractivist elites, coupled with the further concentration of land and thus the polarisation of the social structure, processes of dispossession and social inequality (Kaltmeier, 2020). This situation, with the current pandemic and in the face of a socio-ecological crisis/collapse, far from changing, has accentuated and/or consolidated throughout Latin America. Some even expect a new commodities supercycle considering price trends of commodities during the pandemic and trends towards the greening of infrastructure which require access to resources (Dietz, 2021).

## Socio-ecological conflicts and persistent multiple dispossession

The multiple crisis as well as the extractivist development model and its socio-ecological dimension have disproportional social, economic, territorial and cultural impacts for more vulnerable territories or social groups, which is also reflected in the characteristics and the rising number of conflicts. Conflicts arising in this field can be described as 'glocal' to the extent that national and global processes, actors and power dispositives as well as disputes over the economic systems and understandings of development materialise as dynamics of extraction and as local conflicts, forms of activism, resistance and mobilisation (Hoetmer, 2013; Paredes, 2016). It is a field in which the interests of different countries to gain access to Latin America's resources, of international and national capital, Latin American states, economic and environmental policies, the labour market and the populations living in the vicinity of mining projects are confronted. The local, often rural population—who live and reproduce their lives depending on the land and natural ecosystems—are directly affected by the expansion of commodity frontiers, pushed by the intensive use of resources to meet the needs of capitalist production and accumulation on a global scale (Fini, 2016). Externalities such as ecological degradation and destruction, deterioration of the quality of soil and water as well as health, changes in landscapes, social relations, territorial fragmentation and dispossession are shifted onto them (Loayza and Rigolini, 2016). This leads to ecological distribution conflicts, that 'emerge from the structural asymmetries in the burdens of pollution and in the access to natural resources that are grounded in unequal distributions of power and income, and in social inequalities of ethnicity, caste, social class and gender' (Martinez-Alier and Walter, 2016: 60), as well as the asymmetrical international and territorial division of labour.

Recent dynamics of the acceleration and deepening of extractivist activities led to a rising number and an 'eco-territorial turn' of socio-ecological conflicts (Svampa, 2015) with aspects such as the right to and control over scarce resources, with agricultural land and water at the forefront. They revolve around the interruption of traditional productive activities, repression and the threat to rights, such the right to Indigenous consultation and the resettlement of population. In this scenario, struggles for self-determination and (territorial) autonomy, defending collective cultural, economic and territorial rights became more visible. Considering different existing modes of production, values, cultures, languages and authority structures (Tapia Mealla, 2013: 103), conflicts can be understood as a manifestation of contradictions of different ways of understanding development, democracy and a desired alternative society, based on different and contradictory values, valorisations, beliefs, necessities and ontologies (Blaser and de la Cadena, 2018).

New dynamics have been characterised by a generalised tendency to increase the modalities of 'multiple dispossessions' (Navarro, 2018): territorial spaces of extractivist exploitation and dynamics of dispossession configure so-called 'sacrifice zones' (Bolados and Sánchez, 2017; Svampa and Viale, 2020), denying already existing social, ecological, economic and productive activities within historically constructed territories that contain a set of collective identities, social relations and cultural practices. Thus, 'The space-time of capital seeks to impose itself on space-times of peoples and communities [...]. The new colonizing enterprise appears today more ambitious than before' (Makaran and López, 2018: 18). This 'territorial coloniality' (Rivera, 2010), defended by the dogmas of economic and 'productive' growth, 'development' and 'overcoming poverty', puts 'pressure on natural goods, land and territories', and conditions exclusion, domination, poverty and inequality, cultural racism and social as well as environmental devastation. This has led to increasing and sometimes violent confrontations between local communities, 'peasant-Indigenous organizations, socio-territorial movements, environmental collectives, (on the one hand) and, on the other hand, governments and large economic corporations' (Svampa, 2019: 12).

## Multi-actor roles

How disputes shape local life is influenced by the relations of local forces, which are rooted in local histories and the attribution of meaning to processes on a global scale (Hoetmer, 2013; Paredes, 2016). In that sense, Dietz and Engels (2020) stress the need for a radical contextualisation when analysing extractive conflicts, as each conflict has its own logic, history and rules and is influenced by 'diverse social, political, institutional and discursive factors' (Dietz and Engels, 2020: 208).

To address socio-ecological conflicts, we focus on the analysis of a multi-actor approach, which allows us to read and think about current conflicts within a framework of multiple and complex power relations, negotiations, agreements, tensions and disputes, not only between different or confronted positions and interests but also between visions, languages, meanings and ways of valuing society, nature, territory and life. Concerning specific local conflicts, companies, the state and local communities are the central actors defining its characteristics. Global processes, power relations, development visions and further actors such as the media, (inter)national NGOs, consulting firms, universities, international or regional financial institutions, multilateral organisations, trading agreements and the subnational governments influence the conflicts rather indirectly and materialise through decisions taken by central actors, dynamics of extraction and structural shifts, expressed amongst others in changes in access and control over land (Dietz and Engels, 2020).

On these premises, below we specify and characterise the role and narratives of the state, companies and social movements, which we consider central to a greater and more general understanding of the socio-ecological conflict in the region. We will consider their interests, respective resources of power to influence structures and discourses (Dietz and Engels, 2020). We recognise that actors adapt to changes depending on the context, opportunities and risks and form alliances with actors across the spectrum and thus should not be essentialised (De Echave et al., 2009). Further, we present a generalised approach to those actors, which, on the one hand, can help to approach the analysis of specific conflicts while, on the other hand, must be adapted to specific conflicts.

### *The state*

The state, with its multiple mechanisms such as laws, its political-institutional decision-making, administrative practices, development plans and visible and invisible policies, defines rules within which a conflict is taking place (Dietz and Engels, 2020). It controls people and territories, their natural resources as well as who has access to them (Duit, Feindt and Meadowcroft, 2016) and sets the macro-political rules of environmental management of subordinated territories. Thus, the State can be considered the 'gran distribuidor originario' influencing current distribution conflicts (Alimonda, 2011: 45).

A common characteristic of Latin American States is rooted in their origin as spaces of accumulation dependent on the world market (Thwaites and Ouviña, 2012), its demand and investment and economic structures based on the export of natural resources and the import of industrial products. Further, national markets are weak, which limits an independent orientation of the economy and leads to dependence on this globalised relation concerning fiscal revenues as the basis for state action. Nevertheless, René Zavaleta understood Latin America's dependence not only as a result of external factors but also highly influenced by internal power structures (Costilla and Pimmer, 2014). The hegemony of global capital strongly influenced but did not dispense instances of the national state—which constitute the central space in which substantive struggles for the social direction are settled for its consolidation (Thwaites and Ouviña, 2019).

Further, the Latin American context has been characterised by the implementation of 'development' models imposed from technocratic approaches of international financial organisations such as the International Monetary Fund, the World Bank and the Inter-American Development Bank since the late 1980s. Known as the Washington Consensus, this process set the base and institutional arrangements for the emergence of the current phase of neoextractivism in neoliberal as well as progressive governments (Andreucci and Radhuber, 2015): it was focused on neoliberal structural adjustments within indebted Latin American countries towards privatisation, liberalisation of markets and the reconversion of the state. Latin America's resources as the core of capitalist development regained centrality.

Also, environmental standards and politics started to advance (O'Ryan and Ibarra, 2016). Transnational enterprises gained importance and became the principal agents and beneficiaries of this global order (Brand and Dietz, 2014). Those processes led to a gradual reduction of the states' political-institutional capacity to territorially, politically, culturally and symbolically reorder a given community. Nevertheless, they maintained importance in the organisation of domination, the enforcement of capitalism and remained thus a site of its dispute (Tapia Mealla, 2014). The changed access to resources was eventually politised through social movements and led to a generalised crisis in the context of the neo-liberal nation state at the beginning of the 21st century and progressive reorientation of some governments (Brand and Dietz, 2014).

In all countries, despite the progress of environmental regulation based on ideas of technical solutions in neoliberal governments and/or discourses of *Buen Vivir* and the Rights of Nature in progressive governments, this last decade was marked by the accentuation of socio-ecological conflicts related to the processes of expansion or intensification of extractive policies. The State, in compliance with capital, had a central role in terms of the promotion and viability of development projects and productive activities under the banner of 'progress', 'economic growth' and 'modernisation'. The invisibility and lack or disregard of formal and declarative recognition of historically subordinated subjects, such as Indigenous peoples, have been key to the intensive exploitation of 'natural resources' and dispossession supported by the public sphere, amongst others, through the prioritisation of extractive policies and international treaties over environmental regulation and collective rights. This generated a wave of protest processes and resistance movements against the States and their policies. Thus, also progressive governments reached limits:

The tendency is not precisely that the national state becomes a mega-actor, or that its intervention guarantees fundamental changes in the instruments of regulation. On the contrary, the predominant hypothesis points to the return of a moderately regulatory State, capable of installing itself in a space of variable geometry (Svampa, 2016), that is, in a scheme with multiple actors (of civil society complexity, illustrated by social movements, NGOs and other actors), but in close association with transnational capital.

### *Companies*

Extractive companies, essential for the monetary valorisation of nature and thus for global capitalist accumulation—providing investment, know-how and technology—have gained considerable influence on the global, national and local scale and receive preferential treatment within public policies (Durand, 2016). The state profits and is partly sustained from rents realised in this sector (Bebbington et al., 2018), and subordinates to private interests, willing to flexibilise environmental and social regulations to maintain private investment into the sector.

We refer to the concept of enclaves, which helps to explain the power of extractive companies in the current phase of neoextractivism. They can be understood as 'a large extractive-exporting company (…) that dominates a large territory with state support' (Durand, 2016: 8). Usually, they are decoupled from other productive activities in the region and externally oriented, as they operate in 'internationalized sectors with high economic dynamism and whose surpluses are directly transferred abroad' (Ramírez, 2018: 302). They can be understood as 'a projection of global power at the national and regional/local level', and at the same time, they exercise a multi-dimensional (economic, political, territorial, discursive, social and coercive) power with local, national and global influence (Durand, 2016: 9). Bebbington et al. (2018) refer to the concept of political settlements—holding 'different relationships of power together in stable form' and shaping institutions and policies (Bebbington et al., 2018: 8)—to make sense of how governing relations in the context of extractive industries are negotiated among economic and political elites with their bargaining power. In this context, due to the economic importance and thus economic power of the extractive sector, (transnational) mining companies gain the role of a powerful interest group and 'become "national" elites, because they have accrued resources which allow them to exercise influence over the state and the overall distribution of assets and rights in society' (Bebbington et al., 2018: 13).

Understood as capitalist enterprises, owned by and managed in the name of capitalists, they aim to fulfil their social responsibility to increase profits and serve capitalist interests (Friedman, 1970). Concerning its negative ecological and social record, and the creation of spatial inequality concerning the burdens (Bebbington et al., 2018), extractive companies respond to comply with international standards and a certain image. Companies vary depending on the type of ownership, being private or public, national, foreign, transnational or mixed. Nevertheless, they operate administratively and discursively in a similar way, presenting themselves as 'modern', 'civilizing' and 'good citizen' (Durand, 2016: 11), based on the image of responsible activity, high international standards and imaginaries of high technical capacity capable of preventing most environmental deterioration. Criticism based on alternative forms of knowledge is denounced (Damonte, 2014). They also promote their image as a driving force, one necessary for territorial development and social investment. In the face of an 'absent state' in remote territories, companies often assume 'government roles' as the providers of public goods, constructing infrastructure and promising the provision of basic services (Damonte, 2014: 44; Durand, 2016: 8). Further, by promoting voluntary, self-regulation mechanisms such as policies of social responsibility, 'companies recognize certain negative externalities (…), but which they consider to be controllable without (…) the need to create new public regulation', monitoring and sanctions (De Echave et al., 2009: 328).

Companies are in direct relation with communities. They need to obtain the 'social license to operate' and to handle the (at times) unstable local context. Both for companies and for states it is important to counteract social unrest and local conflicts (De Echave et al., 2009: 230) as the interruption of operations harms accumulation and profitability. It can further create uncertainties and a 'bad reputation', impacting future investment (Composto and Navarro, 2014). To persuade, prevent or respond to possible tensions and conflict and to organise social relations, companies adopt different strategies ranging from 'positive' interventions to gain consensus, legitimacy and support, such as through clientelistic behaviour (Durand, 2016: 35–36), programs of 'corporate social responsibility, payments for losses, Indigenous and local development funds [or] fiscal transfers to subnational governments' (Bebbington et al., 2018: 15); negotiations with the population, cooptation and capture, discipline and normalisation, or with 'negative' interventions to prevent the mobilisation of communities or to stop opposition, such as by controlling the local space by influencing flows of information and institutions; to criminalisation, repression, militarisation and using public and non-public force to suppress mobilisation (Composto and Navarro, 2014: 58).

Leiva (2019) refers to 'novel political technologies (such as collaborative agreements for territorial development) (...) to enact new modes of manufacturing consent (...) targeting local relational, emotional, dialogic, identitarian, memory, interpersonal place-based subjectivity-making processes, to yoke them into the service of transnational capital' (Leiva, 2019: 146).

## Social actors: movements and socio-territorial re-existences

The reproduction of transnational capital and dialectical processes of colonisation/decolonisation/recolonisation imply uprooting and expulsion for subaltern groups. In the face of this scenario, in almost all regions of *Abya Yala* (Latin America), a multiplicity of eco-territorial movements are emerging. They are led to a great extent by Indigenous peoples, campesino and afro-descendant communities and feminist organisations and make visible the struggles for territory and for the common, disputed territorialities, as well as new languages of valorisation (Svampa, 2016) and imaginaries of *r-existence* (Escobar, 2018). They usually situate themselves outside and against existing state-sanctioned governance arrangements. Nevertheless, they often develop alliances with key elites within and outside the state to help them advance their goals (Silva, Akchurin and Bebbington, 2018).

In Latin America, many social movements revolve around defending, constructing and gaining political control over territory (Fini, 2016). Territory not only contains natural resources and population but also is a dense sociological and geographical category that 'presupposes a process of appropriation/territorialisation which fosters the formation of territorialised identities' (Porto Gonçalves, 2002: 230). In that context, territory is discussed as a space of social construction that is the result of the exercise of power relations as well as the basis for the reproduction of collective life. Processes of 'territorialisation' are understood, from the perspective of geography, as the social production of the territory, as a material and symbolic appropriation of a certain space, as an important source of culture, as structuring elements of subjectivities, social imaginaries and dynamics of collective action (Porto-Gonçalves, 2010). This understanding highlights different meanings of space (Moreano, Molina and Bryant, 2017), how the territory is transformed and dominated and how it moulds, controls and signifies social disputes over its ecosystem elements, such as its resources, cycles and human beings (Porto-Gonçalves, 2010).

The struggles of diverse social sectors appear as 'territories in dispute' (Zibechi, 2008), threatened to be subordinated by insertion into the dominant system. The concept of territoriality has served as an instrument of resistance against the expropriation of natural resources, unequal power relations and against economic territoriality that is being imposed by the state and large corporations, promoting a socio-environmental rationality based on their cultural, social and economic values and reclaiming ancestral heritage. (Moreano et al., 2017). That way, many socio-environmental conflicts address the preservation of territoriality that is not submitted to the logic of capital and challenge the consolidation of a 'territoriality of domination'.

These territories are—for the most part—crossed and influenced by hegemonic capitalism and coloniality (Zibechi, 2008) often appear subaltern to the hegemonic schema of territorialisation. These territorialities are maintained in the subsoil and invisible (Tapia, 2008) but emerge once again as alternatives, with their own universe of meaning, myths and realities linked to territory when confronted with conflict. In these 'territories in dispute' (Zibechi, 2008) social actors reconstruct and re-signify these determined geographical spaces, inhabiting, transforming and recreating them according to their interests, forms of life and social reproduction. These processes of socio-territorial construction and recreation are open and not definitive processes that potentially configure new forms of sociability; as such, they are experiences marked by uncertainty and contingency.

## The transformative character of conflicts

Conflicts, as a symptom and a revelatory crisis of the underlying injustice, are inevitable and necessary, as they challenge structural and cultural forms of violence (Chaparro et al., 2013; Le Billon, 2015) and can lead to policy changes, institutional innovation that promote more ecological and just governance, and to the strengthening of the governance of local commons (e.g. Silva, Akchurin and Bebbington, 2018) It requires the capacity of mobilisation, making proposals and of negotiation (Chaparro et al., 2013), depends on the power balance within and between competing coalitions, cyclical political opportunities, on the extent to which authorities allow for social demands and on the support of relevant international and national actors. However, even if conflicts and mobilisation can be a factor for transformation or institutional change, as emblematically shows the new constitution in Bolivia, or advances in environmental regulation and the introduction of the right to previous consultation of Indigenous communities in Peru, reforms are often insufficiently implemented, not respected, or used to legitimise the continuation of extractivist activities, which have led to those conflicts in the first place. Reasons for conflicts therefore often do not disappear, and at times even deepen (Dargent et al., 2017). As De Echave et al. (2009) emphasise, due to different developmental conceptions and needs, conflicts around extractivist activities cannot be solved, but only transformed, and 'displaced to other political and social scenarios' (De Echave et al., 2009: 10). Nevertheless, as conflicts remain necessary to challenge forms of violence and to push policy change, it is crucial to consider alternative horizons proposed both within social movements and other contexts, especially in face of the socio-ecological crisis.

## Post-extractivist and alternative horizons in Latin America

In Latin America, as Svampa (2016) points out, the scope and speed of current extractivist development projects have put organisations, activists and intellectuals of diverse backgrounds on high alert, on the need to develop viable alternatives to extractivism and to the mercantilising, patriarchal, colonial and destructive logics of modern capitalism (Lang and Hoetmer, 2019), proposing the transition through a matrix of scenarios of multi-dimensional intervention. Alternative social/societal experiences throughout the region are presented and manifested in a framework of plurality, heteronomy and geographical as well as contextual diversity. The dynamics of socio-environmental resistances on a local and regional scale laid the foundations for an 'eco-territorial turn' as a common language of valuation on territoriality (Svampa, 2015, 2019).

In this chapter, we are interested in highlighting some of the regional proposals, discussions and experiences around post-extractivist, post-developmental and/or post-capitalist societal alternatives and horizons. For this purpose, we point out at least three dimensions as possible frameworks to be able to conceptualise alternative horizons facing the current multi-crisis, particularly its socio-ecological dimension.

### *Post-extractivist transition scenarios*

Discussions from a more general perspective demand alternatives to development; alternatives within a conventional development model would not be insufficient. It implies seeking alternatives beyond this civilisation shaped by capitalist modernity, which is focused on economic growth, instrumental and destructive social relations with nature, and on a rational, profit-maximising and individualistic conception of humanity, which has led us to this crisis.

Debates and proposals of the Group of Alternatives to Development centre around an agenda and transitional scenarios to overcome extractivism (Brand and Lang, 2015), based on two different levels of action: (1) a set of public policies that act at a macro-social and global level and (2) intervention at a local and regional level, aimed at detecting, valuing and enhancing the existing models of 'alter-development' (Svampa, 2016: 395). In a similar perspective, Gudynas (2015) proposes that the transition from a 'predatory extractivism' to a post-extractive scenario requires a set of public policies: as a first step towards a 'cautious extractivism' which actually respects social and environmental standards and reduces social and environmental costs and as a next step towards an 'indispensable extractivism' which reduces extractivist activities to its necessary minimum, rethinking the articulation between environmental and social issues within strategic horizons of change towards *Buen Vivir* (Gudynas, 2015).

Acosta and Brand (2017) discuss post-extractivism and the notion of 'degrowth' in Europe and thus combine proposals for alternatives from different political and geographical contexts. Those notions emphasise the unsustainability of the imperial consumption models spread globally, both in the North and in the South, and serve to consider new horizons of change and alternatives, based on another 'environmental rationality' (Leff, 2018).

The current COVID-19 pandemic demonstrated that capitalist accumulation and ecological destruction could be paused in times of emergency and thus represents an opportunity for change: 'to build our future based on caring for life'. Therefore, a group of Latin American people and organisations proposed a *Social, Ecological, Economic and Intercultural Pact for Latin America* with alternative perspectives, as a base for a common discussion for social change, change in legislation and institutions and the alteration of the balance of power, including discussions about post-extractivist economies and societies, food sovereignty, autonomous, sustainable local societies that are rooted in society and the creation of national and local systems of care (*Pacto Ecosocial Del Sur*, n.d.).

### *New political and valuation languages*

Within the pluriverse of alternative visions (Escobar, 2018) exist an integral environmental perspective, linked to the notion of strong sustainability and post-development; an Indigenous perspective, with emphasis on *Buen Vivir*; an eco-feminist perspective, associated with the ethics of care and depatriarcalisation; an eco-territorial perspective, linked to social movements criticising 'bad development' and emphasising the concept of territoriality and the defense of common goods. Beyond the differences, all these perspectives are based on a critique of extractivism (Svampa, 2016: 371). As Svampa (2016) points out, this criticism is linked to the eco-territorial turn. Peasant-Indigenous resistance, but also socio-territorial and environmental movements, have been multiplying, resulting in an organisational framework of collective action, which produces an alternative collective subjectivity. Also, the role of women in resistance against neoextractivism has become central both in large organisational structures and in small collectives, as well as in 'proposing another model of life, based on reciprocal relationships, on the resignification of territory, not only spatially but also in relations to women's body' (Hofmann and Cabrapan, 2021: 44). This plurality of actors and the convergence of different matrices and languages, opens the doors to a dialogue and valorisation of different forms of knowledge and accounts for an articulation of languages, alternative concepts and of what Svampa (2016) calls 'horizon-categories': such as the 'defense of the territory', 'eco-feminism', 'common goods', 'communality', 'rights of nature', 'autonomy' and 'ethics of care', ecofeminist language of the 'body/territory' and the criticism of patriarchy, Living Well (*Buen Vivir*) and the Rights of Nature and Mother Earth (Svampa, 2016: 375) including a perspective of a participatory democracy.

These concepts tend to develop an important mobilising capacity and install new themes into societal debates, while guiding the interactive dynamics towards the production of a common subjectivity in the Latin American space of struggles.

### *Practices of re-existences in the territories*

In face of the expansion and deepening of multiple forms of dispossession (Navarro, 2018) and destruction of nature, struggles for self-determination and the processes of autonomy (on a local scale) assume vital importance inasmuch as they constitute territorial resistances and *r-existences* (Porto-Gonçalves and Leff, 2015). Territorialised social movements (Porto-Gonçalves, 2010) are largely manifested either through social rebellions or claiming and building autonomy, both locally, within and outside the frameworks and logics of the state (Esteva, 2011) or as forms of Indigenous self-government. Several of these societal processes manifest themselves as processes of socio-territorial re-existence (Porto-Gonçalves and Leff, 2015): social actors activate specific, spatially situated forms of resilience in the face of multiple dispossession and territorial reconfigurations—deterritorialisation/reterritorialisation of capitalism—and construct or reconstruct socio-territorial relations of their collective life.

These groups not only resist dispossession and de-territorialisation but also redefine their forms of existence through emancipatory movements and the reinvention of their identities, their ways of thinking and their modes of production and sustenance. These diverse processes of re-existence are presented, for example, in the experiences of community agroecology practiced by peasant or/and Indigenous communities, in certain forms of community management of the territory, Indigenous agroforestry and integrated management of recognised community territories and the commons: ancestral forms of forest protection (Guardians of the river in the Bolivian Amazon or guardians of the forest in the Brazilian Amazon) and socio-community reappropriation of land for collective work, such as the case of the liberators of mother earth in the Cauca region of Colombia.

## Conclusion

In this chapter, our particular interest is directed to the socio-ecological dimension of the multiple crises, which characterises dynamics in South America. In the last two decades, the modalities of appropriation, exploitation, commodification and destruction of nature and the accentuation of multiple forms of dispossession are directly related to the changes and reconfigurations of expanding and intensifying dynamics of capitalist accumulation, mainly resulting from the consolidation and generalisation of development models and state policies based on enclaves and neoextractivist ventures. This has led to dynamics of alteration and affectation of the natural cycles of reproduction of life, subordinating them to the demands of global and regional processes of capitalist accumulation. Therefore, we suggested a framework for comprehensive, contextual and temporal analysis, which is based on current approaches and discussions from or about Latin America. We call this work 'reloaded neoextractivism' to account for its central element in the current configuration and manifestation of the socio-ecological dimension of the multi-crises in this region.

In the chapter, we have analysed and problematised how socio-ecological conflicts, manifest as phenomena that converge diverse actors, some of these in open tension and opposition. We propose a multi-actor perspective of conflicts for a more complex reading of the multiple relationships and the different visions and interests compatible or contrasted, but also of the diverse imaginaries, discourses, strategies and political and societal horizons of these actors. For the analytical axis of this work, we have suggested some actors that we consider key to analyse current processes. We also consider that to account for socio-environmental conflicts, mainly located in specific territorial enclaves, it is necessary to link processes on a local, national/regional and global scale ('glocal' conflicts).

The first fundamental actor we refer to is the State, as a multi-dimensional central political-territorial actor, as a place of assemblages, a space of hegemony and field of power relations which materialise in specific institutional and normative structures. In this sense, the State—beyond the identity and political-ideological orientation (conservative neoliberal or progressive neoliberal)—is a bearer of a certain vision of development and facilitator and executor of policies and extractivist ventures which are functional to processes of capital accumulation, exploitation and commodification of nature. As a second actor, we refer to companies, mainly transnational extractive companies (mining, hydrocarbon, energy, forestry, agro-industrial, etc.) that since the neoliberal period consolidated their presence and influence in the region in alliance with the States. The third actor, with its discursive protagonist claiming alternatives, are socio-ecological movements of territorial base, which proliferated in the face of an increase in extractive deterritorialisation. They have a key role, are complex, contentious and sometimes contradictory, manifest in struggles but also in negotiation and tensions with the other mentioned actors. Considering the current crisis, we have emphasised their capacity for resistance, proactive and prefigurative re-existence of alternative horizons to the current neoextractivism. In sum, we believe that a more detailed multi-actor problematisation of the interrelationship between these and further actors may allow a greater understanding of the complexity of the current context in which the contemporary socio-ecological crisis unfolds in the region.

For a comprehensive reading of the current processes of capitalist accumulation, the dimensions and scope of the ecological crisis, as well as the criticisms of the development models and the alternatives that are woven from the territories, we consider it necessary to analytically link the plurality, complexity of visions, interests, dynamics and interrelation of actors. Without diminishing the importance of the specificity, context and concrete scales of the conflicts, we set out to highlight the vertiginous confluence and structural inherence between socio-environmental conflict and ecological and climatic crisis.

## Note

1 This work is part of the results of the research project "Post-extractivist horizons in Bolivia and Peru: Socio-environmental dimension of the crisis," developed within the CALAS-Tándem-Trasatlántico research grant, 2020–2021 (Maria Sibylla Merian Center for Advanced Latin American Studies in the Humanities and Social Sciences, CALAS).

## References

Acosta, A., and U. Brand. (2017). *Salidas del laberinto capitalista. Decrecimiento y postextractivismo.* Quito: Fundación Rosa Luxemburg.

Alimonda, H. (2011). La colonialidad de la naturaleza. Una aproximación a la Ecología Política Latinoamericana. In H. Alimonda (Ed.), *La naturaleza colonizada : ecología política y minería en América Latina.* Buenos Aires: CLACSO, CICCUS Ediciones, pp. 21–60.

Andreucci, D., and I.M. Radhuber. (2015). Limits to "counter-neoliberal" reform: Mining expansion and the marginalisation of post-extractivist forces in Evo Morales's Bolivia. *Geoforum*, 84, August, 280–291. https://doi.org/10.1016/j.geoforum.2015.09.002

Bebbington, A., A.-G. Abdulai, D. Humphreys Bebbington, M. Hinfelaar, and C.A. Sanborn. (2018). *Governing Extractive Industries. Politics, Histories, Ideas.* Oxford: Oxford University Press.

Benites, G. V., and A. Bebbington. (2020). Political settlements and the governance of COVID-19: Mining, risk, and territorial control in Peru. *Journal of Latin American Geography*, 19(3), 215–223. https://doi.org/10.1353/lag.2020.0081

Blaser, M., and M. de la Cadena (Eds.). (2018). Introduction, Pluriverse. Proposals for a World of Many Worlds. In *World of Many Worlds.* London and Durham: Duke University Press, pp. 1–22.

Bolados, P., and A. Sánchez. (2017). Una ecología política feminista en construcción: El caso de las "Mujeres de zonas de sacrificio en resistencia", Región de Valparaíso, Chile. *Psicoperspectivas,* 16(2), 33–42. https://doi.org/10.5027/psicoperspectivas-vol16-issue2-fulltext-977

Brand, U., and K. Dietz. (2014). (Neo-)extractivism as development option? Towards current dynamics and contradictions of resource based development in Latin America (Neo-) Extraktivismus als Entwicklungsoption? Zu den aktuellen Dynamiken und Widersprüchen rohstoffbasierter Entwic. *Politische Vierteljahresschrift*, 48, 88–125.

Brand, U., and M. Lang. (2015). Entry "Green Economy". In P. Pattberg, and F. Zelli (Eds.), *Encyclopedia of Global Environmental Politics and Governance.* Cheltenham: Edward Elgar, pp. 461–469.

Brand, U., and M. Wissen. (2021). *The Imperial Mode of Living: Everyday Life and the Ecological Crisis of Capitalism.* London: Verso.

Burchardt, H.-J. (2018). Bienestar del tiempo: respuesta latinoamericana frente a la crisis socioecológica. *Nueva Sociedad,* 273, 136–150.

Chaparro, A., M. Scurrah, and A. Bebbingon. (2013). Movimientos sociales, conflictos y posibilidades de cambio institucional en el sector extractivo. In R. Hoetmer, M. Castro, M. Daza, J. De Echave, and C. Ruiz (Eds.), *Minería Y Movimientos Sociales En El Perú.* Lima, Madrid, Barcelona: PDTG, CooperAcción, AcSur Las Segovias, EntrePueblos, pp. 391–402.

Composto, C., and M. Navarro. (2014). Claves de lectura para comprender el despojo y las luchas por los bienes comunes naturales en América Latina. In C. Composto, and M.L. Navarro (Eds.), *Territorios en Disputa. Despojo capitalista, luchas en defensa de los bienes comunes naturales y alternativas emancipatorias para América Latina.* México, DF: Bajo Tierra Ediciones, pp. 33–75.

Costilla, L.O., and S. Pimmer. (2014). Konfigurationen von Staatlichkeit in Lateinamerika. Eine Kartographie der historischen Debatte. In S. Jenss, and A. Pimmer (Eds.), *Der Staat in Lateinamerika: Kolonialität, Gewalt, Transformation.* Münster: Westfälisches Dampfboot, pp. 34–57.

Damonte, G. (2014). El modelo extractivo peruano: discursos, políticas y la reproducción de desigualdades sociales. In B. Göbel, and A. Ulloa (Eds.), *Extractivismo minero en Colombia y América Latina.* Bogota, Berlin: Universidad Nacional de Colombia, Ibero-Amerikanisches Institut, pp. 37–74.

Dargent, E., J.C. Orihuela, M. Paredes, and M.E. Ulfe (Eds.). (2017). *Resource Booms and Institutional Pathways. The Case of the Extractive Industry in Peru (Latin Amer).* London and New York: Palgrave Macmillan.

Dietz, K. (2021). Rohstoffboom und Ausbeutung. Die drohende Ausweitung des Bergbaus zerstört Lebensgrundlagen. *OXI. Wirtschaft Anders Denken,* 4(21) April, 15–16.

Dietz, K., and B. Engels. (2020). Analysing land conflicts in times of global crises. *Geoforum,* 111, February, 208–217. https://doi.org/10.1016/j.geoforum.2020.02.019

De Echave, J. (2018). El fin del superciclo de precios y las presiones para seguir desregulando: el caso peruano. In S. Ramírez, and M. Schmalz (Eds.), *¿Fin de la Bonanza? Entradas, Salidas y Encucijadas del Extractivismo.* Ciudad Autónoma de Buenos Aires: Biblos, pp. 219–232.

De Echave, J., A. Diez, L. Huber, B. Revesz, X. Ricard, and M. Tanaka. (2009). Minería y conflicto social. In *Instituto de Estudios Peruanos,* pp. 1–428. http://repositorio.iep.org.pe/handle/IEP/639

Duit, A., P.H. Feindt, and J. Meadowcroft. (2016). Greening Leviathan: The rise of the environmental state? *Environmental Politics,* 25(1), 1–23. https://doi.org/10.1080/09644016.2015.1085218

Durand, F. (2016). *Poder político y gobierno minero.* 30. Lima: CooperAcción.

Escobar, A. (2018). *Designs for the Pluriverse: Radical Interdependence, Autonomy, and the Making of Worlds.* Durham, NC: Duke University Press.

Esteva, G. (2011). "Otra autonomía, otra democracia", en *Pensar las Autonomías.* In Jóvenes en Resistencia Alternativa (Ed.), *Alternativas de emancipación al capital y el Estado.* México, DF: Editorial Bajo Tierra, pp. 121–150.

Esteva, G. (2082). *La batalla en el México rural,* México : Siglo XXI, 1982.

Fini, D. (2016). Territorio como paradigma en las luchas sociales contemporáneas. In D. Navarro Trujillo, and F. Mina Lorena (Eds.), *Despojo capitalista y luchas comunitarias en defensa de la vida en México. Claves desde la Ecología Política.* Mexico: Instituto de Ciencias Sociales y Humanidades "Alfonso Vélez Pliego", pp. 93–110.

Friedman, M. (1970). The social responsibility of business is to increase its profits. *The New York Times Magazine*, pp. 31–35. (13 September). https://doi.org/10.1007/978-3-540-70818-6_14

Gudynas, E. (2015). *Extractivismos. Ecología, economía y política de un modo de entender el desarrollo y la naturaleza.* Cochabamba: CLAES/CEDIB.

Gudynas, E. (2018). Extractivismos: conceptos, expresiones, impactos y derrames. In S. Ramírez, and M. Schmalz (Eds.), *¿Fin de la Bonanza? Entradas, Salidas y Encucijadas del Extractivismo.* Ciudad Autónoma de Buenos Aires: Biblos, pp. 19–36.

Harvey, D. (2004). The "new" imperialism: Accumulation by dispossession. *Socialist Register*, 40 (The New Imperial Challenge), 63–87.

Hoetmer, R. (2013). Minería, movimientos sociales y las disputas del futuro: claves de lectura y pistas de reflexión-acción. In R. Hoetmer, M. Castro, M. Daza, J. De Echave, and C. Ruiz (Eds.), *Minería Y Movimientos Sociales En El Perú.* Lima, Madrid, Barcelona: Programa Democracia y Transformación Global, CooperAcción, AcSur Las Segovias, EntrePueblos, pp. 265–282.

Hofmann, S., and D.M. Cabrapan. (2021). Gender and natural resource extraction in Latin America: Feminist engagements with geopolitical positionality. *European Review of Latin American and Caribbean Studies*, 111(111), 39–63. https://doi.org/10.32992/ERLACS.10653

Kaltmeier, O. (2020). *Refeudalisierung und Rechtsruck. Soziale Ungleichheit und politische Kultur in Lateinamerika.* Bielfeld: University Press.

Lander, E., and S. Arconada. (2019). *Crisis civilizatoria. Experiencias de los gobiernos progresistas y debates en la izquierda latinoamericana.* Guadalajara: CALAS, Universidad de Guadalajara.

Lang, M., and R. Hoetmer. (2019). Introduccion. Buscando alternativas más allá del desarrollo. In M. Lang, C.-D. König, and A.-C. Regelmann (Eds.), *Alternativas en un mundo de crisis. Grupo de Trabajo Global Más Allá del Desarrollo.* Quito: Fundación Rosa Luxemburg; Universidad Andina Simón Bolívar, pp. 8–27.

Le Billon, P. (2015). Environmental conflict. In *The Routledge Handbook of Political Ecology*, pp. 598–608. https://doi.org/10.4324/9781351268646-13

Leff, E. (2018). *El fuego de la vida. Heidegger ante la cuestión ambiental.* México: Siglo XXI Editores.

Leiva, F. (2019). Economic elites and new strategies for extractivism in Chile. *European Review of Latin American and Caribbean Studies*, 108, 131–152. https://doi.org/10.32992/ERLACS.10511

Loayza, N., and J. Rigolini. (2016). The local impact of mining on poverty and inequality: Evidence from the commodity boom in Peru. *World Development*, 84, 219–234. https://doi.org/10.1016/j.worlddev.2016.03.005

Luxemburg, R. (2007[1913]). *La Acumulación del Capital.* Edición de Laurat Lucien. La Plata, Argentina: Terramar ediciones.

Makaran, G., and P. López. (2018). *Recolonización en Bolivia. Neonacionalismo y resistencia comunitaria.* México/Buenos Aires/La Paz: Bajo Tierra, El Colectivo, Plural.

Martinez-Alier, J., and M. Walter. (2016). Social metabolism and conflicts over extractivism. In F.M. de Castro, and B.B. Hogenboom (Eds.), *Environmental Governance in Latin America.* New York: Palgrave Macmillan, pp. 58–85.

Moore, J.W. (Ed.) (2016). *Anthropocene or Capitalocene? Nature, History and the Crisis of Capitalism.* Oakland: Kairos.

Moreano, M., F. Molina, and R. Bryant. (2017). Hacia una Ecología Política Global: aportes desde el sur. In H. Alimonda (Ed.), *Ecología política latinoamericana: pensamiento crítico, diferencia latinoamericana y rearticulación epistémica/.* Buenos Aires, Mexico: CLACSO, Universidad Autónoma Metropolitana, CICCUS Ediciones, pp. 197–212.

Navarro, M. (2018). Despojo múltiple y separaciones del capital sobre el tejido de la vida. In F. Sierra (Ed.), *Teoría del valor, comunicación y territorio.* Madrid: Siglo XXI, pp. 277–296.

O'Ryan, R., and C. Ibarra. (2016). Environmental policy in Latin America. In A. Farazmand (Ed.), *Global Encyclopedia of Public Administration, Public Policy, and Governance.* https://doi.org/10.1007/978-3-319-31816-5

Pacto Ecosocial Del Sur. (n.d.). Retrieved December 10, 2020, from pactoecosocialdelsur.com

Paredes, M. (2016). The extractive industries and society the glocalization of mining conflict: Cases from Peru. *The Extractive Industries and Society*, 3(4). http://dx.doi.org/10.1016/j.exis.2016.08.007

Porto-Gonçalves, C.W. (2010). *Territorialidades y lucha por el territorio en América Latina: Geografía de los movimientos sociales en América Latina.* IVIC: Caracas.

Porto-Gonçalves, C.W. (2002). *Geo-grafías. Movimientos sociales, nuevas territorialidades y sustentabilidad.* Siglo XXI: México.

Porto-Gonçalves, C.W., and E. Leff. (2015). Political ecology in Latin America: The social re-appropriation of nature, the reinvention of territories and the construction of an environmental rationality. *Desenvolvimento e Meio Ambiente*, 35. https://doi.org/10.5380/dma.v35i0.43543

Quijano, A. (2000). Coloniality of power, eurocentrism, and Latin America. *Nepantla: Views from South*, 1(3), 533–580. https://doi.org/10.1515/9780822388883-009

Ramírez, M. (2018). Redes de extracción y conflictos sociales en Latinoamérica. In M. Ramírez (Ed.), *¿Fin de la Bonanza? Entradas, Salidas y Encucijadas del Extractivismo.* Buenos Aires: Biblios, pp. 297–314.

Rivera, C.S. (2010). *Ch'ixinakax utxiwa: Reflexión sobre prácticas y discursos descolonizadores.* Tinta Limón: Buenos Aires.

Silva, E., N, Akchurin, and A. Bebbington. (2018). Policy effects of resistance against mega-projects in Latin America: An introduction. *European Review of Latin American and Caribbean Studies*, 106, 25–46. https://doi.org/10.32992/erlacs.10397

Svampa, M. (2015). Commodities consensus: Neoextractivism and enclosure of the commons in Latin America. *South Atlantic Quarterly*, 114(1), 65–82. https://doi.org/10.1215/00382876-2831290

Svampa, M. (2016). *Debates Latinoamericanos. Indianismo, desarrollo, dependencia, populismo.* Ciudad Autónoma de Buenos Aires: Edhasa.

Svampa, M. (2019). *Las fronteras del neoextractivismo en América Latina. Conflictos socioambientales, giro ecoterritorial y nuevas dependencias.* Guadalajara: CALAS, Universidad de Guadalajara.

Svampa, M., and E. Viale. (2020). *El colapso ecológico ya llego. Una brújula para salir del (mal)desarrollo.* Buenos Aires: Siglo XXI Editores.

Tapia, L. (2008). *Política Salvaje.* Buenos Aires: CLACSO, Waldhuter Editores.

Tapia Mealla, L. (2013). *De la forma primordial a América Latina como horizonte epistemológico.* La Paz: CIDES-UMSA; autodeterminación.

Tapia Mealla, L. (2014). Den Staat aus dem Zentrum rücken. Staatstheorie im bolivianischen Kontext. In A. Jenns, and S. Pimmer (Eds.), *Der Staat in*

*Lateinamerika. Kolonialität, Gewalt, Transformation.* Münster: Westfälisches Dampfboot, pp. 155–170.

Teran Mantovani, E., and Svampa, M. (2019). "En las fronteras del cambio de época Escenarios de una nueva fase del extractivismo en América Latina". In *¿Cómo se sostiene la vida en América Latina?* Quito: Fundación Rosa Luxemburg/Ediciones Abya-Yala, pp. 169–218.

Thwaites Rey, M. and H. Ouviña. (2012). La estatalidad latinoamericana revisitada Reflexiones e hipótesis alrededor del problema del poder político y las transiciones. In: M. Thwaites Rey (Ed.), *El Estado en América Latina: Continuidades y Rupturas.* Santiago de Chile: Arsis/CLACSO. http://biblioteca.clacso.edu.ar/clacso/gt/20121127121700/ElEstadoenAmericaLatina.pdf

Thwaites Rey, M., and H. Ouviña. (2019). El ciclo de impugnación al neoliberalismo en América Latina. In H. Ouviña, and M. Thwaites Rey (Eds.), *Estados en disputa*, Buenos Aires: El Colectivo, Bajo Tierra, Desde Abajo, Editorial Zur, pp. 17–63.

Veltmeyer, H. (2016). Investment, governance and resistance in the new extractive economies of Latin America. In K. Deonandan, and M.L. Dougherty (Eds.), *Mining in Latin America. Critical Approaches to the New Extraction*, pp. 27–44. https://doi.org/10.4324/9781315686226-2

Wallerstein, I. (2005). *Análisis del Sistema-Mundo.* México: Siglo XXI.

Zibechi, R. (2008). *Autonomías y emancipaciones. América Latina en movimiento.* México: Bajo Tierra Ediciones.

# 10 Beyond Corporate Social Responsibility

## New territorial management strategies for defeating community-based resistance to extractivism

*Fernando I. Leiva*

In response to escalating struggles against extractivism in Chile, transnational extractive capital began devising after 2011 more effective strategies to defeat community resistance. Through these new strategies, transnational capital intervenes upon the inter-subjective realm of identity, memory and imaginaries so as to embed themselves in the socio-cultural fabric of communities, while simultaneously taking on control over the territorial planning and management of entire provinces where it operates. These emerging corporate initiatives merit close scrutiny as they pose new challenges for activists, communities and scholars as they further narrow possibilities for building genuinely democratic societies.

This chapter offers a succinct overview of these strategies, emphasizing what is distinct and novel about them, exploring how and why they arise, while at the same time presenting lines of sight to assess their impact. It underscores how a flourishing ensemble of transnational capitalist corporate entities, private consulting firms, state agencies, national and transnational non-governmental organizations (NGOs) and academic institutions became a key protagonist in conceptualizing and operationalizing these strategies in targeted territories and communities. This emerging 'epistemic community' of thinkers, practitioners and political, corporate, academic and civil society operatives exercise an increasingly influential 'intellectual, political, and moral leadership' over how Chilean society makes sense of and imagines policies to addresses issues posed by extractivism.[1]

As argued below, these strategies imply a major shift in how transnational extractive capital envisions the tasks, scales and modalities of political intervention it must deploy to successfully defend existing operations and in coming years to expand the extractive frontier. Some scholarly literature describes recent shifts enacted by global corporations as a replacement of traditional Corporate Social Responsibility (CSR) by the more robust Political Corporate Social Responsibility (PCSR) approach (Scherer and Palazzo, 2011), or as a welcomed rise in Multi-Stakeholder Initiatives (MSI) (de Bakker, Rasche and Ponte, 2019a, 2019b). While PCSR and MSI approaches indeed capture recent turns in corporate discourse and business management practices, they

DOI: 10.4324/9781003301981-15

blur key aspects for they deflect attention from a more critical understanding of how these strategies emerge. As Chile shows, these strategies stem from efforts to strengthen a territorialized domination of capital over society in the face of mounting popular opposition.

This chapter examines two emerging strategies piloted by transnational extractive capital in Chile, both of which shift the focus of corporate action to the 'early' socio-cultural embedding of extractive corporations at the local scale. This turn to local socio-cultural embedding aims to preempt communities from relying on citizen participation and Indigenous consultation mechanisms during the environmental permitting stage, which despite their many limitations, have enabled communities that combine social mobilization with litigation to successfully delay and even defeat extractivist projects. This turn to 'early' socio-cultural embedding has also allowed transnational capital to forge new modes for seizing control over territorial planning and management of entire valleys, municipalities and provinces where it operates. Through 'voluntary pre-investment agreements' and the creation of private-public community development corporations, multinational extractivist capital replaces the state as the main actor responsible for territorial management and the production of legitimacy and social cohesion. In a nutshell, these strategies aim to radically reconfigure the relationship between capital, the state and society.

The first variant of these new strategies is the Management of Controversies approach pioneered by the center-left private consulting firm Tironi Asociados that has guided extractive corporations like Antofagasta Minerals in enacting a 'governability from below' in many sites where its operations have been contested by communities.[2] Based on this approach, Tironi Asociados crafted the Somos Choapa initiative to shield Minera Los Pelambres from continued disruptions by community mobilizations and legal actions. Minera Los Pelambres is the crown jewel of the five mines controlled by Antofagasta Minerals and responsible for roughly 50% output and profits generated by this transnational controlled by Chile's Luksic conglomerate. Thanks to its Los Pelambres operation, Antofagasta Minerals has become the tenth largest copper producer in the world.

The second strategy, based on the Análisis Estratégico de Sostenibilidad Territorial (AESOT), has been designed and operationalized by Dinámica Plataforma (DP), a consulting firm hired by Newmont Goldcorp-Teck Resources to ensure successful permitting of its Nueva Union project located in the Huasco Province. Nueva Union's $7.2 billion venture is said to be the largest undeveloped copper, gold and molybdenum project in the world.[3] International development agencies such as the Inter-American Development Bank (IDB) and business management journals praise Somos Choapa and Nueva Union, the two projects associated with each of these variants as shining examples of 'best practices of engagement between governments, companies and civil society' (Milano, 2018).

This chapter is organized in five sections. First, I discuss the general context that foregrounds the 'paradigm shift' transnational extractive capital has undertaken in Chile's strategic mining sector after 2011. Second, I thumb-sketch these two strategies, separating the moment of conceptualization from the moment of their operationalization in concrete socio-territories. Such differentiation underscores the network of actors, interests and processes behind their formulation and deployment. The third section discusses the unique traits of these strategies that allow them to alter power relations and re-furbish capitalist hegemony in sites of extraction. After presenting a compressed summary of some of their outcomes in the fourth section, the chapter closes itemizing challenges posed by these new strategies.

## A paradigm shift

In the span of just the past decade, transnational mining capital operating in Chile thoroughly reconceptualized its approach to dealing with community conflicts and introduced major innovations in how it deployed its cadre and resources in disputed territories. In this process, it revamped the scope and nature of its alliances with a wide range of social actors. Indeed, between October 2011, when Santiago's First International Seminar on Social Responsibility in Mining convened to address why companies can no longer afford to take granted their 'social license to operate'[4] and May 2021, when the Catholic University's Centre for Public Policies inaugurated its 10th annual Certificate on Community Relations and the Prevention of Socio-Environmental Conflicts designed 'to provide concepts and tools for community development so as confront the challenge of involving private firms, public services, the State, and local governments with the community', transnational mining corporations managed to successfully craft strategies seeking to more effectively realign the balance of social and political forces in their favor. Joaquín Villarino, the CEO of Consejo Minero, the business organization that groups the largest mining, gold and molybdenum multinational corporations operating in Chile, described such repositioning and new doctrine as a veritable 'paradigm shift' in how these firms strategically manage relations with surrounding communities (Villarino, 2013).

At least six factors explain this paradigm shift unfolding in the world's top copper producing nation: (1) the capacity of socio-territorial resistances to significantly delay, block and shutdown mega-extractivist projects; (2) the increased economic and financial pressure cascading down the 'chain of command' upon mining executives in charge of operations in the Choapa and Huasco Valleys reflecting how intensely 'local' success impacts global corporate operations and markets (volatility in copper and gold prices, quarterly profits, price of shares, etc.); (3) influence by international bodies such as the International Council on Metals and Mining (ICMM) and the University of Queensland's Centre for Social Responsible Mining (CSRM) in revamping the thinking of mining companies (embrace of the UN's Sustainable Development Goals [SDGs], guidelines for community engagement, policies toward Indigenous communities, etc.); (4) plans by the Chilean state for a society-wide effort to significantly increase copper mining output by 2035 which in 2013 led to funding public-private initiatives like Alianza Valor Minero tasked with 'promoting dialogue and agreements among multiple actors'; (5) two decades of center-left administrations disseminating a more ordoliberal perspective for managing conflicts and crises; and (6) the solid track record established by progressive; consulting firms (i.e., Casa para la Paz, Tironi Asociados, Dinámica Plataforma, Espacio Público, Consultora Estratégica) in wielding their soft-power talent, community engagement, media and design skills in paid service to the needs of transnational extractive capital.

A full explanation for transnational extractive capital's paradigmatic shift over the past decade requires explicative frameworks that carefully consider

> the specificities of other levels (local, regional, and national), their history and geography, and the strategies and interests of local actors. [That] not only question the manners in which global forces impact the local level but also ask how local conditions shape global forces and how local actors negotiate or adapt to global dynamics.
>
> (Schorr, 2019: 510)

Indeed, a genealogy of these strategies reveals a dialectical interplay between local, national, transnational actors and scales. Thus, to explain why in Chile (and I believe increasingly elsewhere) CSR has been discarded as a primary tool for neutralizing community resistance to extractivist projects, we not only require an analysis that moves back and forth across scales but one also capable of illuminating how material and meaning-making dimensions co-constitute the hegemonic capabilities of capitalist economic actors, as well as the popular resistance to them.

## Two strategies

> *The ability of any social actor to promote its interests and alter the balance of forces in their favour depends to a great extent on their capacity to learn, craft a guiding set of ideas and unifying discourse, and forge unity of action in the face of ever-changing circumstances. In the case of the strategies considered here, the role played by situated actors —the Chile-based executive teams of Antofagasta Minerals and Nueva Union— and the constellation of relationships with the staff of consulting firms like Tironi Asociados, Dinámica Plataforma, and Columbia University's Centre for Sustainable Investment (among others) becomes a key entry point. Tracing out how these actors simultaneously intervene upon different geographic, temporal, and semiotic scales helps us to understand the genesis, innovation, and evolution of these strategies.*

A shared background condition for both cases discussed below is that they involve multi-billion dollar mining projects in narrow valleys with relatively small populations and towns, and where livelihoods has been historically linked predominantly to small-scale agricultural activities. Community concerns about water and the threat which large-scale copper and gold mining represents to this vital resource has fueled community contestation for decades (i.e., Caimanes, El Mauro tailings dam, El Morro, Barrick Gold, AgroSuper). In both the Choapa and Huasco valleys, an upsurge of resistance to extractivist operations has been the main factor pushing transnational extractive capital to adopt the emerging territorial management strategies described below.

## Somos Choapa—managing controversies—Tironi Asociados

Jean Paul Luksic, CEO of Antofagasta Minerals, owner of Los Pelambres mine in Choapa Province, explains the shift in corporate thinking as follows:

> Los Pelambres is inserted in a geographically narrow agricultural valley. It has little more than 91 thousand inhabitants, distributed in 42 communities. This makes Los Pelambres a unique case of a large-scale copper mine, located in an area surrounded by nearby towns and farms....The blockage of roads made it very easy to interrupt our supply chain. There was judicialization and we faced legal defeats in court. The result: growth stopped, investment 'stagnated' for years. All this in a mineral-rich zone with reserves for the next 100 years. In sum: we did everything all wrong.
>
> (Luksic 2018, 4 [my translation])

The solution was a major rethink of how Antofagasta Minerals conceived its relationship to the territory and communities surrounding Los Pelambres. This meant abandoning both its earlier transactional approach and short-term CSR perspective which had led the company to juggle over the years more than 60 separate clientelist agreements with different community members:

> In the long run, such [approach] became a risk for our operation. (...) So, the first task was to rethink our connection with the territory. Is it enough to manage our operational risks with a short-term view, or should we understand that we are relevant neighbors in the generation of development dynamics that extend well beyond the direct impact of our operations?
>
> (Luksic, 2018: 5 [my translation])

Thanks to support from Tironi Asociados, and the political technologies articulated in Somos Choapa—the entity created in 2014 after years of field work by Tironi Asociados in the province—Minera Los Pelambres radically reconceived its role in the Choapa Valley where it had been present since 1996. This meant changing not only how it saw its relation with surrounding communities but also reconceptualizing how MLP connected to the overall development of the entire province. Thus, the unit of analysis for conceiving its territorial embedding expanded from just the mine's 'surrounding communities' to the entire Province of Choapa and the four municipalities of Canela, Salamanca, Illapel and Los Vilos conforming it. Through the creation of a public-private entity like Somos Choapa, Minera Los Pelambres strove to 'rebuild trust lost' thanks to a comprehensive province-wide portfolio of development projects defined through a participatory and consultative process that involved community organizations, local and provincial government representatives, schools and cultural centers from all four municipalities. Somos Choapa enabled Minera Los Pelambres to establish a single centralized platform for managing a broad portfolio of infrastructure and community development projects managed legitimized through hegemonic participatory techniques.

## Nueva Union—Dinámica Plataforma in the Huasco Valley

The second case study involves the Nueva Union project in Atacama's Huasco Valley, one of the largest greenfield mining projects in the Americas. For Newmont-Goldcorp/Teck's Nueva Union project, the AESOT strategy endorsed by Dinámica Plataforma and Valor Minero, purports to be more of 'forward looking'. Through 'early community participation', and 'territorial dialogues', the Nueva Union/Dinámica Plataforma team sought to embed this project in the social and cultural fabric of the Huasco Valley. Planned to be in operation for four decades, Nueva Union would allow transnational capital to extract 190,000 tons of copper and 315,000 ounces of gold per year. Though a 'new project', Nueva Union's consultants were acutely aware that since the 1990s decades of community resistance successfully paralyzed Barrick Gold Pascual Lama's project and derailed the AgroSuper and El Morro project in the province, events that had created a sense of empowerment among community members (Lorca and Silva-Escobar, 2020). It is worth noting that in 2012, before deciding to a joint-venture, Goldcorp faced a major defeat when the Chilean Supreme court ratified a decision that rendered its environmental assessment for the El Morro mine null, due to irregularities 'including the company's failure to properly consult with the Diaguita Huascoaltinos Indigenous and Agricultural Community, whose lands would be destroyed if the mine is built'. Thus, just like in the case of Los Pelambres in Choapa, the adoption of a more effective strategy for territorial embedding in Huasco was also informed by community resistance.

Glossing over Goldcorp's 2012 failure in the Huasco Valley, one Nueva Union consultant from Columbia University's Centre for Sustainable Investment and current Program Officer for Sustainable Management of Mineral

Resources for Germany's development agency (GIZ), Nicolas Maennling, claimed that, '[a] good example of a multi-stakeholder planning process around a mining project comes from Huasco Province in Chile where Columbia University's Centre for Social Investment (CCSI) and Dinámica Plataforma supported Nueva Union in the elaboration of a development roadmap for the region' (Maennling and Correa, 2020: 12). The reason why this initiative gets such attention is that it piloted a new political technology carefully created by public and private actors with support from the IDB:

> To receive the backing and support of local stakeholders, the project proponents engaged in *an exemplary bottom-up community participation process even prior to obtaining the necessary approvals* from the authorities to develop the mine. The value proposition of the project seeks to move towards a scenario of co-existence with all the interests present in the territory
>
> (Maennling and Correa, 2020: 13 [emphasis added])

This new approach christened as a Strategic Analysis of Territorial Sustainability (AESOT), offers a methodology that 'frameworks early on dialogues, so that they lead to the sustainable development of territories where large investment projects operate' (García 2021: 55 [my translation]). These dialogues bring together community members, government officials and corporate executives, for an early identification issues of high concern to community members. If not addressed in the stage of project design, the issues have the potential of fueling protracted conflicts that will delay construction and starting date for extraction. In the case of large-scale mining projects (those between US$3 to US$5 billion), these delays can mean losses estimated to run US$20 million per day (Garcia, 2021).

In light of these considerations, through deployment of AESOT, Nueva Union attempted to territorialize its influence and leapfrog over those potential snags that could arise from state-sanctioned citizen participation during the environmental permitting stage. With the assistance of the private consulting Dinámica Plataforma and supported by CSSI, Nueva Union and its collaborators spent two years doing 'field work' in the Huasco province, contacting local organizations, organizing 'open houses' and 'community dialogues' so as to launch on March 29, 2019 its comprehensive plan for the 'holistic' development of the region, the *Hoja de Ruta para el Desarrollo Sustentable de la Provincia de Huasco* [Roadmap for the Sustainable Development of the Huasco Province]. In offering a grand plan for the development of the entire province, Nueva Union sought to deeply embed itself in the social, economic and cultural fabric of the region, claim its place as one more legitimate and good-hearted neighbor and control the direction of the territorial development of the region.

The devised Roadmap consists of five pillars for territorial development that converge in a 'common vision' crafted through a series of social dialogues that, in a province of more than 70,000 inhabitants, involved only 100 individuals. Enrobing itself with the mantle of the UN's SDGs, the Roadmap reflects the many dimensions extractivist multinational corporations are incorporating into their discourse and political attention. Thus, the Roadmap includes the following sections:

1 **Our Huasco,** which recognizes the value of heritage and the cultural roots of the territory.
2 **Human Huasco,** which puts at the center the need for inclusive and equitable development.
3 **Prosperous Huasco,** which promotes economic growth and productivity.
4 **Integrated Huasco,** which highlights the importance of multi-stakeholder partnerships that promote participation of its citizens and collaboration between the public and private sectors.
5 **Natural Huasco,** where the challenges of ecological sustainability and climate change are addressed (Nueva Union, 2019).

The process designed by the Dinámica Plataforma/CCSI/Nueva Union team did not require that dreams for a better future life be extracted from the community through technologies of hybrid forums preferred by Tironi Asociados.[5] Rather, the Huasco Valley, Nueva Union and its consultants could readily use those off the shelf imaginaries provided by the UN's 17 SDG framework: 'Using the SDGs as a guiding principle throughout the process helped to get the various stakeholders to agree on development objectives' (Maennling and Cortes, 2020: 13).

## Stylized sequence of territorial deployment of these strategies

Despite their different orientation ('backward-looking in the case of Choapa vs forward-looking' in the case of Huasco), both strategies share important methodological aspects. These can be depicted in stylized manner as consisting of seven stages or facets.

1 Map local actors and perform an initial assessment of the socio-economic and politico-cultural situation in the territory using techniques drawn from the social sciences. Most of the consultants from Tironi Asociados and Dinámica Plataforma have university studies and graduate degrees from European and North American Universities, and some are researchers affiliated to the Centro de Estudios sobre Conflicto and Cohesion Social (COES) located in Santiago.
2 Organize 'social dialogues' in different localities and municipalities using a consciously designed methodology to collect from neighbors and community organizations their sentiments, aspirations and dreams about the future (i.e., hybrid forums, territorial dialogues, open houses). Through consultation with community participants, these events help identify

priority areas and goals. This kind of 'early citizen participation' prior to and outside the norms established by Environmental Impact Assessment (EIA) procedures, allow corporate agents a well-timed identification deeply felt issues that need to be addressed by extractivist projects so as avoid large-scale community resistance.

3 Process collected information to formulate a territorial development plan containing specific goals, priorities and time frames. The plan should reflect deliberate commitments from the multinational extractivist corporation, different government agencies and local community organizations to implement the crafted 'shared vision' of local development that conveniently incorporates the extractivist project at the core (i.e., Portfolio of Development Projects; Roadmap).
4 Present this plan to the community, creating visually attractive means for the community to monitor progress in each of the agreed upon objectives (viz Tironi Asociados and Elemental, 2017; 2020).
5 Create a central entity, a private-public-civic consortium or community development organization tasked with managing agreed upon projects. This entity coordinates technical teams from the private and public sectors, with involvement from different community organizations (i.e., Somos Choapa, CreoAntofagasta, Calama PLUS, Somos Illapel, PRES Contitución).
6 Align municipal and provincial government development plans and procedures to the establishment of the mega-extractivist project in the territory, so that the goals in the territorial development plan can be monitored using data-driven analysis of indicators and the latest digital technologies (GIS, Satellite Imaging, Real Time monitoring). Such efforts justified on the basis of the need to have a comprehensive view and means for assessing the plan's unfolding provides a unique opportunity to drive the local restructuring of the state to better serve the needs of capital.
7 Produce documentary film and well-designed media campaigns that continuously celebrate the emergent local identity normalizing the presence of the extractivist corporation in the territory.

These strategies and methodologies have received wide praise from international development agencies and corporate media. In the case of Nueva Union, its strategy has been presented as enacting of the world's best practices for community and government engagement with extractivist corporations:

> In August 2016, an early citizen participation process was initiated, with the purpose of informing and including local communities at an early stage in the development of the project's Environmental Impact Assessment (EIA), and finding a consensus on the mechanisms for dialogue that could help discover the topics of interest and concern, while including them in the progress and outcomes.
>
> (Milano, 2018: 24)

One should note that the Nueva Union project has not received official permits by the country's environmental authority or moved even beyond the feasibility stage. Such lavish praise is bestowed on Nueva Union's AESOT initiative, perhaps because it prefigures how to overcome community resistance and accelerate the circulation of capital, the very heartbeat of neoliberal capitalist modernity. As one of Nueva Union's endorsers points out: this process was the first of its kind in the country and sought to respond to the problems of the community *in such a way that the company's operations could be carried out without significant delays* (Milano, 2018: 31).

Using the procedures schematically presented here, transnational extractivist corporations seek to reformat power relations, identities and imaginaries in the territory of operations so that the accumulation of capital can proceed unimpeded.

## Distinctive traits

So what are the unique and novel characteristics about these strategies? Why do we need to pay much closer attention to them? As pointed out elsewhere, these new corporate repertoires, 'represent a nascent form of politics which disputes the role of the state and reconfigures statecraft, enacting artisanal politics targeting local relational, emotional, dialogic, identitarian, memory, interpersonal place-based subjectivity-making processes, to yoke them into the service of transnational capital' (Leiva, 2019: 146). From a broader perspective, these strategies ratchet up the reliance of capitalist domination on hegemonic participatory politics and the 'socio-emotional turn' (Leiva, 2021). They prefigure thus new modalities through which transnational capital aims to overcome the prolonged political, economic, social and ideological crises of 40 years of global neoliberalism.

> Although older political technologies like on-going state repression and targeted assassinations (*sicariato*) in Wallmapu (ancestral territory of the Mapuche people) and against territorial defenders, cooptation of social movements through clientelism, and disciplining through the 'cruelties of the market' (subjection through debt), all remain in use by Chilean state and corporate actors, the new strategies discussed above rely on a different set of levers and dispositifs.
>
> (Leiva, 2018)

There are at least five distinctive traits that have been intentionally designed as part of the 'intellectual processing of reality' underpinning these strategies. Just like the self-valorization of capital perpetually strives to colonize new realms of social existence, these strategies reveal a quantum leap in the political technologies wielded by capital. They illustrate how capitalist domination transforms place-based identities, territorial memory, imaginaries become a field of capitalist domination and contestation Each of these traits is briefly and separately listed below.

## Dialogue is harnessed as a technique of domination

Given the failures of the old CSR approach, the promotion of 'early citizen participation' and 'territorial dialogues' are celebrated as mechanisms that allow investors to opportunely incorporate local knowledges in the design stage of mega-mining projects. Dialogue is used to detect early on potential 'conflict hot spots', so as to achieve greater levels of support for project execution (Schaeffer, 2013). Community involvement and territorial dialogues organized by Tironi Asociados and Dinámica Plataforma are carefully orchestrated affairs.[6] Based on the contributions of Action Network Theory, French pragmatic sociology and the 'regimes of worth' social science literature (Thevenot, Boltanski, Chiapello), these 'territorial dialogues' seek to unearth information that will allow consultants to accurately map the emotional scaffolding and moral structure behind a community's arguments and stances (see Leiva, 2019). This mapping allows for more effective corporate interventions for manufacturing community consent. After more than a decade and half of organizing such dialogues for corporate employers, Consejo Minero and Chilean state agencies (Ministry of Energy, Consejo de Producción de Energía Limpia, Agencia de Sustentabilidad y Cambio Climático), one can draw the conclusion that inviting communities to sign binding 'voluntary pre-investment agreements' can be an effective method to preempt conflicts.

To ensure that 'territorial dialogue' serves the interests of mega-investment projects, actors like the Consejo de Producción de Energía Limpia and Valor Minero have gone to great lengths to design ways of institutionalizing legally binding protocols establishing how corporate and community members must agree to participate in said dialogues.[7] After two years of work, in late 2018, an ensemble of public, private, non-governmental and academic entities, such as Valor Minero, Focus Consultores, Rubik Sustentabilidad, Espacio Público, Casa de la Paz, Centro de Políticas Públicas of Universidad Católica and the Program on Conflict Mediation of Universidad Alberto Hurtado, unveiled the grand proposal presented to the Chilean Congress for the creation of an Agency for Territorial Dialogue (ADT).[8] Behind its conception, one finds that the liberal myth of the market as a site where voluntary exchanges among equals, has been transposed onto the realm of territorial dialogues. Thus, in the ADT proposal, the recently arrived representative from Newmont-Goldcorp/Tech Resources planning a US$7.2-billion project has equal valence and is just a 'good neighbor' as don José, the small-scale Indigenous agricultural producer with limited or no water rights and who has lived his entire life in the valley. Hence, these new political technologies for territorially embedding extractivist capital rest on the myth that both the representative from Antofagasta Minerals or Newmont/Teck can sit next to community members to discuss the future of the valley under the same conditions and arrive at a shared vision of the future. And all of this, thanks to the allegedly disinterested technical support provided by the ADT and its phalanx of certified NGO facilitators to be funded by transnational extractive corporations and the state (Leiva, 2019).

## New mechanisms for territorial planning and control

Under the umbrella of discourses about 'creating value in the territory', a new political entity thrives and multiplies: the 'private-public-social' consortium begotten through carefully orchestrated territorial dialogues. With extractivist transnational corporations firmly at the center, this new community development entity is entrusted with conceiving, directing and managing a portfolio of investments designed to promote 'sustainable territorial development' of entire provinces where extractive capital operates. The two variants considered here—Somos Choapa and the Roadmap for a Sustainable Development of Huasco—enable transnational extractive capital to create a centralized platform from which to articulate and control all 'stakeholders'—both proximate and distant—in their sphere of influence. Such dispotifs allow extractive capital to better and legitimately directly control a broad spectrum of variables affecting present and future operations.

## Synching temporalities to the needs of extractive capital

These strategies emphasize the importance of promoting 'territorial dialogues' and 'early community participation' for the purpose of 'unblocking' investment projects, and in so doing aim to synch the temporalities of communities and state bureaucracies to the quicker temporalities of capital. The Agencia para el Diálogo Territorial proposed by Valor Minero clearly states that its goal is to 'anticipate problems afflicting investment projects to that they can become viable... What we are proposing is a pre-judicial institutional framework capable of resolving these conflicts to avoid their litigation, and that this early step be legally binding'.[9]

Hence, citizen participation guaranteed by the state during the environmental permitting stage is privatized. By preempting conflicts in an earlier stage of project development, encasing them in private agreements that are signed before a notary public, this mechanisms strips communities of the right to use the court system during the environmental permitting stage. One important outcome is the subordination of vastly different temporalities to that of the owners of capital and investors in large mega-mining projects.

## Alter place-based identities and historical memory

Through the use of films,[10] carefully curated exhibits, staged events, visually attractive and carefully designed websites, extractive corporations and their consultants attempt to reconfigure place-based identities. Mining is represented as an ancestral practice existing in these valleys since pre-Inca times, an activity that has always co-existed with agriculture. Emphasis is placed on how these valleys' unique identity has allowed them historically to adapt to new developments and continue thriving while retaining their identity. In this manner, transnational extractive corporations and their mega-mining projects are naturalized and passed off as 'one more neighbor' with equally legitimate rights to shape the future of the valley and province as everyone else. A right that can't be denied, since the ones convening, hosting and financing the 'social dialogues' where community aspirations are expressed, codified and represented, many times for the very first time, are the extractive corporations themselves.

## Produce supplicant subjectivities

These strategies, particularly as deployed by Tironi Asociados in Choapa, produce new supplicant subjectivities where the possible horizon for a life with dignity is tied to the magnanimity of the extractive corporation invading not only the socio-spatial territories of communities but also all aspects of political decision-making and cultural life.

These strategies invite to dialogue as equals, but the culmination of such endeavors is legally binding agreements that will produce acceptable behaviors on the part of the community along with certainty for the owners of these extractivist corporations. Social peace and dignity thus become dependent on the largesse of extractivist capital; the only access to better material conditions, even modernity, depends now on a friendly treatment of extractivist corporations. Jean Paul Luksic makes clear that transition from 'competition to collaboration' with communities in the territory has a price, one he is not afraid to make crystal clear:

> Nevertheless, if these efforts to reach broad and legitimate agreements are not binding or lack validity in the courts, then legal conflicts will increase, just as will the fractures within communities, as has already happened, affecting their social fabric and checkmating the country's development options. A word of caution here: I am speaking here not only about the possibilities of generating new business opportunities but about the community's access to greater levels of wellbeing and social justice.
> (Luksic, 2018: 6)

The above overview suggests that at least in Chile transnational extractive capital with the help of private consulting firms, state planners, civil society allies and academia has engendered more sophisticated modalities for preempting and defeating community resistance. The literature on CSR, PCSR and MSI manages to ski on the surface of such developments. The content of the last seven International Conferences on Social Responsible Mining held Chile in 2011, 2013, 2015, 2017 and 2019, and the just concluded 2021 event, indicates that there is an evolution to much more refined approach that focuses on assuming the task of direct territorial management, the production of legitimacy and social cohesion, all tasks previously left to the state

## Outcomes

What have been the outcomes of the two strategies presented above? What results have they afforded the Luksic conglomerate's Antofagasta Minerals Minera Los Pelambres in Choapa province and Newmont-Goldcorp and Teck Resources' Nueva Union project in Huasco?

A preliminary assessment is presented along three different axis: (1) project approval/prevalence of conflict, (2) creation of new institutions for territorial management/local embedding; and (3) erasure of the public/private divide.

### Project approval/reduced prevalence of conflict

These strategies were designed to achieve two crucial aims. First of all, it was to preempt a further escalation of socio-environmental conflicts thus avoiding economic costs for stockholders and investors. Second, and most importantly, they aimed to clear a path for obtaining the required EIA certifications. In the case of Minera Los Pelambres, this would allow it to expand the scale of its operations; for Nueva Union to jumpstart its installation in Huasco well ahead of formal Servicio de Evaluación de Impacto Ambiental (SEIA) approval. In both Choapa and the Huasco Valley, the deployment of these strategies succeeded in creating new expectations, channeled local social and political energies through the Open Houses and 'social dialogues' and set the stage for further dividing community members. These strategies succeeded—albeit temporarily—in isolating more critical community voices and in delegitimizing more combative repertories of contention.

### New institutions for territorial management/ local embedding

In both cases, the efforts funded by Antofagasta Minerals and Nueva Union led to the legitimation and establishment of new institutions and instruments for territorial planning—Somos Choapa and the Roadmap for the Sustainable Development of Huasco. Antofagasta Minerals publicly praises 'Somos Choapa', an initiative promoted by Los Pelambres together with the municipalities of Salamanca, Illapel, Canela and Los Vilos that seeks to contribute to the sustainable development of the region and the wellbeing of its inhabitants, as a great dispositif 'for dialogue and conversation' that consolidates a plan for joint work, 'the outcome of a development vision shared among all the actors that live together in this territory, materialized in a portfolio of initiatives jointly supported by the communities, local authorities and the government of the province'.[11]

In the case of Nueva Union, the *Hoja de Ruta* sanctioned a more technocratic endeavor. By choosing the framing provided by the UN's SDGs, and then stressing the importance of establishing quantifiable indicators, Nueva Union, Dinámica Plataforma and Columbia University's Centre for Sustainable Investment performed a crucial power move: align the long-term planning horizon of municipal and provincial governments to the vision and needs of Nueva Union. As the CCSI website states, 'CCSI is also supporting the local governments in Huasco Province, Chile, to develop a data-driven long-term development strategy *that takes into account the large-scale mining investment by Nueva Union, a joint venture of Teck and Goldcorp*'.[12] This is extraordinary as the implicit and explicit assumption behind such statement is that the Nueva Union project, which as mentioned earlier, has not yet gone through the legally sanctioned process of permitting by the country's environmental authority and the citizen participatory approval process, is assumed to be a *fait accompli*. CCSI is already working with local governments to set up a 'data collection system with metrics that are aligned with the SDGs that best captures the development concerns and priorities'[13] outlined in the Hoja de Ruta.

## Erasure of public/private boundaries

Thanks to these strategies important state functions are transferred on to the private sector. Not only is territorial planning and management made to increasingly depend on the initiative of private transnational capitalist actors like Antofagasta Minerals and Newmont/Teck, but with proposals for binding voluntary pre-investment territorial agreements and an Agencia de Diálogo Territorial enthusiastically endorsed by Consejo Minero the country's judicial system is also privatized. Thanks to an ordoliberal discourse, Pinochet's neoliberal state of Pinochet is further transformed into an even more useful instrumentalist role of pimping for extractivist transnational capital. Non-existent public goods, like roads, playgrounds, clinics and vocational high schools, will now be funded by private extractivist corporations seeking to embed and legitimize their operations. Such funding for public goods will be forthcoming not from taxing the rich and mining multinationals but will only come into existence if they have been identified and included in the portfolio of investment projects sanctioned by Somos Choapa or the Roadmap for Huasco Province. This ensures that such investments, co-financed with the public sector, better serve the accumulation and domination requirements of transnational extractivist capital. And such a maneuver will be celebrated as a triumph of new 'collaborative agreements for local development' thanks to NGO facilitators skilled in trafficking in the socio-emotional and deputized to scaffold and puff life into simulacra of dialogue. The erasure of the private/public divide is required to manufacture illusions of equivalence between transnational behemoths such as Antofagasta Minerals, Newmont, BHP-Billiton, and Anglo American and Don Jacinto, Señora Juanita and other 'good neighbors' from communities ravaged by extractivism.

As the Coordinadora por la Vida del Valle de Huasco stated the very day that the Nueva Union's Road Map was unveiled:

> We denounce the cooptation and privatization of the power and role of the state undertaken by those transnati0nal corporations behind Nueva

> Union (Newmont that just bought Goldcorp and Teck). It should not be allowed that a mining corporation be tasked with drawing up the plans and directives, in the last analysis, the development policies for an entire province. This is unacceptable; we cannot allow it, and therefore we call upon public opinion to become alarmed, to wake up, think deeply and see what is really happening.[14]

## Challenges

The conceptualization, operationalization and continuous improvement of these strategies poses numerous challenges for communities, citizens and scholars. These are complex, multi-scalar and multi-dimensional techniques of control and attempts to fully account for them here is necessarily inadequate.[15] Given space limitations, I eschew discussing what these strategies imply for community resistance and opt rather for painting with a very broad brush what these tell us about contemporary efforts by extractive capital to reshape state, economy and society relations so as to better anchor capitalist domination at the local level.

### *1. A new self-aware capitalist-state-civil society-academic complex supporting extractivism*

Capitalist extractivist elites and their allies have learned that governmentality and hegemony must be ensured by constantly acting at the local level and by intentionally intervening upon the corporation's 'eco-system' composed by investors, providers, consumers, employees and residents involved in their business operations. Such effort demands corporate managers embody a new 'mindset' and retool their 'soft-power' skill set so as to more effectively reformat the identity, culture, historical memory and imaginaries of local communities.

Forged by an expanding coalition of corporate executives, consulting firms, state agencies, center-left cadre, NGOs and academic institutions, the emergent political technologies (territorial dialogues, early community participation, voluntary pre-investment agreements, collaborative territorial planning) and accompanying discourses aim to defeat community resistance by lodging extractivist imaginaries and forms of governance deeply within the socio-territorial and socio-emotional spaces whence such resistance nestles (Leiva, 2019). These novel efforts to construct 'governmentality from below' signal a qualitative leap in the learning capacity and political action of transnational extractive capital. Additionally, they imply qualitatively new articulations among different factions of capital and a reconfiguration of circuits of valorization that connect in new ways the mining, water and sewage, electricity and financial sectors. In the case of Chile, the fundamental role played by center-left intellectuals and progressive epistemic communities (UNDP, ECLAC, Acción Ong, academic institutions, private and semi-private consulting firms led by center-left cadre with cosmopolitan graduate training and governmental experience (Tironi Asociados, Valor Minero, Dinámica Plataforma, Espacio Público, Consultora Estratégica, etc.) cannot be ignored. The current 'commodity consensus' is being forged at the interstices of transnational capitalist firms, government agencies, civil society organizations and academia, and this capitalist/government/NGO/academia/international development agencies collaborative is laboring to embed extractivism in the socio-spatial territories of 'communities in movement'. This complex conforms the integument, muscle and sinews of the emerging apparatuses for capitalist domination.

### 2. The omnipresence of capital and the 'new citizenship' of capitalists

These strategies significantly redraw a multiplicity of previously existing boundaries including those separating the 'public' from the 'private' sphere. These strategies further privatize the role of the state and shift responsibility for producing 'social cohesion', 'public goods' and territorial management away from the state and the hallowed institutions of procedural liberal democracy onto the shoulders of a new troika of private sector, local governments and civil society actors. The logic of transnational capital, which during previous decades of global neoliberalism colonized (captured some say) the nation-state and thanks to 'free-trade agreements' forged a bill of rights for capital, has now set its sights on extending their domination to the local territorial level In order to do that, it cannot rely on ministers, generals, bought and paid politicians or international trade lawyers: it must devise new discourses, public persona and agents, to socio-culturally insert itself and be accepted as 'one more member of the community'.

### 3. Updating scholarly frameworks and research agendas

Over the past decade, scholars have made important contributions to the study of extractivism in the region. Critically engaging with the latest analytical frameworks —including calls for an 'expanded notion of extractivism' (Gago and Mezzara, 2018), a 'circuits of extraction' analytics (Arboleda, 2019) and a 'world ecology' perspective (Moore, 2015). The analysis offered in this chapter suggests that such efforts must be complemented by paying much closer attention to emergent 'political technologies' seeking to deeply embed extractivism within the local social, ecological and cultural fabric of communities.

In other words, to fully unravel the scope and politico-ideological implications of the 'new commodities consensus', 21st century 'planetary mine' or 'geographies of extraction in the era of the Pacific Century' and digitalized global logistics networks that make these possible, we must begin paying attention to these emergent strategies.

In the vein of updating the focus of research, transnational extractive capital, at least in Chile, has discarded the notion of CSR and embraced strategies that allow it to more directly enact a new citizenship of capital.

The analysis presented here, underscores the need for examining the conflicts created by extractivism through the lens of an expanded strategic relational approach grounded on critical cultural political economy (Sum and Jessop, 2013; Leiva and Chiasson-LeBel, 2018; Leiva, 2021).

Anthony Bebbington and his collaborators, in their book *Governing Extractive Industries: Politics, Histories, Ideas* (Oxford University Press, 2018) defend the use of a 'political settlements approach' to examine how it informs different territorial projects. Their comparative perspective is heavily focused however on 'the importance of pacts, bargains and elites; the significance of relationships among elites, excluded horizontal factions and lower-level vertical factions; the political drivers of institutional form and performance; and the sources of stability and instability in settlements' (Chapter 1). Such attention to *institutional politics,* though necessary, misses more attentively investigating the new articulations outside traditional institutional channels, where the socio-territorial dimensions of domination, corporate refurbishment of hegemony and grassroots counter-hegemonic struggles currently unfold. Drawing on Marx, Gramsci, Foucault and feminist scholars, among others, we need a much broader framework for examining politics and discursive practices not bounded to institutional politics or the alleged dilemmas of 'resource governance'. If we accept the notion that the mine and extractivism needs to be reconceived as a 'global infrastructural system' as Arboleda (2017) suggests, we also must craft more comprehensive theoretico-analytical and methodological frameworks than what currently prevails in academic discussions.

## 4. *An optimism of the will, the power of resistance and visions of transition*

A last but important point is that despite their apparently sophisticated and comprehensive nature, and the legions of intellectuals, academics, civil society and center-left political cadre committed to continuously upgrading them, these strategies are riven with contradictions.

One resident of the Choapa Valley and early critic Tironi's Somos Choapa initiative, illustrates the fundamental contradiction inherent to these corporate efforts to harness place-based identities, subjectivities and temporalities of life to the valorizing needs of capital:

> ... they have convinced us over time that we are a mining valley, nobody remembers anything of what we were before, and this Thursday will be the final blow thanks to that famous 'Somos Choapa' town meeting, a program that is nothing but a sting of scorpions arrived from the outside, pure poison for our own possibility of conceiving a different economic

> imaginary as a solution to 'extractivism' and its hegemony over something so vital as the human right to have access to uncontaminated safe water.
>
> It is urgent to stop extractivism now! Not only the extractivism promoted by the Luksics but that of all these 'bloodsucking' corporations that are drying up the soul of our valley. To stop them now, is a life-or-death matter.
>
> (Leighton, 2014)

In valleys like Choapa and Huasco, historically based on agricultural activities, the promises of 'virtuous, sustainable, and inclusive mining', by Antofagasta Minerals and Newmont-Goldcorp/Teck and their hired hands from Tironi Asociados and Dinámica Plataforma, CCSI, are sagely understood by popular wisdom as involving nothing more than 'gold plating a turd'. Despite 'early participatory territorial dialogues' being a much glossier wrapping than the old tired CSR packaging, mega-mining remains a form of dispossession involving the loss of land, resources, ways of life and ecosystems. On October 7, 2019, despite all their efforts, Nueva Union declared that it was postponing its much-announced presentation of its EIA. The Movimiento Socio-Ambiental por el Huasco declared,

> This is a victory for the organized community of the Huasco Valley since this action by the corporation is linked to the serious environmental impacts that come with the Nueva Union project and which it can no longer hide from the eyes of increasingly empowered communities; communities that know full well that extractive projects at the headwaters of the Andes and on top of glacial ecosystems are unviable, and that these always attempt to minimize their environmental impact, as we saw with Pascual Lama.[16]

Critics have pointed out how extractivism and neoextractivism (extractivism carried out by progressive governments) 'establishes a vertical dynamic that invades the territories and de-structures regional economies, destroys biodiversity, deepens the process of land concentration evicting or displacing rural, indigenous or peasant communities, and violates processes of citizen decision-making' (Svampa, 2015: 48). We need to deepen this critical perspective to the current strategies making fully visible all of the transnational, national, regional and local actors involved.

Ushering in a social, economic, cultural and ecological transition into more sustainable and equitable society requires finding ways to transition out of current extractivist economies, societies and cultures as pointed out by the July 2020 call for an Eco-Social Pact from the South. And the new emerging strategies for territorial embedding and territorial management operate in the opposite direction by promoting the ontological colonization of these territories by the extractivist logics of transnational capital.

## Notes

1 Following Peter Haas (1992) an epistemic community can be understood as those broad networks of intellectuals, leaders, and academics who, unified on the basis of shared values, diagnosis of societal problems, expertise, and knowledge practices, produce action-oriented policy proposals. For Chile, the evolution of this 'epistemic community' can be traced by examining the proceedings of the seven International Conferences on Social Responsible Mining held in 2011, 2013, 2015, 2017, 2019, and 2021. These show how CSR has been abandoned as a useful framework by extractive capital and very name of the conference changed from Social Responsible Mining to Sustainable Mining. See https://gecamin.com/sustainablemining/index.php#home.

2 Tironi Asociados Management of Controversies evolved into Abierta® as the proprietary political technology at the heart of the Tironi Asociados incorporates the latest trends in progressive social science research produced at elite cosmopolitan universities. It relies on conceptual resources such as soft power, Action Network Theory (ANT), subjectivity, justificatory regimes, transcending technocratic knowledge, harnessing inter-personal dynamics and shared dreams through 'placemaking' (Tironi, 2011).

3 "Newmont, Teck to invest $152 m in Chilean copper-gold project," February 20, 2020. https://www.mining.com/newmont-teck-to-invest-152m-in-chilean-copper-gold-project/.

4 https://gecamin.com/srmining/2011/index0c51.html?option=com_frontpage&Itemid=1.

5 "Hybrid Forums for Urban Controversies" [Foros Hibridos para Controversias Urbanas]. http://helsinkidesignlab.org/blog/hybrid-forums-for-urban-controversies-the-ten-commandments.html.

6 See Brickstarter. "Conversation with Rodrigo Araya from Tironi Asociados". http://brickstarter.org/conversation-rodrigo-araya-tironi-asociados/.

7 See Agencia de Sustentabilidad y Cambio Climático, 'Acuerdos Voluntarios de Pre-Inversión,' https://www.youtube.com/watch?v=drC3fZ4bW10.

8 https://www.espaciopublico.cl/agencia-de-dialogo-territorial.

9 "Valor Minero presentará propuesta para destrabar inversiones," *La Tercera*, April 17, 2018. https://www.latercera.com/pulso/valor-minero-presentara-propuesta-destrabar-inversiones/Mytranslation.

10 See the project and film "Tesoros de Choapa" funded by Minera Los Pelambres." https://www.tesorosdelchoapa.cl/.

11 https://www.antofagasta.co.uk/media/3607/antofagasta-2018-sustainability-report.pdf.

12 Columbia Centre for Sustainable Investment Website, "Localizing the SDGs: Data-driven Development Planning" [my emphasis].

13 Columbia Centre for Sustainable Investment Website, "Localizing the SDGs: Data-driven Development Planning".

14 Valle del huasco, 29 March 2019. Comunicado Cordinadora por la vida del valle del Huasco declara luego de la presentación de "hoja de ruta para el desarrollo sustentable de la provincia del Huasco" por parte del proyecto minero Nueva Unión en Vallenar.

15 I discuss these challenges more thoroughly in the book manuscript *Embedding Extractivism: Political Technologies for Capital Accumulation in an Era of Crises.*

16 Valle del Huasco: Comunicado por retraso de presentación EIA proyecto Nueva Unión. https://www.mapuexpress.org/2019/10/08/valle-del-huascocomunicado-por-retraso-de-presentacion-eia-proyecto-nueva-union/.

## References


Arboleda, M. (2017). "Planetary Mine and the Modes of Existence of Capital," *World-Ecology Research Network Conferences*, September 12. https://www.youtube.com/watch?v=zt5OuTnt8Y0

Arboleda, M. (2019), "From Spaces to Circuits of Extraction: Value in Process and the Mine/City Nexus," *Capitalism, Nature, Socialism*, 31(3), 1–20.

de Bakker, F.G.A., A. Rasche and S. Ponte. (2019a). "Multi-Stakeholder Initiatives on Sustainability: A Cross-Disciplinary Review and Research Agenda for Business Ethics," *Business Ethics Quarterly*, 29(3), 343–383. https://doi.org/10.1017/beq.2019.10

de Bakker, F.G.A., A. Rasche and S. Ponte. (2019b). "Business Ethics and Multi-stakeholder Initiatives on Sustainability: Examining Hidden Issues and Proposing a Research Agenda," *Paper presented at 35th EGOS Colloquium 2019*, Edinburgh, United Kingdom.

Gago, V. and S. Mezzadra (2018), "A Critique of the Extractive Operations of Capital: Toward an Expanded Concept of Extractivism," *Rethinking Marxism*, 29(4), 574–591. DOI: 10.1080/08935696.2017.1417087.

García, A. (2021). "Una nueva forma de crear valor en los territorios: Análisis Estratégico de Sostenibilidad Territorial (AESOT)," *Revista Minería Chilena*, 478(Abril), 55–56.

Haas, P.M. (1992). "Introduction: Epistemic Communities and International Policy Coordination," *International Organization*, 46(1): 1–35.

Leiva, F.I. (2021). *The Left Hand of Capital: Neoliberalism and the Left in Chile*: Albany, NY: SUNY Press.

Leiva, F.I. (2019). "Economic Elites and New Strategies for Extractivism in Chile," *European Review of Latin American and Caribbean Studies*, 108, 131–152. http://doi.org/10.32992/erlacs.10511.

Leiva, F.I. (2018). "El diálogo territorial y la participación temprana como dispositivos de despojo: El capital transnacional extractivista y sus nuevas estrategias." Unpublished monograph.

Leiva, F.I. and T. Chaisson-LeBel (2018). "Sharpening Our Tools, Linking Endeavours. Research on Recent Transformations of Latin America's Capitalist Class. Corporate Strategies and the Role of Economic Elites". https://www.academia.edu/39896082.

Lorca, M. and J.P. Silva-Escobar. (2020). "Conflictividad y acción colectiva en el Valle del Huasco 1990–2019," *Revista Izquierdas*, 49, 4564–4583.

Luksic 2018 (see page 9… two occurrences; page 22; page 24;).

Maennling, N. and J. Correa. (2020). *Best Practices in Data Driven Development in Mining Regions*. New York: Columbia Centre on Sustainable Investment.

Milano, F. (2018). *Extractive Sector and Civil Society: When the Work of Communities, Governments and Industry Is Synonymous with Development* [IDB Monographs]. Washington, DC: Inter-American Development Bank. https://publications.iadb.org/en/extractive-sector-and-civil-society-when-work-communities-governments-and-industries-leads).

Moore, J. (2015). *Capitalism in the Web of Life*. London: Verso.

Nueva Union. (2019). *Huasco: Hoja de Ruta para el Desarrollo Sustentable de la Provincia del Huasco*. http://ccsi.columbia.edu/files/2018/03/Provincia-del-Huasco-Sustentable.pdf.

Schaeffer, J.P. (2013). "Prevencion y resolución de conflictos socio-ambientales," Presentation to the Second International Conference on Social Responsibility in Mining. Santiago.

Scherer, A.G. and G. Palazzo. (2011). "The New Political Role of Business in a Globalized World: A Review of a New Perspective on CSR and its Implications for the Firm, Governance, and Democracy," *Journal of Management Studies*, 48(4), 899–931. Available at SSRN: https://ssrn.com/abstract=1824946 or http://dx.doi.org/10.1111/j.1467-6486.2010.00950.x.

Schorr, B. (2019). "Extractivism in Latin America: The Global-National-Local Link," *Latin American Research Review*, 54(2): 509–516. http://doi.org/10.25222/larr.392.

Sum, N.-L. and B. Jessop. (2013). *Towards a Critical Cultural Political Economy. Putting Culture in Its Place in Political Economy.* Cheltenham UK & Northampton USA: Edward Elgar Publishing.

Svampa, M. (2015). "Commodities Consensus: Neoextractivism and Enclosure of the Commons in Latin America," *South Atlantic Quarterly*, 114(1), 65–82.

Tironi Asociados and Elemental. (2017). *Somos Choapa: Provincia Sustentable, Memoria Anual 2016. Colaboracion para el Desarrollo Territorial.* Santiago. https://somoschoapa.cl/memoria-2016/.

Tironi Asociados and Elemental. (2020). *Somos Choapa/Provincia Sustentable. Memoria 2019. Una mirada a 6 años de trabajo. Colaboración para el Desarrollo Territorial* (preparada para). Los Pelambres: Antofagasta Minerals.

Tironi, E. (2011). *Abierta: gestión de controversias y justificaciones.* Santiago de Chile: Uqbar.

Villarino, J. (2013). "Relacionamiento comunitario: cambio de paradigma y materias de especial reflexión," Presentation to the Second International Conference on Social Responsibility in Mining. Santiago, Chile.

# 11 Communities in resistance

## Forging a communitarian revolutionary subject

*David Barkin*

Who are the peasants/Indigenous people? What role have they played in the history of Mexico? What are their roles in Mexico today and in the future? These are some of the burning questions we face today. I propose: addressing these questions requires rethinking the history of the country since the 1917 Revolution, to question the dominant version of the Mexico's socio-political dynamics. To ask these questions, it is essential to start with maize, because this grain shaped the country and its population over millennia. It is not of minor significance that maize was created in Mesoamerica, the product of the work of generations of Indigenous peoples who carefully transformed it from the original plant, teosinte, with crosses among plants and selection of varieties, to develop the milpa, one of the agroecological systems most admired today in the world.[1] It is also noteworthy that the milpa has contributed to the good nutrition and health of countless generations of Mesoamerican peoples, (re) shaping their social structures and the territory itself. It is not surprising then that, in all the original peoples, there were deities related to corn, be it the Nal of the Mayas, the Cintéotl of the Mexica or those of many other ethnic groups.

In this chapter, we trace the marginalisation of maize in recent decades, as a result of the political vision of the peasantry's irrelevance in Mexican society. This reframing was a deliberate product of the dominance of the imposition of a new model of 'civilisation' guided by pecuniary values and an individualist ethos that promotes destructive competition, built on the basis of a class struggle that is undermining society and threatening the future of humanity on the planet. The argument of this chapter is that it is the peasants who insist on protecting maize, maintaining the great genetic diversity that they inherited and strengthening the traditions that venerate its consumption. Despite their marginalisation, it is the peasants, many of whom are Indigenous, who cultivate, protect and enrich the native varieties, the *criollas*. It is they who assume responsibility to maintain the complex ecosystems where it was born and where it continues to be planted.

The marginalisation of maize and its peoples are not just a peasant tragedy. Nor can they reverse this collapse alone. The peasants insist on growing maize but putting it back in its proper place will require the collaboration of many. That native maize varieties continue to be cultivated seems a miracle,

DOI: 10.4324/9781003301981-16

but it is not so once it is understood that the poetry of the *Popol Vuh* continues as a part of the culture, the belief systems, beyond the lands of the Maya K'iché from which it originated.[2] In a VERY profound sense, Mexicans are still 'made of maize': as the text recounts, it was the very creation of maize that allowed civilisation to flourish, entering into the flesh of people who created it; this was their blood, and from this people were moulded. 'Thus, the maize entered (into the formation of people) through the work of the Progenitors, the Forefathers'.

Although today the peasants seem to be in a precarious situation, it is remarkable that they continue to produce most of the maize that we Mexicans consume. They constitute a very important and misunderstood part of the national population; their ways of living, their communities, their organisations and their production processes offer models of persistence that controvert the long history of predictions of their disappearance. But they are a neglected, misunderstood social group; many consider that their continued existence is a stumbling block for the country's advancement, since these 'globalisers' cannot accept that their traditional productive practices, forms of organisation and worldviews offer alternative paths towards models of society and sustainability that are realistic solutions to many of the crises that overwhelm us today: especially the social and environmental ones.

## A little history

The rural sector suffered enormously in the years following the armed conflict of the Revolution that led to the promulgation of the 1917 Constitution with its unique Article 27. A part of the original text read like this[3]:

> *The property of all land and water within national territory is originally owned by the Nation, who has the right to transfer this ownership to particulars. Hence, private property is a privilege created by the Nation.*
>
> *Expropriation is authorized only where appropriate in the public interest and subject to payment of compensation.*
>
> *The Nation shall at all times have the right to impose on private property such restrictions as the public interest may demand, as well as to regulate, for social benefit, the use of those natural resources which are susceptible of appropriation, in order to make an equitable distribution of public wealth, to conserve them, to achieve a balanced development of the country and to improve the living conditions of rural and urban population. For this purpose, the necessary measures will be dictated for the division of large estates; for the development of the small property; for the creation of new agricultural population centres with the lands and waters that are indispensable to them; for the promotion of agriculture and to avoid the destruction of natural elements and the damage that property may suffer to the detriment of society. The towns, ranches and communities that lack land and water, or do not have them in sufficient quantity for the needs of their population, will have the right to be endowed with them, taking them from the immediate properties, always respecting the small property.*

Although land distribution began even before the end of hostilities, it was not until the presidential administration of General Lázaro Cárdenas (1934–1940) that large areas were (re)distributed among the rural population. In the first 19 years of the agrarian distribution (1915–1934), 11.6 million hectares were distributed to 866 thousand beneficiaries. In contrast, during the Cardenista administration, 729 thousand people received almost 18.8 million hectares, instilling a new dynamic in the Mexican countryside that would continue for almost 30 years.[4] A new era of agrarian progress directly improved the quality of life in 18,000 localities throughout the whole country.

It was a time of great optimism in the Mexican countryside. The Bureau of Experimental Farms (becoming the Instituto de Investigaciones Agrarias—IIA—in 1947) was staffed by a group of agronomists committed to working with the peasants to transform the agrarian reform into a program to inject dynamism into the sector, increasing agricultural productivity and improving social welfare. Their efforts rapidly bore fruit among a population eager to put the land into production. However, in 1943, the Rockefeller Foundation sponsored an 'Office of Special Studies' (OEE),[5] that engendered a deep epistemological and political conflict that continues up to the present day, challenging the way forward to ensure prosperity in the countryside and how to face the world problem of famine, and the definition of who would be the main actors in the process. The Mexican agronomists insisted on the possibility of and need to continue collaborating directly with farmers to improve productivity, taking advantage of their vernacular knowledge of ecosystems and plants and enriching this relationship with the results of the work in their experimental fields. For their part, the team led by North American agronomists insisted on the need to use state-of-the-art technologies to develop new seeds, creating planting areas in areas especially suitable to promote high yields, an approach that would soon be labelled 'The Green Revolution'.

In essence, the dispute between the two approaches was rooted in the role of science and technology in shaping and transforming society; *pari passu*, the different epistemologies reflect contrasting views of who would be the main actors in and beneficiaries of social dynamics (Jennings, 1988). The agronomists and specialists of the IIA were trained in the Revolution, contributed to the Cardenista dynamic, bringing the fruits of the political transformation to all regions of the country and especially to the 'favoured children of the revolution', paraphrasing Arturo Warman (1972). The program was to increase the production of the new land recipients, accompanying the expansion of the social programs of the revolutionary regime. In contrast, the OEE group, and even more so later on with its formalisation as CIMMYT (the Mexican affiliate of the World Bank group of research centres around the world), was strongly influenced by the Malthusian doctrine that dominated the American vision of the 'underdeveloped' world; their specialists focused on breeding new seeds and 'technology packages' supplied by transnational agroindustrial corporations to increase yields. The international team did not consider the differential effects that their approach would have on the use of resources, such as water and agrochemicals, nor were they troubled by favouring one social group or region at the expense of others. These so-called 'second generation' effects were mentioned at the time and remain important as part of the criticism of the 'Green Revolution' response to the problems of famine in the world (Jennings, 1988; Lappé et al., 1999; GRAIN, 2014).

The success of the land distributions with the collaboration of the Mexican agronomists from the IIA did not take long to manifest itself in Mexico. The continuous increases in local food production were significant, driven by a public policy to support the countryside, helping to improve the health and nutrition of the rural population while encouraging the peasantry to supply part of the growing urban demand. In this new political environment, the countryside began to play an important role in prolonging the 'Mexican Miracle', that period of more than three decades of sustained economic growth with price stability (Barkin, 2018: Chapter 1). So spectacular was the impact that President López Mateos was able to declare towards the end of his term (1958–1964) that 'From now on, Mexico will never have to suffer the ignominy of producing tortillas with imported corn!'[6] Rural Mexico was responding to the confidence placed in its protagonists by President Cárdenas.

## Class struggle rears its head

In the two decades following this victory cry, food production stagnated, falling to the point that at the end of the 1960s the country was importing almost half of the maize it required for human consumption. As a result of growing social conflicts and faltering policies, the peasants responded by diverting a greater part of their production to local consumption and diversifying their productive and social activities. Of course, it did not take long to cause crisis and alarm, since increasing parts of the foreign exchange of oil exports had to be redirected from industrial projects to basic foodstuffs.

But falling food production was not the only result. Agricultural policy that had favoured the modernisation of the countryside, with its emphasis on large-scale water projects and investments in the new irrigation districts, began to have dramatic results, benefitting a new class of *neo-latifundistas* (Stavenhagen, 1973; Barkin, 2018, Chapter 6). They found expedited access to credits and subsidised prices for some key inputs produced by state-owned companies. Agricultural research also took a dramatic turn from the improvement of comprehensive diversified production systems towards the production of new high-yield hybrid varieties that could be planted with increasingly mechanised and industrialised systems, taking advantage of the wide availability of virtually free water from dams and underground aquifers and very cheap labour.

To try to counteract this trend, in the 1970s the State created a new organisation, CONASUPO, to promote peasant production by offering guaranteed prices for their crops and subsidies for needed inputs and for basic consumer products. This new approach was complemented by the hiring of brigades of technical advisers who relied on and strengthened peasant organisations to try to increase agricultural productivity. Other complementary initiatives included the creation of agencies to support coffee and sugar output, important export products.

These initiatives provoked strong opposition from different sectors of society. Initially, the business reaction was quieter than the academic one, which mounted an intellectual onslaught to demonstrate that the peasantry was a social group condemned to disappear; its population was redundant and public policy should be devoted to removing it from the countryside. As a consequence, they argued that the diversion of public resources to prolong its existence weakened the advance of the inexorable historical tendencies towards the modernisation of the countryside. Their arguments were supported both on a practical level—the need to encourage the development of modernising agriculture, following the North American model—and encouraged by CIMMYT's research and development programs—on an ideological level. The intellectuals asserted that Marx was clear that only two classes would survive as a result of the development of the productive forces in the evolution of capitalism (Bartra et al., 1975; Bartra, 1978).

A heated debate ensued. Beginning in 1975 (e.g., Escobar, 1978, 1980; Esteva, 1982), another group of intellectuals who defined themselves as '*campesinistas*' (peasantists), responded with a broad discussion of the meaning of historical perseverance in Mexican society of 'the campesinos, this stubborn and clinging protagonist of our history' (Bartra Vergés, 2008: 6). It was not limited to the corridors of the academy, since these advocates were immersed in the formulation and implementation of national agricultural policy and had the ears of the rural organisations that would play a decisive role in the evolution of rural Mexico during the subsequent years. This is not the place to recall the well-documented avalanche of materials that filled the columns of national newspapers and opinion magazines, resulting in important books that will serve to inform future generations of the depth of the social conflict that was brewing.

In this chapter, it is sufficient to briefly elucidate the background of the visions of the rural sector in contention. They represent two opposing models of the country as well as a profound difference in who controls the reins of power, with different approaches to meeting the basic needs of society. On the one hand, productive specialisation based on 'comparative advantages', defined by the relative prices of products in international markets, organised by business groups who would mobilise the necessary resources to apply productive systems and cutting-edge technologies. to organise their activities. In contrast, the opposing model was based on strengthening rural societies, granting them increasing measures of autonomy to organise production and ensure the conservation of their natural environments. This apparently academic discussion reflected the growing class tensions in Mexican society and politics.

In both cases, the State would be responsible for promoting research to take advantage of state-of-the-art knowledge and ensure the availability of productive inputs at affordable prices. However, there would be important differences regarding the direction and use of public research, via property rights and patents, in one instance, while in the other there would be an obligation for the State to identify the benefits of the biocultural heritage created and developed by the communities, protecting it and ensuring that its benefits would contribute to the well-being of these domestic producers.

These contrasting views would manifest themselves as a struggle between competing societies, in very different social structures and production processes. The differences reflect the profound contrast between the diverse worldviews of the many Indigenous and peasant communities and the dominant worldview of the Judeo-Christian world, that surfaced as a powerful business model guided by the principles of 'free-market' capitalism, based on productive efficiency and individual accumulation. Luis Villoro, an influential Mexican philosopher, dramatically expressed this schism in several of his latest books (2001, 2004, 2009) and especially in the last one: *La Alternativa* (2015). In the prologue to this book, Luis Hernández Navarro, summarised it clearly:

> He saw the indigenous societies as promoters of an independent movement with enough power to end the fiction of the hegemony of modernity. A movement with the ability to go from a homogeneous state to a plural one, respectful of their differences, as the path to a radical democracy. A movement with the vision to move from a centralised government to a participatory democracy, and from individualistic association to a true community.
>
> (2015: 17)

## Who are the peasants?

Posing this question involves addressing a history of neglect, abandonment of that part of society that is heir to part of the most brilliant and, at the same time, most neglected history of Mexico. Without going into greater detail, a very important part of this group is Indigenous: in 1987, Guillermo Bonfil Batalla spoke of 'a civilisation denied' (1987) referring to this group; at the time, he quantified it as something more than six million people. A few years later, with the Zapatista uprising (1994), more than eight million were registered in the census and in the INEGI Intercensal Survey of 2015, 25.7 million people self-identified themselves as Indigenous, that is, 21.5 per cent of the total population.[7] They are part of 68 linguistic groups, spread over more than 43,000 localities and constitute a segment of the most vulnerable part of society, according to descriptions by international organisations (IWGIA, 2020). Much of this population is included in the discussion of peasants in Mexico.

Identifying the other groups that make up the peasant ranks is much more difficult. It begins with people living in communities with less than 2,500 inhabitants, the inadequate definition that is still used to define the rural world in Mexico. In 2020, it reported 27.8 million living in these communities (22 per cent of the total population). It is likely that a significant proportion of these people are working in the fields during important periods of the year, when agricultural work requires it. With the information currently available in Mexico, there is no way to estimate the numbers of other demographic groups that could be considered campesinos.

However, workers in the field make a very important contribution to the national economy. The day labourers on whom commercial agriculture depends for their domestic and export markets, especially in the north of the country, constitute a social force of great economic importance, even though their work is poorly paid, and their working conditions pose great risks to their lives and health and that of their family members who often accompany them. To these groups must be added a substantial part of the more than 11 million Mexicans who are working in the rural North American economy and in the various industries that process agricultural and livestock products in the region.

With the profound changes in the Mexican economy and society during the last four decades, there has been a similar transformation in the activities of the rural population—the peasants and their families. The marginalisation that affected the Mexican countryside as a result of the '(neo) liberalisation' of economic policy since the eighties of the last century, including the entry into force of the North American Free Trade Agreement (1994), forced many people to seek employment in urban areas or in the United States. One consequence of these structural changes is the 'feminisation' of the management and cultivation in traditional agriculture, that of small family and/or ejidal plots that has been the territorial and social base for maize production (mainly in the polyculture of the milpa). This development is of considerable import since it is resulting in a diversification of small-scale production and positively influencing the quality of life of families. Continuous increases in the productivity of the milpa in the peasant sector are also reported.

Official data on the quality of life of these social groups suggest a marked marginalisation. However, it is important to consider the profound differences in their worldviews, their lifestyles, social organisation and the relationship with their natural environments when trying to understand the reasons why more than a fifth of the national population (substantially underestimated due to the inadequate definition of 'rural') chooses to remain in these regions. With the growing proliferation of opportunities for peasants to broaden the range of occupations in which they engage, labour pluriactivity has become increasingly important, artistically portrayed in the Mexican films, *El Mil Usos* (1981) and its sequel *El Mil Usos Llegó de Mojado* (1984). This phenomenon also became the subject of academic debate in Mexico, as some preferred to characterise it as the 'semi- or sub-proletarianisation' of these individuals, instead of considering it as part of a complex survival strategy that would strengthen rural society, as we are asserting here.

This process of labour flexibility, migration and feminisation contributed to another important phenomenon in the Mexican countryside: the re-peasantisation that is evidence that their communities are becoming strong institutions contributing to the consolidation of rural societies. The complex transformation of the labour market and the reorganisation of social relations within the communities contributed to the social dynamics that were unfolding during the last quarter of the 20th century as a consequence of the recognition of the futility of trying to achieve a better quality of life and control of their territories within the national economy. To escape from the oppressive cycle of unfulfilled political promises and heightening marginalisation, the communities found themselves obliged to demand and then assert their political and economic autonomy. In a quiet way, one of the first groups to organise to protect their territory and the culture of the Totonac and Nahua groups in the region, by constructing viable cooperatives to organise the production and marketing of their commercial products, coffee and pepper, was Tosepan Titataniske, founded in 1977 in the Sierra Norte de Puebla; its range of activities and services has dramatically expanded since then, improving the lives of the more than 48,000 families who presently participate (Bartra et al., 2004; González Rosales, 2020; Rojas and Mendez, 2020). In other regions, the struggle for autonomy required differing degrees of militancy. This was begrudgingly recognised as legitimate in Oaxaca, with the incorporation of the figure of '*usos y costumbres*' as a mechanism to select people for leadership and ceremonial positions in some local communities. The redefinition of the communities themselves is leading many campesinos to reaffirm their roots as 'communitarian subjects' (Barkin and Sánchez, 2019).

Of course, there is also the Zapatista alternative. Since the dramatic emergence of the Zapatista Army of National Liberation (EZLN) in 1994, a very large area in the southern state of Chiapas has remained under the control of a complex collective governance structure that continues to administer the region in which as many as 500,000 people participate. During the more than a quarter-century they have established the basic institutions and productive systems to assure an improving quality of life while building on the inherited cultural and cosmological processes of the many ethnicities of the Mayan world co-existing in their territory (Mora, 2017). As suggested above, since then numerous other organised efforts to exercise autonomous control community territories and governance structures have emerged throughout Mexico; one of the most dramatic of these is the experience of Cheran, a Purhepecha community in the highlands of Michoacan, where a group of women faced down an organised gang of forest poachers, sparking a collective movement to re-claim traditional customs and governance processes, creating a process to protect their forest and create a new process for improving the community's well-being (Gasparello, 2021).

As a consequence of these complex dynamics, today we find Mexican peasants almost everywhere. They are not only in their communities of origin or in the cities where others were born, survivors of millennia of extraordinary cultures and five centuries of terrible exploitation and marginalization. We find some in the universities, preparing to return, to contribute to realising their productive potential, to assume social and political management responsibilities. Others are abroad contributing by sending remittances that have grown significantly to ensure the survival of their relatives and the strength of local productive systems. In short, today's peasant is a complex figure that reflects a new reality: a world in which millions of people are recognising the need to build new models of civilisation with social and productive structures that contrast markedly with the dominant models in the regions shaped by capitalist accumulation. They are societies marked by their demand for autonomy and control of their territories, their search for social justice, and for forging internal solidarity and with other communities. In these models there are other ways of relating to nature, to forge a different social metabolism that considers the limits of inherited generosity and the possibility of rehabilitating some institutions weakened by past generations.

## The peasantry facing its future

Perhaps one of the most important characteristics of many of the peasant communities in Mexico is the profound difference between their worldviews and that of Judeo-Christian society. Antonio Elizalde, a Chilean philosopher, puts it synthetically in the introduction to a collection of essays on Latin American identity: 'We have gone from being nations proud of our autonomy to being countries dependent on the hegemonic imperial centre'; now, we must realise the urgency of forging:

> A "Patria Grande", (Great Homeland) [which] allows for creating spaces that would allow for a greater and better expression of the enormous cultural diversity that characterises us as peoples. The American people are a melting pot of racial, ethnic, and linguistic identities; of diverse forms of musical, literary, pictorial, artisanal expression, of legal institutions, worldviews and religious conceptions, and many other resources and capabilities that abound among us, that differentiate and enrich us.
>
> (2007: 4)

Increasingly, the societies that are part of this melting pot are demanding more respect and more attention to their traditions, their heritages and their rights recognised and codified in international legislation and incorporated into national jurisprudence with its ratification by most of the countries of the region. The recovery of the heritage of philosophies of their ancestors has become the work of the peoples themselves, even as academics and politicians are taking advantage of them for their own purposes. The claims of the various groups of native peoples and growing numbers of peasant groups for the importance of their origins are more frequent. New discussions proliferate about the meanings of these cosmologies, of the recent systematisation of ways of organising, governing and managing their ecosystems. They are translated into demands for autonomy that are repeated in different ways throughout the region: the alliance of the groups in Canada coalesced into 'Idle No More'; in Ecuador, the Confederation of Indigenous Nationalities of Ecuador (CONAIE) is taking an increasing role in national and regional elections and with the lawsuit against Chevron for ecological damage in the Amazon (Serrano, 2013); in Panama, the formalisation of the institutions of the Kuna people (Bley, 2020); in Chile, the increased stridency with which the Mapuche people are demanding recognition (Meza-Lopehandía, 2019). In Mexico, the discussion of the meaning of 'communality' has become a common theme, even outside the Oaxacan societies from which it emanates, after the publication of several books on the subject (Robles and Cardoso, 2008; Martínez Luna, 2010). These discussions include expressions of other ways of conceiving the paths to the future, another vision of 'the good life'; there are similar expressions embedded in the beliefs of other peoples, throughout Mexico: *Lekil chahpanel* among the Tseltales of Chiapas (Paoli, 2019), *sesi irekani* in Purhépecha de Michoacán (Magaña Mejía, 2017), among several others, including urban organisations (Díaz et al., 2017).

There are many societies that have strategies to advance in process of consolidating their visions of these other worlds. Some have a vision of what Porto Goncalves (2003) calls 'r-existence', a path towards the future, 'reappropriating nature, reinventing its territories and building an environmental rationality' (Porto Goncalves and Leff, 2015; Rivera-Núñez, 2020). To understand these efforts, the need to build a new theoretical lexicon is suggested, in a decolonial framework to accompany them in overcoming the obstacles that are preventing their consolidation as 'community subjects' (Porto Goncalves, 2015). We distilled five fundamental principles that are common to the various groups involved in forging these worlds:

- Autonomy;
- Solidarity;
- Self-Sufficiency;
- Productive diversification; and
- Sustainable management of the local environment (Barkin y Lemus, 2015).

It requires a social capacity for collective living, respecting their traditions and taking advantage of their cultural heritages. It implies the implementation of direct democracy that includes all segments of the population, with a special emphasis on overcoming the historical reluctance to include women in the process. In addition, it implies mechanisms to organise productive activities, considering the limitations in the exploitation of the environment to develop a responsible social metabolism (Fuente et al., 2019).

The peasants will endure. The debate of half a century ago of their disappearance in Mexico seems outdated by reality. Even the textual references to the interpretations of Karl Marx proved inaccurate: in 1881 he wrote a letter to Vera Zasúlich recognising the revolutionary potential of the peasants in Russia (https://www.marxists.org/espanol/me/1880s/81-a-zasu.htm). Today their presence on the world stage is unquestionable: La Via Campesina is the largest social organisation in the world, with more than 200 million members in active organisations located in more than 80 countries (https://laviacampesina.org). Its presence in international and national forums makes it a force that offers a significant dynamic, promoting food self-sufficiency through the combination of traditional knowledge and important innovations of a peasant-informed agroecology (Rosset et al., 2021); The innovations introduced into its practice since its founding in 1993, such as the peasant-to-peasant schools, modelled on the Mexican and Brazilian experience, and its insistence on governance from below, have made LVC a respected and effective voice, particularly in this period of pandemic (James et al., 2021).

Another organisation that is made up of peasants is the Consortium of Indigenous Communities and Conservation Areas, or Territories of Life, which was officially formed in 2010 (https://www.iccacorsotium.org). It represents more than 150 organisations in 81 countries committed to supporting each other in promoting strategies to advance their capacities to improve their quality of life and enforce their claims for autonomy at the regional, national and international levels. These Indigenous communities occupy more than one-quarter of the planet's land area (Garnett et al., 2018; Fa et al., 2020); they are internationally recognised as making important contributions to conserving and enhancing the world's biodiversity, while their accumulated knowledge of natural systems is now considered essential for environmental management (Fernández-Llamazares et al., 2021).

At this time, when the 'world' economy is demonstrating its inability to face social, productive and environmental challenges, there is a great urgency to seek alternatives (Esteva, 1982). Peasant societies and Indigenous peoples are not limiting themselves to outlining strategic proposals. They are building the many worlds we need to overcome today's problems with models that could perhaps contribute something to the quest that many in the 'globalised' societies have not found. The Global Tapestry of Alternatives is another example of the way in which individual communities are weaving their experiences together into a broader framework on a worldwide scale (https://globaltapestryofalternatives.org/) (Kothari, 2020).

## The communitarian revolutionary subject

The proud history of the Mexican peasant and Indigenous communities is still being (re)written. Just as Mexico is still coming to grips with events that unfolded with the waves of landings of the first Spanish adventurers at the beginning of the 16th century, years before the 'fall' of Tenochtitlan in 1521 (Salmerón Sanginés, 2021), we have yet to realise the full import of the renewed assertiveness of the thousands of communities that are no longer content to accept their place as obedient subjects in the globalising order in which Mexico has placed itself.

This confidence is now evident in myriad examples of groups of communities that are insisting on 'going their own way'. Consolidating their societies and developing new paths for strengthening their productive systems, attending to the basic needs of their members and assuring adequate educational opportunities and health care, while taking care to minimise their abuse of the environment and conserving its biodiversity and ecological balance.

This litany of responsibilities is imposing. And yet, the communities are assuming them with vigour and seriousness. But they are not doing it alone. Long ago, they learned that the struggles of single groups are easily defeated by the deliberate nation-building strategies of the systems within which they live. Alliances and networks among the communities are being carefully shaped, and bridges constructed with organisations in the civil societies that understand and share some or all of their values. A new global dynamic is emerging that explicitly acknowledges the dangers of the consolidation of the international capitalist system and is mobilising peoples to realise the promises of a decentralised pluriverse that is emerging in all parts of the globe (Kothari et al., 2019; Escobar 2020a; 2020b).

Many of the Indigenous and peasant societies analysed in these pages are becoming 'anti-systemic'. Some observers, especially those whose frame of reference is 'North Atlantic', are sceptical that these peoples lack the knowledge, skills and institutional structures to implement effective alternatives to the overwhelming force of global capitalism. But throughout the Global South, and especially in Latin America (and parts of the Indigenous world in North America), the effervescence of rural and Indigenous peoples belies this disbelief: these communities are convinced that they have no alternative: firmly grounded in the recognition that the existing global order will not contribute to their well-being, they are instigating social, productive, political and environmental processes that reinforce their demands for autonomy. Indeed, it might be just as Latin America is on the frontlines of the global resistance against the neoliberal policy agenda and extractive capitalism so does the activism of Indigenous communities in Latin America in regard to constructing possible alternative futures provide important lessons for activists and communities elsewhere.

This activism takes many forms. Some groups are still trying to negotiate with the State, with local, regional and national institutions to eke out support for their projects, developing strategies to assert their independence, advancing towards differing degrees of autonomy; building mechanisms to protect their communities and territories and improve the quality of life of their members. In their own ways, each of these peoples are reacting collectively to demonstrate their ability and commitment to build the new societies that will be better positioned to provide for their members and to care for their territories, offering examples of ways in which other groups still encrusted in the globalised socio-political structures of capitalism might begin to experiment with new organisations while modifying their behaviour. As such, then, many Indigenous and peasant societies are becoming the Communitarian Revolutionary Subject pointing the way to a brighter future (Barkin and Sánchez, 2019).

## Notes

1 The literature on the significance of the milpa as one of the most innovative agricultural systems is abundant. The 38 articles published in *Agroecology and Sustainable Food Systems* on the subject are indicative of its importance; of particular note are recent studies by Astier et al. (2017) and Rivera Nuñez et al. (2020).

2 The *Popol Vuh* is a sacred narrative of the Maya K'iché people in Mesoamerica from long before the Spanish colonisation of the Americas. Preserved through the centuries as oral tradition, the "Book of Community" or "Book of the People", offers a version of the creation in which humanity emerges from and remains a part of nature, in sharp contrast to the Judeo-Christian story in which humanity is expelled from the Garden of Eden for violating the laws of nature. A popular version of the text was distributed by the Fondo de Cultura Económica in México; since its original publication in 1947, it has been reissued dozens of times.

3 See the analysis of the many subsequent reforms of Article 27 of the Constitution in Mexico in Garduza Machin (2019). The original text is presented on p. 4.

4 The data come from the very useful publication of the National Statistical Agency (INEGI), *Estadísticas Históricas de México*, which is updated regularly and available online (https://www.inegi.gob.mx).

5 Transformed into the International Center for Corn and Wheat Improvement (CIMMYT for its initials in Spanish) in 1961, as part of the Consultative Group on International Agricultural Research (CGIAR), with headquarters in the World Bank.

6 Hearing that, I commented to the scientist who brought me to the meeting: 'When a president declares a problem solved, it is time to start worrying!'

7 https://www.inali.gob.mx/es/comunicados/701-2019-02-08-15-22-50.html.

## References

Astier, M., J. Argueta, Q. Orozco-Ramírez, M. González, J. Morales, P. Gerritsen, M. Escalona, F. Rosado May, J. Sánchez-Escudero, T. Martínez Saldaña, C. Sánchez-Sánchez, R. Arzuffi Barrera, F. Castrejón, H. Morales, L. Soto, R. Mariaca, B. Ferguson, P. Rosset, H. Ramírez, R. Jarquín Gálvez, F. García-Moya, M. Ambrosio Montoya and C. González-Esquivel (2017). "Back to the roots: understanding current agroecological movement, science, and practice in Mexico," *Agroecology and Sustainable Food Systems*, 41(3–4): 329–348.

Barkin, D. (2018). *De la protesta a la propuesta : 50 años imaginando y construyendo el futuro.* Mexico: Siglo XXI.

Barkin, D. and B. Lemus (2015). "Construyendo mundos pos-capitalistas," Revista *Cultura y Representaciones Sociales*, 10(19): 26–60.

Barkin, D. and A. Sánchez (2019). "The communitarian revolutionary subject: New forms of social transformation," *Third World Quarterly*, 41(8): 1421–1441.

Bartra, R. (1978). *Estructura Agraria y Clases Sociales en México.* México: Ediciones Era.

Bartra, R., E. Boege Schmidt, P. Calvo, J. Gutiérrez, V. Raúl Martínez Vásquez and L. Paré (1975). *Caciquismo y Poder Político en el México Rural.* México: Siglo XXI editores.

Bartra Vergés, A. (2008). "campesindios. aproximaciones a los campesinos de un continente colonizado," *Boletín de Antropología Americana*, 44: 5–24.

Bartra Vergés, A., R. Cobo and L. Paz (2004). *Tosepan Titataniske. Abriendo horizontes. 27 años de historia*. México: Ed. Circo Maya-Sociedad Cooperativa Agropecuaria Regional Tosepan Titataniske.

Bley, F. (2020). "Rethinking law from below: Experiences from the Kuna people and Rojava," *Globalizations*, 17(7): 1291–1299.

Bonfil Batalla, G. (1996 [1987]). *México Profundo: Reclaiming a Civilization*. Austin: University of Texas Press.

Díaz Muñoz, J., M. Sánchez Ramírez, C. Ortiz, T. Kelly, M. Monroy Gómez and F. Pöhls (eds.) (2017). *Buen Vivir y Organizaciones Regionales Mexicanas: Miradas de la diversidad*. Guadalajara: ITESO.

Elizalde, A. (ed.) (2007). "Identidad Latinoamericana hoy: tensiones y desafíos," *Polis—Revista Latinoamericana*, No 18. https://journals.openedition.org/polis/4008.

Escobar, A. (1980). *La Batalla en el México Rural*. México: Siglo XXI editores.

Escobar, A. (2020a). "Alternative paths of transformation," *Globalizations*, 17(2): 225–231.

Escobar, A. (2020b). *Pluriversal Politics: The Real and the Possible*. Durham: Duke University Press.

Escobar, A. (ed.) (1978). "¿Y si los campesinos existen?," *Comercio Exterior*, 28: 1436–1439.

Esteva, G. (1982). *La batalla en el México rural*, México: Siglo XXI.

Fa, J., J. Watson, I. Leiper, P. Potapov, T. Evans, N. Burgess, Z. Molnár, Á. Fernández-Llamazares, T. Duncan, S. Wang, B. Austin, H. Jonas, C. Robinson, P. Malmer, K. Zander, M. Jackson, E, Ellis, E. Brondizio and S. Garnett (2020). "Importance of Indigenous Peoples' lands for the conservation of Intact Forest Landscapes," *Frontiers in Ecology and the Environment*, 18(39): 135–140.

Fernández-Llamazares, Á., D. Lepofsky, K. Lertzman, C. Armstrong, E. Brondizio, M. Gavin, P. O'B. Lyver, G. Nicholas, P. Pascua, N. Reo, V. Reyes-García, N. Turner, J. Yletyinen, E.N. Anderson, W. Balée, J. Cariño, D. David-Chavez, C. Dunn. Garnett, Spencer Greening (La'goot), S. Jackson (Niniwum Selapem), H. Kuhnlein, Z. Molnár, G. Odonne, G-B. Retter, W. Ripple, Lįszló Sįfiįn, A. Sharifian Bahraman, M. Torrents-Ticó and M. Blaich Vaughan (2021). "Scientists' warning to humanity on threats to indigenous and local knowledge systems," *Journal of Ethnobiology*, 41(2): 144–169.

Fuente Carrasco, M., D., Barkin, and Clark-Tapia (2019). "Governance from below and environmental justice: Community water management from the perspective of social metabolism," *Ecological Economics*, 160: 52–61.

Garduza Machín, X. (2019). "El Derecho Agrario: El Artículo 27 de la Constitución y sus reformas," *Perfiles De Las Ciencias Sociales*, 7(13): 263–300.

Garnett, S., N. Burgess, J. E. Fa, Álvaro Fernández-Llamazares, Z. Molnár, C. Robinson, J. Watson, K. Zander, B. Austin, E Brond.izio, N. French Collier, T. Duncan, E. Ellis, H. Geyle, M. Jackson, H. Jonas, P. Malmer, B. McGowan, A. Sivongxay and I. Leiper (2018). "A spatial overview of the global importance of Indigenous lands for conservation," *Nature Sustainability*, 1(7): 369–374.

Gasparello, G. (2021). "Communal responses to structural violence and dispossession in Cherán Mexico," *Latin American Perspectives*, 48(1): 42–62.

González Rosales, S. (2020). "Discursos y Prácticas del Ejercicio del Yeknemilis (Buen Vivir) en La Unión de Cooperativas Tosepan, Sierra Nororiental de Puebla,

México," pp. 233–253 in B. Marañon (ed.) *Economías alternativas y buenos vivires. El debate.* México: Instituto de Investigaciones Económicas UNAM – CLACSO.
GRAIN. (2014). "Hungry for Land: Small farmers feed the world with less than a quarter of all farmland". https://grain.org/article/entries/4929-hungry-for-land-small-farmers-feed-the-world-with-less-than-a-quarter-of-all-farmland.
Hernández Navarro, L. (2015). "Prologue," in L. Villoro (Ed.), *La Alternativa: Perspectivas y posibilidades de cambio.* México: Fondo de Cultura Económica.
IWGIA – International Working Group on Indigenous Affairs. (2020). *The Indigenous World, 2020.* Copenhagen: IWGIA.
James, D., E. Bowness, T. Robin, A. McIntyre, C. Dring, A. Desmarais and H. Wittman. (2021). "Dismantling and rebuilding the food system after COVID-19: Ten principles for redistribution and regeneration," *Journal of Agriculture, Food Systems, and Community Development*, 10(2): 29–51.
Jennings, B. (1988). *Foundations of International Agricultural Research: Science and Politics in Mexican Agriculture.* Boulder, CO: Westview.
Kothari, A. (2020). "Earth Vikalp Sangam: Proposal for a global tapestry of alternatives," *Globalizations*, 17(2): 245–249.
Kothari, A., A. Salleh, A. Escobar, F. Demaria and A. Acosta (eds.). (2019). *Pluriverse: A Post-Development Dictionary.* Delhi and New York: Tulika Books/Columbia University Press.
Lappé, F., J. C. Moore and P. Rosset (1999). *World Hunger: Twelve Myths.* 2nd Ed. New York: Grove Press.
Magaña Mejía, D. (2017). "Educación purhépecha: La configuración del sesi irekani y la reproducción cultural," *Ethos Educativo*, 50: 129–172.
Martínez Luna, J. (2010). *Eso que llaman comunalidad.* Oaxaca: Conaculta; (Colección diálogos, Pueblos originarios de Oaxaca).
Meza-Lopehandía, M. G. (2019). *Principales demandas mapuche como reivindicaciones de derechos humanos Derechos Políticos, Económicos, Sociales y Culturales.* Santiago de Chile: Biblioteca del Congreso Nacional de Chile, Asesoría Técnica Parlamentaria.
Mora, M. (2017). Kuxlejal *Politics: Indigenous Autonomy, Race, and Decolonizing Research in Zapatista Communities.* Austin: University of Texas Press.
Paoli Bolio, A. (2019). *Lekil chahpanel y Derechos Humanos: Prácticas e ideales tseltales del Comité de Derechos Humanos.* Ocosingo Chiapas: Universidad Intercultural de Chiapas, Fray Pedro Lorenzo de la Nada, A. C.
Porto-Goncalves, C. (2003). "A geograficidade do social: uma contribuiēćo para o debate metodológico sobre estudo de conflito e movimentos sociais na América Latina," pp.141–150 in: J. Seone (ed.), *Movimientos sociales y conflicto en América Latina.* Buenos Aires: CLACSO.
Porto-Goncalves, C. (2015). "Por la vida, la dignidad y el Territorio: Un nuevo léxico teórico político desde las luchas sociales en Latinoamérica/Abya Yala/Quilombola," *Polis: Revista Latinoamericana*, 41: 238–251.
Porto Goncalves, C. and E. Leff (2015). "Political ecology in Latin America: The social reappropriation of nature, the reinvention of territories and the construction of an environmental rationality," *Desenvolvimento e Meio Ambiente*, 35: 65–88.
Rivera-Núñez, T., L. Fargher and R. Nigh (2020), "Toward an historical agroecology: An academic approach in which time and space matter," *Agroecology and Sustainable Food Systems*, 44(8): 975–1011.

Robles Hernández, S. and R. Cardoso Jiménez (eds.) (2008). *Floriberto Díaz. Escrito, "Comunalidad, energía viva del pensamiento mixe"*. México: UNAM, Programa Universitario México Nación Multicultural.

Rojas Herrera, M. and D. Alejandra Méndez Rojas (2020). "Educating for solidarity: The experience of the Union of Tosepan Titataniske Cooperatives," *Textual*, 76: 45–73.

Rosset, P., L. Pinheiro Barbosa, V. Val and N. McCune (2021). "Pensamiento Latinoamericano Agroecológico: The emergence of a critical Latin American agroecology?," *Agroecology and Sustainable Food Systems*, 45(1): 42–64.

Salmerón Sanginés, P. (2021). *La Batalla por Tenochtitlan*. México: Fondo de Cultura Económica.

Serrano, H. (2013). *Caso Chevron-Texaco: Cuando los pueblos toman la palabra*. Quito: Universidad Andina Simón Bolívar, Sede Ecuador.

Stavenhagen, R. (1973). "Aspectos sociales de la estructura agraria en México", in R. Stavenhagen, et al. (eds.), *Neolatifundismo y Explotación: De Emiliano Zapata a Anderson Clayton & Co.* Mexico: Nuestro Tiempo.

Villoro, L. (2001). *De la Libertad a la Comunidad*. México: Fondo de Cultura Económica.

Villoro, L. (2004). *Crecer, Saber Conocer*. México: Siglo XXI.

Villoro, L. (2009). *Tres retos de la sociedad por venir. Justicia, democracia, pluralidad*. México: Siglo XXI editores.

Villoro, L. (2015). *La Alternativa: Perspectivas y posibilidades de cambio*. México: Fondo de Cultura Económica.

Warman, A. (1972). *Los campesinos: Hijos predilectos del régimen*. Mexico: Nuestro Tiempo.

# Part V

# Post-Extractivist Alternatives

# 12 Post-extractivist transitions

## Concepts, sequences and examples

*Eduardo Gudynas*

The impacts of so-called extractivisms have been well known for many years, raising the oft-repeated question: What is the alternative? Conventional views hold that there are no alternatives because they are indispensable for development, and the discussion should therefore focus on reducing their impacts and better distributing their economic benefits.

A different answer might be termed 'post-extractivist transitions' in that they propose to leave extractivisms behind. This answer includes a theoretical framework and concrete proposals for action, most of them designed for public policies. Such post-extractivist transitions have been elaborated in South America for more than ten years with the purpose of offering guides and options that are feasible and defensible from the perspective of civil society.

This chapter provides an introduction to post-extractivism: Its conceptual bases, the organisation and sequence of proposed actions and their possible implications are described. A summary of this type is shared for the first time in English in that the contributions in this area and associated discussions have taken place mainly in Spanish, and more or less independently of the academy. Therefore, and given the space limitations, there is no detailed discussion with the academic literature and only a summarised bibliography is provided.

### Definitions and concepts in extractivism and transitions

As a first step in addressing post-extractivist transitions, it is necessary to specify the meanings of both the category 'extractivism' and that of 'transitions'. Extractivism is defined here as a mode of mass appropriation of natural resources, characterised by the extraction of large volumes or high intensity, to be exported for the most part (more than 50 per cent), as unprocessed raw materials or with minimal processing (corresponding to the conventional definition of 'commodities'). This approach is based on the Latin American experience of the capitalist development process in recent decades and is explained in detail in Gudynas (2021).

From this perspective, extractivism is a plural concept with diverse connotations; thus, different types can be described (such as mining, drilling for

DOI: 10.4324/9781003301981-18

oil and gas, agro-extraction, forestry and fishing). Extractivisms so understood designate a mode of *glocal* appropriation in that they depend on natural resources located in specific sites but that are marketed globally. In addition, prices, demand and investments in these sectors are also determined by international markets. Extractivisms are manifest in enclaves, such as an open-pit mine, oil drilling camps or monocultures, but are always found together with their connection networks (such as roads or waterways) and support areas (such as dams as a means of irrigation). These extractive activities and associated infrastructure, regarding which there is voluminous evidence, trigger multiple local impacts that are social, territorial and environmental and that in turn in many cases trigger citizen conflicts.

But in addition to those local impacts, we can also identify so-called spill-over effects, which are not spatially determined and may even arise before an extractive operation is initiated. The best-known examples are reductions in social demand and deterioration of and damage to health and the environment. These spill-overs impose changes in public policies and in political categories such as participation or democracy, to mitigate the negative impacts of extractivism so as to make them more palatable.

It can be argued that extractivism has become the continent's main environmental and social problem. Latin America is the world's largest net exporter of natural resources per capita. Its exports went from an estimated seven million metric tons in 1980 to 1,035 million tons in 2016—the greatest growth occurring in metallic minerals. In much of the 20th century, the most important net export flows were to the US and Western Europe, but in the 21st century the largest destination point became China, where exports reached a huge volume (527 million tons), tripling the flow to European destinations (Infante-Amate et al., 2020). This situation explains the urgency in the search for alternatives to extractivism.

The concept of transitions has a long history behind it. Among the best-known uses, it should be remembered that the change from capitalist economies to others conceived as socialist was described as a transition; the European debate in the 1960s and 1970s had a lot of influence. But since the collapse of the Soviet Union, the same word was used to describe the passage from real socialism to capitalism in Eastern Europe. In turn, in other fields this term has been used to describe other gradual changes, such as social and ecological modelling (e.g., the Network of Cities in Transition).

Here the term 'transitions' is used to describe a succession of changes that allows us to abandon the current dominance of extractivism in economics and politics. The word refers to change from one condition or stage to another, one that is different regarding both the process and its effects. The changes here are successive and gradual since it is recognised that they cannot be abrupt given that extractivism is deeply rooted in politics and the economy as well as the dominant culture (of incessant accumulation, possessive individualism and the dominion of humans over nature). Likewise, changes must affect several dimensions at once and are not simply a different technocratic management in, for example, mining or agriculture.

Transitions that are specifically post-extractivist are then defined as follows: they are a set of politics, strategies and actions to reduce, nullify or eradicate the most serious and acute impacts of current extractivism; to successively reduce them until they disappear to be replaced by an indispensable extraction. The focus is to eradicate poverty and ensure *buen vivir* (living well) and the protection of Nature. It should be noted that here the appropriation of natural resources is not rejected, but that only those resources that are indispensable for human well-being and ensuring environmental protection must be extracted.

The definition of extractivism must always be kept in mind since not all modes of appropriation of Nature, such as mining or agriculture, satisfy this condition. This implies that post-extractivism does not imply prohibiting these activities, and they will be able to continue these activities in other ways.

Transitions include a set of measures, actions and instruments, on various planes, and which are chained and linked together. All these components in one way or another refer to changes in public policies. The sequence of components of post-extractivist transitions can be separated into two phases (Figure 12.1). The first corresponds to emergency and emergency measures, whose essential purpose is to stop the most serious and acute local impacts that are affecting human health or survival and destroying Nature. The second represents measures of deeper transformation by which the spill-over effects are dismantled, the productive structures and the political framework, including the cultural bases, are modified to diminish modes of resource extraction by replacing them with others. The two phases are superimposed,

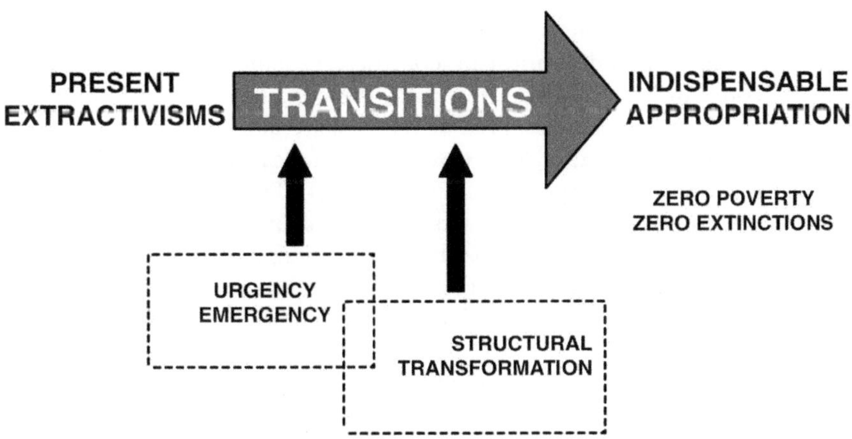


*Figure 12.1* Schematic representation of transitions to post-extractivism as a set of measures, actions and instruments divided into two phases.

since the most urgent measures must be selected to allow structural changes to move forward to a next stage.

In these transitions there are common components and others that are specific to each type of extractivism and to the conditions of each country. A sequence for mining extractivism is then presented as an example, which is then complemented by key elements for other sectors.

## Emergencies and urgencies in the face of mining extractivism

Emergency and emergency measures begin by evaluating the ventures in operation as future projects. Both terms are derived from medical practice. Emergency refers to dangerous and critical situations that require immediate action as human and non-human life face imminent risks; the main objective is to prevent death and secure life, while urgent response deals with severe and dangerous conditions that must be addressed as quickly as possible, but not immediately, with the objective to restore human health and environmental quality. Examples of emergency measures include stopping mercury contamination in alluvial gold mining from harming health and the environment, while urgent environmental restoration measures are applied in contaminated soils.

These measures consider social aspects (such as health and labour conditions), ecological (such as effects on biodiversity or pollution) and territorial (spatial). Accident risk analyses are included, clearly identifying those that are identified as unacceptable because if an accident were to occur, its consequences would be severe and could not be remedied. These assessments are not restricted to mining sites but incorporate their connection networks and support areas, and in all phases (from exploration to abandonment). Procedures must be rigorous, ensuring local participation to prevent data manipulation or corruption, and monitoring controls and standards accepted by the scientific community. Following this path, the conditions and thresholds by which mining ventures are accepted or rejected are determined.

Applying these criteria, at least three situations can be distinguished for mining extractivisms in operation (Figure 12.2). The first corresponds to those who are responsible for impacts considered unacceptable, and which cannot be resolved or remedied by technological or managerial means, which makes their effects inevitable. Emergency measures require that they be shut down. The same goes for ventures that involve such high risks that they cannot be properly managed, as can happen with certain tailings dams. After a closure, the priority should be focused on environmental restoration and the health and viability of the communities.

The second situation corresponds to operations for which there are environmental, health and territorial management options to avoid these severe impacts, but which nevertheless were not implemented due to their high cost to ensure profitability, where corruption existed, to not meet those

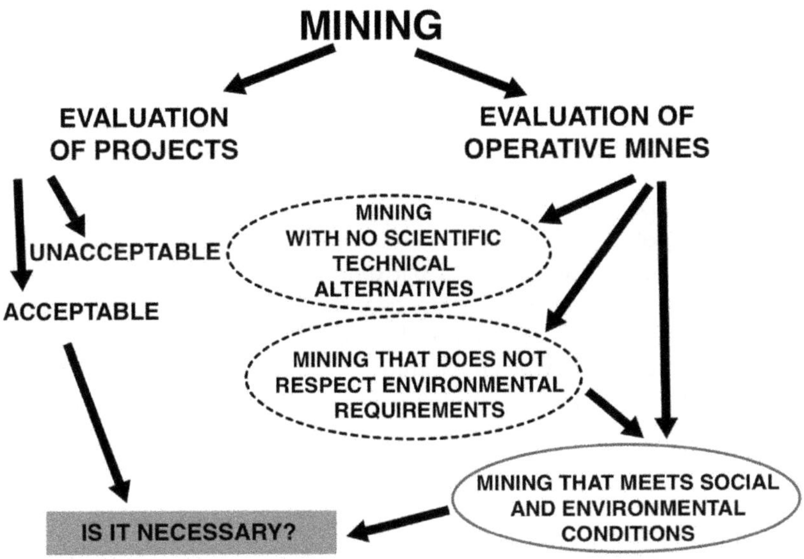


*Figure 12.2* Sequence of evaluation of projects and ventures in mining extractivisms in the urgency and emergence phase of post-extractivist transitions.

requirements or hide their effects, or that were not monitored. The emergency measures in this case require that several of these enterprises be closed to allow communities and the environment to heal. There will be others that can be reconverted in compliance with social, environmental and territorial requirements and that can be subject to adequate monitoring and therefore are referred to in the third situation.

The third condition refers to mining ventures that meet social, environmental and territorial requirements or can be reformulated to meet those requirements, either by technological or managerial adjustments and that can be monitored appropriately. These are activities that can continue to operate during this first phase of transition.

Evaluations for projects into the future follow the same steps and can then lead to proposals that will be unacceptable and others that could be concretised.

At the same time, in parallel, economic assessments that are very different from the current ones must be applied. Conventional procedures such as cost/benefit analyses are inadequate as social and environmental costs are ignored or poorly accounted. Alternatively, transitions emphasise that they must incorporate costs that are usually ignored or outsourced, such as costs of water pollution, damage to public health, etc. Similarly, conventional assessments systematically relegate technological reconversion options to reduce environmental and social impacts, so as not to increase operating costs. Thus, they generate an illusion of extractivism as almost always profitable businesses but at the cost of externalising to society and the environment the costs of their impacts.

Considering the mining situation in several South American countries, it can be argued that the application of all these assessments will lead to the closure of many enclaves, which will lead to a significant reduction in that sector, and at the same time, the abandonment of several future projects.

Assessments must also be adjusted to each type of mineral, as well as to ecological and social contexts. For example, the technology of extraction and separation of gold is not the same as that of iron, and that means that the evaluations must be adjusted to each natural resource. The determination of social and environmental requirements and limits also depend on other dimensions, since, for example, the possible options in the Amazon are very different from those of the Andean páramo.

The sequence of evaluations implies a final aspect that corresponds to consider whether it is necessary to extract that type of mineral or it can be supplanted or there are reuse and recycling options (this condition is discussed below).

## Measures in other sectors

As for the diversity of different types of extractivism, the sequences are similar, addressing on the one hand future projects and on the other the emergency and urgent measures applied to the ventures in operation. They are not described here in detail due to space limitations, but some particularities can be mentioned.

In the case of extractivism in the sector of hydrocarbons or fossil fuels, from the perspective of transitions, fracking is considered unacceptable under any option, both for its impacts and for its terrible energy balance. Unlike mining extractivism, conventional oil and gas extraction must be limited by the need to reduce greenhouse gas emissions. At the same time, limitations should also be imposed on both current enclaves and future projects in tropical and subtropical forests, due to their impacts on biodiversity, water and local communities and the high risk of accidental spills.

In agriculture, livestock and forestry ventures, emergency measures are focused on stopping deforestation in areas of high biodiversity or ecological fragility, on ensuring water quality and on reducing the use of agrochemicals that are risky for wildlife and human health. In addition, deforestation and changes in land use are the main sources of greenhouse gases in several countries, where commitments to climate change reinforces the need for such measures. Much attention is also paid to export monocultures, due to the use of transgenic varieties, their effects on soil quality and the consequences of the intensive use of some agrochemicals such as the herbicide glyphosate. In these extractivisms, the impacts of connection networks, especially roads and highways in wild sites, and support areas such as irrigation dams, are also very relevant.

## Evaluations, limits, indicators and zoning

The sequences of assessments summarily described above address at least five aspects (social, environmental, territorial and economic). In each of them, limits, thresholds or standards that, for example, establish limits on the emission of pollutants into the air or on the safety of workers, are recognised. This recognition is key to being able to distinguish between acceptable and rejected ventures according to the sequences just described.

The environmental limits and thresholds in several cases depend on each ecosystem; for example, the water quality requirements in Andean rivers are not the same as those of an Amazonian watercourse. Conditions in the social dimensions include, among others, the demands that ensure the health of workers and local communities. Thresholds such as these rest above all on expert knowledge (for example, blood lead levels), although in others, scientific input is articulated politically and culturally (such as decisions about whether to protect a historic site).

In Latin America, there is a wide range of regulations in constitutional mandates, laws and decrees that cover many of these conditions, but that their enforcement is deficient, either due to self-limitations of the State itself that serves to protect certain extractivisms, or due to inefficiencies and a lack of personnel and funds, or corruption. Economic assessments also suffer from constraints, many of them based on conventional academic positions on how to understand economic value, on accounting for social and environmental costs, or on the role of economic growth as indispensable for development. The emergency measures aim to rigorously apply these regulations, understanding that if they were applied with seriousness, effectiveness and independence, they would allow the excesses to be adequately evaluated at the beginning of the transitions. This requires strengthening enforcement, ensuring the capacities of the government and the judiciary for that application and above all, eradicating corruption. Business and political pressures must also be faced to establish cuts or flexibilisations under these conditions. In those issues where notable absences are identified, new instruments will be promoted.

Some of these evaluations have peculiarities for extractivisms that rely on new types of indicators. Among the best known are the evaluations on the intensity of the appropriation of matter, energy or water (which have received different names, such as ecological rucksack, material inputs per unit of service and ecological footprints). For example, in the case of mining it is necessary to consider all the matter removed from Nature, considering the debris or waste, described as ecological rucksacks, which almost always represent larger volumes, have enormous responsibility for impacts; as they do not have commercial value, they are invisible to economic analysis. Similarly, there are also ecological rucksacks in water and energy. In the case of fossil fuels, their energy balances (known as EROI—energy return on investment) should be considered.

Another set of instruments defended by post-extractivist transitions are spatial zoning, where areas are delimited in which certain types of extractivism are not accepted. The procedure is based on the well-known economic and ecological zonings used in countries such as Brazil or on demands to exclude mining in Páramo environments in Colombia or in the Amazon of Ecuador.

As a result of these evaluations, ventures will be found that will be unacceptable. This is the case of open-pit mega-mining, characterised by large-area enclaves associated with corporations, almost always transnational. The 'mega' rating indicates that more than one million tons of matter are removed per year (including both the mineral and its ecological rucksack), and more than a thousand hectares of surface are committed. As can be seen, this characterisation is not determined from a productive or economic perspective, but ecologically.

This type of extractivism implies 'ecological amputations', understood as the large-scale physical removal of an ecosystem, destroying not only the biological framework with its living species but also the material base. These amputations are evident in the large pits or quarries, which can be very deep, along with the implantation of deposits of rocks and debris without commercial value that become new hills. Being an amputation, it is not possible to return to the original ecological state. However, conventional environmental impact assessments avoid recognising this and focus on mitigation measures that only manage collateral impacts, such as dust generation or water management. In this way, they serve to justify the myth of a kind of mining that can be ecologically managed, but they do so by avoiding the primary impact, that is amputation. The post-extractive analysis reveals these ecological amputations and therefore the decision must be to abandon this type of venture.

The final step in this sequence of evaluations is to consider whether it is necessary to extract the resource from Nature. Returning to the case of mining extractivism, several aspects must be considered. For example, there will be minerals that are indispensable or irreplaceable, and therefore, their exploitation can be defended. But there are minerals that are not necessary, their use is not justifiable, they can be replaced, or there are volumes already removed that can be reused. Under these conditions, exploitation is not acceptable.

The evaluation of gold mining illustrates the post-extractivist perspective. It is a type of extractivism oriented almost exclusively to export, and with very low national consumption. It is responsible for very severe environmental, health and territorial impacts, such as deforestation and mercury pollution, with a very high ecological rucksack (an average estimate indicates that 540 tons of matter are extracted to obtain a kilo of gold) (NOAH, 2005). It is a practice that invades Indigenous lands, has high levels of violence and is associated with corruption networks in many regions. Its main destinations are superfluous: the current demand for gold is concentrated in around 51 per cent in jewellery and more than 40 per cent as an investment or in bullion or coins, while technological uses are estimated at about 8 per cent.[1] Therefore, gold is extracted from Latin America for markets especially in Asia, for purposes that are not essential for the quality of life but the banal and unnecessary, such as jewellery or financial speculation.

At the same time, it does not make sense to continue mining for new gold, because with the ore that has already been removed, all needs such as industrial needs can be met. It is estimated that 'above ground' gold is almost four times the volume of gold that remains 'underground'. In fact, it is estimated that almost 200,000 tons of gold have been removed (two-thirds of that total is due to operations carried out since 1950), while some 54,000 tons remain in the fields. This available gold allows all the future needs of the industrial and medical sector to be met through recovery, recycling or reuse programs. Therefore, from a post-extractivist perspective in the case of gold, the alternative is a moratorium on this type of mining.

Considering other natural resources, analyses of this type will indicate which are the indispensable resources and whose extraction is legitimate, as is obviously the case with several foods.

## Compensation, indemnity, ownership and prices

The best-known justifications of extractivism maintain that they generate economic benefits, both to the State and to society, conceived as essential for national economies. These conceptions have support in almost all political perspectives, in much of academia and society. Associated with this is the idea that these incomes in money can serve as compensation for the impacts of extractivism, and even that they are indispensable to finance poverty reduction, as the progressive South American governments argued.

Post-extractivist transitions pose a radical critique of the commodification of society and the environment. A purported barter for money does not solve the environmental impacts or the significant effects on people, such as lead contamination in mining enclaves. The thresholds in health and environment are not modified according to the money collected by the State or even by transfers to local communities. This makes it possible to avoid falling into the trap of social and environmental flexibilisations linked to economic performance. This does not imply refusing or not using monetarised reparation measures for damage to people and their property, whether by companies or the State, which must be applied anyway.

Similarly, the evaluation sequence also does not depend on the ownership of the resource. This avoids another trap that is the acceptance of an extractivism if it were state or national. A change in ownership, leaving transnational corporations behind, does not ensure that environmental and social impacts disappear, or acceptance thresholds are modified.

This allows us to differentiate post-extractivism from alternatives that bet on replacing private and transnationalised extractivisms with others under state ownership, or that only seek to increase taxes or royalties. If you consider an alternative that, for example, nationalises an open-pit mega-mine and distributes all its profits among local communities, this does not ensure better social or environmental performance anyway. The property regime or taxation does not change the thresholds or requirements, such as the level of lead in blood or the survival of local biodiversity (assessed as described above). This does not imply denying the importance of changes in both ownership and taxation, but they are necessary in other dimensions of post-extractivism, such as economic and productive reforms to enhance other sectors that are not extractivist.

Beyond all these precisions, it must be recognised that society can decide that it accepts certain irreversible impacts, whether environmental, human, or territorial, to privilege what it understands as an economic benefit that it considers more important or more urgent. That is a political discussion that must be pursued, but that can only be properly addressed if real and substantive information is available. One of the strengths of post-extractivism is that it makes these dilemmas explicit and obliges us to provide adequate and reliable information to make those decisions. On the other hand, what is happening today is that serious or irreversible environmental impacts are minimised, the dogma of economic benefit is repeated and access to information is hindered.

One of the central aspects in the reproduction of extractivism lies in the distortions in the allocation of prices to raw materials and the economic invisibility of many of the impacts. This results in the natural resources exported being 'cheap', and this in turn sustains their commercial insertion.

In the conventional calculation, for example of a ton of ore, its price responds to components such as the so-called extraction costs, but these do not include different components, or do so to a limited extent, such as social and environmental externalities. Nor does it properly account for the cost of ecological rucksack (as is the case with dumps, tailings deposits, etc.). It is an incomplete and distorted accounting, shielded by companies and governments and legitimised by conventional economic academia.

Given this, post-extractivist transitions postulate what can be called a social and ecological correction of the prices of removed natural resources. The cost of operation of extractivism must incorporate these aspects, and that will result in their increase, and from there an increase in prices. At the same time, it is necessary to dismantle the hidden or explicit subsidies that extractivism receives. They distort market distortions and contribute to externalising social and environmental effects, to end up financed by society or by the State. Recent studies reveal the inaccuracy of the classic defences of extractivism as large businesses that ensured a lot of money for the country, since the State grants them enormous economic support or imposes very low taxes on them (for example, De Echave and Flores (2020) on royalties and taxes in Peru, or FARN (2020) on subsidies and state support for oil exploitation in Argentina).

## Employment, economy and state expenditures

The emergency measures just described, by reducing the number of extractive enclaves in operation, will lead to a drop in the removal of material for export. The social and ecological correction of prices and the use of rigorous accounting leads to another type of cost-benefit analysis, where some ventures would be financially unviable. In some cases, it will be evaluated whether this extractivism is necessary or legitimate, where some items may be abandoned. Therefore, the ventures that continue will surely offer resources with much more expensive prices. This will have various consequences for international trade, as there will be buyers who will be willing to pay higher prices and others will not accept it (seeking to exploit their own resources or appealing to recycling, reuse, recovery measures, etc.).

Faced with this type of scenario, the defenders of extractivism denounce that the consequences will be negative, especially due to the loss of jobs, and due to a fall in tax and royalty collection, a decrease in the income of dollars through exports and lower investment income. These arguments contain the basic core of the economic defence of extractivisms, which focused all of them on the alleged economic benefit. This type of reductionism is based on the rationality that legitimises extractivism. Faced with them, post-extractivist transitions offer several responses that imply moving towards structural transformations. Some of these proposals are presented in this section and the following.

Job losses in post-extractivist transitions have a limited impact and can be overcome. It should be borne in mind that mining and oil extractivisms are very limited generators of employment; for example, in Peru, direct and contracted jobs in mining reach one-per cent of the economically active employed population.[2] For these reasons, reductions in these sectors can be offset by the strengthening of other, more labour-intensive sectors, such as agriculture, livestock and forestry.

In the face of post-extractivist proposals, conventional discourses argue that an economic catastrophe will occur. An examination of the evidence indicates that the contribution of these sectors to domestic product is limited, although it increases in periods of high commodity prices (see Gudynas, 2021). It is clear that it is not really one of the main sources of tax collection, which rests mainly on conventional internal taxes (an example is Colombia; see Pardo, 2017). But the sources that can compensate for these reductions in economic income must still be indicated.

On the one hand, structural reforms are needed on the royalties and taxes applied in these sectors. In several countries, the tax on these activities is very low, and at the same time companies resort to different manoeuvres to reduce their payments (a well-known example occurs in Peru) (De Echave and Flores, 2020). Reforms should increase royalties, taxation, including automatic tax mechanisms at times of extraordinary profits, and nullify illegalities or fiscal corruption.

On the other hand, it should be noted that by reducing extractivism there is *also* a fall in subsidies and in the costs that the State and society assume for the outsourcing of social and environmental impacts (for example, it will not have to pay for water decontamination works). This leads to a net saving of state and social spending. In any case, it should be borne in mind that some of these subsidies must be redirected to legitimate support for an alternative productive reconversion to extractivism.

These economic changes, like other measures indicated above, impose substantial changes in state economic management, which are typical of the structural reform phase. Adjustments and changes will be necessary to achieve greater precision and effectiveness in the allocation of state spending, for example, in education, health, or housing, reducing superfluous expenses for example in the state bureaucracy or in perverse subsidies. This need also responds to the multiple evidence that public spending in Latin America is messy, inefficient and that in the case of extractivism, it is associated with subsidies or tax waivers.

In these ways, structural reforms would support productive sectors that meet social and environmental conditions, promote jobs and have good balances in terms of energy and water use and their greenhouse gas emissions. An agricultural reconversion plays a key role in this regard.

There must also be substantial changes in investment policies. These monies should also be focused on initiatives of environmental restoration, energy reconversion, strengthening of public health and education, which require contemplating larger time scales and recognising returns that will not only be financial but also social and environmental.

## Limits, poverty, opulence and sustainability

Post-extractivist transitions do not postulate an untouched Nature. On the other hand, they argue that the use of natural resources should be necessary to ensure the quality of life of people but at the same time preserve Nature. Extractivism violates these limitations by sustaining consumerist lifestyles, especially on other continents, and especially in the privileged classes.

Structural reforms must therefore recognise, on the one hand, that there are ecological limits by which appropriation must be adjusted to the rates of recovery or renewal in the case of renewable resources and must comply with ecological conditions that, for example, prevent pollution, and that apply to all types of resources. In other words, this limit of appropriation requires exploitation within the carrying capacities of ecosystems.

On the other hand, such removal of resources must be necessary to ensure that people do not live under conditions of poverty; it must ensure, say, access to water, adequate food, materials for housing, etc. This makes it necessary to recognise a poverty line that must be overcome in transitions. But at the same time, a limit of opulence must be identified, where the consumption of material resources, water, energy or greenhouse gas emissions exceeds those necessary for a good quality of life and instead is typical of sumptuous and consumerist styles. The discussion of poverty is associated with the discussion of wealth.

Within these limits and thresholds, a field of sustainability can be recognised, within which different options or preferences in the use of natural resources can be followed. Post-extractivist transitions operate within that space (Figure 12.3). They do not impose deterministic models on what to consume or which resources to take advantage of, since each society and culture will be able to follow different options, in turn adjusted to their ecological contexts, but the structural transformations it postulates operate within that field to ensure its goals of eradicating poverty and preserving nature.

At present, the removal of resources is totally distorted. An enormous volume of natural resources is extracted, exceeding ecological limits, but most of them are exported to meet consumerism and opulence in other countries. An economic unequal exchange that is also ecological is consolidated (see Alonso-Fernández and Regueiro-Ferreira, 2022). Meanwhile, in Latin America, large sectors of the population are below the poverty line, and there are also national minorities with consumption characteristic of opulence. Post-extractivist transitions face this distortion, on the one hand, drastically reducing the appropriation of natural resources that are exported, while structural reforms aim to ensure that those resources that remain appropriate effectively serve to eradicate poverty.

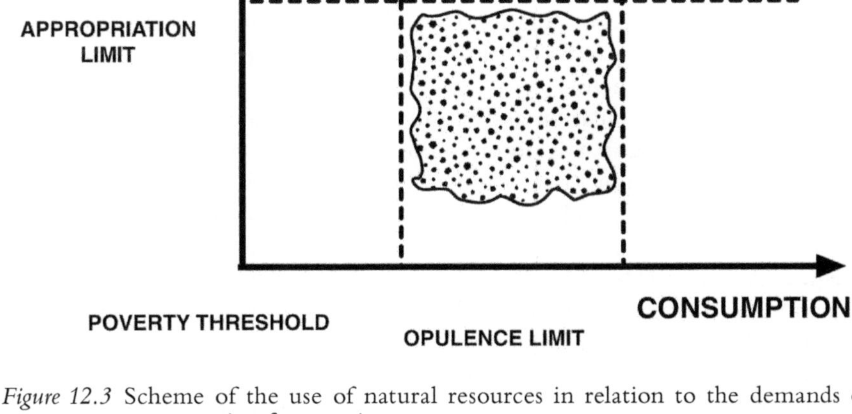


*Figure 12.3* Scheme of the use of natural resources in relation to the demands of consumption from society.

## Bioregions, autonomous reorientism and selective decoupling from globalisation

The need to stay within the sustainability space allows us to address other distinctive aspects of post-extractivist transitions. Obviously, the availability of natural resources and ecosystem capacities are different from country to country, and more specifically from one ecological region to another. At the same time, the available resources and the options to take advantage of them with the least environmental impact change. For example, there are environments that allow agricultural practices through polycultures that conserve ecosystems, while in other places the best balance can be achieved, instead, with the grazing of livestock.

This makes it more appropriate to consider that the balances between appropriation and types of natural resources are defined by bioregions, which do not follow political boundaries but are shared between countries. In this way, the transitions decrease, the productive options, let us say for the bioregion of the Páramo de los Andes will be few, and these are different from those found in another bioregion, such as the coasts of the Pacific Ocean. Any of these bioregions are shared among more than one country.

The structural reform measures propose an articulation between bioregions that is both ecological and productive. Resources will be used according to these bioregional conditions both within each country and by exporting the surpluses that are possible to neighbouring nations. As can be seen, post-extractivism does not imply isolating countries nor is it against international trade in natural resources, but reforms it to stay within the framework of sustainability. In fact, this type of mechanism allows for a reduction in the pressure on different ecosystems. Regional trade will be generated between neighbouring countries, taking advantage of the ecological and productive advantages of each one. If it will be geared towards national needs, the volume of resources exchanged will be substantially lower.

Regional integration agreements in Latin America, such as MERCOSUR or the Andean Community, do not contemplate this type of coordination while their extroverted orientation towards globalisation prevails. But these agreements provide a party institutional framework for structural reforms to modify and reorient them.

The ecological articulation and productive complementarity seek to configure a regionalism that is autonomous in the face of global conditions, demands and institutions. Let us remember that it is global markets that determine the price, demand and availability of investments, which feeds extractivism. In particular, free trade agreements have enabled extractivism and unequal exchange (Delgado Wise, Chapter 1 in this volume; also, Alonso-Fernández and Regueiro-Ferreira, 2022). The recovery of autonomy in the face of globalisation is an imperative need to advance in post-extractivism. This would also make it possible to coordinate social and ecological corrections of prices, social and environmental management of resources and basins shared between countries, and other measures, to avoid ecological and social dumping.

This autonomous regionalism allows a selective disengagement from globalisation. Participation in international trade should not be done from subordination, but countries should have autonomy to choose the practices they deem appropriate. To advance on this path, there are multilateral agreements on trade in natural resources that can be strengthened and reformed (especially the agreements on commodities promoted by UNCTAD). That autonomy also implies freedom from financial dependence (including subordinate relationships administered by the IMF and other multilateral bodies) and institutional (such as global governance that for example rests on the WTO).

## Spill-over effects and extractivist culture

In parallel to the local impacts of extractivism, so-called spill-over effects occur. These are defined as modifications in public policies and basic political conceptions, to make these extractivisms possible and tolerable (see Gudynas, 2021). They include processes such as lowering environmental, labour or social requirements to favour the arrival of future projects, and that once granted, they 'spill' over other sectors. As can be seen, they are not direct impacts of a venture, but even occur before, and are also not locally limited but are 'spilled' into public policies and throughout the country.

Among the most alarming spill-over effects is the reduction in coverage and effectiveness in rights and even in the quality of democracy. Safeguarding rights should, for example, protect local communities, but on the contrary, there is a growing deterioration directly related to extractivism, including the assassination of its leaders. A recent study that addresses in detail the spill-over effects on the rights of people and Nature in Bolivia showed that there are violations related to extractivism in all of them, without exception (Campanini et al., 2020). This deterioration explains, for example, the prevalence of violence around extractivism.

At the same time, the quality of democracy is weakened. Participation and access to information are limited, citizen consultations are prevented, criminalisation is encouraged and corruption is tolerated. Hyper-presidentialism is reinforced, which is functional to extractivist expansion by dismantling citizen, political and judicial controls.

For these reasons, post-extractivism seeks not only to nullify local impacts but also to dismantle these spill-over effects. The phase of structural reforms includes, among others, measures that ensure the fulfilment of rights, prevent the use of violence and strengthen democratic mechanisms of information, consultation and control. These have a more ambitious and deeper scope than the environmental 'governance' reforms promoted by academics, governments and regional bodies such as ECLAC (Economic Commission for Latin America and the Caribbean), which aim to appease environmental conflicts while maintaining extractivism. It also aims to safeguard the rights of both the environment and people, including the adequate protection of life in local communities. This makes post-extractivism inseparable from a debate to radicalise democracy, with a broader agenda that imposes enhancing the role of the legislative powers (local and national), the reform of the judiciary, and reversing the hyper-presidential verticality.

The spread of spill-over effects has naturalised environmental destruction and violence in extractivism. This occurred under governments of different ideological perspectives (whether conservative or progressive), showing that they rest on deeply rooted cultural and affective foundations. Post-extractivism must reach those roots, such as the cultural myths that conceive that a nation is mining itself to death, or those that feed the idea of a Nature as a basket of inexhaustible resources that must always be exploited. An extractivist 'common sense' has been built, shielded from criticism and unable to conceive of alternatives. This foundation behaves like a political theology and is therefore an act of faith that is not abandoned from one day to the next.

To dismantle this theology, post-extractivism must also operate in that cultural field, to dismantle the words, ideas and affectivities that sustain extractivism. An example of this is the call for a change in vocabulary. There is no 'production' of copper or oil, but it is an 'extraction'; it is also not correct to speak of 'extractive industry' since these do not represent an 'industry' but are a mere removal and sale of commodities. By this we mean that the construction of another vocabulary is in itself an important component of transitions to make clear their limits, their impacts and allow us to think or imagine alternatives.

In this sense, the critical importance of changes in valuation must be underlined, and within them the recognition of values intrinsic to the non-human. This implies abandoning the restriction due to exclusively anthropocentric valuations (based on use and exchange values, and from there, in sustaining the prevalence of price as an indicator of privileged value). The change in valuation leads to the recognition of the rights of Nature, as approved in the constitution of Ecuador and similar changes in Colombia.

## Sensible extractivisms and indispensable extractions

In transitions it is possible to describe a sequence with three situations. The first is the starting point that corresponds to current extractivism, which can be characterised as predators due to the high level of their impacts. The beginning of the transitions with the emergency measures occurs here, with the purpose of stopping or reversing those enclaves with the most severe impacts. As a result, a second situation will be reached that can be called sensible extractivism. In it, extractivisms are reduced but not eliminated and social, environmental and economic effects that are otherwise managed are dealt with. Structural transformations continue until the third situation is reached, which can be characterised as an indispensable extraction of natural resources. The aspect that defines extractivism, the massive export of natural resources, disappears, and instead there is a use of Nature to ensure the quality of life.

In this sequence, the measures, both initial and structural transformations, follow the objective of eradicating poverty and preserving nature. The process is not focused nor is it a response to a particular venture, but the transitions assume complete sectors and their scale is national, and even regional. In other words, they imagine countries that are structured and functioning in other ways.

The granting of measures aims to reduce the volume of natural resources removed for export, considering not only those final resources exported but also their ecological footprints and rucksacks (in matter, water and energy). This is possible as some enclaves will be closed and others will be able to continue operating although under other social, economic and environmental demands.

The recent situation in Latin America shows a physical trade balance with a deficit that exceeded 600 million tons in 2016 (Infante-Amate et al., 2020). This net loss of natural resources has occurred since the early 20th century, with a notable increase since the 1990s, making the continent one of the largest providers of natural resources for globalisation. In a schematic way, and as an illustrative example, the emergency and urgent phase of the transitions aims at a reduction of at least 50 per cent in the total of the natural resources exported, and a substantive reduction of the deficit in the trade balance.

The stage of deeper structural changes must strengthen the non-extractivist sectors. The criterion for this transformation is to ensure genuine jobs, economic balances that consider social and environmental impacts and that serve to eradicate poverty. The clearest priorities aim to strengthen and expand in the agricultural, livestock and forestry sectors. There is a huge and rich tradition of agroecological and organic practices that can nurture these changes, which not only contemplate environmental demands but also reduce dependence on fossil energy, pollution by agrochemicals and the greenhouse effect. At the same time, an industrial reconversion is necessary to manufacture necessary products, with long periods of obsolescence, and directly linked to the quality of life.

All these transitions lead to an indispensable extraction. Continuing with the schematic example, the appropriation of those resources that directly ensures the necessary domestic consumption for each country and the possible trade with neighbouring countries under autonomous regionalism will be maintained. It defends a scenario without poverty but also without opulence, quality of life—but a more austere daily life.

As is evident, the transitions do not postulate an abrupt change by which predatory extractivism is abandoned from one day to the next; this is impossible for many reasons, and even any attempt to impose it would violate the democratising demand that is defended from these alternatives. It must be made clear that the stage of sensible extractivism is not an end goal; it is a stage that must inevitably be contemplated and then continue advancing in these alternatives. The summary description presented here should be interpreted as successive steps by which extractivism is reduced while at the same time promoting cultural and political conditions to accept and design alternatives and at the same time implement them so that they serve as an example.

These transitions aim to abandon extractivism in any of its expressions. It is not the replacement of a conservative-style extractivism with a progressive one with greater state participation. This must be borne in mind since in Latin America there have been changes between extractivisms under different political regimes that in no case solved the underlying problems.

It is also important to note that it is not acceptable to label post-extractivism as 'anti-extractivism', as is the case in several countries. In many places this qualification was initially used by businessmen, politicians or journalists who defended extractive enclaves and denounced local groups as anti-extractivist or anti-development. This contemptuous attitude seeks to disqualify citizen mobilisations.

## The citizen experience

Post-extractivist transitions do not express academic exercises, although they are nourished by the contribution of many independent technicians and university students. Nor are they reduced to describing or listing or denouncing the impacts of extractivism, although it incorporates such diagnoses. They are not a set of vague and imprecise demands but provide roadmaps to get out of extractivism, with options that are practicable as soon as possible, that respond to social and ecological urgencies and that are understandable by citizens. In other words, post-extractivism aims to provide public policies that are accurate, effective and replicable.

The most important initial experiences occurred in Ecuador, and especially in Peru from 2010 onwards. Civil society responded to demands, participating in the political debate, and in conceptual elaborations that addressed different sectors and reforms, postulating urgent measures (summarised in Alayza and Gudynas, 2011). This was followed by an exploration of options in the other Andean countries, including ideas about an autonomous regionalism (contributions in Alayza and Gudynas, 2012). Since then, these proposals have spread in different South American countries, alternating moments of greater and lesser intensity in public debates. In recent years, the most intense discussions have occurred in Bolivia, Colombia and Peru, they retreated in Ecuador but expanded in Chile, Argentina and Uruguay, and their scope is smaller in Brazil, Paraguay and Venezuela.

The contributions are nourished by a rich repertoire of experiences that already exist, many of them at the local or regional level. Among some of the most emblematic are the proposals for an oil moratorium in Ecuador, the granting of rights to Nature in Ecuador and similar initiatives in Colombia, the moratoriums on open-pit mining in Costa Rica, El Salvador, and recently in Honduras, the territorial defence that peasant and Indigenous groups that deploy in Bolivia, or local alternatives for other water management and mining in Chile.

The relevance of post-extractivist transitions is evidenced by the heated backlash from governments, companies and conventional academia. These questions, in addition, come from the entire political spectrum; on the right, in Peru, conservative actors repeatedly describe these ideas as an expression of a radicalism of the Left, and in Bolivia, from the Movement towards Socialism, they are denounced as functional to the Right. As an example of the current discussion, the associations of mining companies in Colombia and those of mining and oil in Peru identify as the main risk the 'utopia' of a world without extractivism and harshly question the proposals of post-extractivist transitions (for example, ANDI, 2014). In their opinion, these alternatives cause all extractive sectors to lose their livelihood.

## Imagining other futures

Building alternatives to extractivism requires imagining other futures. This openness to visualise a non-extractivist condition is not simple given the broad and deep roots of the imaginary of a continent very rich in natural resources that must be exploited at all costs (Gudynas, 2013). In turn, conventional ideas about development actively block options for change and even make certain alternatives unimaginable or inconceivable.

That different future must necessarily abandon extractivism since options that invoke reformed, sustainable, or any other variety of extractivism are not acceptable. There are no ecological solutions to the environmental impacts of a removal of natural resources at such huge volumes and scales as wide as those involved here. That same scale and intensity means that extractivism ends up fatally involved in conflict and violence. Any attempt to make extractivism economically profitable requires massive subsidies, distorting social and environmental costs and widespread externalisation of its effects. These are all unacceptable conditions. At the same time, extractivism is only possible coupled with global markets and therefore will always end up in production networks, trade regulations and capital flows that are capitalist. The idea that a southern country would use the money generated by extractivist exports in productive diversification or endogenous industrialisation does not solve any of these problems, while reinforcing the asymmetrical order of globalisation. To be clearer, extractivism is an indissoluble part of today's varieties of capitalism.

All this makes post-extractivism part of a broader agenda of alternatives to capitalism, and from there, an opening that transcends contemporary ideas of development and progress. This perspective also has a South American inspiration corresponding to the notion of *Buen Vivir*. Post-extractivisms are based on these conceptions and have incorporated much of their contents, such as the rights of Nature. It is an effort that seeks alternatives, both in ideas and in affectivity, tinged by the hope of reorganising the economy, life in society and the link with Nature in another way.

## Notes

1 Data and trends in www.gold.org.
2 Estimation from data in the annual labour report; MTPE (2021).

## References

Alayza, A. and E. Gudynas (eds.). (2011). *Transitions. Post extractivism and alternatives to extractivism in Peru.* Lima: CEPES and RedGE.

Alayza, A. and E. Gudynas (eds.). (2012). *Transitions and alternatives to extractivism in the Andean region. A look from Bolivia, Ecuador and Peru.* Lima: CEPES and RedGE.

Alonso-Fernández, P. and R.M. Regueiro-Ferreira. (2022). "Extractivism, ecologically unequal exchange and environmental impact in South America: A study using Material Flow Analysis (1990–2017)," *Ecological Economics* 194, 1073.

ANDI. (2014). *Modern mining for Colombia's progress.* Bogota: ANDI (Cámara Asominores), Cámara Colombiana de Minería and Federación Nacional de Productores de Carbón.

Campanini, O., M. Gandarillas and E. Gudynas. (2020). *Rights and violence in extractivism. Extra-works in Bolivia and Latin America.* Cochabamba: La Libre.

De Echave, J. and C. Flores. (2020). *Mining and taxation in pre- and post-pandemic times.* Lima: Grupo de Justicia Fiscal Perú, Cooperacción.

FARN. (2020). *Fossil fuel subsidies 2019–2020 is everything still just as 'good'?* Buenos Aires: FARN (Fundación Ambiente y Recursos Naturales).

Gudynas, E. (2013). "The construction of other futures and alternatives to extractivism," pp. 567–581 in *Minería y movimientos sociales en el Perú* (R. Hoetmer, et al., eds). Lima: PDTG, CooperAcción.

Gudynas, E. (2021). *Extractivism. Politics, economy and ecology.* Black Point: Fernwood Publications.

Infante-Amate, J., A. Urrego Mesa and E. Tello Aragay. (2020). "The open veins of Latin America in the Anthropocene era: A biophysical study of foreign trade (1900–2016)," *Diálogos. Revista electrónica de Historia, Universidad Costa Rica and CALAS* 21(2): 177–214.

MTPE. (2021). *Annual report on employment in Peru.* Lima: Ministry of Labour and Employment Promotion (MTPE).

NOAH. (2005). *Ecological rucksack for material used in everyday products.* Copenhagen: NOAH Friends of the Earth.

Pardo, L.A. (2017). "The fifteen myths of big mining in Colombia," *Green Ideas* 1, Bogotá.

# 13 Sumak Kawsay for Indigenous women

*Gabriela Gallardo*

*Sumak Kawsay* (SK) *or Buen Vivir* (BV)[1] appears as a central concept in one of the most important currents of reflection on the development process that Latin America has provided in recent years. This concept and associated principles mark the recovery of the experience of Indigenous peoples on the continent, which encompasses 500 years of struggle against extractive imperialism and colonial rule, and a reconstruction of the way of life and communal ethics of the *pueblos originarios* (First Nations people) in the Americas. According to García Álvarez (2014), this Indigenous civilisational concept of SK, deeply rooted as it is in Indigenous Andean culture and history, has profound ecological, social and political and cosmological connotations. Awareness of the transcendental importance of this concept concerning an alternative way of thinking about the world and the development process reached new heights when it was embedded in the new political Constitution enacted by the governments of Bolivia (Estado Plurinacional de Bolivia, 2012) and Ecuador as a fundamental principle regarding the Rights of Nature (Mother Earth, or *Pachamama*). These Constitutions that converted the republics of Ecuador and Bolivia into plurinational and multiethnic States are widely recognised as the most progressive and radical in the world as regards recognition and protection of the Rights of Nature. According to Magdalena León (2008), the constitutional adoption of *Sumak Kawsay* (Buen Vivir in Ecuador, Vivir Bien in Bolivia) took place in a context of a widespread crisis of neoliberalism as a policy agenda in Latin America, and she points out that in broader terms it also reflects the impact of the global crisis of capitalism that provoked widespread discontent and a search for an alternative way of living and development. Petras and Veltmeyer (2005, 2009), in the same context, attribute this crisis in development thinking and the neoliberal policy agenda to the activism of the socio-political peasant movements in the 1990s. Another motivation for the emergence of SK was a growing concern for Nature in the context of a multidimensional crisis of global proportions (Houtart, 2011).

As for the conceptualisation of Sumak Kawsay or Buen Vivir as a uchronia of post-development, Unceta et al. (2014) point towards an alternative approach to living in solidarity and harmony based on ancestral knowledge,

DOI: 10.4324/9781003301981-19

Indigenous ways of being in a relation of harmony with each other and Mother Earth. Thus, from an Indigenous cosmological worldview, SK is presented as a new, albeit old, way of understanding human life as part of Nature and in harmony with it. In addition, Buen Vivir (Living Well) implies a critique of the idea and practices of western modernist development, especially when it comes to a fetish-like attachment to ideas of material progress and economic growth based on the incessant accumulation of capital,[2] and the evident inability to solve the problems of poverty and also the failure or inability to understand that their ideas and practices lead to destructive social and environmental outcomes (Gudynas, 2011: 2).[3] As Choquehuanca Céspedes, Bolivian foreign minister in the 'progressive' government headed by Evo Morales, the first Indigenous leader in history (at least in modern times) to have captured the levers of state power, put it: *Vivir Bien* is a 'culture of life' based on the ancestral knowledge of Indigenous peoples that aims to strike a balance, striving for harmony between humans and nature alike, and which foresees a return to a way of life that had been suppressed by colonisation. 'We must return to being because colonisation has made us into "wanting to be." Many of us want to be, but as of yet we are not. We now want to return to our own path to our being' (Fatheuer, 2011: 19).

In summary, all of the authors that have tackled these issues in recent years such as Acosta (2008, 2010, 2012, 2017) and Acosta et al. (2013), as well as Gudynas (2009, 2011a, 2011b), Ramírez (2019), León (2010), Zaragocín and Varea (2017) and De Souza de Santos (2010), agree that SK relies on Indigenous cultural traditions and is expressive of and reflects a worldview in which humans live in communal solidarity and in a relationship in harmony with nature. However, this does not mean that other elements fluctuate in its constitution. Gudynas (2011a) for one argues (and many would concur) that *Buen Vivir* is 'a concept under construction' and is unfolding in a wide variety of contexts; it is, he argues, characterised precisely by its plurality.

As an example of this Ana Cubillo-Guevara (2017), an academic and expert on the subject, applies the idea of living in harmony to three spheres: harmony with oneself, with human beings and with other beings of nature. In this context, the concept of Sumak Kamsay (Living Well) cannot be simplistically associated with '[the] western [concept of] wellbeing' (Cubillo-Guevara, 2021). Likewise, René Ramírez, formerly Minister of Education in Ecuador under the government of Rafael Correa, argues that BV is concerned with 'time', what he terms 'the time of the good life or living well' (Ramírez, 2019). In this proposal the author proposes the socio-political ecology of the good life or living well as a theoretical, conceptual and methodological platform for researching and debating the possibilities of realising a totally reconstructed non-linear idea of development.

In addition, as noted, for some (Acosta, Ramírez, Gudynas, Hourtart, Zaragocín) Sumak Kawsay is a concept under permanent construction. But to be clear this does not imply that basic principles such as living in harmony between all living beings can be eliminated or changed (Cubillo-Guevara,

2017). What it does mean is that—notwithstanding its cultural roots in an Indigenous cosmology and worldview—the concept of SK in its reconstruction has been nourished and enriched by other philosophical principles such as feminism, humanism (re: the unrestricted defense of human rights), post-development, co-operativism, environmentalism and social ecology, as well as Marxism (Acosta, 2010). Similarly, for Cristina Carrasco (see Garcia Álvarez, 2014) the BV paradigm is convergent with proposals that have existed for decades in feminist and ecological economics, since both had already rejected classical and neoclassical economics, and contrarily, they propose notions of development and wealth as a function of environmental sustainability and a people-centred ('as if people mattered') approach.

## Sumak Kawsay as feminism—a way of deconstructing and reconstructing gender relations in a colonial context?

In regard to feminism or feminisms, Sofía Zaragocín maintains that Buen Vivir and decolonial feminism[4] '*share important desires such as the decolonization of knowledge as well as an emphasis on affections and feelings as their own forms to go beyond materialism, the dominant form of modern ontology*' (Zaragocin and Varea, 2017: 18). In addition, the economy of work/home care can be seen as an expression of Sumak Kawsay in that it recovers the idea of life as the axis and central category of the economy. On this point (care from a Sumak Kamsay perspective) and the surrounding debate regarding economic activities assigned to women (women's work), see in particular 'Subversión feminista de la economía: aportes para un debate sobre el conflicto capital-vida' (*Feminist subversion of the economy: contributions to a debate on the capital-life conflict*) by Amaia Pérez Orozco (2014).

To all appearances, there seems to be no *Sumak Kawsay* for Indigenous and rural women given that societies like Ecuador where this concept has been articulated remain spaces of oppression for women. That is, one cannot speak of *Sumak Kawsay* if women are violated or evicted from their lands for economic interests. In Ecuador, for example, six out of ten women have experienced some type of violence, a figure that increases when it comes to Indigenous or Afro-Ecuadorian women. Some 67.8 per cent of Indigenous women have suffered some type of violence, compared to 61 per cent of mestizo women (INEC, 2011). To which we can add that most women do not own their land. For example, in Ecuador only 21 per cent of women heads of household own their land, and the traditional territories of Indigenous peoples have greater deprivations as to access to sanitation, which places an additional burden of unpaid work on Indigenous women and girls and exposes them to an increased risk of disease (National Survey of Employment, Unemployment and Underemployment, INEC, 2016).

Regarding the time available to women for undertaking diverse activities throughout the day, it is important to note that women in general—and this phenomenon can be observed worldwide—have less time for *living well.*

This is particularly so when it comes to Indigenous women's time. Indigenous women work without pay on average 25–35 minutes longer than Indigenous men (INEC, 2012). Thus, the gap for an Indigenous woman to get out of poverty of time on average is seven hours a week. And poverty among rural women is also high. On average, a rural woman spends two more hours on domestic work than a woman, mostly mestizo, in the urban area. That is, from the perspective of intersectionality,[5] women are much more likely than men, both within and across households, to experience and suffer from conditions of social inequality and oppression—in clear contradiction to the concept of SK (Patiño, 2017).

Given this reality it is not surprising, but even so important to note and emphasise, that it is women who are mainly supporting, promoting and putting themselves at the forefront of the resistance against neoliberalism and against extractivism. This is clearly evidenced by the fact that Indigenous women throughout the region have been and remain at the forefront of the struggle against extractivism. This was evident, for example, in the most recent transcendental social protests in Ecuador against extractivism and the associated neoliberal policy agenda that took place in October 2019. Also, among the Amazonian Indigenous leaders the best-known and loudest voices against mining and oil extraction in their communities have been those of women. For example, in cases such as Intag in Ecuador in regard to the *March for Life, Water and Dignity of Peoples* promoted by the Confederation of Indigenous Nationalities of Ecuador (CONAIE), the participation and leadership of women (the Assembly of Women and Diversity of Ecuador) was prominent (Villarreal and Muñoz, 2019).

Regarding the political discourse on Buen Vivir—as with the post-development theoretical discourse in the academy—the feminist movement (especially the current of decolonial feminism concerned with decolonising the power matrix of male domination—the decoloniality of gender)[6] has maintained that BV is not possible without gender equality. Nevertheless, notwithstanding these facts, evidently and surprisingly there have been relatively few encounters between the feminist and Indigenous movements and Sumak Kawsay. Thus, the criticism levelled against the conceptualisation of SK in the literature: that it has been constructed without a serious questioning and deep understanding of the lives of subaltern women—a matter of both class and gender-based inequalities and oppression. In fact, unlike other issues such as nature, development and interculturality, the connection of Sumak Kawsay with political and academic feminist activism has not been a pillar for its conceptual construction. Perhaps this is why Amaia Pérez Orozco (2014) insists that Buen Vivir needs to be reconstructed democratically to take into account the voices of subaltern women.

In fact, in the discourse and voices of Indigenous and peasant women there is scant reference to Sumak Kawsay. And surprisingly, according to a study by Mantilla and Vercoutere (2021) entitled *Bibliometric and contextual analysis of scientific production around Sumak Kawsay in Scopus*, the vast majority of those responsible for the production of scientific knowledge about *Sumak Kawsay* have been 'privileged white men' such as Alberto Acosta, Philip Altmann and Eduardo Gudynas (Arturo Escobar, Acosta, Gudynas are the most cited authors). Ana Cubillo-Guevara, a university teacher and researcher with a specialised interest in the subject, is one of the few women with an Afro- and Indigenous identity who has taken up the issue. This shows that there is an absence of women's and Indigenous voices in the academic production of studies on Sumak Kawsay.

Given all the above, it is useful to contribute to a collective reconstruction of the concept of SK regarding both the debate surrounding extractivism and the struggle of women to escape and improve their social condition. In this connection, the chapter aims to contribute to the debate on the concept of KS from the perspective of Ecuadorian Indigenous women and to raise and visibilise the voices of these women who are seeking to incorporate Buen Vivir into their daily lives. To this end, I propose to address the following questions: (i) Are the values of Sumak Kawsay, and the term itself, part of the cultural heritage of Indigenous peoples and nationalities, and is it used by Indigenous women? (ii) What does Sumak Kawsay mean to Indigenous and peasant women? and (iii) What are the limitations that these women have to confront in order to achieve the condition of Living Well?

## Methodology

The theoretical-methodological approach used in my research into the meaning of SK for Indigenous women in Ecuador could be termed decolonial feminism and constructivism. The hallmark of this approach—see, inter alia, Byrne and Imma (2019), Zaragocin and Varea (2017), Lugones (2016) and Pérez Orozco (2014)—is to deconstruct the experience of these women in their own voices and to reconstruct their increased self-awareness of their potential power and agency. To this purpose—a discourse analysis of Indigenous women's voices regarding their experiences and understandings[7]—I conducted seven interviews with Indigenous and peasant women leaders and women who have written about SK or BV in depth.[8] Below is the list of women interviewed and their identity:

| *Name* | *Identity*[9] |
|---|---|
| **Luisa Lozano** (Lozano, 2021) | • Indigenous woman of the Saraguro Quichua people<br>• Former Leader of the Women's Commission of CONAIE (Confederation of Indigenous Nationalities of Ecuador)<br>• Designated Capa (President) of the community of The Lagoons<br>• Mother, wife, worker and social fighter<br>• Counsellor of the Intirraymi School |

(*Continued*)

| *Name* | *Identity* |
|---|---|
| **Monica Chuji** (Chuji, 2021) | • Ecuadorian Kichwa of the Amazon<br>• Activist and human rights advocate<br>• Director for Latin America at Indigenous Peoples Rights International-IPRI<br>• Former Secretary of Communications and former constituent assemblywoman of the government of the Citizen Revolution (Rafael Correa as President) |
| **Haro Luz** (Haro, 2021) | • President of the women of the rural parishes of Ecuador<br>• Peasant woman and leader, born in a rural parish in Pastaza (province in the Ecuadorian Amazon)<br>• Woman committed to fighting for the least disadvantaged sectors, for women and rurality. |
| **Katy B. Machoa** (Machoa, 2021) | • Indigenous woman from the Quichua community of Shamanto-Napo Runa.<br>• Leader and activist in Confeniae and CONAIE.<br>• Former technical-political advisor of CONAIE<br>• Part of a School of Indigenous women |
| **Nemo Andy** (Andy, 2021) | • Indigenous leader of the lwaorani (Amazonian) nationality<br>• Health Director of the Confederation of Indigenous Nationalities of the Amazon—CONFENIAE (includes 11 peoples and nationalities)<br>• Leads the Antisuyu Warmikuna School |
| **Ana Cubillo-Guevara** (Cubillo-Guevara, 2021) | • Professor at the University of Huelva interested in development alternatives<br>• Expert on Buen Vivir<br>• Of Afro-, Indigenous and Spanish ancestry. |
| **Tamia Vercoutere** (Vercoutere, 2021) | • Indigenous woman and mother<br>• Professor at the University of Otavalo<br>• Researcher at the Institute of Anthropology on issues of identities, race, gender and Sumak Kawsay.<br>• Political scientist, graduated from the Institute of Political Science of Paris with a master's degree in International Relations |

## Sumak Kawsay in the daily life of women

Much has been said and written about the origin of *Sumak Kawsay*. On the one hand, some authors maintain that it already existed before it was established as a legal and constitutional issue (Hourtart, Álvarez, among others). Such is the case of Alberto Acosta, who was a key player in the Constituent

Assembly where the concept of BV was debated and established. Acosta has affirmed that discussions about BV were promoted to this Constituent Assembly and that the concept originated in the Indigenous world long before it was incorporated into the Constitution as a national principle (2012). On the other hand, there are those who suggest that BV is of recent origin and was constructed in the context of the constitutional debate (León, Vercoutere, LeQuang). According to Vercoutere (2021), the concept of SK is linked to the ups and downs of the country's political sphere, rather than to social reality. In any case, what is interesting to know is whether it currently exists within the tangible and daily life of women in the Indigenous communities, or if this concept only remains as a political slogan of the past.

As a result of the interviews conducted, it can be observed that as in the academy there are two positions as to whether the concept of Sumak Kawsay has a life of its own after it was abandoned by the governments that succeeded Correa's tenure as President. For Nemo Andy, representative of CONFENIAE, SK is not a term used by women of peoples and nationalities; nor is it recognised as an alternative way of living. '*It has nothing to do with the vision of indigenous women*' (Nemo Andy, 2021). Her answer was that Buen Vivir or Sumak Kawsay was a creation 'from above' promoted by former President Rafael Correa and used as a political propaganda tool. In any case, Nemo Andy added that the principles of living in harmony with nature and living in community are nevertheless specific to Indigenous peoples and nationalities, and that they are translated into other terms according to the language of the community (but none similar to Buen Vivir or Sumak Kawsay). Similarly, Tamia Vercoutere mentioned that in Otavalo, from where she originates, these terms or concepts are not used in everyday life. '*Sumak Kawsay is a concept that has no real hold in real communities. It is a polysemic conception* that *depends on the actors where it is located or where it comes from*' (Vercoutere, 2021). However, she suggested that in-depth research be carried out with more Indigenous women to confirm this hypothesis. Here, Ana Guevara-Cubillo, another academic, joined in by saying that the concept is in disuse, if not obsolete, from an institutional point of view. She argued that the three actors who from the beginning fought for SK—Indigenous communities, the Ecuadorian government and activists or alternative movements such as ecologists or cooperatives—have abandoned the concept. In addition, she suggested that '*now, mainly the current Ecuadorian government is drafting a development plan without Buen Vivir (living well)*'.

In contrast to this position, Mónica Chuji, who was one of the main Indigenous assemblywomen in the creation of the Ecuadorian Constitution of 2008, argued that Sumak Kawsay is a concept and term that is recognised by Indigenous women both in language and in practice:

> From the Amazon, where we are very connected to the jungle, *Sumak Kawsay* is a word that is always in everyday life and we are always questioning if we are living in a *llaki kawsay*, which is the opposite of *sumak*

> (and which, translated into Spanish, is to have a sad experience or life). Also, we put it in another dimension. For example, we say: that before we had a *sumak* life. Given that in the Amazon, where we are in permanent mobilisation and organisation for all current issues of exploitation, it is a concept that we use very often. Each nationality in its own language because *sumak kawsay* is a word in Quichua.
>
> (Chuji, 2021)

From the same position, Katy Machoa (2021), who prefers to use her mother's surname, argues that SK is present in the practices of peoples and nationalities but that the concept is a generality that denotes different things according to people and nationality. In addition, the Indigenous leader and former advisor to CONAIE, highlighted the fact that SK takes different names depending on the languages and languages where it is expressed. Luz Haro, peasant and leader, adheres to this idea:

> *Buen Vivir*, or *Vivir Bien* as the Bolivian comrades say, can have different perspectives. For example, I myself have heard the concept from different points of view in different situations. For example, I once heard a Quichua man say that Buen Vivir was having education, accessing a good workplace, having a vehicle, having roads in good condition. Whereas for a Shuar woman it was to be able to sow on her land, to supply food for the family. They are two different looks, so I think everyone can think about Buen Vivir from within their own space and time.

According to the President of the women of the rural parishes of Ecuador, BV can denote different subjectivities depending on space and time, to which Katy Machoa responded that although SK can have different meanings and elements, in general it is still in all cases a tool and an argument to fight and defend their ways of life and nature, as well as values that are put into practice in the communities. Machoa explained that when there is a conflict or violation of rights in some territory, the concept of SK is used because it allows them to argue more firmly when it is in the Constitution.

Given this, Luisa Lozano, former Leader of the Women's Commission of CONAIE and recognised Indigenous leader, pointed out that SK is a daily practice rather than a concept. For her, SK has been misunderstood by the State and she makes it clear that BV is to live with dignity, in community and in harmony:

> I believe that if there is BV in my community because there is solidarity, respect, living in security, living in community through practices such as community *mingas* (collective work and struggles), taking care of our territories. In the community territories we continue to talk about living well, but more than talking we live with those principles.

## Sumak Kawsay for women and their limitations

Talk of the Sumak Kawsay of women has generated much controversy among many Indigenous peoples of the Amazon, since although defending territories and nature have been the flag of struggle of the SK, it has not been allowed to connect it with the lives of Indigenous women (Chuji, 2021). That is, there has been an invisibility of Indigenous women in SK.

As for writings on this, the question has arisen as to whether the discourse on *Buen Vivir* has been influenced or shaped by feminism, a key question in feminist meetings that have taken place in Ecuador. A meeting entitled '*Towards a new State without patriarchy*' held in 2013 and a second in 2015 were organised by the Institute of National Studies (IAEN) where meanings, proposals and interpretations of Buen Vivir of several feminists of different currents were shared (Zaragocín and Varea, 2017). From these meetings, a book has been produced entitled: '*Feminism and Buen Vivir*' that sought to glimpse a gendered approach and feminist policies that are absent in the dominant discourse of BV in Ecuador, to generate a line of thought on existing proposals of what is the feminism of living well and the living well of gender. Faced with this question, Ana Cubillo-Guevara (2021) responded that BV has not been influenced by feminisms and that for the same reason one of the biggest criticisms of existing publications concerning BV is that what is needed is the perspective of decolonial feminism.

On this point, most of the interviewees joined in with the argument that what was needed is for women themselves to fill this concept with meaning from the point of view of Indigenous women. As Katy Machoa (2021) put it:

> Sumak Kawsay is a potential concept for indigenous women, but right now women have not appropriated the concept or linked it to gender equality. As to what is Buen Vivir for women has not been talked about or discussed. In fact, it is external processes that have come to position gender inequalities.

In effect, the interviewees supported the idea that that a discussion and collective construction of the concept of SK or BV could serve to promote a dialogue regarding the feelings and thoughts of Indigenous women. To this end—the collective construction of the concept of SK—the interviewees were asked to consider what might appear to be common aspects of the question 'What is the Sumak Kawsay of women?'

The first aspect that stood out is that no interviewee forgot to ask: the Sumak Kawsay for which women? This shows that an intersectional perspective is present in all the visions they evoked regarding gender. The answer given to this question was that SK is not the same for mestizas or white women in the urban areas and cities as for Indigenous or peasant women in rural areas or those living in communities. Tamia Vercoutere (2021) in this regard raised the question: *What is Sumak Kawsay for black, Indigenous, racialised, poor women?* Therefore, subsequent discussions focused on the question as to what SK means for Indigenous and peasant women in the rural area of Ecuador.

A second aspect of the Sumak Kawsay problematic that drew our attention was that all the interviewees agreed that in considering SK from the perspective of Indigenous women one should not lose sight of the need to defend the essential principles of its concept, namely, the importance of (i) living in harmony with nature, which also implied the defense of the territorial rights of Indigenous communities, and (ii) to live in community, i.e., in a relation of solidarity and harmony with others as well as nature, which is to leave aside the individualism of modernity. On the defense of nature, what was emphasised was that living in harmony is a question of respecting nature as a whole as well as its fundamental life cycle and bio-rhythms regarding time. SK in this communal context also implies: 'to have a territory of life, and to have a space to create life. For Amazonians it is a physical and spiritual space both on the ground, as well as in the subsoil' (Machoa, 2021). Nemo Andy, in the same context noted that to live in harmony with nature means 'being able to access everything [the commons], our medicine, our food, harmony that encompasses having a clean river, to be in fullness with the other beings of the communities'. On the other hand, for Monica Chuji (2011), the SK is:

> to think about the lives of women without disconnecting ourselves from the right to our territory (…) A what to do, living…a being in this world in which we consider that everything is alive and in motion. Sumak Kawsay in terms of our Indigenous people is that if we want to live well the integrity and well-being of our ecosystem have to be respected [and secured]. We are but one element of it.

On living in harmony with nature, all interviewees considered that women are much more connected to nature than other members of the community. It is a reality that Indigenous women devote more time to work on the farm compared to their peers [men] (Ana Cubillo-Guevara, 2021; Luz Haro, 2021). It is Indigenous and peasant women who are most connected to the food they serve to take care of their families and their community. In the same way, women occupy a special role since they are the guardians of the seeds. Luz Haro (2021), in this connection, added that 'women are always thinking of planting, even if it is a plant, that nature takes care of. We are guardians of nature'. In addition, *it is women who are leading the anti-extractivist movements in Latin America* (Ana Guevara-Cubillo, 2021). And Luisa Lozano explained that the reason why women are more attentive to their sheep, guinea pigs, orchard, relatives, food is because Indigenous women are 'caretakers of life'.

On the question of community or communalism, Katy Machoa (2021) described this as meaning that '*collective well-being overrides that of the individual*'. All the women were of the view that the SK of women will be plural (collective) since their thinking accompanies others constantly. For Tamia Vercoutere '*Sumak Kawsay has several hearts or nuclei and one of them is the community*', while for Nemo Andy and Luisa Lozano, practices such as *mingas*, which are constantly carried out in the communities, give and strengthen a sense of solidarity between those who make up the community.

The third element found in common is that they all the interviewees agreed that there can be no SK if women are being raped, if there are clear inequalities in their time and work and if discrimination against Indigenous women continues. On the question of violence, they were clear that '*violence against women is not Sumak Kawsay*' (Machoa, 2021). The interviews revealed the worrisome violence suffered by Indigenous and peasant women in the rural areas of Ecuador. All the women denounced the gender violence suffered inside and outside the communities. Mónica Chuji (2021) denounces the femicides and rapes that exist in Indigenous communities and emphasised that this happens, especially in the communities furthest from the roads. As a cause of gender violence, Nemo Andy and Luisa Lozano blamed the alcoholism of men (very much present within Indigenous communities) as an inciting factor of male violence. Here are some testimonies of the interviewees about gender violence:

> In a hospital in Puyo I met a woman who had a baby in her hands. I say, 'What a beautiful daughter,' to which she replied with pain: 'Ay, number 11 is beautiful and number 12 is on the way. My eldest daughter turned 15 and I couldn't even go out to the store to buy her something. My husband can't see me outside if I'm not pregnant.
>
> (Luz Haro, 2021)

> In Sucumbíos, where I am from, I conducted research and found cases of femicide and several cases of rape by family members and community members. They have asked us to rescue from the indigenous justice system indigenous comrades who are imprisoned, according to them for simple things such as rape.
>
> (Chuji, 2021)

> Women in some communities can't sell even their own corn that they have produced if their husbands don't authorize them.
>
> (Luisa Lozano, 2021)

> 'Violence is in all nationalities and alcohol is a determining factor for this violence.' 'In the communities it is difficult to access a complaint of gender violence. Those who can find help are those who live near the roads. In remote communities there is nowhere to file a complaint'.
>
> (Andy, 2021)

It should be noted that violence has diverse dimensions and causes and is found in different institutional and social contexts: the State, couples, relatives and community. On the question of state violence, one of the interviewees proceeded to describe a case that occurred in 2016 between *nanqui* women and the Ecuadorian State. Katy Machoa (2021) narrated how pregnant women with children in their hands were confronted with military pistols to be evicted from their lands, lands that were turned over to Chinese mining companies. Here she noted that for her, extractivism has a clear patriarchal image: military men targeting pregnant women with children in their arms. Luisa Lozano (2021), who was imprisoned for 16 days for protesting against the closure of schools and community nurseries and for indiscriminate extractivist practices, maintained that it was contradictory for the State (in the times of Rafael Correa) to speak of *living well* when they displaced, clubbed with batons and dragged Indigenous women of the land.

In addition to widespread and endemic violence, the interviews revealed that it was women who continued to spend more time working than men. Andy Nemo in this regard related how Indigenous women get up before their partners to cook and that they are also the ones who fall asleep at the end when they finish making the *chicha* (traditional fermented corn drink) that is shared within homes and in communities. Luz Haro (2021) reiterated that peasant women are expected to do double or triple work, such as cooking, taking care of the farm and taking care of their children at the same time. As far as Luz Haro is concerned, Buen Vivir for women has to do with the three 'C's': **(comida, casa y cama) food, house and bed** (emphasis added).

On the other hand, quite apart from the common aspects of the reality confronted in their lives by Ecuadorian Indigenous women, it is worth considering certain particular elements of SK highlighted by some of the interviewees. For example, for Katy Machoa (2021) another essential element of SK is the connection with spirituality, which is intrinsically connected to women. The leader of CONFENAIE describes her and her community's beliefs in *ayas* (spirits) and the rituals through singing and dancing that Indigenous women undergo when planting. To which Luisa Lozano joined in by indicating that her grandmothers connected with the moons to talk to the earth.

Another finding derived from this exercise of collective reconstruction relates to the denunciation of the material conditions of rural women. For example, their rights such as the right to health and education are not guaranteed. The interviewees confirmed that the lack of access to education for them and their children cannot be SK. Luisa Lozano referred to the fact that SK means 'dignity' and dignity refers to the respect for 21 collective rights; that there be social justice; and that women have decent jobs. What was also emphasised was that products that are healthy and free of chemical products must be valued beyond economic considerations and that the traditional work of Indigenous women as collectors and producers of the countryside should be recognised and valued.

Luz Haro (2021), in the same context, mentioned that

> [f]or us, women from the rural areas, Buen Vivir means that we have access to quality goods and services. Since unfortunately, we have many disadvantages even though we are always attentive to the well-being of the family and in service to others.

Similarly, Katy Machoa (2021) claimed that given current conditions, Indigenous women in Ecuador are destined to be domestic workers. Given the legacy of colonialism, it is very common for paid women in the household who work for mestizo or white families to be Indigenous or Afro-Ecuadorian women.

Luisa Lozano former Leader of CONAIE, in the same context recognised that the discrimination of Indigenous women should not overlooked. In this connection she portrayed how more than Indigenous woman have been fired for being pregnant, noting that 'the same would not happen to a mestizas or white woman' (Lozano, 2021). She also observed that the discrimination against Indigenous women is everywhere, from when they go to hospitals, on the streets when police evict them for informal selling, to markets when they are discriminated against by the buyers of their products themselves. Added to this point, several interviewees noted that the oppression of women goes well beyond discrimination; that it originates in patriarchy, a deeply rooted culture of male domination, the effects and consequences of which have been greatly magnified by centuries of colonial rule and a capitalist culture of economic exploitation and possessive individualism.

The conclusion that the interviewees and I have come to in this exercise of social construction is that for SK to exist, the collective rights as well as the individual rights of Indigenous women need to be respected. Also, relations and the role played by women within their communities need to change, i.e., to be changed, because they currently serve to exploit and oppress Indigenous women. Another conclusion, of great import regarding the possibilities and the prospect for Indigenous women to live well in solidarity and harmony with nature, is that these women have been empowered by an increasing awareness of their power and are in fact taking action to change their social status and their situation.

Also, a conclusion that I have come to as an Indigenous Ecuadorian woman who has managed to look at the question of Buen Vivir for women from an academic perspective, from outside the communities within which most Indigenous women live their lives, is that further dialogue between Indigenous women and the feminist movement, especially the current of decolonial feminism, would be mutually empowering.

## Sumak Kawsay limitations for Indigenous women

Among the limitations regarding SK that the interviewees pointed out are: (i) the penetration of capitalism in their communities in the form and prevalence of genetically modified products (GMOs), which has seriously undermined their role as protector of seeds and custodian of nature; (ii) the lack of food sovereignty (Haro, 2021); (iii) the use of pesticides that endanger both the health of the people who use them and the land; (iv) the lack of respect for their collective and territorial rights by the State, which has failed to provide or guarantee the Indigenous communities the right *to prior and informed consent* before allowing for the exploiting of their natural resource wealth and the inability of these communities to exercise their responsibilities as custodians of the integrity of mother earth (Chuji, 2021); (v) thinking only about the macro economy and not about the humble women of the countryside; and (vi) the fact that large-scale capitalist production monopolises the best lands, leaving the most humble small producers the worst land, where there is less water (Haro, 2021).

All the interviewees shared a concern for these issues as they relate to or threaten the SK of Indigenous women. However, some of them had other or additional concerns. Macho (2021), for example, expressed concern for the loss of spiritualism brought about by the spread of Western ideas and a capitalist culture (Machoa, 2021). Both Machoa (2021) and Lozano (2021) bemoaned the capitalist logic of market economics—to follow the demands of the market rather than the natural way. Other concerns had to do with the social inequalities that put Indigenous people below other people, the increasing migration of women from the countryside to other countries, forcing them to not only abandon agriculture and their rural communities but also their children (Lozano, 2021); patriarchy and extractivism, which is largely exclusive regarding women, providing meagre benefits (jobs in the mining sector, for example) that go predominantly to men. Ana Cubillo-Guevara (2021) added that those in high positions and that see themselves as lords of nature are predominantly if not exclusively men. To sum up, in the words of Monica Chuji:

> There is no Sumak Kawsay if there are injustices, or if you don't have access to education. You do not have Sumak Kawsay if you live an intracommunal, intrafamily, or State violence. You don't have a Sumak Kawsay if your territories are threatened, if you don't have a right to health, or if your right to self-determination is threatened
>
> (Chuji, 2021)

In terms proposed as a theoretical framework constructed by Ana Cubillo-Guevara (2021): there is no SK if you do not live in harmony with nature and with others and as part of a community, which is to share equitably in society's productive resources and wealth.

## Conclusion

Both the origin and use of Sumak Kawsay has been heavily debated and disputed. The controversy centres on whether or not the concept is currently part of the culture or reality of Indigenous peoples and nationalities or is something external used by political actors. In this regard, it would seem that when SK ceased to be supported and promoted by the State as in the case of Ecuador, it becomes clearer whether Sumak Kawsay lives or still lives where it supposedly came from: in the communities of Indigenous peoples and nationalities, and not only as a political slogan or a constitutional article. In any case, it is clear enough that in the conception of Buen Vivir or Sumak Kawsay there is the defense of nature, and the spiritual belief in the need to live in harmony with all living beings is alive and well, and present in the life and practices of Indigenous women in rural communities in Ecuador.

In addition, given the complexity of SK as a concept, it is difficult to believe that there is a single Sumak Kawsay or a single Buen Vivir for everyone and in all times and spaces. Thus, it is useful to add to this concept under construction what has been largely left in oblivion to date: the lives of Indigenous women themselves. Thus, we conclude that SK owes a special and important debt to Indigenous women since it has not landed in their lives. For Indigenous women Sumak Kawsay cannot coexist with gender violence, discrimination, the omission of rights, the lack of opportunities, the eviction of lands, the triple day of women's work, among others. Most importantly, it cannot be said to exist for Indigenous women if they do not live in dignity.

## Notes

1 For most authors, *Sumak Kawsay* and *Buen Vivir* are essentially the same, only that one is in Quechua and the other in Spanish. Although it is widely understood that there is no precise or adequate translation of the term Sumak Kamsay (in Spanish and even more so in English) that captures its full meaning. However, Ana Cubillo-Guevara (2021) argues that Buen Vivir (Living well) is a Westernised idea of Sumak Kawsay. Huanacuni Mamami, an intellectual of Aymara ethnic extraction argues that in the Bolivian context of the Aymaran language Sumak Kamsay appears as '*suma qamaña*', translated as 'Buen Vivir' (living well) or '*a full life*' (*vida en plenitud*), which in general terms means 'living in harmony and equilibrium, in harmony with the cycles of Mother Earth, of the cosmos, of life and of history, and in equilibrium with all forms of existence' (Huanacuni Mamami, 2010: 21).

2 As emphasised by Gudynas and Acosta (2011) the concept of Buen Vivir represents the dissolution of the Western or modernised idea of progress. Buen Vivir implies a substantial break with the appropriation of the natural world to feed a development understood as economic growth, and a progress understood as evolution in a straight line (Gudynas and Acosta, 2011).

3 As Bolivian Foreign Minister David Choquehuanca Céspedes (2010) put it: 'the excessive and unbridled industrialization resulting from Western accumulation models does not offer humanity a solution'.

4 This current of 'southern feminist' thought (decolonial feminism) has its roots in post-development, a modality of development theory formed in the 1980s in conditions of a 'theoretical impasse' characterised by a rejection of both materialism and structuralism in all of its forms, including Marxism (see multiverse). Another pillar of decolonial feminism is the concept of the 'coloniality of gender' formulated by Maria Lugones (2016), who based her approach on the concept of

the coloniality of power elaborated by Anibal Quijano in the Latin context. The coloniality of power, in Quijano's formulation (2000), interrelates the legacy of European colonialism in forms of social order and social orders and knowledge, Latin American subaltern studies, and the subsequent process of decolonisation initiated by the empowerment and activism of the colonised, including—as it happens—indigenous women who in the current context have assumed a leading role in the resistance to the advance of extractivism in the development process (Quijano, 2000). It is worth emphasising that the coloniality of gender is part of a tradition of thought associated with women of colour who criticise hegemonic feminism precisely for ignoring the intersectionality of race/class/sexuality/gender (Lugones, 2016). Indeed, Decolonial thought draws on the thoughts, reflections and voices of Afro-Caribbean, Indigenous, mestizo, and racialised feminists who promote the visualisation of the oppression of women who have been visibilised. This group of feminists seek the creation of knowledge from a non-hegemonic geopolitical place, what might be termed 'decolonial feminism', which incorporates the views of Afro-Caribbean, Indigenous, peasant and academic feminists who, with a subaltern feminist analysis and praxis, criticise feminist political theories and proposals that remain Western, white, heterosexual, and bourgeois (Montanaro Mena, 2017).

5 Feminism in its diverse forms makes reference to theoretical-methodological approaches to framing the 'woman question' in development studies, usually with explicit or implicit reference to patriarchy, a system of male domination in the relationship between men and women in different institutional and social contexts. This fact resonates particularly well with 'Southern feminism' and contemporary critical feminist studies of intersectionality (Byrne and Imma, 2019; Crenshaw, 1990). Intersectionality is based on the idea that women are not a homogeneous category—on the contrary, women experience different realities based on oppression and privilege. These oppressions are not one, nor do they operate in isolation, given that' when it comes to social inequality, people's lives and the organization of power in a given society are better understood as being shaped not by a single axis of social division, be it race, or gender or class, but by many axes that work together and influence each other (Hill Collins and Bilge, 2020). The first to introduce the term intersectionality was Kimberle Crenshaw (1990), who highlighted how society has hidden the vulnerability of women, especially racialised women. The importance of using intersectionality as a perspective is based on contemporary feminist thinking concerned with the issue of differences through understanding the combined effects of race, class and gender on women's identities, experiences and struggles (Gallardo, 2020).

6 On this decolonial feminist current of post-development thought see Byrne and Imma (2019), Zaragocín and Varea (2017), and Pérez Orozco (2014).

7 The methodological implications of a post-development emphasis on culture as a missing dimension in social scientific analysis, and a consequent of rejection of structuralism and materialism, is a predisposition towards discourse theory—the idea that a deconstruction of the meaning that individuals and groups viewed as 'actors' attach to their own experiences and actions allows for a better understanding than an analysis of the political and economic system and its structural dynamics. In any case, for the sake of analysis this researcher and writer has adopted the methodological principles of constructivism and discourse analysis.

8 The interviews were conducted via zoom and telephone, by means of a semi-structured questionnaire. The difficulties encountered were that Indigenous women have little time to grant interviews, and the internet or telephone signal in some communities is weak or absent.

9 Information regarding identity was obtained with the question: Who are you? This question allows one a wider look and perform an analysis intersectional analysis.

## References


Acosta, A. (2008). "El Buen Vivir, una oportunidad por construir," *Ecuador Debate*, Quito, 75: 33–47.

Acosta, A. (2010). *Living Well on the Post-Development Path in the Montecristy Constitution*. Quito: FES-ILDIS.

Acosta A. (2012). *Buen vivir y Sumak kawsay. Una oportunidad para imaginar otros mundos*. Quito: Abya-Yala.

Acosta, A., et al. (2013). *El correísmo al desnudo*. Quito: Montecristi Vive.

Acosta, A. (2017). "Post-Extractivism: From Discourse to Practice—Reflections for Action," *International Development Policy*, 9: 77–101. DOI: 10.4000/poldev.2356.

Andy, N. (2021). *Buen Vivir for Women*. (G. Gallardo, Interviewer).

Byrne, D. and Z. Imma. (2019). "Why 'Southern' Feminisms?," *Agenda*, 33(3): 2–7. DOI: 10.1080/ 10130950.2019.1697043.

Choquehuanca Céspedes, D. (2010). "Hacia el reconstrucción del Vivir Bien," *Revista América Latina en movimiento, Sumak Kawsay: recuperar el sentido de vida*, Edición 452, Febrero 13. Quito: ALAI, 8–13.

Chuji, M. (2021). *The Buen Vivir of Women*. (G. Gallardo, Interviewer). 8 September.

Collins, P. H. and S. Bilge. (2020). *Intersectionality*. Hoboken, NJ: John Wiley & Sons.

Crenshaw, K. (1990). "Mapping the Margins: Intersectionality, Identity Politics, and Violence against Women of Color," *Stanford Law Review*, 43: 1241.

Cubillo-Guevara, A. (2017). *Living Well in Ecuador: Political Dimensions of a New Approach to the Political Economy of Development*. Huelva: University of Huelva.

Cubillo-Guevara, A. (2021). *Sumak Kawsay of Women* (G. Gallardo, Interviewer). 10 September.

De Souza Santos, B. (2010). "Hablamos del socialismo del Buen Vivir," *ALAI, América en Movimiento*, 452: 4–7.

Estado Plurinacional de Bolivia. (2012). *Ley marco de la madre tierra y desarrollo integral para vivir bien*. La Paz: Asamblea Legislativa del Estado Plurinacional de Bolivia.

Fatheuer, T. (2011). *Buen Vivir a Brief Introduction to Latin America's New Concepts for the Good Life and the Rights of Nature*. Berlin: Heinrich Böll Foundation. Retrieved from http://montreal2012.wordpress.com/2011/10/19/buen-vivir-a-brief-introduction-to-latin-ameri ca%E2%80%99s-new-concepts-for-the-g-ood-life-and-the-rights-of-nature/.

Gallardo, G. (2020). "Political Representation of Women in the Ecuadorian Legislature," pp. 180–206 in P. Quiñonez and C. Maldonado-Erazo (Eds.) *Gender Inequality in Latin America: The Case of Ecuador*. Leiden: Brill.

García Álvarez, S. G. (2014). *Sumak Kawsay or Buen Vivir as an Alternative to Development in Ecuador. Application and Results in the Government of Rafael Correa (2007–2011)*. Madrid: Universidad Complutense de Madrid.

Gudynas, E. (2009). *El mandato ecológico. Derechos de la Naturaleza y políticas ambientales en la nueva Constitución*. Quito: Abya Yala.

Gudynas, E. (2011a). "Buen Vivir: Germinating Alternatives to Development," *Latin America in* Motion-ALAI, 462: 1–20.

Gudynas, E. (2011b). "Buen vivir: Today's tomorrow," *Development*, 54(4): 441–447.

Gudynas, E. and A, Acosta. (2011). La renovación de la crítica al desarrollo y el buen vivir como alternativa. *Utopía y praxis latinoamericana*, 16(53): 71–83.

Haro, L. (2021). *The Buen Vivir of Indigenous Women*. (G. Gallardo, Interviewer). 4 September.

Houtart, F. (2011). "El concepto de Sumak Kawsay (Buen Vivir) y su correspondencia con el bien común de la humanidad," *Ecuador Debate*, 84: 57–76.

Huanacuni Mamami, F. (2010). *Buen Vivir/Vivir Bien: Filosofía, políticas, estrategias y experiencias regionales andinas.* Lima, Peru: Coordinadora Andina de Organizaciones Indígenas – CAOI. Retrieved from http://www.reflectiongroup.org/stuff/vivir-bien.

INEC. (2011). *National Survey of Familiar Relations and Gender Violence against Women.* Quito: INEC.

INEC. (2012). *Time Use Survey.* Quito: INEC.

INEC. (2016). *National Survey – Employment, Unemployment and Underemployment.* Quito: INEC.

León, I (ed.) (2010). *Sumak Kawsay/Buen Vivir y cambios civilizatorios.* Quito: FEDAEPS. Retrieved from http://www.kavilando.org/images/stories/libros/Sumak_Kawsay_Buen_Vivir_y_cambios_civilizatorios.pdf.

León, M. (2008). "El buen vivir: objeto y camino para otro modelo" (Living Well: The Goal and Path of Another Model), ILDIS-La Tendencia, agosto {Quito], pp.105–123.

Lozano, Luisa. (2021). The *Living Well of Women.* (G. Gallardo, Interviewer).

Lugones, M. (2016). "The Coloniality of Gender," pp. 13–33 in W. Harcourt (Ed.) *The Palgrave Handbook of Gender and Development.* London and New York: Palgrave Macmillan.Machoa, K. (2021). *The Living Well of Women.* (G. Gallardo, Interviewer).

Mantilla, J. and T. Vercoutere Quinche. (2021). "Bibliometric and Contextual Analysis on Scientific Production Concerning Sumak Kawsay in Scopus," *Universidad y Sociedad* [online], 13(3): 321–332. Epub 02-Jun-2021. ISSN 2218-3620.

Montanaro Mena, A. M. (2017). Una mirada al feminismo decolonial en América Latina (*Una mirada al feminismo decolonial en América Latina*). Madrid: Editorial Dykinson.

Pérez Orozco, A. (2014). *Subversión feminista de la economía: aportes para un debate sobre el conflicto capital-vida,* Madrid: Editorial Traficantes de sueños.

Petras, J. and H. Veltmeyer. (2005). *Social Movements and State Power: Argentina, Brazil, Bolivia, Ecuador.* London: Pluto Press.

Petras, J. and H. Veltmeyer. (2009). *What's Left in Latin America?* Burlington, VT: Ashgate.

Quijano, A. (2000), "Coloniality of power, Eurocentrism, and Latin America," *Nepantla: Views from South,* 1(3): 533–580.

Unceta, K., A. Acosta, and E. Martinez Eds. (2014). *Desarrollo, postcrecimiento y buen vivir (Development, Post-Growth and Living Well).* Quito: Abya Yala.

Vercoutere, T. (2021). *The Living Well of Women.* (G. Gallardo, Interviewer). 12 September.

Villarreal, M. and E. Muñoz. (2019). "Women's Struggles Against Extractivism in Latin America and the Caribbean," *Contexto Internacional,* 41(2): 303–325.

Zaragocín, S. and S. Varea. (2017). *Feminism and Buen Vivir: Decolonial Utopias.* Basin: Pydlos.

# 14 Commune socialism

## Self-management, popular power and autonomy in Venezuela

*Dario Azzellini*

This chapter analyses the construction of local self-government in Venezuela through the Communal Councils (CC) and Communes. The Communes are considered by the organized popular bases and most popular movements as spaces in which the communities can build their autonomy. CC in urban areas encompass 150–400 households, in rural areas about 20 and in Indigenous territories about ten households. Communes are constituted by several CCs and other organizations present in the self-defined territory. At the end of December 2021, there were 49,096 CC and 3615 officially registered in Venezuela. Among the organized popular bases if the Bolivarian process – understood as a historical project of radical social transformation – the horizon of the transformation is a communard or communal socialism with its characteristics of local self-government, workers' control, popular participation, direct democracy and horizontal relationships. The strategy of transformation is based on the construction of communal cycles of production and consumption. Although this normative orientation was co-developed and shared by former president Hugo Chávez, the relationship between constituent power and constituted power has always been one of cooperation and conflict. While the popular bases see the local government as autonomous and plural form of organization for self-management, constituted power and its representatives at all levels try to coopt, control and instrumentalize the forms of self-management. Under the government of Nicolás Maduro, state-centred and vertical views were strengthened and the conflicts increased further.

### Revolutionary Bolivarianism and communal socialism

Bolivarianism refers to Simón Bolívar (1783–1830), Venezuelan liberator who fought for independence throughout South America and promoted the unification of the continent. In Venezuela, most popular movements and the governments since 1999 define themselves as Bolivarian. The social transformation process envisioned is called Bolivarian Process or Bolivarian Revolution. The Bolivarian process was characterized since the first election of Hugo Chávez as President at the end of 1998 by a 'two-sided' construction: from the popular bases and from the institutions; from a state-centred perspective and from

DOI: 10.4324/9781003301981-20

an antisystemic perspective. In the 21st century, Venezuela Bolivarianism has become a set of political ideas, collective experiences and values without a clearly defined program or theoretical framework and thus is a work in progress rather than a meticulous ideology or theory. Bolivarianism reaches across a wide ideological spectrum reflecting the diversity of political, social and cultural influences feeding it. Chávez' extraordinary ability was to keep the different currents together while developing further and strengthening a perspective of social and political transformation with a normative orientation of *revolutionary Bolivarianism*.

I differentiate between Bolivarianism as state-centred and increasingly pragmatic government policy and *revolutionary Bolivarianism* as political-ideological set of ideas and practices. Revolutionary Bolivarianism is a genuinely Venezuelan socialist project that started to take shape in the guerrilla movements of the 1960s (Azzellini, 2009). Over the following decades, it permeated the Venezuelan left and became the dominant set of ideas for the transformation of society during the presidency of Chávez (1999–2013). Revolutionary Bolivarianism encompasses different currents in a decolonial and socialist project. It is a collective construction and delineated in certain central ideas and discourses expressed by Chávez. One important reference is his last speech on 20 October 2012 at the first meeting with the ministers of his government after winning the presidential elections. He strongly criticized the government and demanded a great leap forward in the construction of a democratic communal socialism (Chávez Frías, 2015). According to the normative orientation Chávez had launched, the state is not the agent of transformation. The central role corresponds to the popular movement and the organized pueblo. The state is supposed to accompany them, to be the facilitator of the processes from below, so that the constituent power can develop mechanisms to transform the society (Azzellini, 2017a; Chávez Frías, 2008).

In the year 2000, shortly after the beginning of Chávez' first presidency, popular organizations and revolutionary organizations, organized communities and even some institutions started developing different initiatives of local self-government. The CC as mechanism of self-government on a small neighbourhood level arose in 2005 from those experiences. Soon, the organized communities realized that the scale of the neighbourhood alone was too small to respond to all their needs and, in 2007, the Communes became widely visible as next higher level of self-government. The community as living space, rural or urban, is the strongest self-identification for a significant part of Venezuela's inhabitants. For the popular majority, it is at the centre of the construction of social relations. It can be affirmed that class is built as community through shared histories of struggle and existing social relations.

Other council initiatives were also initiated (as workers' councils, students, fishermen, disabled and others). Some of them were developed from below and met the fierce resistance of the institutions although Chávez promoted them, as is the case of the workers' councils (Azzellini, 2017b, 2018, 2021). Others were promoted by institutions as a kind of consulting mechanism for lawmakers but were rather short-lived. In 2007, Chávez also launched the idea of so-called Communal Cities as level of self-government above the Communes.

Revolutionary Bolivarianism sees the 'councilist structures' in various areas of the society as the foundations of a Venezuelan socialism in development. Chávez picked up this debate and generalized it as proposed strategy for social transformation (see Aló Presidente 290, 19 August 2007 in Chávez Frías, 2008: 67). A central theoretical reference for the construction of the 'communal system' is the book *Beyond Capital: Capital: Towards a Theory of Transition* by Istvan Mészáros in which he conceptualizes strategies for a transition to socialism (Mészáros, 1995: 739–770).

Beyond the obvious connection with the Paris Commune and council democracy, the historical lineage of communard or communal socialism shares also ideals and practices with experiences of Indigenous and Afro-Venezuelan organizing. Many Communes in mainly Afro-Venezuelan regions of the country identify themselves as *cumbe* (the Venezuelan name for the historical Maroon towns). The idea of the Commune is also in line with many popular movements and the experiences of building popular power.

Parallels can also be found to the thought of philosopher and educator Simón Rodríguez (1769–1854), the teacher of Simón Bolívar and a central reference of Bolivarianism. Rodríguez proposed in 1847 a form of self-government he named 'Toparchy'(from the ancient Greek term 'topos', meaning place). According to his ideas the government should be built as a confederation of self-governed communities, in which the power of the church, the rich and the military had been abolished. He considered direct local self-government the only effective mean against despotism (Rodríguez, 2001: 542).

Communal socialism connects also with currents of Latin America Marxism, as with Peruvian José Carlos Mariátegui (1894–1930). Mariátegui advocated in favour of an original Latin American socialism and a transition rooted in Indigenous collective forms of organization and practices. He rejected the supposition that the Indigenous communities were based in abstract juridical principles or sentimental traditionalism and the notion as primitive economy that would be gradually displaced. He recognized them as concrete forms of social and economic organization relying on collective principles and analysed the semifeudal latifundium as unable to advance technologically (Mariátegui, 2010: 75–122).

The construction of the new socialism as two-sided process, from below (the movements and organized communities) and from the top (the government and the institutions), was defined as normative orientation by Chávez and adopted by most movements. But it revealed to be much more conflictive than originally assumed. Beyond the fierce resistance of the political opposition, traditional powers, private capital and foreign powers, the relationship between constituted and constituent power was controversial and conflictive from the beginning. The logics of constituted and constituent power clash constantly. Even if constituted power promotes, supports and finances popular participation and self-organization (at least until 2014), it tends also inherently toward the control, homogenization, bureaucratization and planning of the initiative from below. This is antagonistic to what constituent power is, which draws its potential from the unleashed 'creative power of the people'.

The vast majority of Venezuela's popular movements and popular organizations are autonomous, although they supported the government and cooperated with it: They have their own political agenda and make their own decision. Protests, demonstrations, strikes and the occupation of land, companies and institutions have always been part of their instruments of struggle in conflicts with constituted power (Azzellini, 2017a). Even some movements that were promoted by the state have built their autonomous structures and struggles, as it is the case of the Urban Land Committees (Comités de Tierra Urbana, CTU), which were self-organized following an institutional initiative for the collective legalization of informal urban neighbourhoods and housing (Azzellini, 2012).

Autonomy is not a self-isolation from government power, nor is it a counterweight to it. It is self-administration and the construction of a network that overcomes the division into the political, the social and the economic sphere and tends to turn superfluous the state in its known form. As Andrés Antillano, one of the founders of the CTUs, sums up:

> We [as CTU] have always said we have to advance in the construction of a new society with the state, without the state or against the state. It is not us who define the relationship with the state, it is defined by the willingness of the state to subordinate to the interests of the people.
>
> (Antillano, 2008)

## Communal Councils

The CC is a mechanism of local self-government based in participation and direct democracy. They are not part of the institutional representative structures. They were created from below and spread rapidly because of institutional support. Several popular organizations in various regions of the country promoted since the year 2000, the construction of local self-government. From 2005, even some local institutions started to promote the construction of local self-government. In January 2006, Chávez presented various initiatives of local self-government in his TV program 'Aló Presidente' as example to follow and coined the term 'Communal Councils'. He saw the CC as mechanism of self-government to maintain the pressure of constituent power on constituted power (Massey, 2009: 21).

The first *Law of Communal Councils* was sanctioned in April of 2006. At that time, some 5,000 CC existed already. Eduardo Daza, who had promoted and supported the construction of local governments in rural areas before 2005 and later worked in promoting them in the Greater Caracas area, clarifies: 'It's not that the president said, here's a new law, from now on it's going to be like this …, we went all the way to the National Assembly to fight for the Law of Communal Councils' (Daza, 2007). In 2009 a reform of the law, elaborated with great participation of many CC, was sanctioned (ANdRBV, 2009).

The CC is the assembly of all neighbours of 15 years and older. The working bodies are the committees formed according to the interests and needs of the inhabitants (for example housing and habitat, health, culture, sports and others). The committees have spokespeople that are elected by the CC that means by the whole community. The committees elaborate proposals and projects for the community that have to be approved by the CC. The level of participation, organization, autonomy and the ability to plan and execute projects varies obviously considerably among the existing CCs, and many have even ceased to exist or reduced their activities to a minimum when the economic support by the government vanished because of the deepening crisis. Prior political and organizational experience, general participation, access to education and information, and the political orientation of the inhabitants are some of the factors that play a role in determining the councils' activity. In more general terms it can be stated that the CCs in popular urban and rural areas experience more participation and function better than CCs in middle-class or impoverished middle-class areas, where they come into existence less often and where the expectation of representation is stronger than in popular strata (Azzellini, 2017a: 114–152).

The popular communities have appropriated the CCs as mechanism of self-government and modify the functions, contents and rules of CCs and Communes according to their needs and abilities. The law plays more the role of an orientation than of a strict rule to follow. The priority is to create structures of self-government, as Luz Carrera underlines, a long-time political activist and director of the Political Secretariat of the Mayor's Training Commission in 2007–2008, that offered political and methodological training to neighbourhood activists to support the construction of CCs:

> What people do with their Communal Councils goes beyond the law. … For example, the elections of spokespeople, … are a full day of ballot-box elections, where you mobilize the entire population. … [T]he law says it has to be in assembly. But who gives legitimacy to the council? It is the people! People say how they will hold their election, and that is how they do it. … [W]hich committees are formed, how they are formed, how the control of instances works, and how the community bank works: all that is transformed by the people according to their reality… We stick with the people… What is written is the product of systematizing previous experiences and turning that into a law, which is not bad, but it does not reflect what exists right now.
>
> (Carrera, 2007)

I could also verify this during my work in the support and training programme for some 150 CCs in Caracas 2007–2008 and later (Azzellini, 2017a: 100–102).

Following the negative experiences with the CLPP and problems in the initial phase of the CCs, Chávez urged that the projects of CCs (and later also Communes) should mainly be financed directly by institutions of the central state and special funds. The intention was to reduce pressure and interference by local entities, mainly the municipal governments. The law does also not specify that the institutions in charge can reject projects presented by the CCs. From 2007 until 2014 state funding for CCs and Communes amounted to several billion US Dollars per year.

However, the relationship between CCs and institutions is generally not harmonious. Conflicts are frequent and mainly due to the slow response of government institutions and their attempts of interference or cooptation. The state funding led also to the accusation that the CCs are only built because of the available money. While this might be the case for some of the CCs (especially in middle-class neighbourhoods), all activists of CCs I interviewed or spoke with over many years, categorically rejected the accusation. Especially in communities with low financial resources the access to state funds and the ability to decide on how to use them, is seen as a legitimate right that is not questionable (Azzellini, 2017a: 108–156). State funding is nevertheless ambivalent. It is facilitating institutional instrumentalization and cooptation because of the asymmetry of power between financing entity and recipient and increases the risk that the CCs and Communes become an executive institution. Although observation suggests that the majority of active communities has learned to impose their interests and to defend themselves against attempts of cooptation, which originate mostly at the municipal level. With the deepening of the political crisis after Chávez' death in 2013, the government party PSUV (United Socialist Party of Venezuela) and the institutions of the central state have also increased interference and attempts of cooptation.

The CCs promoted a qualitative leap of the participation in the communities and led to a politization with aspirations for a systemic change:

> Communities discussing the budget… I am going crazy, peasants planning streets, building their own power supply system, their direct gas pipes. A quick job training and ready. Before they taught you that the technician was essential and it turns out that is not the case… there is the labor movement, the self-management, the co-management, the endogenous development, all those are the key issues for that future that we are envisioning.
>
> (Álvarez, 2007)

During the first years of their existence, most of the CCs concentrated on remodelling homes, roads and common spaces and creating access to basic services. Over time more and more CCs took on productive projects.

First, agricultural and fishing projects emerged in rural areas, an increase in productive projects in urban areas followed. Small companies of communal collective property were born: bakeries, fish farms, production of school shoes and uniforms, transportation services, distribution of building materials and others. The communities themselves looked for ways for the collective communal administration of the companies.

That communities and their inhabitants begin to take control of their environment and the definition of their needs, allows them to develop perspectives and plan their lives by making decisions. They are not limited anymore, as before, to sheer survival. Participation also transforms the individuals. Personal change is often described as 'humanization' or sensitization, indicating the importance of having transformed into a 'social being' and emphasizing their satisfaction and personal growth due to community activism and the transformation of social relations in the community (Azzellini, 2017a: 133–151).

The formation of CCs (and Communes) is a process of social construction that transforms the communities themselves. Although the community as such exists previously, it is, at the same time, always an act of active construction and not a given territory, and its social fabric is reinforced through work with and in the CC. The collective dimension and solidarity become central features of community life: 'Needs that until recently were resolved at the domestic level of each household, now come to have a collective character and are seen as problems that the community should participate actively to solve, thus enhancing the collective space' (Lacabana and Cariola, 2005: 37). A central activating effect for participation in the popular urban neighbourhoods and rural communities has been played by the experience of being an agent for overcoming one's own marginalization. The accumulated self-confidence makes the communities and the previously marginalized or excluded population confront the institutions demanding their rights. Gender relations are changing too. As is common in processes of deep social transformation, women have been the driving force. They make up a vast majority of the activists in the CCs and Communes (Azzellini, 2017a). This is recognized explicitly at the El Maizal Commune, where women are organized in the *Movement of Communard Women*, which defines its own means and ends, and brings them into the general struggle. El Maizal is a highly organized rural Commune that has occupied private and state-owned farmland, greenhouses and a pig farm. The majority of its activists are women, a fact that has defined the character of the Commune's endeavours, actions and victories (Comuna El Maizal, 2019).

## Communes, communal cities and the communal state

Communes are not decreed by the government but are built in a collective process by CCs and other popular organizations in a certain territory. Its conformation responds to the socio-cultural-economic relational space (Harvey, 2006) and does not have to correspond to the official political-administrative (absolute) space. There are Communes that cross municipal or even state borders since it is in the hands of the population to define and to model their socio-cultural-economic spaces. The Communes can develop long-term and far-reaching projects and measures, while decisions are still made in the CCs. The construction mechanism of Communes (and Communal Cities) is flexible. The communities themselves decide around which common tasks the Commune begins to be built. Initially, Commune building has proven to be easier in rural and suburban areas. In rural areas, Communes are usually made up of fewer CC (between five and twenty) and the common demands are more obvious than in urban areas (where a Commune usually encompasses between 20 and 40 CCs).

The Communes are seen by the rank and file as the most important instrument of self-organization to overcome representative democracy, the bourgeois state and the current capitalist model. At the centre of local self-government is the 'participatory and protagonist democracy' with its characteristics of horizontality and direct democracy, as described by Delbia Rosa Avilés, spokesperson for a CC of the 'Commune of the 7 Socialist Pillars', Anaco, Anzoátegui State:

> We make decisions in the Commune and the Communal Councils in assemblies, and we also have planning meetings every Saturday with a start time of 9 a.m. and no finish time. During the week we plan what has to be done and the following Saturday we get together again to continue making decisions.
>
> (Avilés, 2012)

The Communes arose from below and evolved from the need for the communities to come together at a higher level than the CCs, to undertake projects of greater scope. Shortly after the first CCs began to form, cooperation between various CCs came also into existence. As in the case of the CCs, Chávez's initiative was also essential for the development of the Communes. Atenea Jiménez Lemon of the National Network of Communards (RNC) and involved in the construction of Communes since the beginning, describes the origins of the autonomous communards' movement and of the Communes:

> In answer to a call by Chávez in 2007, debates began in each community over what the commune should be. [...] There was the risk that the Commune would replace the municipality or the parish in terms of politico-administrative organisation... one more body of the bourgeois liberal state.
>
> We began to build in that sense and to study other historical experiences of the commune. We created a space for debate and invited international guests who have considered the subject. We began the work of visualizing the entire country in communes. It is a process of building, it is being able to resume constituent popular power, which is in the

> constitution, which is the creator that permits the opening of spaces and the collective creation of a number of things.
>
> [...]
>
> In 2008 we started to work with a team on the issue of the communes under direct instructions from the president of the Republic. We started to explore what commune experiences were evolving in the country from their own initiative. A mapping was begun, identifying 21 pilot experiences. .... The Ministry of Communes was created, and they kicked us all out. We decided then and there to begin a process of articulation by popular power. We articulated the idea of not working from within the state but from ourselves ... We worked with popular education, with the interchange of knowledge ... We started out in 2008 with 16, and right now there are more than 80 experiences at the national level in the Network and we add more experiences with every activity. The process of building the commune without subordination to any kind of power outside the community brings us together.
>
> (Jiménez Lemon, 2012)

The Communes began to spread throughout the national territory. A Law of Communes (ANdRBV, 2010a) was approved only at the end of 2010 when there were already hundreds of Communes under construction. The structure of councils is thought to cooperate and converge at higher levels of organization, in order to replace the bourgeois state with a communal state. The term was coined by Chávez in January 2007. As he further specified, the future communal state must be subordinated to popular power, which would replace bourgeois civil society. This would overcome the rift between the economic, the social and the political spheres – between civil society and political society – which underlies capitalism and the bourgeois state. It would also prevent, at the same time, the over-centralization that characterized the countries of *real socialism* (Chávez Frías, 2008: 67). This implies a profound transformation of constituted power and a resignification of the state, although it does not fully reflect in the legal definition, according to which the communal state is

> [a] form of socio-political organisation, founded in the Social State of Law and Justice established in the Constitution of the Bolivarian Republic of Venezuela, in which power is exercised directly by the people, by means of communal self-governments with an economic model of social property and endogenous and sustainable development that permits the achievement of supreme social happiness of Venezuelans in the socialist society. The basic structural cell of the communal state is the Commune
>
> (ANdRBV, 2010a)

This concept was widely adopted by popular movements and organizations, opening up a perspective on how to overcome the logic of capital.

## The relationship with constituted power

According to the debate about the communal state, the new structure would tend toward replacing the old institutionality. Chávez had been clear about it even in his speech when he was sworn in as President in 2007: 'a communal city, a city where there is no need for parish boards, where there is no need for mayoralties nor municipal councils, but Communal Power' (Chávez Frías, 2007: 6). Nevertheless, other high representatives of the government have repeatedly declared that old institutions and territorial divisions would remain intact, and the new structures would act as a parallel power. Nicolas Maduro campaigned for the presidential elections 2013 after Chávez' death declaring 'Commune or nothing'. Despite that, the vision of the self-government structures as institutional appendix became the officially declared government interpretation by 2015–2016.

Although several government institutions provided important support for the local self-government, especially to the CCs during the first years, the relationship between constituted power and the new structures of self-government has always been a conflictive one. In contrast to Chávez' declarations and initiatives, negative interference in the organic popular processes occurred by government institutions, the PSUV, mayors, regional governors, representatives to the National Assembly and the Ministry of Communes. They tried to create Communes from above and to impose from territorial boundaries to specific projects and ignored or sabotaged Communes that refused to subordinate. The Ministry of Communes did not register any Communes until 2012, when it had to because of massive protests. Obviously, Communes existed and functioned as such and were called Communes without being registered.

Addys Figuera from the Commune Los 7 Pilares Socialistas in Anaco, Anzoátegui state, describes the struggle of her Commune:

> Everything began in 2010 when the mayoralty of Anaco grouped the Communal Councils by sectors and 17 Communes appeared. Each director of the mayoralty was the representative of one of the Communes. This created a great discontent within the municipality. However, … the only Commune that would not accept this imposition at that moment was ours: Number 2, not even a name … We began to work in the communities. … We did not stay just our seven Communal Councils of the supposed Commune 2, but we extended at the municipal level. … As of right now, our Commune-in-development is made up of 42 Communal Councils. Each community has about 1,000–1,500 people. We have more than 50,000 inhabitants […]
>
> We've had confrontations with the mayoralties … they've called us anti-revolutionaries, troublemakers, etc. At first when we began our work, we asked ourselves, could we be wrong about this? But no, we weren't wrong

> because we believe that this is the right way to go. … The institutions are more of the same, whoever they are, whether a mayor of the revolution or a mayor of whatever… Some people say, 'The staff there is no good.' No. It's the system that doesn't work
>
> (Figuera León, 2012)

## Communal production

During their first years, most CCs and Communes concentrated on repairing homes and infrastructure. Around 2007 productive projects began increasing. The cooperatives were often administered collectively by the CCs or Communes. The necessity of forming community-controlled companies as an alternative to worker-controlled cooperatives emerged in 2006 when it became obvious that the traditional cooperatives created through institutional programs and incentives did not necessarily correspond to the interests of the communities and did therefore not allow advance planning of a communal production cycle (production, processing and distribution).

In 2008, some institutions reacted and began to handle forms of communal cooperatives under different names. The most common term became EPSC, *Enterprises of Communal Social* (or *Socialist*) *Production* (EPSCs). A legal frame followed in 2010 with the Organic Law of the Communal Economic System (ANdRBV, 2010b). The law was elaborated with the participation of Communes, although in the end it did not include all their proposals. Nevertheless, it was a huge step forward for the Commune movement. The law provided also a legal base to the more than one dozen existing local currencies introduced by different Communes.

Communes, and later also the Communal Cities that were formed, have generally considered of great importance to develop productive enterprises under collective communal administration. Over the years, thousands of EPSCs have been founded. They principally operate in sectors that respond to pressing social needs, such as food and construction materials production or transport services; textile manufacturers, agricultural companies, bakeries and shoemakers are also common (Azzellini, 2017a: 164–171, 252–258).

The productive projects not only have the function of improving conditions and quality of life of the communities and creating the basis for autonomous financing of the Communes but are also seen from a perspective of transformation of the relations of production and the capitalist economic model.

> No commune can be autonomous if it does not produce wealth that can be distributed among its members. … How do we imagine these new social economic relationships that the commune provides? … In the commune there has to be workers' control of the companies that are

> already there and of the ones that are going to be established. And not only the workers but the commune itself decides how it will function and how it will produce and what to do with the surplus. The management is socialist because the commune decides.
>
> (Jiménez Lemon, 2012)

Communes and workers have also jointly occupied and taken over underperforming state companies or abandoned private companies. This is the case of the former beer brewery Brahma-AmBev in Barquisimeto, abandoned in 2013. Thirty of its workers occupied it and started managing it together with the José Pío Tamayo Commune. They started selling filtered deep well water, established a car wash and opened a selling point for chicken supplied by the nearby worker-recuperated company Beneagro. In 2014, they founded the EPSC Proletarios Uníos (United Proletarians). The EPSC faced various eviction attempts by the authorities of the oppositional regional government. In 2016, Proletarios Uníos successfully started the production of industrial animal feed.

Communes also created barter networks for regular interchange of products between them, direct supplies from agricultural producers' Communes for Communes in urban areas and communal economic activities along value chains. The autonomous Commune network RNC grew up to more than 500 Communes in 2014, also organizing regional encounters along territorial axes coordinating production, processing and distribution of various products, mainly food, but also construction material, animal feed and others. This raised the opposition of commercial sectors, distributors, big companies in the food sector and politicians and administrations on a local, regional and finally even national level, sharing economic interests with them, having been bribed or simply seeing their central position and power vanish because of autonomous self-organization (state subsidized food distribution programs were controlled by the military and the state-owned oil company PdVSA).

The RNC, the affiliated Communes and other Communes and Commune networks engaged in autonomous construction, like El Maizal or José Pío Tamayo, faced hostilities of different kinds and at different levels. The initiative of the RNC to build a *Greater Communal Enterprises of Socialist Production* (EPS GC) was blocked and sabotaged by the state authorities (Jiménez Lemon, 2022). When the government in 2016 organized an additional subsidized food distribution system to support the popular sectors to face the crisis, instead of entrust the CCs and Communes with it, it created a new parallel structure, the Local Committees for Supply and Production (CLAPS).

Protests and takeovers of land and companies by Communes faced repression by local and regional authorities. For example, when four adjacent Communes occupied the abandoned former state-owned coffee farm Las Lomas of 186 hectare, in the state of Lara in January 2019 when it was supposed to be handed over to a big private coffee farmer. The communards cleaned the land, recuperated many coffee plants and started growing coffee, corn, black beans, pigeon peas and other produce. The regional authorities reacted with harsh repression. Several communards were incarcerated up to 60 days until they had to be released because of the popular pressure. In September 2019, police forces tried to evict the communards from the farm but did not succeed because of the communards' resistance (Martínez and Aporrea.org, 2020). Aroldo Pérez, spokesperson of the Commune Rio Buchí, state of Portuguesa, denounces that the state is handing over state enterprises to private investors: 'There is a mediatic discourse saying that they are with the Communes, but what we can see is the privatization of social production units Chávez created, and we see that with concern' (TatuyTV, 2020).

## Communes and autonomy

The perspective of many communards is one of autonomy, though that does not mean to renounce state funding. On the contrary, they demand state support and control of resources. However, the main focus is on building Communes and Commune networks based on one's own resources and abilities, and following one's own decisions, as we have seen, often clashing with state institutions in the process.

> The Communes of the RNC work to assume the planning of the productive cycle (production, transformation, and distribution, thus promoting the cultural change of the models of consumption and consumerism) ... Accumulate the technical and organic force for the means of production to pass progressively to workers' control (councils of workers) and of the communes in their various levels of aggregation, to develop the communal economy, in transition to Bolivarian socialism.
>
> (RNC, 2011)

In its Fourth National Encounter, the RNC agreed to continue the structuring process by means of a National Council of Commune Members and of national, regional and local commissions of organization, communication, formation, communal project planning and defence. With respect to the latter, the intention was declared to 'assume territorial security and defence, composing the militia with combatants from the Communes, with the intention of safeguarding the strategy of occupy, produce, and defend' (RNC, 2011).

The declared goal of the RNC is 'To progressively dismantle the bourgeois liberal state and construct from the pueblo a new form of government, the Socialist communal state' (RNC, 2011).

Ángel Prado, spokesperson of the Commune El Maizal and member of the Constituent Assembly of Venezuela, explains:

> Chávez put forth the idea of the communal council, and then that of the commune. After the commune, he launched the idea of the communal

> city and then came the communal federation. Finally, at the highest level, we would have a confederation of communes spanning the whole country. [….] We believe it could be a viable way to carry out the territorial organization of the new state as we move towards socialism.
>
> (Vaz, 2018)

When the El Maizal Commune decided in 2017 that Prado should run as candidate for mayor for the local municipality of Simón Planas in the local elections, the PSUV blocked his candidacy on its lists, and when Prado won the elections on the ticket of a small leftist party the National Electoral Council imposed the PSUV candidate arguing that Prado, as a member of the National Constituent Assembly was not allowed to run for mayor. In 2021, finally, El Maizal could impose itself and Prado won the mayor's election on the PSUV lists. El Maizal is a founding member of a new initiative to build a Network of Communes, the Communard's Union (UC). The UC coordinates production among Communes and wants to turn into a political actor also entering the electoral space, although its goal is the construction of the communal state. It does not aim at opposing the government but to advance popular power form a huge pole and continue to occupy land and abandoned production sites (TatuyTV, 2020).

## Some tentative conclusions

The construction of Communes is an expression of construction of autonomy and represents an important qualitative step forward in the popular organization. However, there are inherent contradictions to the relationship between constituent and constituted power. The centrality of the state and its role as a distributor of financial resources, create an unequal power relationship and promote the self-limitation of movements. Attempts at co-option, imposition of agendas and projects and paternalistic and welfare practices on the part of the institutions threaten to distort the autonomous popular organization. Beyond the deviations, the state institutionality continues to operate under logic and with bourgeois structures that do not respond to the necessary transformations. Institutional logic and social logic collide, while institutional logic measures progress with numbers in tables, social logic is recognized in social processes that are rarely quantifiable. The centrality of the state leads also to a growing bureaucratization which impedes transformation and tends toward institutional administration of social processes.

Chávez was aware of the impasse. Less than two weeks after his fourth re-election as President of Venezuela and only months before his death on March 5, 2013, he delivered a very critical speech at the Cabinet meeting. The speech came to be known as 'El Golpe de Timón' (Strike at the Helm) and is still the central reference for revolutionary and rank-and-file Chavistas (Chávez Frías, 2015). Chávez offered a radical critique of the way in which the process of social transformation was obstructed, insisted on fundamental changes in the entire government structure and advocated an immediate leap forward in the creation of the communal state.

After Chávez's death, the new president Maduro, to counter the massive opposition mobilization, gave in to popular demands linked to the legacy of Chávez. He accepted demands of gradual introduction of workers control raised in some workers struggles (Azzellini, 2017b: 2018) and related strongly to the CCs and Communes in his discourse. He promoted changes in the Ministry of Communes and a massive process of registering Communes started. Encounters of Communes on a local, regional and national level happened all over the country, partly autonomous and partly organized with support of the Ministry of Communes. The RNC organized its biggest national encounter with more than 3,000 elected spokespeople and decided to take concrete steps for the creation of a National Communards Council. The Ministry of Communes announced the creation of a Presidential Council of Communes.

However, with the worsening of the crisis caused by the collapse of oil prices, the international siege against Venezuela, the oppositional violence, the economic war of private capital, mafias and financial institutions and the errors of the government in economic and financial matters and corruption, CCs and Communes ceased to occupy a wide space in government speeches and the media. A state-centred vision and the idea of subordination of instances of self-government to the state and the party became dominant in the government. More radical and leftist sectors were pushed out of the government and the institutions and the attempts of cooptation and the attacks on autonomous structures increased. Ángel Prado from the El Maizal Commune states:

> Unfortunately, there are big contradictions inside the state, between the state and the popular social movements, and between the state and the Commune. Because the government is very powerful economically, it has the capacity to make big decisions, and sometimes with a single blow, it can put an end to interesting experiences.
>
> (Vaz, 2018)

Other decisive factors for the weakening of the popular organization and construction were the further deepening of the economic crisis from 2015 on: internal problems of many Communes led them to focus more on the own survival; traveling and financing regional or national encounters became almost impossible; and several activists that had leading functions regarding coordination and communication migrated out of economic reasons or had to dedicate themselves to economic activities for their own and their families' survival (Jiménez Lemon, 2022). Communards of RNC Communes in the states of Lara, Falcón and Yaracuy were arrested in protests and occupations, but among the RNC delegates still meeting in smaller numbers in Caracas until 2019, there was no consensus regarding how to evaluate the acts of repression (Jiménez Lemon, 2022).

According to Atenea Jiménez Lemón a series of faults, weaknesses and problems of the Communes and the RNC became also evident. The Communes did not advance enough on time in building economic projects that would have allowed to face the economic crisis; they relied too much on a number of central activists and did not succeed in training and preparing cadres to keep up the national coordination, this is in part due to a strong culture of personalized leaderships; they did not strengthen enough the idea of democratic practices beyond the structure of the Communes; several regional Commune leaderships switched from the initiative of the autonomous National Communards' Council to the institutional Presidential Council. Finally, a huge setback was caused by internal divisions and contradictions with the spokespeople from the state of Lara, which played a central role in the RNC structure and clashed with other regions (Jiménez Lemon, 2022).

Nevertheless, council structures have endured and are the main and most successful organizational framework through which communities tackle the problems they face as a result of the crisis. There are many production facilities controlled by communities and companies and land taken over by former workers and communities to establish different kinds of production. These types of experiences are very relevant in those moments of a deep crisis that strains social networks by pushing people to greater individualism.

The RNC continues to exist and dedicates itself to strengthening Communes along regional corridors and value chains, while it also intensified the activities in several parts of Caracas. It has important strongholds with impressive organizational and economic advances in the states of Sucre, Trujillo and Lara. There is the Communal City Alba Caribe in Sucre or a communal bank created it Trujillo with housing construction programs with own resources (Jiménez Lemon, 2022).

In the second half of 2019, El Maizal and allied Communes launched the UC: the first regional meeting took place 24–26 January 2020 in the Las Lomas farm in the state of Lara, bringing together more than 300 communards from 60 Communes of the states of Lara, Portuguesa, Yaracuy, Cojedes and Apure. Four other regional meetings were supposed to follow before the foundational congress of the UC, but the agenda had to be suspended until late 2021 because of the COVID-19 pandemic.

Of the more than 49,000 CCs and 3,600 Communes officially registered at the end of 2021, obviously not all function as autonomous democratic popular assemblies. Some are subordinated to government institutions or the PSUV, others ceased to function once state support disappeared due to the crisis, some function thanks to a few activists who have the support, although not the active participation of the community, while many others have assemblies meeting regularly and can count on well-organized communards. They are determined to continue along the path to building self-government and are increasingly developing their skills, still building networks and prefiguring a new economy, a new politics and a new society.

## References

Álvarez, T. (2007). Author's Interview with Talía Álvarez, 62, Retired School Teacher, Housing and Habitat Committee, CC Las Quintas, Artigas, Caracas, 3.1.2ßß8.

ANdRBV—Asamblea Nacional de la República Bolivariana de Venezuela (2009). *LOCC, Ley Orgánica de los Consejos Comunales.*

ANdRBV—Asamblea Nacional de la República Bolivariana de Venezuela. (2010a). *LOC, Ley Orgánica de las Comunas.*

ANdRBV—Asamblea Nacional de la República Bolivariana de Venezuela. (2010b). *LOSEC, Ley Orgánica Del Sistema Económico Comunal.*

Antillano, A. (2008). *Comités de Tierra Urbana (CTU), Antímano, Caracas.* 20 April 2008. Author's interview.

Avilés, D.R. (2012). Author's Interview with Delbia Rosa Avilés, 45 Years, Spokesperson of La Floresta Communal Council, Commune Los 7 Pilares Socialistas, Anaco, Anzoátegui state.

Azzellini, D. (2009). "Bolivarianism, Venezuela," pp. 412–416 in I. Ness (ed.) *The International Encyclopedia of Revolution and Protest.* Oxford, UK: Wiley. doi:10.1002/9781405198073.wbierp0216.

Azzellini, D. (2012). "Movimientos y Construcción Alternativa En Venezuela," pp. 375–410 in F. Rodrigues, H. Novaes and E. Batista (eds.) *Movimentos Sociais, Trabalho Associado e Educação Para Além Do Capital.* São Paulo: Outras Expressões.

Azzellini, D. (2017a). *Communes and Workers' Control in Venezuela: Building 21st Century Socialism from Below.* Leiden: Brill.

Azzellini, D. (2017b). "Class Struggle in the Bolivarian Process: Workers' Control and Workers' Councils," *Latin American Perspectives* 44(1): 126–139. doi:10.1177/0094582X16666016.

Azzellini, D. (2018). "Fighting Against Capitalist Ownership and State Bureaucracy – Labour Struggles in Venezuela," pp. 82–107 in D. Azzellini and M. G. Kraft (eds.). *The Class Strikes Back.* Leiden: Brill.

Azzellini, D. (2021). "Control obrero en el proceso bolivariano. Con, en contra y más allá del Estado," pp. 463–490 in D. Azzellini and I. Ness (eds.) *Poder obrero. Control y autogestión obrera desde La Comuna hasta el presente.* Economía Popular y autogestión. Buenos Aires: Editorial El Colectivo.

Carrera, L. (2007). Author's Interview with Luz Carrera, Director of the Commission of Political Training of the Political Secretary of the Mayoralty of Greater Caracas.

Chávez Frías, H. (2007). "Fragmentos del Discurso de toma de posesión," pp. 2–7 in *El Poder Popular edited by IMU (Instituto Metropolitano de Urbanismo).* Serie Ensayos. Propuestas para el debate. Caracas: IMU.

Chávez Frías, H. (2008). *El Poder Popular.* Caracas: Ministerio del Poder Popular para la Comunicación y la Información.

Chávez Frías, H. (2015). "Strike at the Helm. The First Ministerial Meeting of the New Cycle of the Bolivarian Revolution, October 20, 2012," *Monthly Review Online.* https://monthlyreview.org/commentary/strike-at-the-helm/.

Comuna El Maizal (2019). "Comuna El Maizal: en el camino de construcción del socialismo territorial que el Comandante Chávez nos encomendó," *AlbaTV,* March 3. http://www.albatv.org/Comuna-El-Maizal-en-el-camino-de.html.

Daza, E. (2007). Author's Interview with Eduardo Daza, Community Participation Promoter. Technical Department, Political Secretary of the Greater Mayoralty of Caracas and Activist of ANROS (Asociación Nacional de Redes y Organizaciones Sociales).

Figuera León, A. (2012). Author's Interview with Addys Figuera León, 33 Years, Facilitator of Popular Power. Las Charras Communal Council, Los 7 Pilares Socialistas Commune, Anaco, Anzoátegui State.

Harvey, D. (2006). Space as a Keyword," pp. 270–293 in N. Castree and D.G. Malden (eds.) *David Harvey: A Critical Reader.* Malden: Blackwell.

Jiménez Lemon, A. (2012). Author's Interview with Atenea Jiménez Lemon, 39 Years, National Network of Communards of Venezuela.

Jiménez Lemon, A. (2022). Author's Interview with Atenea Jiménez Lemon, 46 Years, National Network of Communards of Venezuela.

Lacabana, M. and C. Cariola (2005). "Los bordes de La ssperanza: nuevas formas de participación popular y gobiernos locales en La periferia de Caracas," *Revista Venezolana de*

*Economía y Ciencias Sociales* 11(1): 21–41.

Mariátegui, J.C. (2010). "7 Ensayos de Interpretación de La Realidad Peruana. El Problema de La Tierra," pp. 75–122 in J.C. Mariátegui (ed.) *Política Revolucionaria. Contribución a La Crítica Socialista. Tomo II.* Caracas: El Perro y la Rana.

Martínez, G. and Aporrea.org. (2020). "Unión Comunera denuncia amenazas para privatizar tierras en Centro Occidente y uso de las FAES," *Aporrea.* February 2. https://www.aporrea.org/desalambrar/n351689.html.

Massey, D. (2009). "Concepts of Space and Power in Theory and in Political Practice," *Documents d'Anàlisi Geogràfica,* 55: 15–26.

Mészáros, I. (1995). *Beyond Capital: Toward a Theory of Transition.* London and New York: Merlin Press ; Monthly Review Press.

RNC (2011). "Culminó con Éxito iv Encuentro Nacional de Comuneros y Comuneras," *Red Nacional de Comuneros y Comuneras.* http://rednacionaldecomuneros.blogspot.com/2011/08/culmino-con-exito-iv-encuentro-nacional.html.

Rodríguez, S. (2001). *Obras Completas de Simón Rodríguez. Tomo II.* Caracas: Ediciones de la Presidencia de la República.

TatuyTV (2020). "[UNIÓN COMUNERA] ¡'Los que quieran socialismo, vengan con nosotros!'," *TatuyTV.* February 25. http://tatuytv.org/union-comunera-los-que-quieren-socialismo-vengan-con-nosotros/.

Vaz, R. (2018). "The Commune Holds the Solution to the Crisis" – Interview with Ángel Prado'. *Investig'Action.* August 24. https://www.investigaction.net/en/the-Commune-holds-the-solution-to-the-crisis-interview-with-angel-prado/.

# 15 Development beyond extractivism

## Lessons and alternative pathways

*Henry Veltmeyer and Arturo Ezquerro-Cañete*

The forces of production in Latin America as elsewhere, both at the centre and the various peripheries of the capitalist system, since the 1980s have been developed within the institutional and policy framework of the new world order of neoliberal globalisation. This system of global governance, instituted in the form of 'structural reforms' of macroeconomic policies that include privatisation of state enterprises and the deregulation of capitalist markets, as well as the liberalisation of both commerce and the flow of foreign direct investments, unleashed powerful forces of production associated with the advance of resource-seeking 'extractive' capital. However, these structural reforms also generated equally powerful forces of resistance against the neoliberal model and the associated policy agenda, which led the guardians of the capitalist system and the architects of the neoliberal policy agenda to search for and institute a more pragmatic and politically sustainable form of economic development. The solution, devised by economists at ECLAC, was for policymakers in the region to adjust the macroeconomy to the requirements of the neoliberal world order but to bring the state back into the development process in the form of a new social policy targeted at poverty reduction (inclusive development). In the context of a search by governments formed in a progressive cycle in Latin American politics (the so-called 'pink tide'), this neodevelopmentalist model was the keystone of the progressive macroeconomic policy agenda of these governments. The other pillar of this policy agenda was neoextractivism (the use of revenues derived from primary commodity exports to finance the progressive policy agenda).

The neoliberal policy reform agenda of governments in the 1980s and 1990s not only weakened their capacity to pursue an autonomous industrial policy but also resulted in the destruction of forces of production built up over several decades in the industrial sector, and also had a devastating impact on small-scale 'peasant' production in the agricultural sector, which forced many peasants (the 'rural poor', in the discourse of international development) to abandon agriculture and their rural communities—leading many to take the pathways out of rural poverty proposed and facilitated by the World Bank (2007) and other such agencies of international cooperation, namely labour and migration.

DOI: 10.4324/9781003301981-21

However, outmigration of the 'rural poor' (i.e., dispossessed and proletarianised peasants) in the search for an alternative source of livelihood in the form of labour, was but one feature of this phase of the capitalist development process in the region. It also included the rapid advance of extractive capital (foreign direct investments in the extraction of natural resources for exportation on the capitalist world market in primary commodity form) as well as popular resistance against this advance in the form of diverse efforts to move beyond capitalism in its manifest form of extractivism and neoliberalism. This resistance took diverse forms including efforts to construct a social and solidarity economy based on cooperativism and community-based local development, or, as in the case of the Zapatistas in Chiapas and some Indigenous communities in the Bolivia Highlands, a self-governing autonomous commune.

At the level of national politics the search for a more pragmatic and politically sustainable form of neoliberalism—in response to the powerful forces of resistance mounted by the semi-proletarianised peasantry (the rural landless workers movement) and Indigenous communities—as noted above took the form of 'neodevelopmentalism', a policy regime concerned with achieving a more 'inclusive' form of capitalist development by means of a new social policy oriented towards poverty reduction.

This chapter is organised in six parts. In Part 1, we review the proposal for a more pragmatic form of neoliberalism, constructed in response to the forces of resistance mobilised against the neoliberal policy agenda in the 1990s. In Part 2, we review the proposals for alternative development advanced in the agricultural sector, which historically provided capitalism its principal developmental resource (surplus labour force) but that also constituted the major obstacle to further expansion. The principal agency of alternative agricultural development and transformative change has been the peasant movement formed in the 1990s in opposition to the neoliberal policy agenda and the advance of corporate capital in the agricultural sector. In 1993, the dispossessed rural landless workers in the region, together with diverse organisations of small-scale producers and peasant farmers across the world, came together and united in the formation of La Vía Campesina, a transnational social movement that has led the regional and now global struggle against the advance of capitalism in the agricultural sector. The proposals for transformative change and sustainable development advanced by activists in the sector, and its prospects, are briefly reviewed in this section.

In Part 3, we review the proposals that have emerged in the political arena regarding the possibility of combining extractivism with a new industrial production matrix and a new energy policy based on sustainable development in the form of 'green' technology and a shift away from environmentally damaging hydrocarbon fossil fuels towards the production of hydroelectric power and renewable forms of energy resources.

In Part 4, we discuss the proposals for transformative change and a post-extractivist transition associated with the 'progressive cycle' in Latin

American politics—the so-called 'pink tide' of post-neoliberal policy regimes that emerged in the first decade of the new millennium in conditions of a widespread rejection of the neoliberal policy agenda and the search for a more inclusive form of development. The aim here is to draw out the lessons provided by diverse experiments with alternative models and post-extractivist pathways unleashed in this progressive cycle—with specific reference to the search for a post-neoliberal and neoextractivist development pathway by the governments of Bolivia and Ecuador, both of which at the level of the new Constitutions of the Plurinational State paid homage to the Indigenous imaginary of *buen vivir* (living well in social solidarity and harmony with nature). The concern here is with the lessons provided by both countries in their failed efforts to reconcile the post-development and anti-capitalist Indigenous imaginary of *Sumak Kawsay* with a post-modernist extractivist development strategy.

Part 5 focuses on a project constructed by Hugo Chávez as President of Venezuela to bring about what he conceived of as 'socialism of the 21st century'. To some extent, this project can be viewed as part of the 'progressive cycle', the 'pink tide' of progressive policies associated with the rejection of the neoliberal policy agenda of many governments in the 1990s. But whereas most governments formed in this 'pink tide' were unable or unwilling to break with the capitalist system (hence the reference to 'pink' as opposed to 'red', which implies a commitment to systemic change, or socialism), Chávez was explicit in his rejection of both neoliberalism *and* capitalism. It is true that both Morales and Correa also talked of their idea of an alternative future as 'socialism', but in the case of Morales socialism was understood as communalism rather than public ownership or state control of the means of production. As for Correa whatever image he had of it his idea of socialism was at worst confused and at best ambiguous, without any clear reference to policy or the role of the state. President Chávez, on the other hand, had a perfectly clear conception of the role of the state in the process of socialist development, although a defining feature of 'socialism of the 21st century' was communalism understood in terms of community-based autonomous development.

In Part 6, we discuss the alternative proposals and experiments that have emerged from within the popular sector of 'civil society' (rather than the arena of national politics). These proposals in part have to do with experiences across the region related to the construction of a social and solidarity economy based on cooperativism, communalism, and local development. These proposals regarding a post-extractivist transition and a post-capitalist form of development are associated with diverse forces of community-based popular resistance that that materialised on the extractive frontier. The major agency of transformative change in this context, according to David Barkin (Chapter 11), are the Indigenous communities that have managed to transform themselves into what Marx in his Early Works had conceived of as the 'identical object-subject of history', i.e., an agency of transformative or revolutionary change, a 'class in itself' formed in the heat not of academic or political debate but political struggle against the ravages and depredations of what emerged as the world capitalist system.

## 1. The development dynamics of pragmatic neoliberalism (neodevelopmentalism)

The neoliberal policy agenda based on the Washington Consensus on the virtues of free market capitalism was short-lived. By the end of the 1980s, barely six years into the new world order, it had already become apparent even to its functionaries that neoliberalism was economically dysfunctional—rather than delivering on the promise of 'general prosperity' the outcome included a 'decade lost to development'—and destabilising, generating as it did massive social protests and political resistance. In response, the guardians of the new world order such as the World Bank (2000) came together to forge a new consensus and construct a new paradigm. The resulting post-Washington Consensus was formed around the need 'to bring the state back in' and to establish a 'better balance between the state and the market'—as well as a more 'inclusive' and participatory form of 'development from within' (Sunkel, 1993). There were various formulations of this new consensus, including 'structural adjustment with a human face' (UNICEF, 1989), 'growth with equity' (Guimarães, 1989), and 'inclusive development' that were synthesised as 'the new developmentalism' (Bresser-Pereira, 2007, 2009). In fact, there was no consensus as to the best economic model but a broad agreement on principle regarding the need for: (i) structural reform at the level of macroeconomic policy; (ii) a 'new social policy' targeted at poverty reduction; (iii) the formation of human capital via investments in education and health, the basic pillars of social inclusion; (iv) good governance in the form of administrative decentralisation and social (or popular) participation; and (v) empowering the poor to enable them to act for themselves in initiating a process of community-based local development.

There was no consensus as to the best or most appropriate model that would serve as a guide for policymakers to implement a more pragmatic neoliberal policy agenda. To this purpose the architects of the post-Washington Consensus turned to Gonzalo Sánchez de Lozada, Bolivia's Minister of Planning and a convinced neoliberal ideologue who would in a few years assume the Presidency. Bolivia was chosen and used by these architects of a more pragmatic form of neoliberalism as an experimental laboratory, to try out the new policy and construct a new model. The institutional framework of this model was established by the Sánchez de Lozada administration in 1994 in the form of the Law of Administrative Decentralization and the Law of Popular Participation.

This legislation not only provided the institutional framework for a neoliberal policy agenda focused on local development but also opened space for the construction of an alternative social and solidarity economy.

But some on the Left, particularly those engaged in what was increasingly viewed as the 'old politics'—the use of the electoral mechanism and other trappings of liberal democracy such as political parties as a pathway to state power—were critical of the regime's newfound interest in promoting community-based local development. They saw it as a neoliberal stratagem, as undoubtedly it was.

The keystone of the post-Washington Consensus and the search for a more inclusive form of development (the new developmentalism) was a new social policy aimed at the reduction of poverty. By the end of the 1990s, in conditions of a widespread resistance and a rejection of the neoliberal agenda in some policymaking circles, many governments in the region, including governments such as Mexico that continued to hoe the neoliberal policy line, had implemented the new social policy of poverty reduction, in many cases by taking advantage of the growing demand for natural resources on capitalist markets, a policy described by some, among them the social ecologist Eduardo Gudynas (2009), the sociologist Maristella Svampa (2019), and the economist Pablo Dávalos (2013), as progressive neoextractivism, characterised by a stronger role and presence of the state in the extractive sector. By the first decade of the new millennium the combination of forces generated by the anti-neoliberal resistance, a new configuration of economic power in international relations, a post-Washington Consensus on the need to bring the state back in, and a primary commodities boom brought about a seatide change in the political economy of capitalist development in the region. Development policy in this context rested on two pillars: neodevelopmentalism, or inclusionary state activism, constructed by economists at ECLAC in the form of a social policy of poverty reduction; and neoextractivism, viz. the use of revenues derived from resource rents and commodity exports to finance the neodevelopmentalist policy regime.

## 2. The agrarian question: dynamics of post-capitalist agricultural development

The classic form of extractivism unfolded in the form of mining the abundant supply of precious metals (gold and silver), which served as a means of sustaining the lifestyle of the ruling class of aristocratic landowners in Europe as well as a major source of investment of merchant capital—in the context of imperialist conquest and European colonialism. However, extractivism in this context also took other forms, including agro-extractivism—the harvesting of plantation agro-food products and commodities such as sugar in conditions of slave labour. Mining and agriculture in this context provided a major source of merchant capital that played an important role in the development of industrial capitalism in Europe and the evolution of capitalism into a world system. The point of these observations is that these and other forms of extractivism have different and distinct development and resistance dynamics that need to be analytically differentiated (see Chapters 3 and 4).

Within the agricultural sector, in the context of an era of structural adjustments and neoliberal policies that reinforced rural poverty and migration out of the countryside, several countries in the region experienced massive land occupation movements throughout the 1990s, led by the landless peasantry (Veltmeyer, 2005). The most important of these is the Landless Rural Workers Movement (MST), with has developed as the most dynamic, best organised, and effective social movement in Brazil (Wolford, 2010). Similar processes of rural mobilisations emerged to redefine the national political agenda across the region, including the emblematic Zapatista uprising in Chiapas, Indigenous uprising in Ecuador led by the Confederation of Indigenous Nationalities of Ecuador (CONAIE), the marches of the coca growers in Bolivia, and the mobilisations for agrarian reform by the National Peasant Federation (FNC) in Paraguay, among other demonstrations and actions of struggle (see Petras, 1997).

Many of these organisations joined together to build transnational social movement associations at the subregional, hemispheric, and global levels, including the Latin American Coordinator of Rural Organizations (CLOC) and La Vía Campesina, a global federation of some 180 (sub)national rural social movement organisations from 81 countries.

By the mid-2000s, as neoliberalism entered a conjunctural crisis of legitimacy, social discontent among the marginalised majority resulted in a proliferation of protests throughout Latin America, with rural social movements exhibiting the strongest capacity for mobilisation and firmly establishing themselves the most fervent critics of the neoliberal model of development in the region (Petras and Veltmeyer, 2005). Many of these organisations positioned themselves at the forefront of social mobilisation against neoliberalism, even helping to topple national governments as in Ecuador and Bolivia. The Latin American Left benefited greatly from the vitality of these rural movements. Riding this anti-neoliberal wave, a 'pink tide' of left-wing governments rose to power, often with political discourses promising to carry out land redistribution and improve the living conditions of the rural poor (Gascón and Montagut, 2010). Under these conditions, Latin America became fertile ground for the construction of an alternative peasant model of development that revolves around the concept of 'food sovereignty', which is seen by some academics and activists as the dawning of a new anti-systemic movement and alternative for dismantling and transforming the current corporate-driven global food system.

The food sovereignty project is about restoring democratic forms of local and national food systems through participatory decision-making and building viable alternatives based on the foundation of low-input, eco-farming, and consumer rights to adequate and appropriate foods. Such a model can only be viable after a significant programme of redistributive land reform, and at least initial support from the state via provision of technical assistance, rural extension and supporting alternative markets for smaller scale producers.

Some of the ideas behind the food sovereignty movement have been put to the test of policy recently in Latin America. In a few countries, such as Bolivia, Ecuador, and Venezuela, the discourse of food sovereignty was used, and even enshrined in the constitution (McKay et al., 2014). However, the results have not been impressive. Drawing on the findings of a Special Issue and edited volume analysing the main agrarian policies of eight 'pink tide' governments—Argentina, Bolivia, Brazil, Ecuador, Nicaragua, Paraguay, Uruguay, and Venezuela—Kay and Vergara-Camus (2018) conclude that food sovereignty alternatives have been nearly absent, inadequate, and at best represent a vision completely different from that put forward by La Vía Campesina. Instead, the ideological foundation of agricultural policies seems to have been guided by the World Bank's (2007) long-standing agenda of market liberalisation accompanied by the incorporation of small-scale producers into agribusiness-controlled commodity chains to reduce rural poverty. Moreover, in all cases, their policies have continued to promote agribusiness, only funnelling comparatively very few financial resources to small-scale peasant producers and family farmers. This situation constitutes a paradox, since food sovereignty alternatives 'often rely on finances derived from the extraction of natural resources which directly threatens the viability of the alternatives they claim to be supporting' (McKay, 2020: 1386). In other words, food sovereignty and neoextractivism co-exist in a profoundly contradictory relationship as 'the rents derived from natural resource extraction are used to support the livelihoods of the rural poor whom are threatened by these very same extractive activities' (McKay, 2020: 1386). Only in Brazil did the state promote family agriculture through its programme of buying food for school meals from agrarian reform settlers (see McKay, 2012). However, this pales in comparison to all the resources and policies that were mobilised in the promotion of agribusiness (Sauer and Mészáros, 2017). In none of the countries governed by leftist governments was there an extensive redistributive agrarian reform to transform the unequal land structures in the countryside. The landlord classes reacted vehemently to the threat or mere possibilities of a redistributive agrarian reform (Ezquerro-Cañete and Fogel, 2017). In almost all the cases, the needs of rural workers were ignored. This is particularly evident in the undisputed advance of the agro-extractivist model (see McKay et al., 2021) characterised by mechanised large-scale agriculture which can be viewed as 'the antithesis of broad-based development—it eliminates work opportunities and ejects labour to urban sectors that are already overwhelmed with unemployment and underemployment' (North and Grinspun, 2016: 1497). This same model of agrarian extractivsim, particularly because of its enormous use of agrochemicals, is having significant negative environmental impacts across the region, as well as negative health impacts on the population (Ezquerro-Cañete, 2016). None of these governments can be said to have implemented stronger environmental regulations or increased the monitoring of the environmental impact of agribusiness (Kay and Vergara-Camus, 2018).

## 3. Extractivism and a new industrial policy for Latin America

The price of commodities on capitalist markets is notoriously volatile, subject as it is to boom-bust cycles. The progressive cycle of Latin American politics in the first decade of the new millennium a boom-bust cycle. The progressive cycle of Latin American politics in the first decade of the coincided with a boom in commodity prices caused by the demand for natural resources, particularly industrial minerals and fossil fuels, but also agri-food products, a development fuelled by the unprecedented economic growth of China and other 'emerging markets' (the so-called BRICS). This boom began to bottom out in 2012, resulting in a dramatic reduction in the region's rate of GDP growth, as well as conditions that would bring about the end of the progressive cycle (Gaudichaud et al., 2019; Petras and Veltmeyer, 2019). However, in the current context commodity prices are once more on the rise, creating additional pressures in the direction of resource extraction and deepening the current path of commodity-led development and the primarisation of exports (Ocampo, 2017)—what UNCTAD (2021) has defined as 'the commodity dependence trap'.

The solution, proposed and pursued by a number of governments in the region, was a new industrial and energy policy that combined resource development and extractivism with technological innovation in the direction of 'inclusive growth' and sustainable resource development (UNCTAD, 2021). This new resource-dependent and commodity-led industrial policy has been pursued by both the aforementioned pink tide of progressive governments, as well as by conservative regimes on the pacific rim, that continue to hoe the neoliberal policy line. What is common to both progressive and conservative policy regimes is a deepening commitment to a new resource-dependent industrial policy (resource-based industrialisation) and a regulatory regime regarding protection of the environment and engaging with the communities on the extractive regime. The difference between the two categories of regime is that progressive ones are oriented towards 'inclusive development' based on the agency of the State, while conservative regimes generally favour a corporate self-regulatory regime oriented towards 'inclusive growth' based on the agency of the private sector and corporate social responsibility.

In the context of the 'progressive cycle' the governments of both Bolivia and Ecuador concluded that they had no option but to rely on the extraction of their wealth of natural resources and on direct foreign investment to mobilise these resources. But they also believed that they could escape the trap of resource dependency and the 'resource curse' commonly associated with it by means of combining this extractivist policy with a policy of fiscal decentralisation, investing the resource rents appropriated by national governments in the local green economy, together with a neodevelopmentalist emphasis on inclusive development, and constructing an energy matrix based on new industrial policies focused on industrial development of its finite but extensive hydrocarbon reserves (Devlin and Moguillansky, 2012).

Both governments—as well as Mexico, which has pursued a similar strategy but within a neoliberal rather than a post-neoliberal policy framework—sought to reduce a dependence on finite hydrocarbon resources by uniting a strengthened energy infrastructure with industrial competitiveness through the transformation of the country's 'energy matrix'. The aim of the new industrial and energy policy was to lever the generation of cheap energy as a comparative advantage for national industrial development.

Riding high on a boom in global commodity prices at the turn into the 21st century and tapping into a huge stream of Chinese infrastructure investment, the governments of Bolivia, Ecuador, and Mexico massively increased investment in new sources of hydroelectricity and energy infrastructure, including the construction of several hydroelectric dams (Purcell and Martinez, 2018). The problem, as established by Puyana and Rodríguez in their review of the energy production matrix formed in Mexico, Canada, and the US over the past two decades, is that the turn away from fossil fuels towards more renewable and less environmentally damaging resource extraction in the energy sector does not mean abandonment of extractivism. Indeed, they argue, to substitute for coal, oil, and gas, renewable energy sources such as wind, sun, water, and land will extend and prolong extractivism: first, by privatisation of those public goods to transform them in electricity and generate income from its commercialisation in the national and foreign markets and, second, by multiplying the production and consumption of strategic metals and minerals.

Whilst ostensibly bringing about a reduction in energy production costs, implementation of what was a rather ambitious socio-ecological master plan to 'transform the country's productive matrix' has come at the price of leveraging the country's natural resources (oil and minerals) and, paradoxically, creating an oversupply of hydroelectricity. Of greater concern, however, is the failure of each of these three governments to escape what some economists have dubbed a 'resource curse' (Van der Ploeg, 2011; Venables, 2016) and what others (see UNCTAD, 2021) have described as a 'commodity dependence trap' or the 'new dependency' (Borón, 2008).

There were various reasons for this failure, including the ending of a ten-year primary commodity boom and a precipitous fall in the price of oil in 2014, which effectively brought an end to the 'progressive cycle' in Latin American politics. Other reasons, particularly in the case of Ecuador, is a fundamental contradiction between a modernist development model of resource extraction and poverty reduction, which includes a continued reliance on foreign direct investments and the operations of multinational corporations in the extractive sector, and a concern with the communal territorial rights of Indigenous communities that have been systematically violated.

## 4. Sumak Kawsay: panacea or straitjacket?

The governments formed by Evo Morales (Bolivia, 2006–2019) and Rafael Correa (Ecuador, 2007–2017) are widely viewed as the most radical defenders of the so-called 'rights of nature' (*Pachamama*, or Mother Earth)[1] and as a possible post-neoliberal and post-extractivist pathway out of both world capitalism and the global ecological crisis. As declared by Morales on numerous occasions and climate summits, including the Day of Mother Earth (April 22, 2009) in the UN General Assembly: 'The Earth does not belong to us, we belong to the Earth'. Bolivia and Ecuador have among the richest biodiversity systems in the world, which, together with the livelihoods and rural communities of Indigenous peoples are being threatened and seriously harmed by the pollution and deforestation caused by the industrial extraction of society's non-renewable natural resources.

The new constitutions of Ecuador (2008) and Bolivia (2009) are the first in the world to recognise and protect both the territorial rights of Indigenous communities and the 'rights of nature', as well as the collective rights of the diverse nationalities and ethnic groups that make up what the constitution of both countries describes as a plurinational, intercultural and multiethnic state. In recognising and respecting the rights of nature, both constitutions express a transition from an anthropocentric view of nature as a repository of resources to be exploited to one that is more biocentric and respectful (Gudynas, 2011; Ramírez Gallegos, 2012).

In any case, this is the theory embodied in the government's political rhetoric and development discourse. But in practice the situation was rather different. In implementing the new policy regime, both Bolivia and Ecuador, were confronted with powerful economic and political interests in the country that clashed with Indigenous and environmental rights. Also, in the context of nationalising not only the wealth of natural resources but also associated extractive industries—mainly hydrocarbons, agribusiness, and mining—the Bolivian Constitution declares the industrialisation and commercialisation of natural resources to be a key priority of the state, albeit considering the rights of nature and Indigenous peoples, and providing that revenues and government spending are directed at the common good. This is a central policy also of the Ecuadorian government, to a large extent backed up by the 2008 Constitution, subsequent legislation, and the National Development Plan.

With this backdrop, the governments of Morales and Correa stood out in their proposal to abandon capitalism for socialism as an institutional framework for a radical program of ambitious social welfare reforms—poverty reduction, provisions for education and universal health services, improved infrastructure, etc. Nevertheless, like the less 'radical' (capitalist, rather than socialist) social welfare program implemented by the other 'progressive' governments in the region, to finance their 'radical' policies both Morales and Correa continued to rely on the fiscal revenues derived from the exportation of the natural resources in primary commodity form ('neoextractivism' in the discourse of critical development studies).

The end result was momentous. Not only were the progressive quasi-socialist regimes instituted by Morales and Correa unable to escape the extractivist development trap, but also because of the coincidence of economic interests between the state and transnational capital (profits for the corporations, resource rents and export revenues for the governments), both governments were constrained to side with the extractive companies in their relation of conflict with the communities negatively impacted by their extractive projects and operations. As a result, the political landscape in both Bolivia and Ecuador featured a series of unresolved clashes between the government's economic development policies and the demands of the Indigenous communities in their concern for the violation of their territorial rights and the rights of nature—clashes that have been at the centre of recent contentious politics in both countries.

The two symptomatic and most emblematic conflicts in this context, concern the cases of TIPNIS highway project in Bolivia and the Yasuní-ITT initiative in Ecuador. Regarding TIPNIS, in October 2011, large numbers of Indigenous and environmental activists marched for 65 days from the Bolivian lowlands to the capital protesting against a highway construction project through a protected area and Indigenous territories (TIPNIS—*Territorio Indígena y Parque Nacional Isiboro Secure*). The 602-km highway project would connect the lowland Beni department with highland Cochabamba. The protesters presented a list of 16 demands concerning respect for Indigenous territorial and other rights such as the right to free, prior, informed consultation, as well as other social, economic and cultural concerns. After some violent clashes between police forces and the marchers, the government acknowledged that it committed a number of mistakes concerning the construction project and communication with affected Indigenous groups and agreed to all of the demands presented. However, after a few months the highway project was reinitiated, despite heavy resistance and international media and academic coverage. But in the end the conflict was brought to an impasse, as reflected in public statements in 2013, at a conference in Argentina, by vice-president Alvaro García Linera to the effect that construction of the highway is necessary but that it would have to be postponed 20, 50 or 100 years, and carefully carried out with care regarding Indigenous rights and protection of the environment (Lalander, 2014: 162).

As for Ecuador, the government of Rafael Correa developed an alternative to capitalist resource management in the Amazonian territory of Yasuní, home of several Indigenous groups and with the richest biodiversity of the world, but also a territory of unexploited oil richness. With the slogan of 'leaving the oil underground', the government asked the international community for 50 per cent of the revenues that would have been generated by exploitation of the oil reserves in order to protect the biodiversity and the Indigenous peoples of the area, which added to the image of Ecuador as the most progressive country in the world *vis-à-vis* the rights of the environment. To this end, the government together with the UNDP created the Yasuní-ITT trust fund to administer the donations. The initial commitment of the government was to leave approximately 850 million barrels of oil underground without time limits. However, on August 15, 2013, President Correa officially declared the ending of the Yasuní-ITT initiative, giving a green light for oil drilling in this bio-cultural Amazonia reserve. He claimed it was his 'toughest political decision ever' but that in the end (given the failure of the international community to support his proposal—having achieved only 0.37 per cent of the estimated contributions), Correa declared that he had no alternative to signing an executive decree for the liquidation of the Yasuní-ITT trust fund and thus end the initiative (Lalander, 2014: 163–164).[2]

The policies implemented by Bolivia and Ecuador in the context of the 'pink tide' generated a major theoretical and policy debate, particularly as relates to the notion of *Buen Vivir* and the principles and policies associated with it. The debate continues, as do unresolved questions that surround the tensions and contradictions between ethno-environmental concerns and development politics. In both countries the Indigenous principle of *Sumak Kawsay* as well as the rights of the Indigenous peoples to prior consultation (and implicitly to free, prior, and informed consent when new extractive projects are planned) are constitutionally established. At first sight, it appears that the new constitutions would undoubtedly benefit the Indigenous communities in their concern for both their livelihoods and nature, of which they see themselves as custodians, since the constitutions embody and echoes many Indigenous concerns and voices. However, as Lalander (2014) argues, they accentuate tensions and contradictions that are manifest moreover in the legal norms derived from the constitutionally sanctioned so-called 'rights of nature'. The conclusion that he, together with critics such as Alberto Acosta (2013), draws from this is that the rhetoric and professed concern for the rights of nature and the rights of Indigenous peoples has evolved into a straitjacket, an obstacle for progressive development and welfare politics.

But this is not the only contradiction between discourse and practice manifest in the policies pursued by Morales and Correa. For example, despite the nationalist and populist rhetoric of the Bolivian government (that the country's natural resource wealth belongs to the people), the relationship of the state with capital has not substantively changed. In some strategic extractive sectors such as hydrocarbon sources of energy, iron ore, and lithium the Bolivian government has indeed maintained formal ownership of the resources, and even nationalised the associated enterprises, but even so it has not been able to promote any structural change—which would be to process the raw materials for energy production in Bolivia and to manufacture finished products that would allow the country to secure a much larger share of the value of the social product on capitalist markets, value that currently is currently disproportionately captured by foreign capital. In fact, what we have in Bolivia—as well as Ecuador and other countries in the region, regardless of whether the regime is post-neoliberal and progressive or neoliberal—is a state that is dependent on and subordinate to global capital because of a coincidence of economic interest and a relation of economic dependence.

## 5. Venezuela and communal socialism

One conclusion reached by the authors of this volume is that the capitalist system, no matter what form it takes or how it might be revised in the direction of equity, social inclusion, and sustainable development, is unable to elude or escape its inherent contradictions, which are rooted in the incessant drive to accumulate capital at all costs, and the resulting need to put profits before people. Thus, the search for a pathway or transition towards a more inclusive and equitable form of post-development, a society that embodies the principles of social inclusion and environmental justice, dictates the search for systemic or structural change—an alternative system, call it socialism or what you will, that reaches beyond capitalism and extractivism.

One proposal along these lines is associated with the notion of what was understood and described by Hugo Chávez, President of Venezuela at the time, as 'socialism of the 21st century'. Unlike the 'actually existing socialisms of the 20th century', socialism here was predicated not so much on the state's control of the commanding heights of the economy but on communalism—the agency of the state in support of initiatives taken 'from below' (the grassroots) within the institutional framework of the commune and what could be described as municipalisation. In this regard, socialism as conceived of by Chávez reflected the dynamism of diverse experiments in the region in the direction of constructing a social and solidarity society based on cooperativism, workers' self-management and local development.

Apart from the Zapatista project to construct an autonomous and communal society on the margins of the capitalist system in Chiapas, perhaps the most interesting and important experiment in the construction of a social and solidarity economy within the institutional and policy framework of the State can be found in Venezuela, under Chávez. However, although the Bolivarian Constitution of 1999 centred on socialism as a system designed for human development (the equitable development of human capabilities), it also retained support for capitalism. For example, while rejecting neoliberalism and stressing the importance of the state presence in strategic industries, the focus of the government's 2001–2007 Development Plan was to encourage investment by private capital—both domestic and foreign—by creating an 'atmosphere of trust'. To this was added the development of a 'social economy', conceived as an 'alternative and complementary road' paved by both the private sector and the State.

Cooperativism and cooperatives play a part in this social economy, but what is significant if not somewhat puzzling—as in the case of Cuba's latest 'update' of its model ('new guidelines')—is how small a role was assigned to self-managing and cooperative activities. As it was for the development agencies of international cooperation, in Venezuela the development of the social economy seems to be essentially a program for incorporating the informal sector into the national economy. It is necessary, the government's plan argued, 'to transform the informal workers into small managers'. Accordingly, family, cooperative, and self-managed micro-enterprises were to be encouraged through training and micro-financing (from institutions such as the Women's Development Bank) and by reducing regulations and tax burdens.

Therefore, the *social economy* was to play the role it plays in Brazil and elsewhere—islands of cooperation nurtured by states, NGOs, Grameen-type banks, and church charities that serve as shock absorbers for the economic and political effects of capitalist globalisation. Of course, this would make things better for the unemployed and excluded (the half of the Venezuelan working class in the informal sector). But the point is that the social economy here was not envisioned as an alternative to capitalism (except insofar as survival within the nooks and crannies of global capitalism constitutes an alternative). The goal was not socialism as we understand it but rather a different type of capitalism, i.e., socialism understood as a different, more human, form of capitalism—based on popular or social participation—to ensure the complete development of the person both individual and collective.

But there is a fundamental difference between 'development of the social economy' in the context of the Bolivarian Revolution and the solidarity economics as understood and promoted by ECLAC, FAO, ILO, and the development agencies of International Cooperation. For the latter, the social economy is a mechanism of adjustment to the forces of capitalist development, a way of creating spaces within the system for poverty reduction based on local sustainable self-development, the social capital of the poor and the empowerment and agency of the poor—and a means of converting the informal sector into a more productive sphere of economic development. For the theorists and architects of the Bolivarian Revolution—see Articles 62 and 70 of the 1999 Constitution—the social economy or solidarity economics is viewed through the lens of what is described as 'socialist human development', i.e., 'self-management, co-management, cooperatives in all forms' as examples of 'forms of association guided by the values of mutual cooperation and solidarity'. With its emphasis upon a 'democratic, participatory, and protagonist' society, the Bolivarian Constitution contains the seeds of the 'social economy' conceived of not as a supplement to the dominant private and public sectors but as nuclei of the socialism for the 21st century, i.e., as a national not just local development model, brought about from below as well as above.

Cooperatives and cooperativism plays an important role in this model. The framework of endogenous socialist human development brought about by the Bolivarian Revolution is based on the institution of the *Misiones* and the *Comuna* (or Commune), which are oriented towards and designed to bring about the building of new human capacities both by teaching specific skills and preparing people to enter into new productive relations through courses in cooperation and self-management. The effect of this development program was dramatic: the number of cooperatives increased from under 800 when Chávez was first elected in 1998 to almost 84,000 by August 2005.

In January 2005 at the World Social Forum, Chávez explicitly called for the reinventing of socialism—different from what existed in the Soviet Union. 'We must reclaim socialism as a thesis, a project and a path, but a new type of socialism, a humanist one, which puts humans and not machines or the state ahead of everything'. Six months later, Chávez argued the importance of building a new communal system of production and consumption, in which there is an exchange of activities determined by communal needs and communal purposes. 'We have to help to create it, from the popular bases, with the participation of the communities, through the community organisations, the cooperatives, self-management and different ways to create this system'.

On Chávez's re-election in December 2006, a new building block was added: the communal councils (based upon 200–400 families in existing urban neighbourhoods and 20–50 in the rural areas). These were established to diagnose democratically community needs and priorities. With the shift of resources from municipal levels to the community level, the support of new communal banks for local projects, and a size which permits the general assembly rather than elected representatives to be the supreme decision-making body, the councils were envisioned as a basis not only for the transformation of people in changing circumstances but also for productive activity based upon communal needs and communal purposes.

These new councils were identified as the fundamental cell of Bolivarian socialism and the basis for a new state. 'All power to the communal councils!' Chávez declared.[3] An 'explosion in communal power', designated as one of 'five motors' driving the path towards socialism. The logic is one of a profound decentralisation of decision-making and power.

## 6. Post-extractivist alternatives from within civil society

One of the lessons that can be drawn from an examination of the forces of change unfolding in the region is that the major agency for transformative change is likely to emerge from below and from within civil society—from the communities that have shown greatest resistance towards capitalism. One such struggle, which predates by centuries the current advance and onslaught of extractive capital, is the Mapuche resistance and defense of their native lands, described by the Coordinadora Arauco-Malleco (CAM) as a revolutionary struggle against a history of colonialism, 'dispossession, deception, racist tutelage, and militarisation; phenomena that are being repeated today… [in] the pattern of capitalist accumulation and its colonial scaffolding' maintained by the state (CAM, 2021).

As noted above, in the countryside and the agricultural sector the major agency of transformative change and the resistance to the advance of capitalism (in the form of the neoliberal policy agenda) has been the peasantry, or what remains of it (mostly rural landless workers). But in the extractive sector (open pit mining) it has been Indigenous communities contiguous to the sites of extraction—communal responses to structural violence, enclosure of the commons and the appropriation of the community's resources, environmental damage, and the violation of the community's territorial rights (Gasparello, 2021). These dynamic forces of change are operating at the level of local development and the extractive frontier. Here, the economic and political development process is subject to, and reflected in, diverse forces of transformative change and a post-extractivist transition towards different post-capitalist, post-development pathways. These transitions include community-based resistance against the advances of extractive capital and the negative impacts of extractivism on the health, the environment, and livelihoods of the Indigenous population.

Although there is a paucity of studies in this area, there is substantial anecdotal evidence and research that point towards the activism and prominent role played by women in these struggles. Not only have women in diverse contexts been active in the struggle against their subordination and diverse forms of gender discrimination, but also they have played a prominent role on the front line of the political and military struggles against the advances of capitalism and extractivism. The exemplary case in this regard is the role played by women in the Zapatista insurrection and subsequent developments in Chiapas against the incursions of capitalism and extractivism (Hernández Castillo, 2010). Initially, Indigenous women were a minority within the Zapatista movement, but by 2004, ten years into the movement, women made up 50 per cent of the support bases and a third of the Zapatista armed forces (Mariscal, 2001). And it would seem that the prominent role of women in the class struggle and the movement to reclaim the territorial rights of the Indigenous communities is by no means unique to the Zapatista movement. David Barkin, author of Chapter 12, has led a series of investigations by his graduate students and assistants into the dynamics of community-based struggles on the extractive regime—investigations that point towards the protagonism and political activism of women and the prominent role that they have played in the resistance and the actual fighting (Aguilera, 2018), as well as the support bases of the movement where they continue to fulfil their traditional role as caregivers and maintenance of the family.

Other forms of community-based resistance include the experiments across Latin America regarding the construction of a social and solidarity economy or a self-governing autonomous commune—communal socialism as Azzellini describes it in Chapter 14. These experiments include local expressions of what might be described as communal eco- or bio-socialism based on the active participation and autonomy of communities on the extractive frontier in the management of their natural resource wealth.

It is difficult to determine the eventual outcome of these diverse forces of change. It is dependent in part on the changing correlation of forces in the class struggle or the broader albeit quiescent revolutionary struggle for transformative change. It is also dependent on the outcome of conflicting efforts to either advance the forces of extractive capitalism or to derail them, to stop them in their various tracks. In this book, we have explored this issue at some length and in some depth by means of a series of analytical probes into the development and resistance dynamics of extractive capitalism in Latin America.

The conundrum at the heart of the extractive development model: is it really possible to achieve sustainable development with extractivism, and promote manufacturing-based industrial policy alongside extractivism? We are left with a fundamental incertitude. Can we view and treat an industrial policy and extractivism as symbiotic or compatible? Thus far, at least in the Latin American context, the empirical evidence for this is rather thin. Nevertheless, we cannot necessarily conclude that the problem has no solution. We end the book with a brief discussion of the different ideas regarding this problem advanced by the various contributors to the book.

## *In lieu of a conclusion: Whither extractivism in the post-extractivist transition?*

In regard to the search for alternatives, the authors in this volume reflected on the question as to how to move beyond capitalism in its current form of neoliberalism and extractivism, to consider and critically review and assess broad array of proposed pathways to sustainable development. These proposals range from those who consider extractivism as fatally flawed, unable to overcome its inner contradictions, to intellectual and political conversations among social movements and other non-academic knowledge producers about alternative practices in the search for synergy between different theoretical and political developments, including emergent 'new ecologies for the 21st century' (Escobar, 2018). Further considerations and issues confronted by the contributors to this volume included the 'extractive bargains' struck by the agents of extractive capital with state officials and local governments as well as representatives of the communities impacted by extractive projects and processes. These 'extractive bargains' include what in the context of Bolivia in particular could be described as 'resource nationalism' and the assertion of the state's proprietary rights and decision-making power. It also included the construction of a government-mediated social pact between capital and the communities engineered with and secured on the basis of a strategy of corporate social responsibility, a strategy that includes a commitment to secure the informed consent of the communities or community groups to the implementation of any extractive project, as well as their participation in the benefits and the management of the resource extraction process—community-based resource management that recognises and respects the territorial rights of the Indigenous communities as well as the 'rights of nature'.

The narrow pathway towards a more sustainable future in the post-extractive transition, littered as it is with pitfalls and contradictions, has both a local dimension (e.g., resource nationalism, fiscal decentralisation, investment of resource rents in the local green economy, community-based resource management) and an opening to the world market and global economy. This issue of globalisation in the context of the world capitalist system and the emergence of China as a global economic power raises several questions addressed by Nem Singh (Chapter 8) as to the role of China in the mega-financing of the vast infrastructural projects needed to develop extractive industries in the region, and the question of how to secure the insertion of Latin America and other peripheral regions into the global value chains of these industries. In this connection, Gary Gereffi in his 2018 book *Global Value Chains and Development*, compares the differences in the way Latin America and East Asia were inserted in the global value chains of diverse extractive industries. Resource-rich Latin America, he notes, was inserted through production-driven value chains where the idea is to promote state expansion in domestic markets. Resource-poor East Asia, by contrast was incorporated through a buyer-driven commodity chain. Consequently, this avenue of incorporation produced very different state-business relations (pressures for tariff protection, tax subsidies, incentives for export) which, for Gereffi, explained the differential successes of the two regions (also see Kay, 2002).

In moving forward on this front, Nem Singh argues the need to think about how global value chains are opening and closing economic opportunities for sustainable resource extraction and development. Latin America, he argues, will likely end up specialising in the production of lithium, niobium, rare metals, etc., to respond to the rapidly increasing demands for technology-intensive products and clean energy. Here he argues, in agreement with Puyana and Rodríguez Peña (Chapter 7), that it would be useful to go back to the theorists of Latin American structuralism and dependency, as well as Celso Furtado and Albert Hirschman's concept of forward and backward linkages, in the search for entry points and opportunities provided by global value chains to reposition the economies in the region to take better advantage of the their wealth in the development of extractive industries and new ways for capturing a greater share of surplus value and resource rents—to secure a more favourable position in the international division of labour.

If, as Nem Singh argues, producer-driven commodity chains in this scenario will be dominated by large flows and the investment of private foreign capital and Chinese state capital, the prospects for Latin America and the Caribbean in securing a greater share of the total value of the exported commodities, particularly those with value added in the emergent extractive industries, will hinge on the ability to negotiate technology transfers or to innovate Indigenous technology. Here, Nem Singh references the example of Petrobras, a state-owned Brazilian multinational corporation in the oil industry, in securing with its offshore deep-water engineering its own technological niche in the global market. This example reinforces Nem Singh's argument as to the need to go forward by going back to the thinking of Latin American dependency in the 1960s and 1970s regarding the importance of integrating Latin American economies into the global economy under more favourable conditions. In practice, this would include resource nationalism, an appropriate institutional and policy framework, and the availability of the most advanced 'green' production technologies as well as environmentally sustainable practices, to ensure thereby not only an environmentally friendly and sustainable resource development but also the ability for producers and workers in the region to capture a greater proportion of the social product and to share in the benefits from the value added by labour in the production process. What this means is that exporters would supply the market not just with ethically sourced natural resources in primary commodity form but with intermediate and finished processed and manufactured goods that are sold at prices that reflect not only the bounty of nature but also the value added by labour.

Another argument for reaching back into the past (critical Latin American development school of thought) to navigate future turbulent waters in the oceans and seas of global capitalism is a renewed emphasis on the need to provision the decentralised domestic and local markets with basic goods produced on a small scale, to create thereby forward and backward linkages between the local and global economy and a direct interrelation between producers and consumers. In addition to the other benefits of serving the local economy and an expanding domestic market linked to the global economy, the anticipated ecological benefits and the resulting environmental effect would be palpable.

The conclusion drawn by Nem Singh and several other contributors to this volume (Moreno-Brid, Garry, Puyana, Rodriguez Peña) is that it is possible, and indeed necessary, to combine a new industrial and energy policy designed for a more sustainable and inclusive form of capitalist development with a regulatory regime of natural resource extraction—neoextractivism, as we have come to understand it in the South American context of capitalist or socialist development. These authors have concluded that rather than viewing natural resource extraction as a curse and development trap, it has in fact been central to Latin America's economic prosperity and is likely to remain the region's central model for economic growth. The assumption shared by these authors is that the contradictions of extractive capital can be counteracted and socio-environmental conflicts ameliorated; that the destructive and negative socio-environmental impacts of extractivism can be compensated for and mitigated by means of prudent state-regulated community-based resource management, appropriate conservation measures and a regime of corporate social responsibility, together with a technology fix (implementation of advanced convergent green technologies) and a new industrial policy.

On this point, however, the other contributors to the book beg to differ, arguing in effect that the contradictions of capital and extractivism are endemic and cannot be resolved within the confines of the capitalist system; that the *sine qua nom* of a post-extractivist transition towards 'another world' of social and environmental justice and sustainable post-development is to move beyond natural resource extraction, i.e., beyond extractivism, as a modality of capital accumulation and modernist development.

In particular, Eduardo Gudynas in his many writings as well as his contribution to this volume, has most clearly articulated this dissenting view. Addressing the argument regarding the need for Latin America to position itself for insertion into the global production networks and the value chains of the emergent extractive industries, and taking on Nem Singh's argument and example of Petrobras as an agency of post-dependency development, Gudynas argues that in a Latin America committed to the goal of social and environmental justice that there is no place for extractivism as we have come to know it. Furthermore, even the commitment of extractive companies to turn away from the extraction and exportation of environmentally damaging sources of energy towards renewable resources and green technologies do not suffice to prevent the continuation of resource conflicts on the extractive frontier—as confirmed by recent reports on continuing conflicts between the communities of the Mapuche nation and companies seeking to implement green hydrogen projects in Argentina and Chile, that in the case of Chile promise greater fountains of resource rents and fiscal revenues than even the export of copper (Masello, 2022).

The point made by a number of authors is that no matter what policy and institutional reforms are put into place, the systemic workings of extractive capitalism, as well as its local impacts and spill-over effects on public policies, are simply incompatible with the goals of social equity and environmental justice. On the other hand, as Gudynas points out, this does not mean that there is no role for natural resource extraction in the transition towards a more socially inclusive form of development and a future in which people can live sustainably with nature. On this point, he argues that it is important to clearly distinguish between extractivism as a modality of capital accumulation and the appropriation of renewable natural resources under conditions of respect for both territorial rights and the right of communities to sustainable livelihoods. For example, not all mining is extractivism as we have to know it, i.e., as a mode of appropriation and profitmaking within the institutional and policy dynamics of the capitalist system. Nor does resource extraction, or the appropriation of Latin America's natural resource wealth, necessarily entail the predatory practices—the usurpation of the lands and lives of the Indigenous population—associated with extractivism. Indeed, in the post-extractivist transition and beyond (see Chapter 12) there is undoubtedly a place for some forms of sustainable natural resource extraction involving mining and agriculture, forestry, fishing, and maybe even some types of hydrocarbon exploitation.

To conclude this excursus into the dynamics of Latin American extractivisms, what is needed is a closer look at the development and social dynamics of natural resource extraction, and further research into these dynamics from a critical development perspective. However, in consideration of the preponderance of the evidence, and mindful of the arguments advanced in this volume regarding the complexity and diversity of these extractivisms, it is possible to argue that: (i) as dependence on the extraction of natural resources seems inevitable in the short- and even medium-term perspective, commodity based economies will face the need to increase the sustainability and productivity of their extractive sectors, a very tall order under the circumstances and only possible in the context of a post-extractive transition that moves beyond extractivism as a modality of capital accumulation and capitalist development; (ii) many countries in the current context have failed—or are destined to fail—to strike a balance between the purported economic and fiscal benefits of extractive industry growth and the heavy social and environmental costs in terms of environmental degradation, community displacement and social conflict, all of which are particularly acute at the local level; (iii) extractivism is an indissoluble part of today's varieties of capitalism; (iv) extractivism as a modality of capitalist development cannot provide a pathway towards another world of inclusive, equitable and sustainable development; (v) post-extractivism is part of a broader agenda of alternatives to capitalism, which provides an opening towards an alternate future that transcends contemporary ideas of development and progress; and (vi) any such pathway (and a post-extractivist transition) towards a more inclusive and sustainable form of post-development will require mobilisation of the diverse forces of resistance on both the political front and the extractive frontier, as well as the activism and protagonism of the communities negatively impacted by the advance of extractive capital in the development process.

In sum and thus to conclude, regarding extractivism it is not a matter of *celebration or a promise of better things to come, but neither can we write its obituary.*

## Notes

1 Eduardo Gudynas, in a communication with the editors, notes that the common and oft repeated reference by analysts in the Global North to the 'rights of nature' has little resonance in Latin America. That is, it is merely a slogan with no analytical utility.

2 One of the most distinguished scholars on Indigenous studies in Latin America, the anthropologist Xavier Albó, wrote a short requiem of the Yasuni-ITT, viewing it as 'the most radical and bold proposal I know of regarding the relationship between the respect of Mother Earth and development in national parks of high biological diversity and valuable natural resources in the subsoil' (Albó, 2013).

3 This was an ideological declaration of political intent rather than a programmatic statement. In practice it seems that the power of local councils is strictly limited to matters of local development. Even so, it would appear that these local councils are managing to function even with the macro-economy falling or pushed into crisis (Teruggi, 2015).

## References

Acosta, A. (2013). "El Correísmo: Un Nuevo Modelo de Dominación Burguesa," in Acosta, A., et al., (eds.), *El Correísmo al Desnudo*, 9–21. Quito: Montecristi Vive.

Aguilera, A. (2018). "Primer Encuentro Internacional de Mujeres que Luchan." *Data Urgente*, February 21. https://web.archive.org/web/20180315003752/https://data-urgente.com/2018/02/21/primer-encuentro-internacional-mujeres-luchan/.

Albó, X. (2013). "Réquiem por el Parque Nacional Yasuní." *La Razón*, August 18. https://www.la-razon.com/lr-article/requiem-por-el-parque-nacional-yasuni/.

Borón, A. (2008). "Teoria(s) de la Dependencia." *Realidad Economíca*, 238: 20–43.

Bresser-Pereira, L.C. (2007), "Estado y Mercado en el Nuevo Desarrollismo." *Nueva Sociedad*, 210: 110–125.

Bresser-Pereira, L.C. (2009). *Developing Brazil: Overcoming the Failure of the Washington Consensus*. Lanham, MD: Lynne Rienner Publishers.

CAM—Coordinadora Arauco-Malleco. (2021). "Ni con la Derecha ni con el Progresismo Servil: CAM frente a Victoria de Boric." *Desinformémonos*, December 28. https://desinformemonos.org/ni-con-la-derecha-ni-con-el-progresismo-servil-cam-frente-a-victoria-de-boric.

Dávalos, P. (2013). "'No Podemos ser Mendigos Sentados en un Saco de Oro'. Las Falacias del Discurso Extractivista," in Acosta, A., et al., (eds.), *El Correísmo al Desnudo*, 190–215. Quito: Montecristi Vive.

Devlin, R. and Moguillansky, G. (2012). "What's New in the New Industrial Policy in Latin America?" Policy Research Working Paper, 6191. Washington: World Bank.

Escobar, A. (2018). *Designs for the Pluriverse: New Ecologies for the Twenty-First Century*. Durham, NC: Duke University Press.

Ezquerro-Cañete, A. (2016). "Poisoned, Dispossessed and Excluded: A Critique of the Neoliberal Soy Regime in Paraguay." *Journal of Agrarian Change*, 16(4): 702–710.

Ezquerro-Cañete, A. and Fogel, R. (2017). "A Coup Foretold: Fernando Lugo and the Lost Promise of Agrarian Reform in Paraguay." *Journal of Agrarian Change*, 17(2): 279–295.

Gascón, J. and Montagut, X. (eds.) (2010). ¿Cambio de Rumbo en las Políticas Agrarias Latinoamericanas? Estado, Movimientos Sociales Campesinos y Soberanía Alimentaria. Barcelona: Icaria.

Gasparello, G. (2021). "Communal Responses to Structural Violence and Dispossession in Cherán, Mexico." *Latin American Perspectives*, 48(1): 42–62.

Gaudichaud, F., Webber, J., and Modonesi, M. (2019). *Los Gobiernos Progresistas Latinoamericanos del Siglo XXI. Ensayos de Interpretación Histórica*. Mexico: UNAM.

Gereffi, G. (2018). *Global Value Chains and Development: Redefining the Contours of 21st Century Capitalism*. Cambridge: Cambridge University Press.

Gudynas, E. (2009). "Diez Tesis Urgentes sobre el Nuevo Extractivismo. Contextos y Demandas Bajo el Progresismo Sudamericano Actual," in CAAP & CLAES (eds.), *Extractivismo, Política y Sociedad*, 187–225. Quito: CAAP & CLAES.

Gudynas, E. (2011). "Buen Vivir: Today's Tomorrow." *Development*, 54(4): 441–447.

Guimarães, R. (1989). *Desarrollo con Equidad: ¿Un Nuevo Cuento de Hadas para los Años Noventa?* LC/R. 755. Santiago de Chile: CEPAL.

Hernández Castillo, R.A. (2010). "El Zapatismo y el Movimiento de Mujeres Indígenas de México." Montreal Institute of International Studies, March 10. https://www.ieim.uqam.ca/IMG/pdf/el_zapatismo_y_el_movimiento_de_mujeres_indigenas_en_mexico_hernandez.pdfexico_hernandez.pdf.

Kay, C. (2002). "Why East Asia Overtook Latin America: Agrarian Reform, Industrialisation and Development." *Third World Quarterly*, 23(6): 1073–1102.

Kay, C. and Vergara-Camus, L. (eds.) (2018). *La Cuestión Agraria y los Gobiernos de Izquierda en América Latina: Campesinos, Agronegocio y Neodesarrollismo*. Buenos Aires: CLACSO.

Lalander, R. (2014). "Rights of Nature and the Indigenous Peoples in Bolivia and Ecuador: A Straitjacket for Progressive Development Politics?" *Iberoamerican Journal of Development Studies*, 3(2): 148–173.

Mariscal, A. (2001). "Mujeres: 30% de Combatientes Zapatistas." *La Jornada*, April 8.

Masello, C. (2022). "Nación Mapuche. Una vez más, se Tensan las Cuerdas entre Referentes Mapuches y el Gobierno de Rio Negro/Cuestionamiento al Proyecto de Hidrógeno Verde." *Resumen Latinoamericano*, 14 AprilMcKay, B. (2012). "A Socially-Inclusive Pathway to Food Security: The Agroecological Alternative." *International Policy Center for Inclusive Growth Policy Research, Brief* # 23Brasilia: UNDP.

McKay, B. (2020). "Food Sovereignty and Neo-Extractivsim: Limits and Possibilities of an Alternative Developmental Model." *Globalizations*, 17(8): 1386–1404.

McKay, B., Alonso-Fradejas, A. and Ezquerro-Cañete, A. (eds.) (2021). *Agrarian Extractivism in Latin America*. London: Routledge.

McKay, B., Nehring, R. and Walsh-Dilley, M. (2014). "The 'State' of Food Sovereignty in Latin America: Political Projects and Alternative Pathways in Venezuela, Ecuador and Bolivia." *Journal of Peasant Studies*, 41(6): 1175–1200.

North, L.L. and Grinspun, R. (2016). "Neo-Extractivism and the New Latin American Developmentalism: The Missing Piece of Rural Transformation." *Third World Quarterly*, 37(8): 1483–1504.

Ocampo, J.A. (2017). "Commodity-Led Development in Latin America," in Carbonnier, G., Campodónico, H. and Tezanos Vázquez, S. (eds.), *Alternative Pathways to Sustainable Development: Lessons from Latin America*, 51–76. Boston: Brill.

Petras, J. (1997). "Latin America: The Resurgence of the Left." *New Left Review*, 223: 17–47.

Petras, J. and Veltmeyer, H. (2005). *Social Movements and State Power: Argentina, Brazil, Bolivia, Ecuador*. London: Pluto Press.

Petras, J. and Veltmeyer, H. (2019). *Latin America in the Vortex of Social Change*. London: Routledge.

Purcell, T. and Martinez, E. (2018). "Post-Neoliberal Energy Modernity and the Political Economy of the Landlord State in Ecuador." *Energy Research & Social Science*, 41: 12–21.

Ramírez Gallegos, R. (2012). "Izquierda y 'Buen Capitalismo'. Un Aporte Crítico desde América Latina." *Nueva Sociedad*, 237: 32–48.

Sauer, S. and Mészáros, G. (2017). "The Political Economy of Land Struggle in Brazil Under Workers' Party Governments." *Journal of Agrarian Change*, 17(2): 397–414.

Sunkel, O. (1993). *Development from Within: Toward a Neo-Structuralist Approach for Latin America*. Boulder, CO: Lynne Rienner Publishers.

Svampa, M. (2019). *Las Fronteras del Neoextractivismo en América Latina*. Bienefeld: CALAS.

Teruggi, M. (2015). "¿Comuna o Nada? A Tres Años del Golpe de Timón." *Resumen Latinoamericano*, October 20.

UNCTAD. (2021). *Escaping from the Commodity Dependence Trap through Technology and Innovation*. Geneva: UNCTAD.

UNICEF. (1989). *Participación de los Sectores Pobres en Programas de Desarrollo Local*. Santiago de Chile: UNICEF.

Van der Ploeg, F. (2011). "Natural Resources: Curse or Blessing?" *Journal of Economic Literature*, 49(2): 366–420.

Veltmeyer, H. (2005). "The Dynamics of Land Occupations in Latin America," in Moyo, S. and Yeros, P. (eds.), *Reclaiming the Land. The Resurgence of Rural Movements in Africa, Asia and Latin America*, 285–316. London: Zed Book.

Venables, A. (2016). "Using Natural Resources for Development: Why Has It Proven So Difficult? *Journal of Economic Perspectives*, 30(1): 161–184.

Wolford, W. (2010). *This Land Is Ours Now: Social Mobilization and the Meanings of Land in Brazil*. Durham, NC: Duke University Press.

World Bank. (2000). *Beyond Economic Growth: Meeting the Challenges of Global Development*. Washington, DC: World Bank.

World Bank. (2007). *World Development Report 2008: Agriculture for Development*. Washington, DC: World Bank.

# Index

Note: **Bold** page numbers refer to tables; *italic* page numbers refer to figures and page numbers followed by "n" denote endnotes.

For Product Safety Concerns and Information please contact our EU representative GPSR@taylorandfrancis.com
Taylor & Francis Verlag GmbH, Kaufingerstraße 24, 80331 München, Germany

www.ingramcontent.com/pod-product-compliance
Ingram Content Group UK Ltd.
Pitfield, Milton Keynes, MK11 3LW, UK
UKHW020145200926
475702UK00005B/923
* 9 7 8 1 0 3 2 2 9 5 2 1 3 *